Study Guide and Reader

to accompany

Child Development and Education
Third Edition

Teresa M. McDevitt
University of Northern Colorado

Jeanne Ellis Ormrod
University of Northern Colorado (Emerita)
University of New Hampshire

PEARSON

Merrill
Prentice Hall

Upper Saddle River, New Jersey
Columbus, Ohio

Vice President and Executive Publisher: Jeffery W. Johnston
Publisher: Kevin M. Davis
Development Editor: Autumn Crisp Benson
Editorial Assistant: Sarah N. Kenoyer
Production Editor: Mary Harlan
Design Coordinator: Diane C. Lorenzo
Cover Design: Brian Huber
Production Manager: Laura Messerly
Director of Marketing: David Gesell
Marketing Manager: Autumn Purdy
Marketing Coordinator: Brian Mounts

This book was printed and bound by Bind Rite Graphics. The cover was printed by The Lehigh Press, Inc.

Pearson Prentice Hall™ is a trademark of Pearson Education, Inc.
Pearson® is a registered trademark of Pearson plc
Prentice Hall® is a registered trademark of Pearson Education, Inc.
Merrill® is a registered trademark of Pearson Education, Inc.

Pearson Education Ltd.   Pearson Education Australia Pty. Limited
Pearson Education Singapore Pte. Ltd.   Pearson Education North Asia Ltd.
Pearson Education Canada, Ltd.   Pearson Educación de Mexico, S.A. de C.V.
Pearson Education–Japan   Pearson Education Malaysia Pte. Ltd.

10 9 8 7 6 5 4 3 2 1
ISBN: 0-13-225448-4

PREFACE

As we wrote this third edition of *Child Development and Education*, we had two primary goals in mind. First, we wanted to share many of the things that psychologists and other researchers have discovered about how human beings grow and develop and to do so in a way that our readers would find informative, enjoyable, and perhaps even fascinating. Second, we wanted to give future teachers and other professionals a toolbox of ideas about how best to help young people with diverse backgrounds and abilities achieve personal, social, and academic success.

We have done several things in the book itself to help you learn, remember, and apply what you read more effectively. We have been selective about what we've included in the book, focusing on the concepts and principles that we think are especially useful for prospective teachers and others who will work with infants, children, and adolescents. We have incorporated many examples of youngsters in action in the book—both through case studies and through drawings, essays, and school assignments—and in the set of three compact disks (*Observing Children and Adolescents*) that accompanies the book. And we have offered numerous suggestions for professional practice in bulleted sections of the text, in *Developmental Trends* tables, in *Observation Guidelines* tables, and in *Development and Practice* features.

This *Study Guide and Reader* provides additional ways of helping you learn, remember, and apply what you read in your textbook. For each chapter, it includes:

- **Chapter overview:** This overview describes the general topics and themes you will encounter as you read the chapter.
- **Possible knowledge, beliefs, and misconceptions related to chapter content:** This list alerts you to things you may already know or believe about topics in the chapter, with a focus on prior knowledge and beliefs that may affect your ability to understand and accurately interpret what you read.
- **Suggested supplementary readings:** These readings, which appear in a separate section of this *Study Guide and Reader*, expand on particular topics in each chapter.
- **Chapter outline and focus questions**: This table suggests questions you might try to answer as you read various sections of the chapter.
- **Chapter glossary:** This glossary lists and defines the bold-faced *key concepts* you will encounter in the chapter.
- **Completed "Applying Concepts in Child Development" table:** This table provides examples of how you might have filled in the empty cells in the "Applying Concepts in Child Development" table at the end of the chapter.
- **Application exercises:** These exercises present real-life scenarios that encourage you to apply developmental concepts and principles in interpreting children's behaviors and evaluating professional practices.
- **Sample test questions:** These multiple-choice and essay questions can help you spot-check your learning and give you a sense of the kinds of test questions your instructor might ask.

A Companion Website accompanies the textbook as well. The Website provides some of the same features that you see here in the *Study Guide and Reader*, such as a glossary and practice test questions for each chapter and links to other Internet Websites that are relevant to the content of each chapter. You can find the Companion Website at **www.prenhall.com/mcdevitt**.

Enjoy the book!   T.M.M. & J.E.O.

CONTENTS

STUDY TIPS

Both research and our own personal experiences as teachers tell us that many college students simply do not know how to study. Following are a number of suggestions for reading and studying textbooks more effectively:

➤ **Determine your best learning times and use them wisely.** Are you a "morning person"? Are you a "night owl"? Identify the times that you read and concentrate most effectively, and leave the dirty dishes, campus errands, and favorite television programs (use a VCR to record them) for times when you're relatively brain dead.

➤ **Be realistic about how much you can learn in one sitting.** You can think about and learn only so much information in so much time. Don't try to do too much too fast. And certainly don't leave everything until the last minute!

➤ **Minimize distractions.** Find a quiet place to study where you will have few things competing for your attention. Turn off the radio and CD player, or play soft background music that you will barely notice. And definitely turn off that television set!

➤ **Mark up the book.** Underline or highlight the main ideas of each paragraph and section. Mark essential details that support the main ideas. Put brackets or stars beside examples that you find especially helpful.

➤ **Pay attention as you read.** Don't let your eyes wander mindlessly down the pages. Keep your mind as well as your eyes focused on the things you are reading.

➤ **Actively think about and interpret what you read.** Think about how the theories we present are consistent with personal experiences you've had or with ideas you've learned in other classes. Generate your own examples of concepts and principles. Derive implications for the particular age group you hope to work with.

➤ **Use the tables to help you organize and summarize the material.** Use the *Basic Developmental Issues* tables to find similarities and differences among various theories and perspectives. Use the *Developmental Trends* tables to summarize key characteristics of different age groups.

➤ **Use the pictures, photographs, and cartoons to help you remember the ideas they represent.** For most students, visual images provide one highly effective means of remembering information.

➤ **Practice applying concepts and principles.** Do the *Interpreting Children's Artifacts and Actions* exercises. Answer the questions after the case studies at the ends of each chapter. Fill in the empty cells in the *Applying Concepts in Child Development* tables. Do the *Application Exercises* in each chapter in this *Study Guide and Reader*.

➤ **Periodically check yourself to make sure you understand and remember what you've read.** Try to summarize each section as soon as you've read it. Ask yourself questions similar to the focus questions here in the *Study Guide and Reader*, or have a classmate ask you such questions. Try to explain a difficult concept to someone who doesn't yet understand it.

➤ **Know when to quit.** If you're tired or having a hard time concentrating, close your book for the time being. Pick it up again when you're more rested and less distracted.

➤ **Review.** Research is clear on this point: Periodic review of previously learned material definitely helps students remember it more effectively and accurately.

➤ **Reward yourself for your accomplishments.** Give yourself a break or a treat when you've finished a section or a chapter. Get a bite to eat. Call a friend on the telephone. Go to the mall, the movies, or the park.

USING THE COMPACT DISKS
OBSERVING CHILDREN AND ADOLESCENTS

Included with *Child Development* is a set of compact disks called *Observing Children and Adolescents: Guided Interactive Practice in Understanding Development.* These three CDs present 1 to 5 video clips for each of the 14 chapters of the textbook. Each chapter's clips are accompanied by questions asking you to observe children and adolescents and then reflect on and apply what you've seen. Here is a typical example of what you might see on the screen:

To use one of the CDs, insert it in the CD drive of your computer and then double-click on the diamond-shaped icon. When the title page appears, click on the arrow in the lower right-hand corner of the screen to get to the introductory page. If this is your first time, sign in with your name and, if you wish, your course number and a file name (the latter will be the document name for any work that you save). If you have previously viewed a module on this CD, you can retrieve the work you've already completed by clicking on the *Open* button.

At the next screen (the table of contents for the CD), once again click on the arrow button in the lower right-hand corner. On the following screen, you will see what appears to be a photograph on the left-hand side. This is actually the video screen, which currently displays the very beginning of one of the chapter's videos. You can select the chapter you want by clicking on the "down" arrow next to "MODULE" at the top of the screen. You can then choose from the available videos for the chapter by clicking on the "down" arrow next to "Make a Selection." To begin the video you have selected, click on the right-pointing triangle at the lower left of the video screen. The triangle you have just pushed becomes a pair of vertical lines, which you can click to stop the video at any point. You can fast-forward or backtrack through the video by clicking on and dragging the "traveling" circle below the screen. The *Transcript* button provides a written transcript of the video if you should need it.

After you have viewed the video once, click on the *Observation*, *Reflection*, and *Application* buttons to see questions for you to think about and respond to. You can type your responses in the response box that appears below the question box. If you click on the *Consider* button below the response box, you will find hints that can help you zero in on concepts to consider as you formulate your response.

Click on the black *Show Me* button at the bottom of the screen if you would like a video demonstration of how to use the CDs. Click on the *Help* button for a verbal reminder of the procedure. The *Save* button allows you to save your responses up to this point, the *Print* button prints them out, and the *Quit* button takes you out of the CD program.

To switch to another chapter, once again click on the "down" arrow beside the word "MODULE" at the top of the screen.

Following is a complete list of video clips you can find on the three CDs:

Volume 1:

1. Environments
   - Infancy
   - Early Childhood
   - Middle Childhood
   - Early Adolescence
   - Late Adolescence

2. Research
   - Early Adolescence

3. Physical Activity
   - Early Childhood
   - Middle Childhood

4. Cognitive Development
   - Infancy
   - Early Childhood
   - Middle Childhood
   - Late Adolescence

5. Memory
   - Early Childhood
   - Middle Childhood
   - Early Adolescence
   - Late Adolescence

6. Intelligence
   - Infancy
   - Early Childhood
   - Middle Childhood
   - Early Adolescence
   - Late Adolescence

Volume 2:

7. Language
   - Classroom
   - Individual

8. Literacy
   - Infancy
   - Early Childhood
   - Middle Childhood
   - Early Adolescence
   - Late Adolescence

9. Emotional Development
   - Infancy
   - Early Childhood
   - Middle Childhood
   - Early Adolescence
   - Late Adolescence

10. Neighborhood
    - Early Childhood
    - Middle Childhood
    - Early Adolescence
    - Late Adolescence

Volume 3:

11. Intrinsic Motivation
    - Early Childhood
    - Middle Childhood
    - Early Adolescence
    - Late Adolescence

12. Families
    - Early Childhood
    - Middle Childhood
    - Early Adolescence
    - Late Adolescence

13. Friendship
    - Early Childhood
    - Middle Childhood
    - Early Adolescence
    - Late Adolescence

14. After School
    - Early Childhood
    - Middle Childhood
    - Early Adolescence
    - Late Adolescence

USING THE COMPANION WEBSITE

You can find the Companion Website for *Child Development* at **www.prenhall.com/mcdevitt**. The Website includes the following features:

⌨ **Chapter features:** For each chapter, the Website provides:
- A chapter outline and summary
- A chapter glossary
- Multiple choice and essay questions to spot-check your recall and understanding of chapter content
- Links to other World Wide Web sites relevant to chapter content

⌨ **Link to the Family Education Network:** This feature allows you to connect directly to the Pearson Family Education Network, an integrated set of Internet links that can enhance your own learning and give you innumerable ideas for activities and lessons you can use with children and adolescents. We encourage you to explore the network to get a better understanding of all that it has to offer.

Chapter Study Guides

USING THE CHAPTER STUDY GUIDES

Each chapter in this section of the *Study Guide and Reader* includes numerous features that should help you learn, remember, and apply the material presented in Chapters 1 through 14 of *Child Development and Education*. Following is a brief description of each feature.

Chapter Overview. At the beginning of each chapter study guide, we give a brief overview of the topics that its corresponding chapter in the textbook addresses.

Possible Knowledge, Beliefs, and Misconceptions Related to Chapter Content. When students can effectively build on the things they already know, they learn new material more meaningfully and effectively. Conversely, when they have erroneous beliefs about a topic they are studying, they often misinterpret the new ideas they encounter and so learn them incorrectly. Here we alert you to some of the knowledge, beliefs, and misconceptions that are likely to influence your learning, whether for better or for worse. Keep in mind that your existing misconceptions about a particular topic may sometimes wreak havoc with your understanding of important concepts and principles in the textbook. We urge you to read the textbook with the mindset that you will sometimes encounter information that confirms what you already believe but at other times flies in the face of things that you have long thought to be true.

Suggested Supplementary Readings. If we were to include everything in the textbook that we thought would be helpful for our readers to know about children and adolescents, we would have a very long book indeed! In the final section of this *Study Guide and Reader*, we include a number of supplementary readings that can enhance your understanding of the field of child development. In each chapter's study guide, we list those that are most relevant to the chapter's content.

Chapter Outline and Focus Questions. Each chapter study guide includes a two-column table that lists headings for each section, along with "focus questions" that you should be able to answer once you've finished reading that section. Use these questions to test yourself on what you've learned from your reading. Use them again when you study for any quizzes and exams that your instructor might give you.

Chapter Glossary. The chapter glossary presents definitions of all the key concepts that are introduced in boldface print in the chapter.

Completed "Applying Concepts in Child Development" Table. At the end of each chapter in the textbook, we include a table that describes youngsters at five different age levels and, for each youngster, provides an interpretation of his or her behavior, offers suggestions for adults working with the youngster, or both. The empty cells in the table give you an opportunity to apply what you've learned in the chapter. Each chapter study guide presents examples of how you might have filled in the empty cells.

Application Exercises. In the textbook, we provide numerous examples and instructional implications of the concepts and principles we describe. In the chapter study guides, we present additional examples and instructional strategies for you to analyze. As you do these application exercises, we suggest that you proceed in the following manner:

1. First see if you can interpret each situation using only your *memory* of the ideas you have read in the textbook.

2. If you are unable to carry out Step 1 successfully, reread the relevant sections of the textbook and once again try to interpret the situation.

3. As a last resort, refer to the answers that follow each application exercise. Don't look at these answers until you've already made a concerted effort to apply the material on your own.

Keep in mind that the answers we provide are *our* interpretations of the situations based on the concepts and principles presented in a particular chapter. If you disagree with, or perhaps don't understand, any of our analyses, you may want to consult your instructor for his or her opinion.

Sample Test Questions. At the end of each chapter study guide are several sample test questions to help you spot-check your understanding of what you have read. Some are *lower-level* items that assess your knowledge of concepts and principles. Others are *higher-level* items that assess your ability to apply what you've learned to new situations.

Chapter 1

MAKING A DIFFERENCE IN THE LIVES
OF CHILDREN AND ADOLESCENTS

Chapter Overview

This chapter introduces you to the field of child development. It addresses important developmental issues, significant theories, and general trends during five periods: infancy, early childhood, middle childhood, early adolescence, and late adolescence. You can use the information presented in this chapter, and throughout the book, to improve your understanding of children and adolescents. You will also learn—beginning with this chapter—the many implications the field of child development has for teachers and other practitioners who work with children and adolescents.

Possible Knowledge, Beliefs, and Misconceptions Related to Chapter Content

Many of the images and ideas you hold about children—including what you've previously read, experienced with children, heard from other adults, and recall from your own childhood—will serve as a good foundation for gaining increasingly deep insights about children's development. But some of your ideas might actually interfere with your learning of developmental concepts. Because prior understandings play such strong roles in learning, we recommend that you reflect on your beliefs as they relate to key developmental topics. Consider these ideas relevant to Chapter 1's concepts:

1. Most college students have wondered why a child occasionally acts similarly to same-aged peers yet at other times behaves in unexpected and unusual ways. The basic issues in development—*nature* and *nurture*, *universality* and *diversity*, and *qualitative* and *quantitative change*—are powerful dimensions for analyzing all sorts of regularities and exceptionalities among children's thinking and acting (see the section "Basic Issues in Development").

2. Some readers may expect that agents of *nurture* are always *nurturing*, that is, that they consistently exert growth-enhancing effects on children. In fact, developmental theorists use the term *nurture* to describe any environmental factors that affect children's development, regardless of whether their effects are desirable or harmful. Examples of detrimental agents of nurture include toxins in the environment, destructive family relationships, and a severely limited dietary intake.

3   Do you expect that all children learn to sit, crawl, walk, talk, and read at the same ages? This chapter explains that although some developmental sequences are similar from one child to the next, considerable *diversity* exists among children in the timing and form of age-related changes in physical, cognitive, and social-emotional domains of development.

4. Some readers may think that *qualitative* changes are *better* than *quantitative* changes. This misconception sometimes arises because the words *qualitative* and *quality* can both be used to communicate a superior character ("This printer produces higher *quality* graphics," "This essay is *qualitatively* better than the one I wrote yesterday."). However, applied to development, *qualitative* changes are modifications in the underlying structure or essence of

children's thinking, behaving, or body parts; and *quantitative* changes are gradual and trendlike modifications. One is not better than the other—both kinds of changes are essential to children's growth.

5. A second misconception may arise with *qualitative* and *quantitative* changes. Students exposed to research methods may have encountered the distinction between in-depth descriptive accounts (such as a narrative summary of children's conversations on the playground) and patterns in numerical data (such as a statistical measure of the association between children's test scores and family income levels). These two kinds of research are sometimes referred to as *qualitative* and *quantitative methods*, respectively. In contrast, when applied to child development, *qualitative* and *quantitative changes* refer to the nature of the transformation of a skill or structure. Thus the terms *qualitative* and *quantitative* have separate and unrelated uses when applied to research methods and changes in children.

6. Some people use the everyday word *stage* to mean typical age-related styles of acting (for example, "He's at that NO stage— He always says 'No' when I ask him to do something."). Psychologists refer to *stage* in a more precise way. They note that children sometimes progress through qualitatively different ways of organizing their thoughts and actions. That is, they don't simply accumulate more facts—they also occasionally reorganize their thinking. Readers can find an explanation of stage theories in the section "Qualitative and Quantitative Change."

7. Some people expect that *theories* are "true" or "false" in a simple, obvious, objective sense. They may be confused by the numerous theories that exist in the field of development (we summarize seven theories in the section "Theories of Child Development"). In fact, numerous theories are needed to explain the many complex changes in children's physical, cognitive, and social-emotional development. Each of the theories presented in Chapter 1 has strengths and limitations in accounting for particular aspects of children's development.

8. Readers who have had experience working with children from a few different age levels may easily grasp the features of the five age levels in the section "Developmental Periods." Other readers may have more limited experiences, or they may assume that they need only learn about the single age level of children with whom they expect to work. In reality, teachers and other practitioners need to be familiar with a broad span of ages because some of the youngsters they will serve will be advanced—and others delayed—and all will have unique needs. In addition, a child builds on his or her previous understandings, making it worthwhile for adults to learn skills that are apt to come before and those that are likely to emerge later. With this knowledge, teachers and practitioners can build on the skills children do have and nudge them toward more advanced states.

9. Many people look at children and adolescents as lacking the maturity of adults. Admittedly, youngsters are not as dependable or knowledgeable as adults. Nonetheless, they possess their own developmental assets, such as optimism and curiosity (see the section "Preparing for Developmentally Appropriate Practice").

Suggested Supplementary Readings

The following readings, presented in the final section of this *Study Guide and Reader*, are relevant to Chapter 1:

Reading 1-1:   Enhancing Children's Physical, Cognitive, and Social-Emotional Development in Head Start Programs

Reading 1-2:   Guidance for Teachers and Practitioners from the Field of Child Development

Reading 1-3:   Inquiring about Child Development as a Team of Teachers

CHAPTER OUTLINE	FOCUS QUESTIONS
THE FIELD OF CHILD DEVELOPMENT Three Developmental Domains Effects of Context on Development	• What does it mean for children and adolescents to "develop"? • What are three primary domains of child development? • What kinds of context influence children's development?
BASIC ISSUES IN DEVELOPMENT Nature and Nurture Universality and Diversity Qualitative and Quantitative Change Applying Basic Lessons from Child Development	• What are the three basic issues in the study of development? • What are *nature* and *nurture*? How do nature and nurture exert their effects somewhat differently in distinct domains of functioning (for example, in developing the ability to distinguish speech sounds and learning to read)? • How do children make choices that affect the environments they encounter? • What kinds of developmental sequences are *universal*? What kinds reflect *diversity* among children and adolescents? • What is the difference between *qualitative* and *quantitative* change? Identify a particular development that represents a qualitative transformation to an underlying structure, and identify a second change that is the result of a series of quantitative additions.

CHAPTER OUTLINE	FOCUS QUESTIONS

THEORIES OF CHILD DEVELOPMENT
 	
   Biological Theories
 	
   Behaviorism and Social Learning Theories
 	
   Psychodynamic Theories
 	
   Cognitive-Developmental Theories
 	
   Cognitive Process Theories
 	
   Sociocultural Theories
 	
   Developmental Systems Theories
 	
   Taking an Eclectic Approach
	• Briefly summarize the seven types of theories of child development, offering a strength and limitation for each of the theories.
	
	• Which of the theories take a strong position on the effects of nature? Nurture? Which of the theories take a balanced perspective on the roles of nature and nurture?
	
	• Why have so many different theories of child development been proposed? How can you use these distinct perspectives to better understand children?

DEVELOPMENTAL PERIODS
 	
   Infancy (Birth-2 Years)
 	
   Early Childhood (2-6 Years)
 	
   Middle Childhood (6-10 Years)
 	
   Early Adolescence (10-14 Years)
 	
   Late Adolescence (14-18 Years)
	• What human traits and skills do infants have?
	
	• What are the distinctive features of early childhood?
	
	• What kinds of developmental strengths are present during middle childhood?
	
	• What characteristics are typical of early adolescence?
	
	• What are the priorities of late adolescence?

FROM THEORY TO PRACTICE
 	
   Preparing for Developmentally Appropriate Practice
 	
   Strengthening the Commitment
	• What does it mean to use *developmentally appropriate practice* with children?
	
	• How can children's immaturity be interpreted as having a legitimate purpose?
	
	• How can professionals who work with children expand their knowledge of development?

Chapter Glossary

Behaviorism and social learning theory. Theoretical perspective that focuses on environmental stimuli and learning processes that lead to behavioral change.

Biological theory. Theoretical perspective that emphasizes genetic factors and physiological structures and functions of the body and brain.

Child development. Study of the persistent, cumulative, and progressive changes in the physical, cognitive, and social-emotional development of children and adolescents.

Cognitive development. Systematic changes in reasoning, concepts, memory, and language.

Cognitive process theory. Theoretical perspective that focuses on the precise nature of human mental operations.

Cognitive-developmental theory. Theorctical perspective that focuses on major transformations to the underlying structures of thinking.

Context. The broad social environments, including family, schools and community services, neighborhoods, culture, ethnicity, and society at large, that influence children's development.

Developmental systems theory. Theoretical perspective that focuses on the multiple factors, including systems inside and outside children, that combine to influence children's development.

Developmentally appropriate practice. Instruction and other services adapted to the age, characteristics, and developmental progress of individual children.

Diversity. In a particular aspect of human development, the varied ways different individuals progress.

Maturation. Genetically guided changes that occur over the course of development.

Nature. Effects of inherited characteristics and tendencies that affect development.

Nurture. Environmental conditions that affect development.

Physical development. Physical and brain growth and age-related changes in motor skills.

Psychodynamic theory. Theoretical perspective that focuses on how early experiences and internal conflicts affect social and personality development.

Qualitative change. Relatively dramatic developmental change that reflects considerable reorganization or modification of functioning.

Quantitative change. Developmental change that involves a series of minor, trendlike modifications.

Sensitive period. A period in development when certain environmental experiences have a more pronounced influence than is true at other times.

Social-emotional development. Systematic changes in emotions, self-concept, motivation, social relationships, and moral reasoning and behavior.

Sociocultural theory. Theoretical perspective that focuses on children's learning of tools and communication systems through practice in meaningful tasks with other people.

Stage theory. Theory that describes development as involving a series of qualitatively distinct changes.

Stage. A period of development characterized by a qualitatively distinct way of behaving or thinking.

Temperament. A child's characteristic ways of responding to emotional events, novel stimuli, and personal impulses.

Theory. Organized system of principles and explanations regarding a particular phenomenon.

Universality. In a particular aspect of human development, the commonalities seen in the way virtually all human beings progress.

Table 1–1. Applying Concepts in Child Development: Identifying Developmental Strengths in Youngsters

This table is a complete version of the table that appears at the end of Chapter 1 in the textbook. Compare your entries in the blank cells in the textbook table with our entries here. Keep in mind that there isn't necessarily a single "right" entry for any particular cell.

Age	A Youngster's Experience	Developmental Concepts *Identifying Developmental Strengths*	Implications *Building on Developmental Strengths*
Infancy (Birth–2)	An 8-month-old baby, Marita, has an ear infection and fever. She is in distress and cries often, reaching out for caregivers.	Marita is communicating her distress, having learned that caregivers can comfort her when she is hurt, tired, or scared. The baby's developmental strengths are her *expectation that others will help her* and her *ability to communicate her distress.*	Comfort the baby by holding her. Advise family members of the child's distress, and ask if a doctor has recommended physical care for the baby.
Early Childhood (2–6)	A 3-year-old child, Sydney, asks questions constantly. Sydney wants to know why the sky is blue, why the leaves are green, why the doll is broken, and why it is time for a nap.	Sydney has an insatiable and healthy curiosity. The child has also learned that he can engage adults in conversations by asking a series of questions. Sydney's developmental strengths are a *desire for new knowledge* and the possession of *rudimentary conversation skills.*	Answer the child's questions when you can, tell him politely when you are *not* able to answer his questions, and read him books and arrange other educational experiences that address his most pressing interests.
Middle Childhood (6–10)	A group of 9-year-old boys and girls are playing football at recess. The game appears to be fun, but it is punctuated with arguments over whose turn it is to play particular positions and whether or not there has been a touchdown, the ball is in or out, or a tackle has been too rough.	The children understand and respect rules of the game. They are motivated to follow—and to see that others follow—these rules. Their developmental strengths are their *appreciation for rules* and their *emerging ability to work out their different interpretations* of the game.	Tell the children that their football game looks fun and that they seem to be working out their differences. Make sure that no one is bullying other children and intervene if necessary.

table continues

Table 1–1 continued

Age	A Youngster's Experience	Developmental Concepts *Identifying Developmental Strengths*	Implications *Building on Developmental Strengths*
Early Adolescence (10–14)	Between classes, middle school students talk in the hallways, pass notes, and laugh. Boys and girls congregate in separate groups, eye one another, and seem to be self-conscious.	These young adolescents are learning to relate to one another in entirely new ways. Their developmental strengths are *the exuberant way in which they approach peer relationships* and the *heightened interest they show in social networks.*	Permit free talk during passing times between classes, but ask one teacher or staff member to be nearby to intervene if necessary (e.g., if youngsters are inclined to harass one another). Be a receptive listener to young adolescents who feel slighted or ridiculed by peers.
Late Adolescence (14–18)	A group of high school students believes that school is "dumb" and their classes are boring. They see their teachers as hypocritical and out-of-touch. They have some specific thoughts on how rules and classes should be changed. They decide to write a letter to the newspaper and demand that either the school be changed or they be allowed to graduate early.	These adolescents are questioning the way schools are designed. Their developmental strengths are *being able to see how the world could be different* and their *idealism* that school could be improved dramatically.	Let the adolescents have their say. Ask them to make a presentation to the school's accountability team but to do so in a way that does not offend any individual teachers or staff members.

Application Exercise #1: Identifying Accurate and Inaccurate Examples of Developmental Concepts

In the following scenarios, choose whether the teacher or other practitioner is *accurately* or *inaccurately* using a developmental concept or principle in his or her interpretation of the situation. Justify your response based on the material presented in Chapter 1.

1. One of the members of a girl's basketball team, 10-year-old Marta, is exceptionally advanced in athletic ability. Her coach believes that Marta is advanced for one reason: She has good genes (*nature*).

2. A caregiver in a child care center takes a moment to watch the infants in her room. Babies and toddlers are busily handling objects, studying their visual properties, shaking them, listening to the sounds they make, exploring one another's faces, and vocalizing constantly. She smiles at their vitality and reflects, "Ah, yes, this is what my professor means by saying that children's own choices and activities contribute to their development."

3. An eighth-grade boy, Brendan, is unusually short in stature. Compared to other eighth-grade boys, Brendan has retained his round face and boyish appearance. He complains to his advisor that the other boys call him "Squirt." His advisor reassures him that individual boys begin puberty and enter their growth spurt sometime during a broad age range and that he can expect to start adding inches to his height at some point during the next few years. The advisor appreciates that *diversity* exists in ages at which youngsters achieve developmental milestones.

4. A kindergarten teacher observes one of her children, Bonnie, trying to tie her shoes, hold a pencil, and string beads. Bonnie can't do *any* of these things. Her teacher believes that she can't speed up Bonnie's growth in fine motor control. The teacher excuses Bonnie from all classroom centers that enlist fine motor abilities, such as "Puzzles" and "Arts and Crafts." Instead, she asks Bonnie to build big block towers or play in the dress-up area.

5. A middle school student, Francesco, is having trouble in his pre-algebra class. His teacher notices that he *is* trying hard, doing his homework, and paying attention in class. She rules out motivation as a problem and decides she wants to learn more about how he reasons about mathematics. She believes that he's having trouble understanding abstract mathematical principles and doing mental calculations in his head. She says that she is using *behaviorism and social learning theories* to uncover Francesco's thinking.

6. Ms. Perez, an elementary school principal, serves youngsters from varied income backgrounds. Ms. Perez finds herself wondering about the effects that neighborhood, recreation outlets, and other community resources have on children's well-being. In her spare time, she reads some interesting articles written from the perspective of *developmental systems theories*.

7. A middle school teacher devotes a science unit to experimental procedures and scientific reasoning. Over the duration of the unit, she notices changes in students' thinking. As they gain experience, some students show *quantitative* gains: They gradually learn the parts and procedures of an experiment. Others show *qualitative* changes: They add new skills, such as

the ability to imagine an event before it happens and a capacity to reason about the tangible effects of abstract forces. For instance, some students now thoughtfully predict what might happen if copper and iron strips are placed in the flame of a Bunsen burner.

8. Eight-year-old Beth comes inside after free play in her after-school program. She's out of breath from running hard for 15 minutes. Recently, Beth has started to enjoy chasing games on the playground. Her teacher notices that Beth now becomes more quiet and attentive, and less fidgety, after she has had a chance to run around. Her teacher wonders whether Beth is undergoing a *developmental* change in her ability to sustain attention, or alternatively, whether she simply relaxes after exercising.

9. As children arrive each morning in Ms. Nancy's kindergarten class, they spend their first hour and a half copying sentences from storybooks into lined tablets with pencils. A few children enjoy the activity but most do not. Ms. Nancy believes that it's best to disregard children's complaints, and she encourages them to continue to copy sentences. Ms. Nancy tells the parents that this exercise is *developmentally appropriate practice* because the children are *practicing* a skill that is *appropriate* for an educated person to *develop*.

10. A high school counselor works with a group of students who want to revamp the school's improvement plan. The counselor sees that the students are ambitious about how the plan might be revised. Although the counselor wonders if the students can achieve all they want, she interprets the students' idealism as a positive developmental quality.

Answers to Application Exercise #1

1. Inaccurate. Development is the interplay of nature, nurture, and children's own efforts. It is unlikely that Marta's advanced basketball proficiency is due *solely* to the forces of nature. It may be that Marta is genetically inclined to be physically strong and coordinated, but Marta may have siblings and parents who cultivate her passion for basketball; she almost certainly spends a lot of time shooting baskets, dribbling, and running on the court; and she may have older role models in her neighborhood who inspire her to master new moves.

2. Accurate. Nature and nurture are supplemented by children's actions and choices. Children thereby contribute to their own development.

3. Accurate. Brendan's advisor realizes that diversity is present in many developmental characteristics. In this case, diversity exists in the age at which youngsters enter puberty.

4. Inaccurate. Bonnie's teacher understands that fine-motor control requires maturational development, but she does not realize that experience and activity also contribute. The teacher views development as due entirely to *nature* and forgets the importance of *nurture*.

5. Inaccurate. Francesco's teacher is interested in his thinking and reasoning and so would more likely use *cognitive-developmental* and *cognitive process theories*. She's forgotten that the *behaviorism and social learning theories* focus on tangible rewards, punishments, and other environmental stimuli that lead to behavioral change.

6. Accurate. The *developmental systems theories* examine children's development as it is affected by children's own internal resources, their activity, and the multiple contexts in which they live. The kinds of contexts in which Ms. Perez is interested would be typical topics for research in developmental systems theories.

7. Accurate. *Quantitative* changes refer to minor, trendlike growth. *Qualitative* changes refer to significant transformations in thinking.

8. Accurate. Beth's teacher realizes that there is a distinction between *development*—that is, systematic, age-related changes in physical and psychological functioning (e.g., Beth's ability to concentrate)—and temporary responses (e.g., Beth's immediate physiological response to exercise).

9. Inaccurate. *Developmentally appropriate practice* refers to instruction and other services that are adapted to the age, characteristics, and developmental progress of individual children. Ms. Nancy is conducting an activity that seems inappropriate for the age level of children in that it requires fine motor skills many young children do not have and also necessitates sedentary work for an unrealistically lengthy period. The instruction is developmentally inappropriate in another way: Ms. Nancy disregards the individual differences she encounters in children's reaction to the activity.

10. Accurate. Many "weaknesses" of childhood and adolescence serve a purpose for youngsters. The idealism of youth is an asset that fosters initiative and imaginative thinking.

Application Exercise #2: Working With Children in a Developmentally Appropriate Manner

Which of the following teachers are caring for children in a manner that is developmentally appropriate? Justify your answers in terms of typical qualities of youngsters at each age level and the practices that experts find beneficial at that age.

1.   A caregiver understands how essential *infancy* is to later growth. He wants to teach infants all he can while their brains are so eager to learn. When the infants are well fed and rested, he places them in their high chairs and shows them flash cards with letters and words printed on them. He knows that infants' visual acuity is not fully developed, so he has prepared the cards with large letters in bright primary colors.

2.   A *preschool teacher* understands the importance of laying a solid foundation in reading. She is determined to give her children an exceptionally strong, accelerated start so that they will excel in reading later in life. Accordingly, she frequently substitutes the children's morning outdoor play with additional training in letter-sound combinations. She's also concerned about wasted time in the "dramatic play area" and decides to convert the center to a drill and practice station for pre-reading skills.

3.   An *elementary teacher* appreciates the huge variation that exists in his third-grade students. In particular, he observes dramatic individual differences in children's reading comprehension. He establishes cooperative groups and varies his instructional methods (for example, using hands-on activities, explanations, skits and plays, independent research time, seat work, field trips, and center-based assignments) depending on his particular objectives for students' learning. He strives to nurture children's emerging skills while also capitalizing on their interest in real-life events and institutions. He downplays comparisons among children, instead emphasizing the progress that everyone individually is making.

4.   A *middle school* has initiated a new advising system for its students. Each student has daily contact with his or her advisor during a brief group advising session. In every two-week period, each student has at least 10 minutes of one-on-one time with the advisor to talk privately about homework, academic progress, and school activities. In the busy, socially chaotic environment of the middle school, these young adolescents are building stable relationships with adults who care about them. The relationships help students feel supported and grounded during a time when they are undergoing many rapid changes.

5.   A *high school* sets high standards for all of its students. Teachers in the school have translated this to mean having a common core of courses that all students take in small classes. To free up time for direct instruction, teachers decide to end the "Adult Advocate" program (which assigns one teacher to each student as an advisor) and the "Personal Plan for Progress" program (which permits students to pursue a few elective courses and to establish some goals for themselves). Teachers in the school agree that these programs take time from instruction and must be eliminated.

Answers to Application Exercise #2

1. No. Infants need affectionate, individualized, and responsive care in safe and interesting environments. They do not learn most effectively from drill but rather from loving interactions with familiar caregivers and from explorations in safe, well-designed environments.

2. No. Young children need to be physically active, to take initiative, and to make some of their own choices about activities. Excessive time in rigid academic tasks can be counterproductive at this age.

3. Yes. This teacher is determined to help children develop basic literacy skills, while integrating concepts into real-life activities, encouraging children to work together, and discouraging them from making nonproductive comparisons with peers.

4. Yes. Young adolescents face dramatic changes in their bodies, peer relationships, and roles within their families. A solid bond with a caring adult can be a source of protection and security during period of multiple rapid changes.

5. No. Establishment of high standards is a laudable goal, but it should not be the *only* goal for teachers. Teachers in this high school seem to have forgotten the value of personalizing learning for adolescents. What they may find is that students who are not achieving at high levels will tend to withdraw from the school. Without an advocate who keeps track of their academic progress and whereabouts, adolescents may get into trouble or drop out of school. Moreover, without finding ways to personalize learning, such as establishing individual goals, teachers may find that students perceive the school to be large, uncaring, and institutional.

Sample Test Questions

Use the following multiple-choice and essay questions to evaluate and strengthen your understanding of selected concepts in the chapter.

Multiple-Choice

1. Considering the book's explanations of *nature* and *nurture*, which one of the following statements is *true*?
   a. Nature and nurture are equally important in all domains of child development.
   b. Nature is more important for some children, and nurture is more important for others.
   c. Nature and nurture are both important throughout development, but the relative importance of each depends on the particular domain.
   d. Nurture is the only developmental factor that is relevant to teachers and practitioners.

2. Many well-known developmental theorists have focused on all children's progression through common *stages*. In other words, these theorists have emphasized:
   a. Qualitative change and diversity in development
   b. Quantitative change and diversity in development
   c. Qualitative change and universality in development
   d. Quantitative change and universality in development

3. Before reading about the seven theoretical perspectives on child development, Bertha is especially interested in how children learn tangible skills, such as how to prepare a meal and manage a house, from participating in routine activities with family members. Which of the perspectives is Bertha most likely to favor?
   a. Biological theories
   b. Cognitive-developmental theories
   c. Psychodynamic theories
   d. Sociocultural theories

4. _____ refers to genetically guided changes that occur over the course of development.
   a. Maturation
   b. Sensitive period
   c. Physical development
   d. Cognitive development

5. Which of the following best illustrates *cognitive development* as a developmental domain?
   a. Amanda has learned to sing in tune and to march to the beat of a song.
   b. Billy has learned to skip rope without tripping.
   c. Cathy has learned that she can trust some children more than others.
   d. Darla has developed a larger vocabulary, an increasing ability to attend to and recall material from school lessons, and better reasoning skills.

6. Which one of the following teachers best illustrates use of *developmentally appropriate practice* in the classroom?
   a. Ms. Applebee finds several copies of a book on world geography for college students and presents it to the 9- and 10-year-old children in her class. She asks the children to take turns reading several chapters in the book. She reasons that there is no point babying them with simpler material.
   b. Mr. Barnard notices that 4- and 5-year-old children in his child care center are concerned with possession and ownership; he realizes that this tendency is typical and probably serves a purpose for this age group. While respecting children's property rights in some situations (for example, with items they have brought from home), he encourages them to share and take turns in other situations (for example, when playing together in the block area, where there are limited quantities of blocks).
   c. Mr. Christian asks everyone in his high school algebra class to think with their hands. Because development is universal, he reasons, students must be able to build a knowledge base of concrete relationships before they can talk about, or reason through, the meaning of mathematical concepts. His lessons consist of students handling Cuisenaire rods.
   d. Ms. Delia, a physical education teacher, understands that her high school students are preoccupied with their changing bodies, romance, and yearnings for autonomy. From her perspective, an emerging identity and peer relationships are far more important at this age than are athletic goals; she believes that youngsters can make progress in only one developmental area at a time. Thus she lets the students choose to participate in structured physical education lessons or to congregate on the sidelines talking among themselves.

Essay

7. Some children, perhaps because of a disability, a cultural difference, or a restricted environment, are delayed in their academic achievement. Using the basic issues in development (nature and nurture, universality and diversity, and qualitative and quantitative change), describe how teachers might interpret or address a delay in children's learning.

8. Select one primary distinctive feature of youngsters in each of the five developmental periods: infancy, early childhood, middle childhood, early adolescence, and late adolescence. Describe an implication for each of the age levels for adults who wish to offer developmentally appropriate care for youngsters at that age.

Answers to Sample Test Questions

1. c—*Nature* and *nurture* are both important throughout development. The importance of each may vary somewhat across specific domains, however (see the section on "Nature and Nurture"). For example, children may need specific kinds of instruction to learn particular academic concepts, whereas they can develop the ability to discriminate speech sounds without training and in a wide range of environments.

2. c—Many historically prominent developmental theorists formulated stage theories (depicting a series of *qualitative* transformations) that they proposed applied to all children (*universal* changes). Descriptions of the basic developmental issues can be found in the section "Basic Issues in Development."

3. d—Bertha would be most attracted to *sociocultural theories*. Sociocultural theories focus on children's learning of tools, communication systems, and practical skills by participating in meaningful activities with other people. Theoretical perspectives are outlined in the section "Theories of Child Development."

4. a—*Maturation* is the term used to describe genetically guided changes that occur over the course of development (see the section "Nature and Nurture").

5. d—*Cognitive development* refers to systematic changes in reasoning, concepts, memory, and language. Cognitive development and the other two domains—physical, and social-emotional development—are described in the section "Three Developmental Domains."

6. b—Teaching in a *developmentally appropriate manner* means adapting instruction and care to the age, characteristics, and developmental progress of individual children. It entails looking for and building on children's strengths, recognizing that children's immaturity serves a purpose, accepting the diversity that exists in children, and nudging children toward more advanced thinking and behaving (see the section "Preparing for Developmentally Appropriate Practice"). Mr. Barnard uses developmentally appropriate practice when he recognizes that children's struggles over toys may serve an important function for them. Option *a* is incorrect because the teacher is making no accommodations to the abilities of children and assumes that an adult-like thinking is desirable and realistic for school-aged children. Option *c* is incorrect because the teacher expects uniformity in youngsters and fails to nurture the emerging abilities adolescents have in abstract thinking. Option *d* is incorrect because the teacher assumes that children can progress in only one domain of development at a time.

7. Teachers frequently encounter a child who takes longer than other children to learn academic concepts and skills. The developmental dimensions are relevant in the following ways:

    a. Teachers can acknowledge that the abilities and talents that the child has are the outgrowth of interacting effects of *nature*, *nurture*, and the child's own choices. For examples, adults can support the child's preferred ways of processing information (which may have emerged in part by *nature*, his or her genetic tendencies). Adults can also help the young person to learn new strategies that will be needed for later progress (guiding him or her as an agent of *nurture*). Finally, adults can observe the child's choices that affect learning. For instance, if a child always chooses solitary activities such as doing puzzles alone, a preschool teacher might invite the child to join other children in the dramatic play area.

    b. In considering the developmental dimensions of *universality* and *diversity*, teachers can put the learning delays of the child in perspective. Perhaps a child's abilities, even though lower than those of peers, are nevertheless well within the "normal" range. In other circumstances, a child's delays may become a matter of concern and a reason to offer support.

    c. When a child falls behind in a particular area, teachers often analyze how he or she is reasoning about the topic. It may be helpful to consider whether the child thinks in a manner that is *qualitatively* different from peers (e.g., perhaps the child is inclined to reason concretely, whereas peers are able to think more abstractly) as well as whether the child differs *quantitatively* in exposure to relevant concepts (e.g., perhaps the child has had little exposure to the subject).

8. Several sections of the book might inform your response. For example, you might have used information on general age trends and common age-related practices in the section "Developmental Periods" or typical qualities of youngsters and implications in the table "Accomplishments and Diversity at Different Age Levels." Answers will vary but might take a form such as this:

    a. Infants need to form close bonds with responsive and affectionate caregivers. Caregivers can support infants by getting to know them individually and providing attentive and gentle care of their physical needs.

    b. Young children are imaginative and socially inclined. Teachers can arrange a dramatic play area with props and open play areas.

    c. Children in the elementary schools are able to learn basic academic skills and complete realistic tasks. Teachers can support their learning by teaching them basic skills such as reading and writing, implementing realistic tasks for them to complete, and supplementing lessons with hands-on activities.

    d. The rapid changes of early adolescence make it valuable to offer every young adolescent some individualized time with a caring adult who gets to know his or her abilities and needs.

    e. The priority of peer relationships in late adolescence can be accommodated in high schools with extracurricular activities and after-school programs.

Chapter 2

USING RESEARCH TO UNDERSTAND
CHILDREN AND ADOLESCENTS

Chapter Overview

Chapter 2 explains that developmental research is an effective way to gain meaningful insights about children's development. In the chapter, we examine principles of research, such as applying the scientific method, protecting the rights of children, following painstaking steps at every phase of an investigation, and thinking critically about the meaning of data. We suggest that by growing acquainted with the properties of developmental research, you will become able to make reasonable judgments of the worth of investigations. This chapter also introduces you to the informal but systematic research that teachers and other practitioners conduct during their work with individual children.

Possible Knowledge, Beliefs, and Misconceptions Related to Chapter Content

Your previous ideas about research in child development may affect your interpretation of concepts in Chapter 2. Consider these perspectives:

1. Some people see the field of child development (and the social sciences more generally) as being derived from subjective and inexact methods. To some degree, this skepticism is justified: fool-proof methods for analyzing children's thinking, acting, feeling, and physiological states do not exist, and assertions about children are sometimes refuted or qualified when new information becomes available. Nevertheless, the field of child development has attracted brilliant scholars who design ingenious methods and interpret their results cautiously (see the section "Analyzing Developmental Research").

2. You *can* put your skepticism to good use as you read individual studies. Not every developmental investigation is high quality, making it valuable for consumers of research—including teachers and other practitioners—to remain cautious about the claims put forth in research reports. To be able to analyze developmental research, you will need to learn the various methods, their strengths and limitations, and the kinds of conclusions that are warranted with particular research designs.

3. Some readers may believe that researchers "fudge" their results, that is, skew them in a direction that doesn't do justice to the facts. This belief arises, in part, from the misleading statistics and statements used by some (definitely not all) advertisers, marketers, and political figures. Nonetheless, the vast majority of developmental research *is* conducted honorably. Moreover, other scholars besides the original investigators will carefully analyze and often try to replicate any significant but unexpected patterns in results.

4. Some readers may assume that only trained scientists (perhaps imagined as men in white lab coats, adorned with tousled hair and pocket protectors) hold the rights to research. Increasingly, developmental researchers come from a variety of backgrounds and conduct research in children's natural environments. Furthermore, many classroom teachers and other practitioners now conduct their own research on the experiences of children in schools

and other settings. Readers can refer to descriptions of teachers' research in the section "Conducting Research in Schools."

5.   Assorted misconceptions occur in interpretations of research designs. One common one is that correlations imply causal forces (see the description of studies that identify associations and Figure 2-2, both on page 44). Another misconception is that investigations based on large samples and complicated statistics are ultimately more valuable than carefully reported naturalistic studies (see the description of studies that describe children's experiences in natural contexts on pages 45-46). In this chapter, you will learn that a variety of research designs all contribute in unique and important ways to an understanding of children's development.

Suggested Supplementary Reading

The following reading, presented in the final section of this *Study Guide and Reader,* is relevant to Chapter 2:

Reading 2-1:   Considering Your Beliefs and Their Implications

CHAPTER OUTLINE	FOCUS QUESTIONS
PRINCIPLES OF RESEARCH Ethical Protection of Children The Scientific Method Research Participants	• What ethical standards do researchers follow to protect the rights of children? • What are the primary steps of the scientific method? Why is it important that scientists think critically about evidence when drawing conclusions? • What is the relationship between a sample and a population? • What problems arise when researchers select samples from accessible but narrowly defined groups (for example, when they study only children from middle-class, European American, English-speaking families)? • Give an example of a type of research study in which generalization to a larger population would *not* be an objective.

ANALYZING DEVELOPMENTAL RESEARCH	• What are the four major types of data collection techniques? What are the strengths and limitations of each of these techniques?
Data Collection Techniques	
Research Designs	• Under what conditions is a data collection technique *valid*?
Becoming a Thoughtful Consumer of Research	• What does it mean for a data collection technique to be *reliable*?
	• What is an advantage of using more than one data collection technique?
	• What are the characteristics of studies that identify causal relationships, associations, developmental change and stability, and children's experiences in natural contexts?
	• What strategies might you follow as you look for and review particular research studies?
CONDUCTING RESEARCH IN SCHOOLS	• What guidelines can teachers and other practitioners follow in collecting information from children?
Collecting Information on the Job	
Observing Children	• What can you do to enhance your observation skills with children?
Listening to Children	• How can you put children at ease during an interview?
Interpreting Assessments	• Why is it helpful to analyze more than a single piece of work by a child when trying to determine the child's abilities?
Conducting Action Research	
Ethical Guidelines for Teacher-Researchers	• What are examples of questions teachers might ask when conducting action research?
	• What ethical principles should teachers and other practitioners consider when they collect information from children?

Chapter Glossary

Action research. Systematic study of an issue or problem by a teacher or other practitioner, with the goal of bringing about more productive outcomes for children.

Assessment. Task that children complete and researchers use to make judgments of children's understandings and skills.

Control group. A group of participants in a research study who do not receive the treatment under investigation; often used in an experimental study.

Correlation coefficient. A statistic that indicates the nature of the relationship between two variables.

Correlation. Extent to which two variables are related to each other, such that when one variable increases, the other either increases or decreases in a somewhat predictable fashion.

Correlational study. Research study that explores relationships among variables.

Cross-sectional study. Research study in which the performance of individuals at different ages is compared.

Experimental study. Research study in which a researcher manipulates one aspect of the environment (a treatment), controls other aspects of the environment, and assesses the treatment's effects on participants' behavior.

Habituation. Changes in children's physiological responses to repeated displays of the same stimulus, reflecting loss of interest.

Interview. Data collection technique that obtains self-report data through face-to-face conversation.

Longitudinal study. Research study in which the performance of a single group of people is tracked over a period of time.

Naturalistic study. Research study in which individuals are observed in their natural environment.

Observation. Data collection technique whereby a researcher carefully observes and documents the behaviors of participants in a research study.

Physiological measure. Direct assessment of physical development or physiological functioning.

Quasi-experimental study. Research study in which one or more experimental treatments are administered but in which random assignment to groups is not possible.

Questionnaire. Data collection technique that obtains self-report data through a paper-pencil inventory.

Reliability. Extent to which a data collection technique yields consistent, dependable results— results that are only minimally affected by temporary and irrelevant influences.

Sample. The specific participants in a research study; their performance is often assumed to indicate how a larger population of individuals would perform.

Scientific method. Multistep process of answering a carefully defined research question by using critical thinking and analysis of the evidence.

Self-report. Data collection technique whereby participants are asked to describe their own characteristics and performance.

Test. Instrument designed to assess knowledge, understandings, abilities, or skills in a consistent fashion across individuals.

Validity. Extent to which a data collection technique actually assesses what the researcher intends for it to assess.

Table 2-2. Applying Concepts from Child Development: Learning from Children and
Adolescents

*This table is a complete version of the table that appears at the end of Chapter 2 in the textbook.
Compare your entries in the blank cells in the textbook table with our entries here. Keep in mind that
there isn't necessarily a single "right" entry for any particular cell.*

Age	A Youngster's Experience	Developmental Concepts *Considering the Accuracy of Information*	Implications *Drawing Appropriate Conclusions*
Infancy (Birth–2)	An 18-month-old baby, Harriet, is drowsy when an unfamiliar adult examines her recognition of common household words, such as *ball*. The girl fails to point to particular objects when the adult asks her to do so.	The fact that Harriet is not alert, the task is somewhat artificial, and the adult is a stranger raises questions about *the task's validity as an indication of the child's ability*.	The researcher realizes that the task is not a valid measure of the infant's knowledge of object names. The researcher needs to observe the infant on other occasions, particularly when the infant is interacting with a familiar caregiver.
Early Childhood (2–6)	Four-year old Seth takes a children's picture book, points at each page, and tells the teacher what each page says.	An observer wonders whether Seth knows how to read. She realizes that the boy might know how to read, but it is also possible that this book is a favorite of the boy's and one that he has memorized after listening to it repeatedly. Without additional information, the *validity* of her inference about Seth's reading is questionable.	The researcher realizes that more observations are needed to determine whether Seth can read. It may also be helpful to talk with the boy about his interests and abilities in reading.
Middle Childhood (6–10)	A teacher is conducting action research on her students' performance in mathematics. One 9-year-old boy, Ryan, turns in a blank paper each time they do math worksheets. Ryan has recently moved from another state, and the teacher does not yet know what Ryan's skills are. He is very quiet.	The teacher examines each child's written work, talking with children individually about their interests in math and watching them as they perform mathematical operations. The teacher appreciates that she is just getting to know Ryan and that there are many reasons why he might not be completing the math problems. His failure to complete the work may not be a reliable indication of his performance, and the inference that Ryan is not able to do the work may not be valid.	The teacher cannot draw firm conclusions about Ryan's mathematical skills. There are countless reasons why he is not doing well on the worksheets—perhaps he has not yet been exposed to multiplication, feels anxious about math, or is bored with the task. Alternatively, he might be shy and worried about being in the new classroom. The teacher realizes that she needs more information before she can draw any conclusions about Ryan's abilities.

table continues

Table 2–1 continued

Age	A Youngster's Experience	Developmental Concepts *Considering the Accuracy of Information*	Implications *Drawing Appropriate Conclusions*
Early Adolescence (10–14)	Twelve-year-old Mary completes a survey related to sexual harassment at school. Mary reports that she has experienced each and every action, such as being touched inappropriately while walking down the school hall and being the recipient of unwanted comments about her physical appearance.	The researcher realizes that Mary may be exaggerating the amount of sexual harassment she has experienced at school. It is also possible that Mary is giving an accurate report of her experiences. Both *validity* and *reliability* of responses are in question.	The researcher determines that it will be necessary to look at all students' responses before concluding that sexual harassment is pervasive at school. Because Mary's responses are somewhat unexpected, the researcher may choose to follow it up with informal interviews among a few girls. The researcher may also want to look into the school's policies and procedures to see if the school is inadvertently condoning sexual harassment.
Late Adolescence (14–18)	Seventeen-year-old Melinda has had a brain scan. Her scan seems to show that some brain areas, especially those circuits devoted to planning ahead and using good judgment, are less mature than those in typical adult brains.	Adolescent brains are undergoing continuous refinement as they change with maturational processes and experience. The results of a single brain scan should not be taken too seriously, however. Any single result *cannot* be assumed to be completely *valid* or *reliable*.	The researcher realizes that any single physiological measure should be confirmed with other data. If the immaturity is confirmed, it may be age typical and would not mean that Melinda should be excluded from activities that require judgment.

<u>Application Exercise #1: Identifying Problems in Data Collected From Children and Adolescents</u>

In the following scenarios, information collected from children or adolescents is affected by one of the problems identified in Table 2-1 on page 41 of Chapter 2. Identify the specific distortion in the data.

1. Ms. Rathe has several volunteers from a local senior center who come two or three times a week to hold the babies and give them their bottles. Ms. Rathe uses their visit as a time to write notes to parents and catch up with projects. One day when the volunteers come, Ms. Rathe puts up a new poster. At the time, the babies are sleepy and fussy. Ms. Rathe cheerfully points out the new bright, visually complex poster but the babies look away. Ms. Rathe wonders why they don't like it.

2. Children in Mr. Thomas's classroom are usually active and spirited. They generally talk a lot, ask a lot of questions, and move around the room to pick up supplies they need for assignments. Today they have a researcher sitting in their room. They are quiet and still.

3. In early May, the students at Mill Valley Middle School take their state's annual achievement tests in language arts, mathematics, and science. When researchers try to administer a test of spatial abilities a week later, youngsters are anxious, hurried, and careless. Their attitude seems to be, "Just *finish*." They've had it with tests.

4. A group of adolescents is asked to take a test of their reasoning skills—in particular, an assessment of their ability to judge the adequacy of persuasive arguments. The passages that they analyze are selected from reading materials about American history and contemporary American political events. Adolescents from families who have recently immigrated to the United States have far less knowledge about these topics than do native-born American peers. Consequently, these adolescents perform poorly on the test, even though their reasoning skills are equivalent to native-born American peers on topics for which they have equivalent exposure.

5. Dr. Snow-White interviews young children about the television programs they watch at home. She asks them to describe the names and content of cartoons they watched yesterday, last week, and last month. Children give detailed accounts of cartoons they watched yesterday but are less complete in their reports of those they watched last week and last month. Sometimes they say they cannot remember and other times they give answers that sound as if they might be describing programs they've watched more recently.

6. Having read about high rates of violence in large cities, a team of researchers wants to know if such aggressiveness occurs in schools in urban neighborhoods. The team decides to conduct observations of helping and hurting behaviors at school. Because they expect to see more hurting behaviors, they code ambiguous behaviors, such as bumping into peers, as "intentionally hurtful."

7. Adolescents completing a survey on sexual behaviors believe that the survey items are intrusive and not the rightful concern of the researchers. Some of the adolescents also wonder if their access to contraception will be taken away if they admit that they're sexually

active, and so they purposefully underestimate their frequency of sexual contacts. Other adolescents think that they're "uncool" for *not* being sexually experienced; these respondents exaggerate their sexual experience.

8. A researcher is interested in social exchanges among an ethnically diverse group of middle-school students. She decides to conduct an observational study of students' social interactions during the lunch hour. When she goes to the school cafeteria to make her observations, she realizes that she is not able to attend to the many interactions that take place between and among students from different ethnic groups. She discovers that she cannot take notes quickly enough.

9. A group of children participates in a study focusing on attitudes toward physical activity. The children are given a questionnaire and asked to indicate how strongly they agree or disagree with a series of statements (e.g., "I like to participate in sports."). Some of the children are not accustomed to the questionnaire's format and do not follow the instructions to choose a number from 1 (*strong disagreement*) to 6 (*strong agreement*) for each statement. Instead, they simply circle the statements with which they agree.

10. A group of high school students completes a questionnaire about their experiences in studying science. Students complete the questionnaire as an extra credit activity at the end of a chemistry class. The students assume the researchers are focusing on chemistry in particular and answer the items with this scientific field in mind. In reality, the researchers are interested in students' general perspectives on the various scientific disciplines typically taught in high school, including chemistry but also the biological sciences, physics, and earth sciences.

Answers to Application Exercise #1

1. *Participants' attention to stimuli.* The babies in Ms. Rathe's infant center are not attending to the poster. It is not possible to draw conclusions about the infants' interest in the poster. They are too tired to look around the room and notice new stimuli.

2. *Effect of the observer's presence.* The children in Mr. Thomas's classroom may have changed their behavior in reaction to the presence of the researcher.

3. *Response style of research participants.* Youngsters at Mill Valley Middle School are not giving their best effort to complete the spatial abilities test. They seem to associate it with their recent statewide achievement test, are bored with tests, and just want to be done with it.

4. *Cultural bias in test content.* Adolescents who do not have knowledge of American history and politics are at a disadvantage in this test that purportedly assesses analytical reasoning. In reality, the test also assesses knowledge of American culture.

5. *Memory of research participants.* Children interviewed by Dr. Snow-White cannot fully recall viewing programs last week and last month.

6. *Bias of observers.* These researchers expect to see high rates of aggression, and they allow their expectations to influence their observations

7. *Defensiveness of research participants.* Respondents are not providing accurate information about their sexual experiences.

8. *Attention limitations of observers.* This researcher cannot take it all in: The scope of her research project, and the types of observations she wishes to make, are too broad and unfocused.

9. *Participants' familiarity with test format.* Some of the children are unfamiliar with the format of the questionnaire and as a result do not offer opinions of varying intensity. It would not be clear from their responses how strongly they agreed or disagreed with the statements.

10. *Interpretations by research participants.* Research participants are thinking about *science* differently than the researchers are.

Application Exercise #2: Analyzing Research Methods in Child Development

In each of the following investigations, a problem can be identified with respect to the data collection methods, the research design, or the interpretation of the results. Using concepts from Chapter 2, describe the problem.

1. On a day of record-breaking heat in late September, children complete a questionnaire about their attitudes toward school. The air conditioner has already been turned off, and children are listless. They give responses that are more negative than they would typically give. They don't want to be at school today.

2. Researchers are studying young children's beliefs about friendship. The researchers meet individually with a large number of preschool and kindergarten children; after putting the children at ease, they ask them what friends are for, how they choose friends, and how friends help them. They find that children express rather simple and concrete beliefs about friends. For example, they say that friends build block towers with them and play "mommies and daddies." They say nothing about psychological qualities, such as sharing, giving comfort, or enjoying one another's company. However, the same children exhibit these helpful and mutually supportive behaviors when they interact with friends.

3. A team of developmental researchers investigates the relationship between children's musical ability and their later mathematical performance. The researchers assess children's ability to match the pitches of musical notes at age 10 and later measure their pre-algebra and algebra skills at ages 12 and 14, respectively. They find close relationships between musical ability and later mathematical achievement. The researchers argue that musical training causes superior mathematics ability.

4. A developmental researcher is interested in the origins of juvenile delinquency. He compares two groups of teenagers. Those in one group have been convicted of a crime, and those in the other group have not. The teenagers all reside in the same state and come from middle-income families. He finds that the "delinquent" adolescents are more likely to achieve at low levels academically than are the "non-delinquent" adolescents. The researcher concludes that delinquent behaviors are caused by poor academic achievement.

5. A researcher wishes to investigate children's knowledge of their parents' political participation. Without seeking the consent of children or their parents, she asks children specific questions about parents' voting behaviors and about family discussions regarding political issues. The interviews are lengthy (about two hours), and so many of the children become bored and ask to return to their classrooms. The researcher tells the children they can only return to their classroom after they've answered all the questions.

Answers to Application Exercise #2

1. The heat is not within the control of the researcher. Nonetheless, the conditions of administration of the instruments *are* problematic. The researcher may raise questions about *validity* and *reliability* of the data. In terms of reliability, the responses children give are not likely to be the same from one day to the next. Because their scores are not consistent, validity is also questionable (the instrument is not accurately measuring attitudes; see the discussion of accuracy in data collection in the section "Data Collection Techniques").

2. Questions can be raised about the *validity* of information collected from children's verbal reports. Because these children have limited verbal skills, they may have understandings about friendship that they are not able to articulate (see discussions of self-reports and accuracy in data collection in the section "Data Collection Techniques").

3. There are correlations between age-10 musical ability (as measured by sensitivity to pitch) and age-12 and age-14 mathematical ability (as measured by performance on tests of pre-algebra and algebra concepts). However, this correlation does not provide definitive information about causality. It may be that a third variable (e.g., academic motivation, general intelligence, family support, or enrichment activities) influences both musical and mathematical ability. Alternatively, perhaps there is a reverse effect, with early mathematical competencies affecting both musical performance and later achievement in pre-algebra and algebra. Notice as well that *musical training* was not examined in the study (see the discussion of studies that identify associations in the section "Research Designs").

4. In this study, it is not clear which factors affect other things. For instance, it is possible that it is not the low achievement itself that causes delinquency. Instead, perhaps a third factor causes both problems in school and a tendency toward deviant activity. For example, children whose parents are struggling themselves may fail to prepare children for academic expectations at school, leading children to be delayed in academic abilities, unable to concentrate, and easily swayed by negative peer influences. Or students with learning disabilities or attention problems may be impulsive and inattentive in school and at home, triggering an escalating and pervasive pattern of combative behavior. Another possible explanation is that children who achieve at low levels in school are not invested in doing well there and see little hope for themselves in mainstream society either (see the discussion of studies that identify associations in the section "Research Designs").

5. This researcher has failed to comply with basic ethical standards for conducting research with children. The researcher has not obtained the consent of the children or their families and does not permit them to withdraw from the study when they express their discomfort (see "Ethical Protection of Children").

Application Exercise #3: Conducting Research in Schools

Are the following teachers collecting information in a way that is likely to benefit children in their care? Justify your answer for each scenario based on what you have learned about conducting research in schools.

1. A teacher wants to implement cooperative learning groups in his third-grade class. He has observed teachers implementing cooperative groups, read about strategies in teacher magazines, and talked with colleagues about their strategies for forming groups and structuring tasks. He chooses a particular model of cooperative learning and realizes that he should observe children working in the groups. He uses several kinds of observations: running records, anecdotal records, and checklists.

2. A preschool teacher wants to find out how many children have been to places she is considering for a field trip. She asks the children to sit in a circle around her and then fires a series of questions at them: "Who has been to the art history museum? The natural history museum? The post office? The fire station? The police station? Which of these places would you *most* like to visit?" A few hands go up about having visited particular places, but no one answers her question about where they'd like to go. After the conversation, the teacher is not sure if the children would really like to go on a field trip.

3. A school counselor, Cynthia, is surprised to hear that a colleague, Shauna, is conducting a research study. Shauna wants to learn about the assets and risk factors present in her community so that she can design an effective drug prevention program. She is collecting information from students, families, business leaders, school staff, and city personnel. Cynthia wonders why Shauna would bother to conduct her own investigation when there is such fine research produced by professors and research scientists.

4. A few teachers in one school are interested in how well their new anti-bullying program has worked. They give youngsters a survey and ask them if they have recently committed any acts of bullying at school. Youngsters report no acts of bullying. The teachers conclude that the new program is a success.

5. A first-grade teacher is concerned about the difficulty children in her class have with following rules, keeping their hands to themselves, and anticipating the effects of their actions. She wonders whether their problems with impulse control are age-typical; she also wonders about the conditions under which impulsive behaviors are most common. She talks with a few children individually and asks other teachers for their opinions. She also conducts observations of youngsters before and after school, on the playground, and in school hallways. To focus her observations, she employs a checklist of behaviors. After reflecting on the data she collects, she will develop a plan to foster children's self-control.

Answers to Application Exercise #3

1. Yes. The teacher has learned from other people's experiences with cooperative groups. When he implements cooperative learning in his own classroom, he realizes that he needs to observe the children carefully to see how they handle the new instructional approach. He conducts several different kinds of observations to gain systematic information about how the groups are working.

2. No. The preschool teacher has not put the children at ease, and her rapid series of questions may seem like an inquisition to the children. She might be more successful if she has informal conversations with children individually or in small groups.

3. No. Cynthia does not understand the purposes or benefits of research conducted by teachers and practitioners. Shauna will guide the program's design using both existing research and her own findings.

4. No. When collecting information from young people, it is good practice to obtain multiple sources of information and to question the validity and reliability of the data. The teachers do neither—they don't substantiate self-report responses with other kinds of data and they don't consider why the youngsters would give the answers that they did. It is possible that the children have learned from the program that teachers disapprove of aggressive acts and are ashamed to admit to having committed acts of bullying.

5. Yes. The teacher is collecting several different kinds of data that together will provide a useful picture of the behavior of children in her classroom. She is conducting interviews with a few children and other teachers and is supplementing this information with structured observations of children's behavior in several settings.

<u>**Sample Test Questions**</u>

Use the following multiple-choice and essay questions to evaluate and strengthen your understanding of selected concepts in the chapter.

Multiple-Choice

1. A developmental researcher wants to learn about the problem-solving strategies that second-, fourth-, and sixth-grade students use. During October, he collects data from children at these grade levels and then compares the number of strategies that children of the different ages use. What kind of research design is this?
    a. Naturalistic study
    b. Experimental study
    c. Longitudinal study
    d. Cross-sectional study

2. A group of investigators is interested in the school adjustment of adolescents. They have selected an assessment tool that asks students a variety of questions about how favorably they feel about school's value for them. The researchers are concerned that students' mood when they complete the inventory will affect their responses. The researchers also realize that emotional states can change from hour to hour and day to day, and they only have permission from the school to collect data during a single time period. What primary concern do they have about collecting data with their scale?
    a. Collecting data that generalize to other adolescents
    b. Collecting data that are reliable over time
    c. Collecting data that are not distorted by the biases of the researchers
    d. Collecting data that minimize cultural content

3. Which one of the following is an accurate definition of *action research*?
    a. Observational studies that depict the rapid series of motions of young children on the playground
    b. Systematic research conducted by teachers, with the goal of solving specific problems in caring for youngsters
    c. Small-scale replications of published investigations that teachers conduct as a way of learning the procedures of research
    d. High-quality research that maximizes the validity and reliability of data collection and the generalizability of the results

4. A teacher talks with parents who are troubled by the disruptive behavior of their son. The boy is rude to his parents, refuses to do what they say, calls other children nasty names, and is always in trouble at school. The parents have found a research article on the Internet that finds a correlation between disruptive behavior in children and genetic factors. Given the recommendations in the book for analyzing research studies, how might the teacher comment about the research?

   a. The teacher should suggest that the research is likely to be accurate and thus the family should ask their son's doctor to prescribe medication.

   c. The teacher might volunteer to conduct a statewide investigation into the origins of aggression and non-compliance in children.

   c. The teacher might tell the parents that any single study has strengths and limitations, and even if the association is borne out by other research, group trends do not always apply to individual children.

   d. The teacher might ask the boy to read and reflect on the research results.

5. A researcher is interested in conducting a *naturalistic* study of interactions among infants in a child care center. Which one of the following approaches is she most likely to take?

   a. In-depth observations of how infants watch, imitate, and smile and babble at one another

   b. Interviews with infants about preferred playmates

   c. An experimental study comparing the social skills of infants who have participated in a social-skills training program with the skills of infants who have not participated in the program

   d. A longitudinal study tracing changes in parents' survey responses regarding their children's social behaviors

6. Which one of the following is a serious problem that researchers face in obtaining research participants?

   a. Determining how to override parents' refusals to allow their children to participate in the research

   b. Selecting the most optimistic children to highlight in their research reports

   c. Deciding whether to use half or all the children available

   d. Recruiting hard-to-find samples of children

Essay

7. Compare and contrast research conducted by academic scholars in the field of child development with action research conducted by teachers and other practitioners.

8. In Chapter 2, aggression is used as a theme in the four kinds of designs described: (a) studies that identify causal relationships, (b) studies that identify associations, (c) studies that show developmental change and stability, and (d) studies that describe children in natural contexts (for a summary, see Table 2-2 on page 47 of the textbook). Choose another theme in childhood (such as memory, friendship skills, or physical activity) and describe four studies that illustrate the four types of designs.

Answers to Sample Test Questions

1. d—*Cross-sectional studies* compare the performance of individuals across different age levels at a single point in time.

2. b—These researchers are concerned with the *reliability* of data collection. They realize that moods change fairly frequently and that they cannot assume that one measurement of school adjustment will be representative of participants' typical ways of responding.

3. b—Action research is conducted by practitioners to help them understand youngsters and solve the problems they face in working with these young people.

4. c—Teachers can and should evaluate the results of research instead of taking them at face value (see the section "Analyzing Developmental Research").

5. a—*Naturalistic studies* examine children in their natural, everyday contexts.

6. d—Obtaining hard-to-recruit participants is a major problem faced by developmental researchers.

7. Formal research by developmental scholars and action research by teachers and practitioners are *similar* in the following ways:
    *   The desire to obtain information that has integrity (that is, it is valid and reliable)
    *   Consideration of ethical issues related to the participation of children and adolescents, and protection of their anonymity and confidentiality
    *   Reflection and critical analysis, whereby observations and other data sources are scrutinized and interpreted, and alternative explanations are considered

    In addition, there may be some *differences*:
    *   Developmental scholars are motivated more by contributions to existing literature on the topic, whereas teachers and practitioners are usually more concerned with solving a specific, immediate problem.
    *   Generally, research conducted by teachers and practitioners is narrower in scope than research conducted by professional scholars. For example, a teacher might investigate why a child is not attentive in class and which interventions might be successful in securing his attention, whereas a developmental researcher might examine the broader topic of how attention changes in children as they develop. (Note that some qualitative case studies by developmental scholars go into depth about the perspectives and actions of individual children, so sample size is not the only relevant distinguishing factor.)

8. Responses will vary depending on the theme. Here is a sample response focusing on children's memory strategies:

    Study that identifies a causal relationship: An experimenter compares the recall of words by children trained in memory strategies versus children not trained in memory strategies.

    Study that identifies an association: A researcher collects information on children's memory strategies and the amount of reading they do and determines whether there is an association between these two variables.

    Study that shows developmental change and stability: A researcher examines the stability and change in children's memory strategies by collecting information on their memories once a year for five years.

    Study that describes children in natural contexts: A researcher observes children in a classroom while they are studying state capital cities and infers the learning strategies the children spontaneously use while trying to learn the capitals.

Chapter 3

BIOLOGICAL BEGINNINGS

Chapter Overview

Chapter 3 describes three remarkable biological beginnings for children. A child's first beginning is at conception—when two parents give an offspring genetic instructions for growth. The second beginning is prenatal development—the sequenced, orderly changes in the brain and body of the baby-to-be. A child's third beginning is birth—the dramatic move from the warm, nourishing, and insulated environment of the mother's interior to the cool, vibrant, and socially responsive outer world. In this chapter, we explain how nature and nurture are closely intertwined in the marvelous progressions of these three beginnings. Throughout this chapter, we also offer recommendations that parents and adults outside the family can follow to increase children's prospects for having healthy beginnings.

Possible Knowledge, Beliefs, and Misconceptions Related to Chapter Content

Readers may hold a range of beliefs about genetic inheritance, pregnancy, and birth. Some understandings may facilitate new learning, yet other beliefs might be inconsistent with the evidence. Consider the following possible beliefs related to content in Chapter 3:

1. Some readers may expect that they know little about genetic inheritance. Yet most people probably have seen the effects of genes within families. For example, as a child, you may have observed that some biologically related brothers and sisters had striking physical similarities (maybe in height, a distinctive smile, the color and appearance of eyes, or hair color and texture), whereas other related siblings (perhaps in other families) did not resemble one another at all. In Chapter 3, you will find confirmation that genetic effects are powerful but complex (see the sections "Formation of Reproductive Cells" and "Genetic Basis of Individual Traits").

2. Some readers may believe that individual differences in temperament and intelligence are completely environmental in origin. Without dismissing environmental effects, Chapter 3 suggests that genes also play a sizable role in the expression of psychological traits, such as a person's inclination to be verbally talented or temperamentally shy (see the section "The Blending of Heredity and Environment").

3. Some readers may assume that children who share a particular chromosomal or genetic disorder (such as Down syndrome or sickle cell disease) will be very similar. In fact, children who have a common chromosomal or genetic disorder may have symptoms that vary considerably in their severity, depending on other genes they may have; education, medication, and other environmental experiences; and their own unique personalities (see the discussion of problems in genetic instructions in the section "Genetic Basis of Individual Traits").

4. Many people assume that if a trait has a genetic basis, it must be expressed at birth or at least by early childhood. In Chapter 3, you will learn that not all genes are active at birth, and some genes spring into action only after the child has either matured to a certain extent,

other physiological processes have taken place, or an environmental experience has provoked them (see the section "The Awakening of Genes").

5. An important challenge that teachers and practitioners face is accepting that children's skills, emotional expression, and habits are each caused by multiple factors—that children are the product of nature *and* nurture (see the section "Acknowledging Nature and Nurture in Children's Lives").

6. One misconception about pregnancy is that beyond eating well and avoiding alcoholic beverages and drugs, women can do little to increase their chances of having healthy babies. In this chapter we explain that even before conception, a couple can obtain medical advice about preparing for a healthy pregnancy. Those who are concerned about potential genetic problems in offspring can speak with a doctor or consult a genetic counselor. We also review several health-promoting tactics pregnant women can take (see the section "Medical Care").

7. A misunderstanding about women's labor and delivery is that women must choose between only two options for managing discomfort during labor: (a) using entirely natural methods (for example, using relaxation techniques, breathing through contraction, and being massaged by a partner), or (b) relying solely on medical interventions (for example, taking pain-numbing medicines and undergoing intrusive medical procedures). This chapter explains that women have a wide range of options to choose from as they progress through the labor and delivery, and they often combine natural methods with medical interventions (see the section "Complications and Interventions").

Suggested Supplementary Reading

The following reading, presented in the final section of this *Study Guide and Reader*, is relevant to Chapter 3:

Reading 3-1: Hush Little Baby, Don't You Cry: Massage for Infants

CHAPTER OUTLINE	FOCUS QUESTIONS
GENETIC FOUNDATIONS OF CHILD DEVELOPMENT Structure and Operation of Genes Formation of Reproductive Cells Genetic Basis of Individual Traits The Awakening of Genes The Blending of Heredity and Environment Acknowledging Nature and Nurture in Children's Lives	• By what process do genes exert effects on the body? • How are chromosomes, genes, and DNA (deoxyribonucleic acid) hierarchically related? • What direct effects do genes have on the body? How do genes indirectly affect children's activity? How do children's experiences indirectly affect their genetic expression? • Using your knowledge of *meiosis*, explain how children inherit characteristics from both their parents as well as inherit characteristics that distinguish them from their parents and any biologically related siblings they might have. • Select one of the common chromosomal and genetic disorders, and identify strategies you could use as a teacher or practitioner to support a child with this condition. Include strategies that address both the child's special needs and qualities the child shares with other children of the same age. • Why are the effects of some genes evident from birth whereas others are not expressed until much later? • How can a child's genetic makeup affect his or her experiences in particular environments?
PRENATAL DEVELOPMENT Phases of Prenatal Growth Medical Care Supporting Parents, Protecting Babies	• What are the three phases of prenatal growth? What are the primary accomplishments of the growing being during each of the three phases? • What can a woman do before getting pregnant to increase her chances of conceiving healthy offspring? • What are *teratogens*? During what phase of prenatal growth is the offspring most vulnerable to exposure to teratogens? Why? • What medical procedures are sometimes implemented during a pregnancy to check on the status of offspring? • What can practitioners do to support parents and protect their offspring?

CHAPTER OUTLINE	FOCUS QUESTIONS
BIRTH OF THE BABY Preparation for Birth The Birth Process Complications and Interventions Enhancing Caregivers' Sensitivity to Newborn Infants	• Through what kinds of support do prepared childbirth classes help prospective parents get ready for the baby's birth? • What combination of factors seems to precipitate labor? • What happens during the three stages of labor? • How do midwives, partners, coaches, and physicians comfort women during labor and delivery? • What are the two categories of babies that require special care after birth? • What guidelines are offered for the care of fragile infants? • How can practitioners help new parents and other family members become more sensitive to the cues and needs of newborn infants?

Chapter Glossary

Alleles. Genes located at the same point on corresponding (paired) chromosomes and related to the same physical characteristic.

Canalization. Tight genetic control of a particular aspect of development.

Chromosome. Rodlike structure that resides in the nucleus of every cell of the body and contains genes that guide growth and development; each chromosome is made up of DNA.

Codominance. Situation in which the two genes of an allele pair, although not identical, both have some influence on a characteristic.

Dizygotic twins. Twins that began as two separate zygotes and so are as genetically similar as two siblings conceived and born at different times.

DNA. A spiral-staircase shaped molecule that guides the production of proteins needed by the body for growth and development; short for deoxyribonucleic acid.

Dominant gene. Gene that overrides any competing instructions in an allele pair.

Embryo. During prenatal Weeks 2 through 8, the developing being that is in the process of forming major body structures and organs.

Fetus. During prenatal Weeks 9 until birth, the developing being that is growing in size and weight and in sensory abilities, brain structures, and organs needed for survival.

Gamete. Reproductive cell that, in humans, contains 23 chromosomes rather than the 46 chromosomes present in other cells in the body; a male gamete (sperm) and a female gamete (ovum) join at conception.

Gene. Basic unit of heredity in a living cell; segments of genes are contained on chromosomes.

Meiosis. The process of cell reproduction and division by which gametes are formed.

Mitosis. The process of cell duplication by which chromosomes are preserved and a human being or other organism can grow.

Monozygotic twins. Twins that began as a single zygote and so share the same genetic makeup.

Perception. Interpretation of stimuli that the body has sensed.

Polygenic inheritance. Situation in which many genes combine in their influence on a particular characteristic.

Premature infant. Infant born early (before 37 weeks of prenatal growth) and sometimes with serious medical problems.

Prenatal development. Growth that takes place between conception and birth.

Recessive gene. Gene that influences growth and development primarily when the other gene in the allele pair is identical to it.

Reflex. Automatic motor response to stimuli.

Sensation. Physiological detection of stimuli in the environment.

State of arousal. Physiological condition of sleepiness or wakefulness.

Teratogen. Potentially harmful substance that can cause damaging effects during prenatal development.

Zygote. Cell formed when a male sperm joins with a female ovum; with healthy genes and nurturing conditions in the uterus, it may develop into a fetus and be born as a live infant.

Table 3–1. Applying Concepts in Child Development: Promoting Healthy Beginnings for Children and Their Families

This table is a complete version of the table that appears at the end of Chapter 3 in the textbook. Compare your entries in the blank cells in the textbook table with our entries here. Keep in mind that there isn't necessarily a single "right" entry for any particular cell.

Age	The Experiences of Children and Families	Developmental Concepts *Identifying Factors That Affect Children's Beginnings*	Implications *Helping Children and Families to Experience Healthy Beginnings*
Prior to Conception	Kuri and Taro want to have a child. They go to the doctor to discuss their desire to plan for a healthy pregnancy.	The *health of any children conceived by a couple* depends on several factors, including the mother's health prior to the pregnancy and her diet, actions, stress levels, and exposure to teratogens during the pregnancy. The health of their children's genes is mostly beyond parents' control, although some parents may choose to terminate a pregnancy when diagnostic prenatal tests reveal a serious problem.	Encourage prospective parents to talk with their doctor before conception and to make the necessary adjustments to their lifestyle. For example, the woman will want to find out whether any medicines she takes can affect the health of her offspring. Couples concerned about possible birth defects may choose to see a genetic counselor.
During the first few weeks of pregnancy	A pregnant woman, Antoinette, does not know she is pregnant and continues to drink large amounts of alcohol and to smoke a pack of cigarettes each day. Antoinette also contracts a cold virus and takes over-the-counter medicines.	During the *period of the zygote*, the future human being develops rapidly but has yet to implant into the uterus or to form separate body parts. The zygote might not be harmed by the mother's drinking and smoking. During the *embryonic period*, the rapidly growing being is especially vulnerable to harmful substances. Whether embryos that are exposed to teratogens suffer structural damage depends on a variety of factors, including magnitude, timing, and duration of the exposure and individual genetic vulnerabilities.	Encourage women who are sexually active and able to conceive children to shield themselves from teratogens as a matter of course.

table continues

Table 3–1 continued

Age	The Experiences of Children and Families	Developmental Concepts *Identifying Factors That Affect Children's Beginnings*	Implications *Helping Children and Families to Experience Healthy Beginnings*
Between nine weeks after conception and until birth	A pregnant woman, Larissa, is highly anxious about giving birth to a child because she does not have a job or supportive partner. Late in her pregnancy, Larissa and her mother go to prepared childbirth courses at their local community college.	*Excessive stress* can be harmful to both the mother and her unborn child. *Preparation for childbirth* can reassure parents about the birth process and help them to express their preferences for the birth, including who will be present and how they might respond to various scenarios.	Encourage pregnant women to care for themselves as well as to manage their own stress levels through appropriate exercise and relaxation techniques. Encourage prospective parents to prepare for the birth by attending classes and expressing their hopes for a particular kind of birth.
At birth	Kia and Bello give birth to a premature baby, Riley, six weeks early. He weighs only 4 pounds, 2 ounces. Riley receives intensive medical care and is strong enough to go home with his parents 2 weeks later.	The type of medical care given to early and small babies depends on their state of health and physical needs. *Premature babies* are at risk for developing a range of health problems and may benefit from long-term care and intervention. With good care, the developmental outcomes of premature infants are often quite positive.	Offer appropriate and nurturing care to babies at risk. Address the medical needs of fragile infants, and help parents to care for infants in a responsive manner. As premature infants grow, provide them with services, intervention, and educational experiences that help them flourish.

Application Exercise #1: Identifying Accurate Perspectives on How Nature and Nurture Affect Biological Beginnings

In the following scenarios, people take varying perspectives on how nature, nurture, or both factors are responsible for a condition in a child. Decide whether the view is accurate or inaccurate. Justify your choices on the basis of what you have learned about the manner in which genetic and environmental factors exert separate and combined effects.

1. A new mother talks with the pediatrician about her baby's cleft lip. In response to the mother's questions about why this condition developed, he suggests that some birth defects occur because of several interacting factors, such as having particular genes and being exposed to a virus or other potentially harmful substance during a critical phase of prenatal development. The doctor reassures the mother that the baby is healthy and robust and explains that surgery can help to correct the condition. Is the perspective of the doctor accurate or inaccurate?

2. The parents of a child with Down syndrome are moving to a new city and spend a considerable amount of time searching for a school that will be warm and challenging for their son. A friend of the couple thinks they should focus their efforts on a finding a decent house in a good neighborhood. Because the child has Down syndrome, the quality of the school is not really relevant, they reason: the boy will not be able to benefit from instruction. Is the perspective of the friend accurate or inaccurate?

3. A girl is unusually tall for her age. She has an older brother and sister who are also exceptionally tall. When the girl and her friend talk about height and physical characteristics, her friend suggests that the girl's height must be due to her eating lots of vegetables. Is the perspective of the friend accurate or inaccurate?

4. Jack and Jill both have curly hair. Their baby has straight hair. Taking a human development class, Jack learns that curly hair is a dominant trait and straight hair is a recessive trait. He concludes that he and Jill must both have one gene with a dominant trait for curly hair, and a second gene that is recessive trait for straight hair. Their new child must have received two recessive genes for straight hair, one from each parent. Does Jack have an accurate understanding of genetic transmission?

5. At age 5, Amadeus has an exceptional talent for music. His father, an accomplished musician himself, began teaching Amadeus how to play the piano and read music at age 2. When Amadeus enters kindergarten, his teacher concludes that Amadeus has inherited his father's love of music and needs only a piano and sheet music to refine his gift. Does Amadeus's teacher have an accurate or inaccurate understanding of the origins of the boy's ability?

6. Lily is very shy during her infancy and early childhood years. Lily's parents arrange for Lily to play with other children, and her preschool teachers help Lily to relax and ease into new group settings. By the time she enters elementary school, Lily remains somewhat anxious, but she gets along well with others. Lily's parents have an intuitive understanding that temperament—like so many psychological characteristics—is affected by nature and nurture. Do Lily's parents have an accurate understanding of the roles of nature and nurture in a child's development?

7. Darionna has always been mechanically inclined but her talent has blossomed as she has grown. As a toddler, Darionna took apart and reassembled her older brother's Lego sets, and as a 4-year-old, she asked her father if she could inspect the inside parts of his broken watch. As she grew older, she asked her uncle if she could help replace the oil and filter of his car. In high school, she read books about airplane engines and the aeronautical dynamics of the space shuttle. As a high school senior, she is planning to become an astronaut. Darionna's high school advisor believes that the girl's unusual talent is due solely to the enrichment she has received from adults at key points in her life. Does Darionna's advisor have an accurate or inaccurate view of the girl's ability?

8. Cameron is a third-grade boy who is aggressive and disruptive at school. His teacher, Ms. Petsas, believes that Cameron's parents are fully to blame for Cameron's problematic behavior at school. Ms. Petsas has observed Cameron and his parents interact and found the parents to be punitive with him. Does Ms. Petsas have an accurate or inaccurate understanding of the origins of Cameron's behavior problems?

9. Juliette seemed to be a reasonably happy child until her high school years, when she became volatile in her moods and began to withdraw from family and friends. During her senior year in high school, Juliette began to believe that other people were out to harm her. Eventually, Juliette was diagnosed with schizophrenia, a disorder involving thought disorders, hallucinations, delusions, and social isolation. Not having seen any foreshadowing of mental health problems until her high school years, Juliette's parents conclude that the condition must have been entirely environmental in origin. They feel guilty that they must have done (or not done) something during her high school years to instigate this disturbance. Do Juliette's parents have an accurate or inaccurate view on the origins of Juliette's disorder?

Answers to Application Exercise #1

1. Accurate. Some birth defects seem to be the outcome of several distinct factors, including genes that make the prenatal being susceptible to particular substances and exposure to these substances (such as a virus) at a particular time during prenatal development.

2. Inaccurate. Children with Down syndrome and other genetic disorders are strongly affected by their environment. With proper support and good instruction, this child has the capability of learning many skills and leading a happy, productive life.

3. Inaccurate. Complex physical characteristics that vary among people are rarely the outcome of a single factor. Usually, such features are affected by multiple genes as well as by several environmental factors, including good nutrition, opportunities for physical activity, and participation in affectionate relationships that help the person to reduce stress.

4. Accurate. When a child has a dominant gene and a recessive gene in a particular allele pair, the characteristic associated with the dominant gene is manifested and the characteristic associated with the recessive gene is essentially "overruled." When a child inherits two recessive genes for the same characteristic, that characteristic is manifested.

5. Inaccurate. Almost certainly, Amadeus and his father share a rare talent for music that has a substantial basis in heredity. Nevertheless, Amadeus's talent has been fostered by instruction from his father, and the further refinement of his musical skill will likely depend on additional encouragement and training.

6. Accurate. Psychological characteristics, such as intelligence and temperament, are affected by genetic inheritance and environmental opportunities and experiences.

7. Inaccurate. The advisor has an overly simplistic view of the origin of Darionna's talent in mechanical engineering. Adults have been integral to the progression of her abilities, yet Darionna probably also has a disposition that has some genetic basis, as is indicated by her initiative in arranging for her own enriching experiences.

8. Inaccurate. Cameron's way of behaving is the outcome of several factors: his genetic inheritance; his experiences at home, at school, and in other settings; and his own choices. Cameron's parents may be responding to Cameron in a detrimental way, but Cameron also appears to have certain dispositions, such as a tendency to be impulsive and irritable, that may derive in part from genetic factors. Ms. Petsas can help Cameron to express his feelings productively and can coach the family, if they are receptive, to communicating appropriate expectations to Cameron and responding calmly, consistently, and firmly when he is aggressive.

9. Inaccurate. The effects of genes are not always evident early in childhood. Some psychiatric conditions such as schizophrenia are not manifested until late adolescence or early adulthood. Although circumstances in Juliette's environment may have contributed to her disorder, her parents cannot conclude that a genetic tendency toward this illness was not part of her genetic profile.

Application Exercise #2: Nurturing Children's Biological Beginnings and Adaptations

Teachers, caregivers, and other adults can play important roles in children's biological beginnings. Are the following people effectively nurturing children, either by helping them to have a healthy beginning before birth or effectively accommodating biological characteristics during childhood? Indicate yes or no, justifying your responses with concepts from Chapter 3.

1. Rose Marie, a mother of four, has a younger sister, Ruthie, who is now four months along in her pregnancy with her first child. Ruthie is quite anxious about the pregnancy, has experienced fairly steady "morning sickness" during much of the day, worries that she and her husband will not be able to afford the baby's expenses, and is fearful that her baby will be born with a serious health problem. Rose Marie encourages Ruthie to talk about her concerns, offers to take long walks with her to relieve her stress, and offers to lend her baby furniture, such as a crib and high chair. Is Rose Marie helping Ruthie's baby to have a healthy beginning?

2. Sixteen-year-old Brenda is excited to be having a baby and shares the news with her homeroom teacher, Mr. Frank. Mr. Frank offers his best wishes for the baby and encourages Brenda to remain in school. After a few weeks, Mr. Frank suspects that Brenda is drinking alcoholic beverages with friends during the lunch hour. He talks with Brenda privately, expresses his concern about her drinking, explains the damage that alcohol and drugs can do at critical times of prenatal growth, and refers her to the school counselor. Is Mr. Frank helping Brenda's child to have a healthy beginning?

3. Ms. D'Arcy has a third grader, Milton, who is easily distracted. Milton regularly disrupts the class, seems unable or unwilling to get organized, and has trouble reading. When Ms. D'Arcy meets with Milton's parents, she learns that Milton has recently been diagnosed as having attention-deficit hyperactivity disorder (ADHD). Milton's father says that he had the same kinds of trouble in school, leading Ms. D'Arcy to conclude that the condition is inherited. After the conference, Ms. D'Arcy concludes that the best thing she can do for Milton is to wait patiently for the medications to do their work. Is Ms. D'Arcy offering helpful support to Milton?

4. Second-grade teacher Mr. Crestman has a student, Marney, who has been diagnosed with fetal alcohol syndrome (FAS). Marney is small for her age, impulsive, and delayed in cognitive development. Mr. Crestman has met with Marney's foster parents to determine the kinds of classroom strategies he can use to support Marney's learning and development. Mr. Crestman makes sure that Marney receives a combination of direct instruction to build her skills, rich sensory experiences to enhance her learning (e.g., she traces letter shapes with her hand before she practices writing the letters), and quiet, self-directed activities to foster her independence. Mr. Crestman is aware that transitions between classes and activities are difficult for Marney, so he has built in cues that signal an upcoming change of events (e.g., he turns classroom lights off, sings transition songs, allows Marney to carry her teddy bear between activities). Mr. Crestman has learned that it is difficult for Marney to generalize rules to new situations, so he tries to remind her of situations when she needs to apply certain rules. In many other ways, he treats Marney like the other children and encourages her to take part in conversations and outdoor play with classmates. Is Mr. Crestman offering helpful support to Marney?

Answers to Application Exercise #2

1. Yes. The supporting gestures that Rose Marie makes are reassuring and will likely help Ruthie to relax. High stress levels in the mother's body can be detrimental to babies-to-be, so helping Ruthie to relax will also create better conditions for the growth of Ruthie's offspring.

2. Yes. Knowing about her pregnancy and suspecting she is drinking, Mr. Frank is doing the right thing for Brenda's baby by warning Brenda about the tragic effects that alcohol and drugs can have on developing offspring. Since she may not be prepared to take his advice, Mr. Frank has also taken a prudent measure in referring Brenda to the school counselor.

3. No. Ms. D'Arcy is assuming that because Milton may have a condition with some genetic basis, she cannot help him. In fact, every child is affected by nature *and* nurture, and Ms. D'Arcy most certainly could teach Milton reading strategies and help him to stay focused and organized.

4. Yes. Mr. Crestman has aptly analyzed Marney's abilities. He recognizes that Marney's fetal alcohol syndrome means that she is delayed in learning abilities and benefits from tailored instruction. At the same time, he knows that Marney has many of the same social-emotional needs as the other children, and his many gestures of support reveal his expectation that Marney can flourish.

Sample Test Questions

Use the following multiple-choice and essay questions to evaluate and strengthen your understanding of selected concepts in the chapter.

Multiple-Choice

1. How do the processes of *meiosis* affect a child's genetic inheritance?
    a. Meiosis ensures that a child will share all characteristics with both mother and father.
    b. Meiosis ensures that the child is unlike either mother or father in any genetic factor.
    c. A child receives the most chromosomes from whichever parent (mother or father) has the most dominant genes.
    d. Meiosis ensures that a child is like each parent in certain ways and unlike each parent in other ways.

2. Each *gene pair* has two possible sets of instructions, one from the mother and one from the father. Which one of the following statements about *alleles* is true?
    a. The principle of polygenic inheritance means that each allele contributes equally to physiological attributes such as eye color.
    b. Codominance occurs when the two alleles differentiate into specific bodily organs.
    c. Recessive genes take precedence only when dominant genes are defective.
    d. Dominant genes usually override the instructions of recessive genes.

3. *Canalization* refers to which one of the following?
    a. Developments that are strictly controlled by genetic instructions
    b. Developments that result from correlations between the kinds of settings parents provide for their children and the parents' own genetic attributes
    c. Prenatal effects of toxins in local water supplies
    d. Physiological trauma to the brain and associated neurological defects resulting from prolonged oxygen deprivation in the "birth canal"

4. During a certain stage of prenatal development, the baby-to-be grows rapidly from a single cell into a ball of cells that burrows into the uterus, begins to create the nourishing placenta, and forms simple structures that will later differentiate into the nervous system and brain. What is this stage called?
    a. gamete
    b. zygote
    c. embryo
    d. fetus

5. Which of the following describes the effects of teratogens on the developing baby-to-be?
   a. Teratogens refer to the soft, protective greenish-colored layers around the developing baby-to-be that are formed during the final two months of prenatal development.
   b. Teratogens are the irregular contractions in the mother's uterine muscles that prompt the baby-to-be to move away from areas of compression.
   c. Teratogens are potentially harmful substances, such as alcohol and some prescription medications, that are taken by the mother and disruptive of the baby-to-be's growth.
   d. Teratogens are essential vitamins that enhance the ability of the baby-to-be to learn rudimentary patterns, such as the flavor of carrots and the rhythms of music that can be heard faintly in the womb.

6. Which of the following is *not* one of the recommended things a prospective mother might do to prepare for the birth of her baby?
   a. Get organized for the baby's arrival by preparing the nursery
   b. Take prepared childbirth classes
   c. Begin taking narcotics two weeks before the due date so as to ensure a relaxed state
   d. Prepare other family members for the arrival of the baby

Essay

7. Describe three things a person can do to support the health of pregnant women and their offspring.

8. Describe the kinds of care that are appropriate for infants who are born early, are small, or are fragile in some other way.

Answers to Sample Test Questions

1. d—*Meiosis* ensures that children receive genes from each parent, but the structures of chromosomes change slightly during meiosis, and chance plays a role in determining which chromosomes pair up with others in cells.

2. d—*Dominant genes* generally override the effects of recessive genes.

3 a—*Canalization* refers to developments that are tightly controlled by genetic instructions and occur almost universally in a wide range of environmental conditions. Examples of canalized developments include basic motor developments, such as learning to crawl, sit, and walk.

4. b—During the period of the *zygote*, the new being grows from a single cell into a ball of cells that differentiates into distinct parts and finds a home in the interior wall of the uterus.

5. c—*Teratogens* are potentially harmful substances, such as alcohol, viruses, and nicotine, that circulate in the mother's body and disrupt growth of the baby-to-be.

6. c—Women occasionally are prescribed narcotics and other pain relievers during labor, but such medications would rarely be prescribed in advance of labor.

7. Readers might select three from the following recommendations for supporting pregnant and their offspring:
   - Encourage women to review their health before becoming pregnant.
   - Remind sexually active women to take care of themselves.
   - Encourage pregnant women to seek medical care when they first learn of or suspect a pregnancy.
   - Urge pregnant women to stay clear of teratogens.
   - Encourage pregnant women to relax.
   - Ask pregnant women and expectant fathers to articulate their hopes, fears, and experiences.

8. Readers might select three from the following recommendations for caring for fragile infants:
   - Reduce infants' exposure to light and noise.
   - Regulate the amount of handling of infants by medical staff.
   - Position the baby to increase circulation.
   - Encourage parents to participate in the care of the infant.
   - Inform parents about infants' needs.
   - Arrange activities such as diapering and changing clothes so that interruptions to sleep and rest are minimized.
   - Encourage parents to cuddle with the infant and carry him or her often and for long periods.
   - Swaddle the baby in a blanket with arms bent and hands placed near the mouth to permit sucking on fingers or hands.
   - Massage the baby.
   - Educate parents about caring for the child as he or she grows older.

Chapter 4

PHYSICAL DEVELOPMENT

Chapter Overview

Chapter 4 provides an overview of children's physical development. We begin the chapter with a description of the principles that underlie physical changes, such as tendencies of separate body parts to grow at distinct rates and increasingly coordinate their discrete structures and operations. Next, we describe the brain and its developmental transformations. In the third section, we examine noteworthy physical accomplishments for each of the developmental periods: infancy, early childhood, middle childhood, early adolescence, and late adolescence. In reading this chapter, you will learn that adults can cultivate youngsters' brain-supported abilities (such as judgment and restraint), health-promoting habits (such as getting adequate nutrition, physical activity, and sleep), and resolve to avoid health-compromising activities (such as partaking in unprotected sex or using drugs).

Possible Knowledge, Beliefs, and Misconceptions Related to Chapter Content

Readers can draw on their own experiences with physical development as they interpret this chapter's material. Consider the following beliefs related to content in Chapter 4:

1. Physical growth is both publicly visible and profoundly personal. Youngsters' physical stature, appearance, and motor abilities are on public display, but their thoughts and feelings about what they look like, how well they do in sports, and how advanced they are in their sexual maturation are private matters. At one time or another, most children feel insecure about their physical appearance. We hope that our readers will draw on memories of the trials and tribulations of their own physical development when reading this chapter.

2. Rapid expansion of research into brain development has spurred widespread speculation among educators (often enthusiastic, yet sometimes inaccurate) about the meaning and implications of these developmental changes. One common misconception is that the brain is formed during prenatal development, infancy, and early childhood and undergoes no substantive changes after that. You will learn in Chapter 4 that the brain continues to refine its structures and connections during middle childhood and adolescence, and when young people are encouraged to pursue productive long-term plans, the brain supports advancements in judgment, foresight, and restraint (see the section "The Brain and Its Development").

3. Another misconception about the brain is that individual children vary in the particular parts of the brain they use. For example, some teachers talk about their "left-brain" and "right-brain" students. Although the various parts of the brain do specialize in particular functions, children typically use all areas of their brain, and the connections among circuits in discrete regions of the brain continually exchange information (see the section "The Brain and Its Development").

4. One assumption that some prospective teachers make is that they should concentrate on children's academic learning and disregard children's other needs—including their physical requirements for nutrition, activity, and rest. Yet if children's physical needs are *not* met in

child care and at school—for example, if they are antsy from sitting still for an extended time—children may find it difficult to concentrate or exercise self-control. And if vending machines and school cafeterias offer fatty, salty snacks and meals, educators inadvertently contribute to poor diets. In this chapter, we offer recommendations for promoting good eating habits, encouraging physical activity, and accommodating children's needs for rest and sleep (see the section "Physical Well-Being").

4. Some readers will expect that developmental changes inevitably strengthen young people's inclination to make good choices in diet, health, and physical activity. Unfortunately, as youngsters grow, their health may actually deteriorate due to poor choices. Some young people develop a preference for unwholesome snacks; some develop eating disorders; others fail to exercise; many get inadequate sleep; and too many face tempting health-compromising activities, such as drinking alcohol, taking drugs, smoking cigarettes, and engaging in unprotected sex (see "Health-Compromising Behaviors").

5. Sleep is an underrated but essential ingredient of physical health. As busy college students, our readers may view sleep as a nuisance—an impediment to accomplishing all the tasks that require time. In fact, sleep is essential for everyone. Disruptions in sleep are common for many children and cause problems in mood, self-control, and concentration (see the section "Rest and Sleep").

6. Many prospective teachers are unaware that they will have children in their classes who have chronic illnesses and other ongoing medical conditions. Obviously, teachers are not trained medical professionals and do not (and should not) administer treatment, yet teachers can permit children to visit the school nurse when they need to take medication, allow children who need to eat frequently to do so, and alert families when children's conditions appear to deteriorate (see the section "Special Physical Needs").

7. Some readers may not realize that children with significant physical disabilities can participate in sports and physical games. In this chapter, we suggest that it is important for all children to be physically active, and that there are many things teachers and other practitioners can do to help children with disabilities participate in games and sports (see the section "Special Physical Needs").

Suggested Supplementary Reading

The following reading, presented in the final section of this *Study Guide and Reader*, is relevant to Chapter 4:

Reading 4-1:   A Body to Die For: Body Image and Eating Disorders

CHAPTER OUTLINE	FOCUS QUESTIONS
PRINCIPLES OF PHYSICAL DEVELOPMENT	• What regularities are evident in children's physical growth? • What does it mean for the body to function as a dynamic system? • What does it mean for the body to undergo differentiation and integration?
THE BRAIN AND ITS DEVELOPMENT Structures and Functions Developmental Changes Applications of Research on Brain Development	• Describe the three main parts of the brain and their functions. • What major changes occur in the brain during prenatal development, infancy and early childhood, middle childhood, and adolescence? • What are some reasonable ways for teachers and other practitioners to nurture and accommodate children's brain development?
PHYSICAL DEVELOPMENT DURING CHILDHOOD Infancy (Birth-Age 2) Early Childhood (Ages 2-6) Middle Childhood (Ages 6-10) Early Adolescence (Ages 10-14) Late Adolescence (Ages 14-18)	• What are the rapid physical developments that occur during infancy? How do infants express their physical needs? • What kinds of strides in fine motor and gross motor skills occur during early childhood? • What are the primary characteristics of physical development during middle childhood? • How do the sequences of puberty unfold in girls and boys during early adolescence? How are young adolescents affected by the personal fable? • What kinds of developments occur in the brain during late adolescence? • How can teachers and practitioners support children's physical characteristics during each of the five age periods?

CHAPTER OUTLINE	FOCUS QUESTIONS
PHYSICAL WELL-BEING Eating Habits Physical Activity Rest and Sleep Health-Compromising Behaviors	• What kinds of difficulties do children encounter with each of these domains of health: eating habits, physical activity, and rest and sleep? • How can teachers and other practitioners support youngsters' healthful habits in eating, obtaining physical activity, and getting rest and sleep? • Why do some youngsters engage in health-compromising behaviors? What can teachers and other practitioners do to discourage health-compromising behaviors?
SPECIAL PHYSICAL NEEDS Chronic Illness Serious Injuries and Health Hazards Physical Disabilities Promoting Physical Well-Being in All Children	• In what ways can practitioners support children with chronic illnesses? • Identify several strategies that practitioners can use to accommodate the needs of youngsters with injuries and physical disabilities. • How can educators help to prevent injuries in children and protect them from harmful substances?

Chapter Glossary

Addiction. Physical and psychological dependence on a substance, such that increasing quantities must be taken to produce the desired effect and withdrawal produces adverse physiological and psychological effects.

Anorexia nervosa. Eating disorder in which a person eats little or nothing for weeks or months and seriously jeopardizes health.

Axon. Armlike part of a neuron that sends information to other neurons.

Bulimia. Eating disorder in which a person, in an attempt to be thin, eats a large amount of food and then purposefully purges it from the body by vomiting or taking laxatives.

Cephalocaudal trend. Vertical ordering of motor skills and physical development; order is head first to feet last.

Colic. Persistent crying by infants; it is most prevalent in the first three months of life.

Cortex. Part of the forebrain that houses conscious thinking processes (executive functions).

Dendrite. Branchlike part of a neuron that receives information from other neurons.

Differentiation. An increase from general to more specific functioning over the course of development.

Executive functions. Purposeful and goal-directed intellectual processes (e.g., reasoning, decision making) made possible by higher brain structures.

Fine motor skills. Small, precise movements of particular parts of the body, especially hands.

Forebrain. Part of the brain responsible for complex thinking, emotions, and motivation.

Glial cell. Cell in the brain or other part of the nervous system that provides structural or functional support for one or more neurons.

Gross motor skills. Large movements of the body that permit locomotion through and within an environment.

Growth spurt. Rapid increase in height and weight during puberty.

Hindbrain. Part of the brain controlling the basic physiological processes that sustain survival.

Inclusion. Practice of educating all students, including those with severe and multiple disabilities, in neighborhood schools and general education classrooms.

Integration. An increasing coordination of body parts over the course of development.

Left hemisphere. Left side of the cortex; largely responsible for sequential reasoning and analysis, especially in right-handed people.

Menarche. First menstrual period in an adolescent female.

Midbrain. Part of the brain that coordinates communication between the hindbrain and forebrain.

Myelination. The growth of a fatty sheath around neurons that allows them to transmit messages more quickly.

Neuron. Cell that transmits information to other cells; also called nerve cell.

Obesity. Condition in which a person weighs at least 20 percent more than what is optimal for good health.

Personal fable. Belief held by many adolescents that they are unique beings invulnerable to normal risks and dangers.

Proximodistal trend. Inside-outside ordering of motor skills and physical development; order is inside first and outside last.

Puberty. Physiological changes that occur during adolescence and lead to reproductive maturation.

Right hemisphere. Right side of the cortex; largely responsible for simultaneous processing and synthesis, especially in right-handed people.

Rough-and-tumble play. Playful physical "fighting" typical in early and middle childhood.

Schizophrenia. A psychiatric condition characterized by irrational ideas and disorganized thinking.

Spermarche. First ejaculation in an adolescent male.

Sudden infant death syndrome (SIDS). Death of infant in the first year of life, typically during sleep, that cannot be explained by a thorough medical examination; it peaks between birth and 4 months.

Synapse. Junction between two neurons.

Synaptic pruning. A universal process in brain development whereby many previously formed synapses wither away, especially if they have not been used frequently.

synaptogenesis. A universal process in brain development whereby many new synapses appear, typically in the first $3\frac{1}{2}$ years of life.

Table 4–1. Supporting Physical Development

This table is a complete version of the table that appears at the end of Chapter 4 in the textbook. Compare your entries in the blank cells in the textbook table with our entries here. Keep in mind that there isn't necessarily a single "right" entry for any particular cell.

Age	A Youngster's Experience	Developmental Concepts *Factors Affecting Physical Well-Being*	Implications *Supporting Physical Well-Being*
Infancy (Birth–2)	Thirteen-month old Naima appears to her caregiver to be a healthy, spirited child. The caregiver is surprised when Naima's parents point out that Naima occasionally seems to struggle in her motor development, as when she recently began to walk but then returned to crawling for a few weeks. They wonder if they should take her to the doctor.	Naima is showing sequences of progress and typical regressions in her motor skills. Naima's progress and occasional regressions suggest a *dynamic system* at work. Children act on the world, discover that their bodies permit new skills, make preliminary progress in mastering these skills, and often show declines in proficiency as they figure out how to deal with one or more changing factors (e.g., increases in muscle tone).	Reassure parents that infants make substantial progress in motor skills over brief periods. Explain that some retreats are common and usually reflect the child's adjustment to a new factor, such as weight gain, a temporary illness, or a change in muscle tone. Of course, Naima's parents may be noticing something that is unusual about their daughter, so be sure to encourage them to follow up with their doctor if they are worried about her.
Early Childhood (2–6)	In an orientation meeting for families at a child care center, one father asks how the center will help his 3-year-old son Jules develop a "strong brain." Jules's father brings in a newspaper article about the importance of providing enriching educational experiences for young children.	During early childhood, *brain development* focuses on the strengthening of neurological circuits that are used regularly. For example, the front part of the cortex begins to develop and permits children some rudimentary abilities to control their behavior.	Reassure parents that you are eager to support children in all aspects of their development, including their brain development. Further explain that a well-rounded preschool environment with lots of hands-on experiences, opportunities for pretend play, stories and puzzles, stable relationships with teachers and peers, healthful snacks, and outdoor play will offer ample enrichment for children's growing brains.

table continues

Table 4–1 continued

Age	A Youngster's Experience	Developmental Concepts *Factors Affecting Physical Well-Being*	Implications *Supporting Physical Well-Being*
Middle Childhood (6–10)	Seven-year-old Roy is overweight. His doctor recently gave his mother a brochure on obesity in children. It seems that a range of factors contribute to Roy's obesity—his parents are both overweight, Roy has developed a preference for fatty foods, and he spends most of his free time at home watching television and playing video games. His parents ask Roy's teacher, Mr. McGinnis, how much exercise Roy gets at school and wonder if a lack of physical activity is the problem. They also make a passing comment that it may simply be Roy's destiny to be a "big, chunky guy."	*Obesity* is a serious health risk in childhood. It predicts health problems in adulthood. Being obese as a child is predicted by familial weight problems, poor eating habits, and restricted physical activity. Because Roy is only 7 years old, he has a good chance of changing his eating habits and increasing his physical activity levels.	Suggest to Roy's parents that there are several potential contributors to being obese during childhood. Also advise Roy's parents that although you can do some additional things to encourage Roy's physical activity at school, they can do some things at home as well (e.g., stocking the cupboard with only healthful snacks and taking evening family walks).
Early Adolescence (10–14)	Thirteen-year old Helen used to be known as the school "brainiac," but recently she has *not* been acting intelligently. In the last year, Helen has matured physically and now appears several years older than most of her peers. In fact, Helen has been spending her weekend nights doing dangerous things with friends, such as drinking alcohol, driving with older boys she barely knows, and stealing cosmetics at a local store. When her parents recently confronted her with their suspicions, Helen replied that they should not worry.	It is common for young adolescents to engage in some *risky behaviors*. Helen may be an *early-maturing adolescent* who is allowing herself to be ushered into high-risk behaviors by older teenagers. Helen also seems to be affected by the *personal fable* because she discounts any potential harm that could occur to her as a result of her risky actions.	When adolescents begin to experiment with risky behaviors, remind them of their long-term goals, such as going to college and preparing for particular jobs. Provide information about the serious effects that risky behaviors have had for teenagers who, similar to themselves, did not believe that *they* could be harmed.

table continues

Table 4–1 continued

Age	A Youngster's Experience	Developmental Concepts *Factors Affecting Physical Well-Being*	Implications *Supporting Physical Well-Being*
Late Adolescence (14–18)	Ms. Comstock thinks about the high-school seniors she has in her literature courses. Her students appear to be attractive, bright young adults. But from private conversations with them, Ms. Comstock knows that these teenagers can be introspective and thoughtful one moment yet rash and impulsive the next. And although they certainly seem smart enough to stay on top of their homework assignments, they nevertheless frequently forget to complete projects on time. For a second, she would love to see inside their brains. She wonders: Do they have the bodies of adults and the brains of children?	Brains continue to develop rapidly and systematically during adolescence and, in fact, into the adult years. *Brain development* during adolescence builds on the many changes of childhood. It refines the front part of the cortex, which supports planning, emotional control, reasoning, and judgment.	Continue to communicate expectations to adolescents that they have the ability to act thoughtfully and appropriately, but also give them the scaffolding they need to be successful. For example, because it is difficult for them to keep long-term goals in mind, ask youngsters to turn in *parts* of assignments before handing in the final projects.

Application Exercise #1: Assessing Children's Physical Development

In the following scenarios, identify a specific aspect of *physical development* that appears to be affecting a child and make a *recommendation* for adults to accommodate this characteristic.

1. A four-month-old infant, Ross, has a slight respiratory infection, a condition that may be worsened by his mother's cigarette smoke. With this infection, he seems to have trouble falling asleep. Ross's father asks the director of Ross's child care center if the staff can help little Ross fall asleep by placing him on his tummy (as they do at home) and on top of a large, adult-sized comforter folded over into several layers. His parents are willing to bring the comforter from home.

2. It is the second week of the school year. Five-year-old Morey is one of the youngest children in his kindergarten class. Because of his parents' work schedule, he must attend the afternoon session of kindergarten rather than the morning session, when he would be more alert, rested, and relaxed. Every afternoon, he seems tired, irritable, and distracted.

3. Edel is an adolescent with cerebral palsy, a condition caused by oxygen deprivation to her brain during her premature and difficult birth. Edel is growing into a competent young woman who aspires to become a writer. She is mentally bright and socially outgoing, and she has learned to move quickly with orthopedic support. Edel's cheerful nature, wry sense of humor, and intelligence gain her many friends. During physical education class, however, she sits on the sideline and watches her classmates as they learn athletic skills.

4. Brandi is an academically talented high school student. Brandi takes a few honors classes, is on the girls' cross-country team, and volunteers in her church's youth group. The lunch supervisor, who also coaches her cross-country team, suspects that Brandi has an eating disorder. Brandi eats voraciously at lunch and supplements her cafeteria lunches with extra fatty snacks—potato chips, French fries, cake, and cookies. But she runs to the restroom after every lunch and comes back pale and quiet. One of her friends has seen her vomiting, and Brandi is quite slim.

5. Thirteen-year-old Bryan sits in the back of Mr. Wright's science class. Bryan's mood fluctuates from being agitated and restless to being dazed and still. Mr. Wright smells chemicals when he stands near Bryan, and when he gets close to Bryan, he notices that Bryan's eyes are red and tremble slightly. Mr. Wright knows that glue sniffing has become a frequent pastime at his school. He wonders if Bryan has begun to sniff glue or solvents.

6. From the conversations she's overheard, Ms. Campbell knows that some of her middle school students are having sex. She's not certain what to do.

7. Eight-year-old Jesse has asthma. When he's having an asthma flare-up, he wheezes when he breathes and gets out of breath easily. During these episodes, Jesse uses an inhaler-dispenser at school and at home. At his school, the medicine is kept in the nurse's office, but Jesse often neglects to go to her office at the scheduled times. He also seems not to notice when his symptoms get worse.

Answers to Application Exercise #1

1. The director in the child care center will want to talk with Ross's parents about risk factors for Sudden Infant Death Syndrome (SIDS). Medical experts advise against placing babies on their stomachs, smoking cigarettes near infants, and placing them on soft, loose mattresses and bedding materials. The director can explain that this is why they place infants on their backs on firm mattresses. She can indicate that she is not able to place Ross on a soft, folded comforter, as it would be too soft; she can, however, cover him with a light, soft blanket and rub his back or offer other gestures of comfort.

2. Morey is attending school during a time of day when he is tired. It is possible that he recently gave up his afternoon nap (see the section "Rest and Sleep"). His teacher may find that he responds well to quiet and restful activities, such as drawing and listening to music. Perhaps his need for rest in the afternoon will dissipate as the year progresses, but the teacher can continue to offer choices for restful activities and check with Morey's parents to determine if there might be other factors causing his distress.

3. Edel has a physical disability. She is managing well academically and socially but seems not to be included in physical activity. Her physical education teacher can consider ways that Edel can participate in the activities. She might consult with Edel, her parents, and professional organizations devoted to accommodations that promote the inclusion of children with disabilities in physical activities (see the sections "Physical Disabilities" and "Promoting Physical Well-Being in All Children").

4. Brandi may have an eating disorder (bulimia). Brandi's coach will want to talk with the principal, nurse, or counselor to determine how Brandi might be helped (see the discussion of eating disorders in the "Eating Habits" section).

5. It is possible that Bryan is using inhalants or taking other drugs. Mr. Wright can consult with the principal or school counselor regarding his suspicions about Bryan. Mr. Wright might also talk with Bryan, get to know him better, and encourage him to continue his work in school. To address students' drug use more generally, Mr. Wright might consider the extent to which his school has effectively communicated its intolerance of drug, cigarette, and alcohol use. He might also advocate for a drug prevention program at the school (see the "Health-Compromising Behaviors" section).

6. Unprotected sex compromises health by making adolescents vulnerable to pregnancy and sexually transmitted diseases. Ms. Campbell will want to discuss her concern with the principal and school counselor. She can advocate for prevention programs that are acceptable and effective in her community. Ms. Campbell can also encourage adolescents to set long-term goals that will intensify their resistance to high-risk activities (see the section "Health-Compromising Behaviors").

7. Jesse has asthma, a chronic condition. It is fairly common for children to have trouble monitoring their symptoms and status, and his teacher will want to watch him for any signs of emergency (see the sections "Chronic Illness" and "Promoting Physical Well-Being in All Children"). Learning more about asthma from Jesse's parents might be advisable. The teacher can also advise Jesse's parents of his actual schedule in taking (and not taking) medication. Since the nurse does not always have the time to track down Jesse when he

forgets to come take his medicine, a backup strategy may be needed. Since the long-term goal will be for Jesse to monitor his own condition and take his medicine on schedule, Jesse and his parents may want to develop a schedule that fits with natural transitions in the day (e.g., after math and reading) instead of precise times (e.g., 10 AM and 1 PM).

Application Exercise #2: Enhancing Children's Physical Development

In the following vignettes, aspects of children's physical development are described. In each case, decide whether the professional responds in a way that *effectively meets children's physical needs*. Justify your responses with concepts from Chapter 4.

1. It's been a frigid winter, and students at Range View Elementary have had to stay inside all week. Ms. Fryer makes a point to take breaks with the children. They've developed a routine that helps them to release pent-up energy. Several times a day, Ms. Fryer puts on music and asks children to touch their toes, stretch to the ceiling, lean from side to side, and run in place.

2. A team has been assembled to plan menus at Golden Heights Middle School. The team consists of a dietician, the cooking staff at the school, volunteer students and parents, and a teacher with a background in home economics. As part of a health education theme in the school, the team is designing meals that are healthful (adequate protein and nutrition, low fat and sodium) and that include recipes from different cultural groups.

3. At Norton High School, teachers are discouraged about the alcohol and drug use of youngsters. They notice a growing number of adolescents congregating outside the school while smoking cigarettes and marijuana and possibly drinking alcohol. In discussing the problem, teachers decide not to discourage the youngsters from meeting in the lot, as they suspect that students would only find another, more remote spot to meet, and at least their present location leaves them safe, visible, and close to the school building.

4. At Martinez Junior High, teachers are aware that adolescents feel self-conscious about their changing bodies. They make sure that students can shower after exercising and have private areas for changing clothes. They also educate students about sexual harassment and include prohibitions to this form of discrimination in their school conduct manual.

5. At Washington Junior High, sports reign supreme. Teachers promote sports and fund raising and often travel with the teams. Graduates of Washington Junior High tend to move to Luther High School, where the emphasis on athletic programs is equally strong. Occasionally, small groups of parents express concerns about competitive sports, but the teachers respond that students who participate are learning to compete, to be "good sports," and to be prepared for the demands of high school. Even the physical education classes, which enroll both athletes and non-athletes, are highly competitive.

6. Mrs. Sigmund has three infants in her care. Every two months, she asks the infants' parents to update her records on their preferences for physical care of the babies. For example, Mrs. Sigmund asks them to specify sleeping routines (typical time and length of infants' naps), eating routines and food allergies, and the specific formulas and solid foods babies are consuming. Mrs. Sigmund states her own preferences for ages at which she'd like to introduce cereals and pureed vegetables, fruits, and meats, but she always listens to the guidelines of parents. If she has a question or concern, she works it out with the parents. During the day, she completes a simple chart indicating times for diapering, eating, and napping; she also writes down simple notes about the infants' moods and interests (e.g., "Phyllis was so happy today!"), which parents appreciate.

Answers to Application Exercise #2

1. Yes. Ms. Fryer is giving her students opportunities for much-needed physical activity (see the section "Physical Activity"). Not only is this activity good for the children, but it may actually help them to be more attentive during structured class lessons.

2. Yes. Staff members and volunteers at Golden Heights Middle School are working to enhance the diets, and more generally the healthful choices, of students (see the section "Eating Habits").

3. No. Teachers at Norton High School are permitting, and thereby condoning, use of drugs, alcohol, and cigarettes. Their intentions may be good, but the message adolescents may actually hear is that practitioners either do not care or else believe that their actions are acceptable (see the section "Health-Compromising Behaviors").

4. Yes. Teachers at Martinez Junior High School are showing sensitivity to the feelings of adolescents. With the large diversity that exists among students in the age at which they begin puberty, as well as the heightened feelings of self-consciousness that characterize adolescence, respect for privacy is essential (see the discussion of early adolescence in the section "Physical Development During Childhood").

5. No. A strong emphasis on sports and physical activity can be good for students. However, the focus on competitive sports may *not* be good for *all* students. Coaches and teachers are advised to encourage physical activity for everyone and arrange activities that are enjoyable, accept diversity in skills, and allow students to chart their improvement (see the section "Physical Activity").

6. Yes. Mrs. Sigmund is obtaining valuable information from parents about their preferred ways of caring for their babies and she provides them with detailed information about her physical care of infants during the day (see the discussion of infancy in the "Physical Development During Childhood" section).

<u>**Sample Test Questions**</u>

Use the following multiple-choice and essay questions to evaluate and strengthen your understanding of selected concepts in the chapter.

Multiple-Choice

1. Three of the following are *principles of physical development* identified in the textbook. Which statement is *not* an accurate description of physical development?
   a. Different parts of the body mature at different rates.
   b. Different parts of the body become increasingly differentiated.
   c. The effects of genetic instructions outweigh the effects of nutrition.
   d. Physical development is characterized by quantitative and qualitative changes.

2. Which one of the following descriptions accurately portrays the *development of the brain*?
   a. At birth, the brain is simple and unformed. Most children end up with three main parts in the brain, but those who live in enriched environments may form four or more main parts, and those who live in impoverished environments may form only two parts.
   b. At birth, the brain is well structured and ready to grow. Experience is essential to many later refinements in the brain. Some developments depend on exposure to specific stimuli and experiences during sensitive periods. However, the brain retains its capacity for learning throughout early childhood, middle childhood, adolescence, and adulthood.
   c. At birth, the brain is already well structured and has formed the major connections and circuits that will be used throughout life. Experience is important to activate depth perception but is *not* necessary for the maturation of any other capacity.
   d. At birth, the brain is highly susceptible to experience. After the second year of life, the brain's capacity to learn new systems of thinking, such as music, language, and mathematics, is greatly reduced, and the brain loses all plasticity after early childhood.

3. *Growth spurt* refers to which of the following?
   a. A rapid increase in height and weight
   b. The cascade of hormones released during adolescence
   c. The explosive discharge of growth hormone that occurs during sleep
   d. The completion of puberty sequences

4. Which one of the following is a central feature of the *personal fable*?
   a. Experience of physiological changes of puberty as being improbable and almost mythical
   b. Belief that one is unique and invulnerable to normal risks and dangers
   c. Fantasies during rough-and-tumble play
   d. Unrealistic expectations about one's performance in competitive sports

5. Which one of the following is *not* one of the recommendations in the textbook for promoting healthy eating habits in children?
   a. Provide between-meal snacks when children are hungry.
   b. Follow up when you suspect serious nutritional problems.
   c. Regularly review the basics of good nutrition, asking children to set goals for improving their eating habits.
   d. Advise parents that lunches they send in for their children must be prepared as part of a vegetarian diet with organically grown fruit, vegetables, seeds, and whole grains.

6. Which one of the following is the best illustration of *inclusion* as educators typically use the term?
   a. Children in a school make a point to invite a deaf child who attends a residential school to join them for their spring festival.
   b. Children with disabilities are placed in a small classroom with a special education teacher and included in a school's attendance records for purposes of federal accountability.
   c. Children with disabilities are included in regular classrooms and given no special instruction, services, assignments, or accommodations.
   d. Children with disabilities are educated for all or part of the school day within the general education classroom, where they participate in many regular classroom activities and also receive accommodations from the teacher that maximize their opportunities for meaningful progress.

Essay

7. Recall your experiences as a high school student. Using concepts from Chapter 4, describe and evaluate your high school's support for students' physical development.

8. Specify an age level of youngsters with whom you would like to work, and formulate recommendations for addressing their needs for physical activity.

Answers to Sample Test Questions

1. c—General principles of development do not include genetic instructions outweighing the effects of nutrition (see "Principles of Physical Development").

2. b—The brain is structured at birth but depends on experience for many refinements, and it retains considerable ability to learn and grow new connections across the lifespan.

3. a—A *growth spurt* is a rapid increase in height and weight, as occurs in adolescence.

4. b—The *personal fable* encompasses the false sense of invulnerability experienced by many adolescents.

5. d—A vegetarian diet, a preference of some health-conscious people, is *not* one of the recommendations in the textbook for all children.

6. d—*Inclusion* means that children spend most of the day in the regular classroom where they are included in as many regular activities as possible while receiving special accommodations that maximize their learning and performance.

7. Responses will vary but may include a discussion of support (or lack of support) for the following areas of physical development and functioning:
    *   Eating habits (e.g., food served in the cafeteria)
    *   Physical activity and sports (e.g., whether physical exertion was required in PE classes)
    *   Accommodations for students with chronic illnesses or physical disabilities (e.g., whether teachers and other school personnel offered support to students with these conditions)
    *   Rest and sleep (e.g., whether teachers gave lengthy last-minute assignments that necessitated long hours of work and reduced available time for sleep)
    *   Health-compromising behaviors (e.g., whether teachers encouraged students to feel connected to school, to aspire to long-term goals, and to avoid risky behaviors)

8. Responses will vary depending on the age of children. Here are three examples of strategies:
    *   Identify physical activities that children find enjoyable and can participate in between periods of sedentary study.
    *   Approach physical activities with a focus on enjoyment and personal growth rather than on competition and winning.
    *   Ensure that children have mastered prerequisite skills in physical education classes.

Chapter 5

FAMILY, CULTURE, AND COMMUNITY

Chapter Overview

In Chapter 5, we examine three essential contexts for children's development. *Families* care for children's basic needs and foster their increasingly responsible behaviors; *cultures* expose children to beliefs and behaviors that make life meaningful and productive; and *communities* supply playmates for children and give families jobs, social networks, and services. Considerable diversity exists among the contexts individual children experience, including variations in family structures and styles of expressing affection and discipline. Culture and ethnicity also vary among children and are significant features of family life. For example, children from ethnic minority backgrounds face unique challenges but typically—and especially when supported by caring adults—develop effective coping strategies. We also note that communities usually offer children social and material resources, but resources are almost always scarce for children who live in economic poverty. Teachers can help children by reaching out to families, opening lines of communication, and welcoming all families at school. Similarly, teachers can assist children from disadvantaged families by nurturing their strengths, arranging for needed school supplies, and implementing other strategies outlined in this chapter.

Possible Knowledge, Beliefs, and Misconceptions Related to Chapter Content

Studying this chapter may evoke readers' memories of growing up in their own families, including the discipline parents used, the affection parents showered on them (or withheld), and their various relationships with any brothers, sisters, and extended family members. Consider the possible impressions these beliefs and experiences may have on prospective teachers and other practitioners:

1. Your images of healthy family experiences are almost certainly affected by your *own* experiences growing up. If you had a mother and father who jointly cared for you, you may believe that this family structure is "normal" and that other kinds of families are second-rate. If you grew up in a large family, you may see small families as lonely and dull. If you were an only child, you may wonder how the needs of individual children in large families could possibly be met. Yet you will learn in this chapter that families come in *many* healthy forms (see the section "Family Structures").

2. Did your own parents or other family members encourage you to do well in school? Families can indeed play an important role in preparing children for the academic demands of school, and teachers can encourage families' constructive involvement in children's education (see the section "Forming Partnerships with Families").

3. One belief that some people have is that families are ultimately responsible for any difficulties children encounter at school. Should you assume that children passively become what their parents want them to be, you will be surprised to learn that children strongly affect other family members' behaviors with their interests, abilities, temperaments, and actions (see the section "Children's Influences on Families").

4. Although most families are affectionate and responsible, some families do neglect and abuse their children. A few readers may be unaware of their obligations to report their suspicions of abuse to authorities (see the section "Risk Factors in Families").

5. Some people associate *culture* with music, art, drama, poetry, and literature. Certainly artistic products and performances are precious creations within a culture, but Chapter 5 describes culture as a more inclusive phenomenon—as the behaviors and beliefs that characterize a social group and provide a framework for how people decide what is normal and appropriate. Culture defines such common, everyday events as how duties are assigned in families, how meals are carried out, and what sleeping practices children follow (see the sections "Cradles of Child Development" and "Life in the Community for Children and Families").

6. Some readers may believe that ethnic diversity is best ignored. Putting faith in a one-size-fits-all education for children may be well intentioned, but doing so underestimates the power of culture in shaping children's thoughts, feelings, and actions. It also disregards the effects of discrimination for children and families. This chapter includes many ideas for creating supportive environments for children from diverse ethnic backgrounds (see the section "Life in the Community for Children and Families").

7. Some readers will have grown up accepting that the "melting pot" metaphor is the ideal way for immigrants to adjust in their new country. These readers may be surprised to learn that youngsters often develop in healthy ways when they *retain* some allegiance to their original culture (see the section "Ethnicity, Culture, and Gender").

8. Readers will naturally use their experience with particular types of communities to evaluate other settings. City-goers may see rural settings as drab and boring; rural residents may puzzle over the obsession that suburban families seem to have with fenced-in yards; and suburban residents may believe that only *they* have a decent quality of life. Similarly, readers from middle-class families may be unaware of the skills and values instilled in youngsters from low-income backgrounds. In the section "Community Resources" we acquaint readers with resources and challenges for youngsters in different environments and offer recommendations for assisting children from low-income families.

Suggested Supplementary Readings

The following readings, presented in the final section of this *Study Guide and Reader*, are relevant to Chapter 5:

CHAPTER OUTLINE	FOCUS QUESTIONS

CRADLES OF CHILD DEVELOPMENT
 	
    Family
 	
    Culture
 	
    Community
	• What are the primary roles that families play in children's lives?
	
	• How do parents help their children act and think in increasingly responsible ways?
	
	• What are the two major ways in which culture is manifested?
	
	• How does the community affect children?

FAMILY STRUCTURES
 	
    Mothers and Fathers
 	
    Divorced Parents
 	
    Single Parents
 	
    Parents and Stepparents
 	
    Extended Family
 	
    Adoptive Parents
 	
    Foster Care
 	
    Other Heads of Family
 	
    Accommodating Diverse Family Structures
	• What benefits do children in two-parent families experience?
	
	• How do mothers and fathers differ in their parenting?
	
	• What do children learn from parents who have good relationships with one another? How are children affected when parents argue frequently?
	
	• What kinds of adjustments do children make when parents divorce? What factors seem to help children adjust well after their parents' divorce?
	
	• What benefits and challenges do children encounter in families headed by single parents?
	
	• How are children affected by being in blended families?
	
	• How common is it for children to live with grandparents? What kinds of "parents" do grandparents make?
	
	• What recent trends exist in adoption and foster care?
	
	• What additional family structures exist?
	
	• What are some practical things teachers can do to encourage the inclusion of families of diverse structures in children's schooling?
	
	• What can educators do to support children when they are undergoing a family transition?

CHAPTER OUTLINE	FOCUS QUESTIONS
FAMILY PROCESSES Families' Influences on Children Children's Influences on Families Risk Factors in Families Forming Partnerships with Families	• How does children's guided participation in adults' everyday activities affect their learning? • Describe the characteristics and influences of the following parenting styles: *authoritarian, authoritative, permissive, uninvolved*. • What factors affect the parenting style a parent uses and the impact of this style on children? • What kinds of academic lessons take place in families? How do these lessons affect children? • How does parents' employment affect children? • What risks do children encounter when they care for themselves? How can self-care arrangements be made safer for children? • How do children's temperaments, personalities, and talents affect their interactions with other family members? • What kinds of dynamics are present in sibling relationships? What does the research indicate about the adjustment of children who have no siblings? • What is *child maltreatment*, and what different forms does it take? What responsibilities do teachers and other practitioners have if they suspect children are being maltreated at home? • How can educators foster the involvement of families in their children's education? • Select three communication formats teachers can use with families and describe a circumstance for which each format might be especially helpful. • Describe how principles of effective communication (for example, establishing rapport, listening respectfully, and empathizing) contribute to good partnerships between teachers and families.

CHAPTER OUTLINE	FOCUS QUESTIONS
LIFE IN THE COMMUNITY FOR CHILDREN AND FAMILIES Ethnicity, Culture, and Gender Community Resources Educating Children from Low-Income Families	• What is a child's *ethnicity*? What is the relationship between ethnicity and race? • Compare families from two or more ethnic cultures and their distinct values for children. • How do some families socialize girls and boys toward different roles? • Define *acculturation* and describe its four distinct forms. • Explain the kinds of unique challenges faced by children from minority cultural backgrounds and the coping mechanisms these children use to adjust in society. • How can teachers and other practitioners create supportive environments for ethnic minority children? • How does family income affect children's development? • Describe the challenges faced by children and adolescents whose families live in economic poverty. • How can teachers and other practitioners make a difference in the lives of children from low-income families?

Chapter Glossary

Acculturation. Process of taking on the customs and values of a new culture.

Assimilation. Form of acculturation in which a person totally embraces a new culture, abandoning a previous culture in the process.

Authoritarian style. Parenting style characterized by strict expectations for behavior and rigid rules that children are expected to obey without question.

Authoritative style. Parenting style characterized by emotional warmth, high expectations and standards for behavior, consistent enforcement of rules, explanations regarding the reasons behind these rules, and the inclusion of children in decision making.

Bicultural orientation. Form of acculturation in which a person is familiar with two cultures and selectively draws from the values and traditions of one or both cultures depending on the context.

Blended family. Family created when one parent-child(ren) family combines with another parent figure and any children in his or her custody; also, the structure that emerges when a parent already with a child remarries and has another child with the new spouse.

Child maltreatment. Adverse treatment of the child in the form of neglect, physical abuse, sexual abuse, or emotional abuse.

Community. The local neighborhood and surrounding vicinity of a child and his or her family.

Coparents. The two (or more) parents who share responsibility for rearing their children.

Culture. Behaviors and belief systems that characterize a social group and provide a framework for how group members decide what is normal and appropriate.

Ethnic identity. Awareness of being part of a particular ethnic or cultural group and willingness to adopt certain behaviors characteristic of that group.

Ethnicity. Membership in a group of people with common ancestors and shared values, beliefs, and behaviors.

Family structure. In a family with children, the family's makeup; specifically, the children in a family home and the adults who live with and care for the children.

Family. Two or more people who live together and are related by enduring factors such as birth, marriage, adoption, or long-term mutual commitment.

Guided participation. Active engagement in adult activities, typically with considerable direction and structure from an adult or other more advanced individual; children are given increasing responsibility and independence as they gain experience and proficiency.

Multicultural education. Education that regularly includes the perspectives and experiences of numerous cultural groups.

Parenting style. General pattern of behaviors that a parent uses to nurture and guide his or her children.

Permissive style. Parenting style characterized by emotional warmth but few expectations or standards for children's behavior.

Rejection. Form of acculturation in which a person refuses to learn or accept any customs and values from a new cultural environment.

Resilience. Ability of some youngsters (often enhanced with environmental support) to thrive despite adverse environmental conditions.

Selective adoption. Form of acculturation in which a person assumes some customs of a new culture while also retaining some customs of a previous culture.

Socialization. Systematic efforts by other people and by institutions to prepare youngsters to act in ways deemed by society to be appropriate and responsible.

Socioeconomic status (SES). One's general standing in an economically stratified society, encompassing family income, type of job, and education level.

Uninvolved style. Parenting style characterized by a lack of emotional support and a lack of standards regarding appropriate behavior.

Table 5–1. Applying Concepts in Child Development: Accommodating Children's Families

This table is a complete version of the table that appears at the end of Chapter 5 in the textbook. Compare your entries in the blank cells in the textbook table with our entries here. Keep in mind that there isn't necessarily a single "right" entry for any particular cell.

Age	A Youngster's Experience	Developmental Concepts *Identifying Family Conditions*	Implications *Working Effectively with Children's Families*
Infancy (Birth–2)	Eight-month-old Yves sits in his high chair at the child care center. Yves is hungry but cries rather than feeding himself the diced peaches and turkey on his tray. His caregiver, Mrs. Phillipe, talks with Yves's mother and learns that during meal times at home, she holds Yves and places soft, tiny bits of food directly into his mouth.	Little Yves encounters different feeding customs at home and at the child care center. These different practices may be rooted in dissimilar *cultural beliefs* about desirable qualities in social groups (e.g., for being close to one another or showing independence) and in *cultural behaviors* in caring for infants (e.g., encouraging infants to relax as caregivers tend to them or, in contrast, fostering their self-care).	Talk with parents and other heads of family to learn how they care for infants' physical and social-emotional needs. Explain your own practices and your rationale for them and reassure families that you will gradually introduce new routines. Give infants plenty of time to adjust to practices that are very different from what they are accustomed to at home.
Early Childhood (2–6)	Tawaia is the fourth and youngest child in the Hume family. At 4 years, Tawaia seems to her teacher, Ms. Brookhart, to be socially perceptive. Ms. Brookhart notices Tawaia's ability to charm her friends into sharing their toys with her. Ms. Brookhart also observes that Tawaia can hold her ground during verbal tussles with other children, occasionally selecting insults that aptly push the other children's hot buttons.	As one of four children, Tawaia has had lots of time to interact with her siblings. *Siblings* are not vital to a healthy child's development, but when they are present in a family, siblings often form close bonds with one another. Rivalry is also a common dynamic among siblings, and children often gain influential lessons in taking the perspective of other people through their (sometimes competitive) interactions with brothers and sisters.	Show sensitivity to the bonds that children have with siblings, allowing them to comfort one another during times of family loss. Try not to compare children to their siblings, though, and also do *not* assume that children without siblings are lonely or spoiled.

table continues

Table 5–1 continued

Age	A Youngster's Experience	Developmental Concepts *Identifying Family Conditions*	Implications *Working Effectively with Children's Families*
Middle Childhood (6–10)	Nine-year-old Michael is the only child of his single mother, Ms. Clementine. Michael seems to be mature for his age, particularly in the chores he does around the house, including making dinner twice a week when his mother is at work. Michael feels protective toward his mother, whom he knows to be hard working and devoted to him.	Children in *single-parent families* often have close relationships with their parents. Michael enjoys such a close bond with his mother, and he also seems to have been coached by her in making constructive use of his time in *self-care*, when she is at work and he is home alone.	Find out who children's parents and guardians are, and communicate often with them about children's academic progress and school adjustment. Model acceptance of various family structures, and do not tolerate any name-calling in children about one another's families.
Early Adolescence (10–14)	Mr. Drake, a middle school math teacher, holds an advising meeting with one of his students, Janice, and her parents, Mr. and Mrs. Lee. During the conference, Janice answers questions for the family, and Mr. and Mrs. Lee quietly smile and nod their heads. Later Mr. Drake notices that Mr. and Mrs. Lee fail to take him up on his suggestion that they participate in one of the school's many parent-staffed events.	Mr. and Mrs. Lee may hold different *cultural beliefs* from Mr. Drake about the appropriate roles of parents in children's academic learning. Janice's parents are respectful of Mr. Drake but may not feel it is appropriate for them to ask questions of him during meetings. Furthermore, they may be more inclined to help Janice with her homework at home than to become involved at school events.	Invite families to participate as they can in school activities, but also make certain to acknowledge the important roles that families play in supporting children's academic learning at home.
Late Adolescence (14–18)	Mr. Vogel notices that one of his students, Christy, has suddenly become quiet and withdrawn during homeroom period. He talks with her privately and learns that her parents have recently told her they are getting a divorce. Christy explains that her parents have been arguing constantly over the last year, and she finds the divorce to be traumatic.	Changes in *family structure* can be unsettling for children and adolescents for months and sometimes longer. Adolescents tend to adjust to *parents' divorce* somewhat more easily than do younger children, but adolescents still generally need time to sort through the changes, make sense of their parents' conflicts, and regroup with new custody arrangements.	Listen sensitively when children inform you that they are troubled by a family disruption. Help children sort through the practical issues that inevitably arise when children face a change in living arrangements or find that they must move back and forth between their parents' houses.

Application Exercise #1: Applying Concepts from Family, Culture, and Community

The particular settings in which children grow—their families, cultures, and communities—define children's foremost values, goals, and abilities. As you read each of the following scenarios, explain how it illustrates concepts from Chapter 5.

1. *Children's adjustment after their parents' divorce.* After several months of tense interactions and heated arguments, 10-year-old Georgia's parents decided to get a divorce. Georgia was initially heartbroken about the divorce, but two months after the initial separation Georgia is beginning to accept the change in her family. Georgia's mother and father are helping her set up two bedrooms in their separate houses. She spends weekdays with her mother and weekends with her father, and she is getting accustomed to the moves between the two houses. Tensions between her mother and father are subsiding, and they are beginning to converse easily about arrangements for Georgia.

2. *Single Parents.* Fourteen-year-old Martina has a close and affectionate relationship with her mother, Ms. Conel. Ms. Conel is a single parent who is employed full-time and also keeps busy caring for Martina, shopping, cooking, paying bills, and maintaining the house. Somehow, Ms. Conel also finds time to participate in charitable fundraisers and other volunteer activities. Ms. Conel has close friends and is active in her church congregation, and Martina benefits from the concern that these other adults express for her.

3. *Mothers and fathers.* June (mother) and Gus (father) are both dedicated and loving parents to 2-year-old Louis. They have entirely different styles in interacting with him, however. June is the primary caregiver—she gives Louis an evening bath, makes sure he is well fed, schedules doctor's appointments, reads to him at night, and so on. Gus is equally affectionate but is more playful in interactions with Louis and is more apt to discipline Louis for his temper tantrums and disobedience.

4. *Parents and stepparents.* Lester's parents divorced when he was a baby. Since that time, Lester has lived with his father. Lester is now 8 years old. His father has recently remarried, and Lester now has a stepmother and two stepsisters. In his *blended family*, Lester will need to establish new relationships, learn new traditions for spending the holidays, and cope with some feelings of ambivalence about his new family arrangement. Lester is also apt to benefit from the social support given by the new family members.

5. *Adoption.* Ellie was adopted as a 9-month-old baby. She is now a well-adjusted teenager who understands her family origins and is securely attached to her adoptive mother. One day she hopes to travel to the People's Republic of China, where she was born.

6. *Extended family.* Nickie has been raised by her grandparents since her mother—at age 15—gave birth to her. Nickie's grandparents provide a stable and nurturing family for her, although they occasionally worry about their own health, energy, and the expenses of raising another child and saving for college.

7. *Culture and ethnicity.* Carl Schmidt comes from a European American background. He grew up in a rural area of eastern Colorado, where his grandparents had settled after immigrating from Germany and Sweden. While growing up, Carl enjoyed the European traditions that his

family celebrated. When Carl began teaching, he moved to a small city in New Mexico. As a teacher, he enjoyed learning the cultural traditions of the many Hispanic American children in his class. He learned Spanish and he prided himself in teaching in a culturally sensitive manner. He thought he was familiar with the needs of Hispanic American children until he and his family moved to Florida following his wife's job promotion. There he found that the traditions of Hispanic American children were quite different from the children he had previously taught.

8. *Culture and ethnicity.* An experienced middle school teacher, Mr. Suruku has been honored by his school district for his outstanding achievements in meeting the needs of culturally diverse students. At the awards ceremony, he is invited to describe how he meets the needs of students. Mr. Suruku decides to talk about the remarkably different ways that youngsters go about learning, communicating, responding to authority figures, and getting along with one another.

9. *Community resources.* Mr. Aswin teaches in an economically poor, rural community in the south and recognizes the challenges that many of his elementary students face (such as economic poverty, family upheavals, and medical problems). Without minimizing the frustrations that such problems cause, Mr. Aswin encourages children to do their best. He is conscientious in his academic instruction so that they gain basic literacy skills so essential for later schooling and the world of work. He draws them together, celebrating their successes with ice cream parties and after-school social events, inviting their parents and other family members to these events, and in other ways instilling in them a sense of community.

Answers to Application Exercise #1

1. Georgia faces multiple challenges that she must sort through in quick order. She must cope with the conflicts she has witnessed between her parents, her parents' divorce, and her new living arrangements. Given some time, most children cope reasonably well with parents' divorce (see the section "Divorced Parents").

2. As a single parent, Ms. Conel accepts a lot of personal responsibility for her daughter and for keeping the family home operating smoothly. Characteristic of many single-parent families, Ms. Conel and her daughter have a close relationship, and Ms. Conel goes to considerable effort to ensure that she and Martina enjoy ample social support (see the section "Single Parents").

3. Louis benefits from close bonds with both of his parents. When two parents raise a child, they tend to take on slightly different roles. Mothers tend to act as hands-on caregivers, and fathers tend to act playfully with children and correct children's misbehaviors. There are, of course, many exceptions to gender-based parenting roles (see the section "Mothers and Fathers").

4. Blended families offer resources as well as challenges to children. Lester will undergo numerous changes as he adapts to his new family (see section "Parents and Stepparents").

5. Adoptive children tend to thrive and, as Ellie exemplifies, grow into well-adjusted youngsters. Ellie was adopted through an international adoption program, a relatively common practice in adoption (see the section "Adoptive Parents").

6. Grandparents often step forward to care for their grandchildren when the children's own parents are not able to do so. Grandparents tend to be competent caregivers, though they sometimes worry about the financial and personal resources required to rear a second generation of children (see the section "Extended Family").

7. Carl has learned firsthand that he cannot assume that a single ethnic group (Hispanic Americans) is homogeneous in its cultural traditions. It is likely that families in New Mexico have ancestors from Mexico and Central America, whereas the children in Florida may have families with Cuban and other Caribbean origins (see the section "Ethnicity, Culture, and Gender").

8. Mr. Suruku understands what it means to teach in a culturally sensitive manner. To imagine the particular strategies he might use, you can refer to Chapter 5's Observation Guidelines table, "Identifying Cultural Practices and Beliefs" (on page 180 of the textbook).

9. Mr. Aswin does several things to cultivate *resilience* in his low-income students. He communicates high expectations, develops a sense of community, ensures they have basic skills and academic knowledge, and so on (see the sections "Community Resources" and "Educating Children from Low-Income Families").

Application Exercise #2: Forming Partnerships with Families

In the following vignettes, use your understanding of concepts in Chapter 5 to determine whether the educator's response is *appropriate* or *inappropriate*.

1. In preparation for Mother's Day, Ms. MacLean helps her preschool students make a bouquet of paper flowers in a clay vase. With children who have both mothers and stepmothers, she encourages them to make one bouquet for each mom. When other children ask why some of their classmates are making two bouquets, Ms. MacLean explains matter-of-factly that they have two loving mothers they want to honor.

2. Mrs. Brothers has a middle school advisee, Samantha, who's been acting moody lately. One afternoon Mrs. Brothers asks the girl what's going on, and Samantha responds that she's recently learned that her parents are getting divorced. Mrs. Brothers comforts Samantha and invites her to talk when she'd like to do so. Over the next few weeks, Mrs. Brothers makes a point to check regularly with Samantha about how she's feeling and learns that Samantha is beginning to adjust to the change in her family.

3. In his child care center, Mr. Morris has one child, Bronson, who is unusually thin and listless. Bronson is withdrawn from caregivers in the center, and he is aggressive with other children. On cold, snowy days in winter, he arrives at the center in a t-shirt and shorts and with no jacket. One day Mr. Morris notices that Bronson has bruises all over his abdomen. He consults with the child care director, and together they talk with a representative from social services. They suspect neglect and abuse.

4. Mr. Yarrow is concerned about one of his third-grade students, Gerry. Mr. Yarrow has not yet met Gerry's mother but decides she needs to be informed of Gerry's behavior in the classroom. Mr. Yarrow phones Gerry's mother and describes Gerry's latest misbehaviors. He asks her to punish Gerry and communicate to him the need for good behavior at school. Gerry's mother says little but agrees to punish Gerry.

5. During the months between parent-teacher-student conferences, Mr. Small telephones his students' parents at least once. He keeps note cards for each family, listing the phone number, best times to reach parents, and dates of contact. He also jots down notes of children's accomplishments, as well as any problem areas for discussion. In his telephone conversations with parents, Mr. Small begins with a few areas in which the students are doing well. When he must bring up areas that need improvement, the parents are usually receptive to his suggestions and often add ideas of their own.

6. In scheduling conferences with parents and other family members, Ms. Rachel makes herself available numerous times during the day, evening, and weekend so that she can maximize the attendance of working parents.

7. When arranging parent-teacher conferences, Ms. Frye-Mills makes available a list of interpreters that she can recruit if families want her to do so, and she also invites parents to bring someone they know who can translate for them if they prefer.

Answers to Application Exercise #2

1. Appropriate. Ms. MacLean is showing her respect for the roles that two mothers play in some children's lives (see the section "Accommodating Diverse Family Structures").

2. Appropriate. Mrs. Brothers is aware that Samantha is undergoing a major family transition. She offers reassurance during this difficult time (see the section "Accommodating Diverse Family Structures").

3. Appropriate. Mr. Morris takes proper (and legally required) precautions when he discusses his suspicions of neglect and abuse with the director and contacts social services (see the section "Risk Factors in Families").

4. Inappropriate. Mr. Yarrow launches into complaints about Gerry without first establishing rapport or acknowledging the good things that Gerry is doing. Gerry's mother may conclude that Mr. Yarrow is blaming her for Gerry's misbehavior. The conversation is one-sided, and Mr. Yarrow learns little about Gerry's family or his mother's perspective (see the section "Forming Partnerships with Families").

5. Appropriate. Mr. Small is doing several things well. He is staying in close communication with parents and family members, and he makes a point to communicate information about students' accomplishments (see the section "Forming Partnerships with Families").

6. Appropriate. Ms. Rachel is accommodating parents' busy work schedules. She is likely to have better attendance by showing such flexibility (see "Forming Partnerships with Families").

7. Appropriate. Ms. Frye-Mills is accommodating families' language backgrounds (see the section "Forming Partnerships with Families").

Sample Test Questions

Use the following multiple-choice and essay questions to evaluate and strengthen your understanding of selected concepts in the chapter.

Multiple-Choice

1. Which one of the following parenting styles represents *authoritarian parenting*?
   a. The Abrahams expect Joshua to "Snap to it!" when they tell him what to do. They want him to obey without arguing, and they punish him when he asks why he needs to follow particular rules.
   b. The Browns expect their daughter Vera to be a responsible member of the family. They listen to her desires and reasoning, and then work out a set of rules that she is to follow. They routinely explain to her why they have certain rules in their family.
   c. The Coutfords exert little control over their children. They are affectionate with them but let them choose what they eat, when they go to bed, and whether or not they complete homework.
   d. The Dornachters are cool and indifferent with their children, often letting the children do what they want. They are quick to tell their children what they are doing wrong but slow to keep tabs on their activities and whereabouts.

2. Which one of the following statements represents the nature of sibling relationships?
   a. Sibling relationships usually reflect cooperation but in cases of abuse also include rivalry.
   b. Sibling relationships are essential for normal, healthy relationships.
   c. Sibling relationships are based in extreme antagonism.
   d. Sibling relationships reveal both cooperation and competition.

3. Children and parents simultaneously influence one another's behaviors in a process called *reciprocal influences*. Which of the following is a clear example of reciprocal influences?
   a. The joint effects of nature and nurture in family socialization
   b. The affection that is showered among multiple offspring in a family
   c. The cues that children and parents take from each other during their interactions
   d. The progressive adjustment of children to a major family transition

4. Which of the following statements about *acculturation* is true?
   a. Immigrant children seem to adjust most successfully when they undergo full assimilation into their new culture.
   b. Immigrant children seem to adjust most successfully when they learn a new culture while also retaining some customs of their previous culture.
   c. Immigrant children seem to adjust most successfully when they reject all aspects of the new culture and preserve absolute loyalty to their previous culture.
   d. Immigrant children seem to adjust most successfully when they create novel customs in their family that are not present in either their previous culture or the new culture.

5. Three of the following alternatives are strategies that the textbook recommends for forming partnerships with families. Which one does it *not* suggest?
    a. Encourage family members to get involved in their children's education.
    b. Persuade parents that they really need to do what experts tell them to do.
    c. Find out what family members do well (e.g., cooking or woodworking) and ask them to share their talents at school.
    d. Use a variety of communication formats in reaching out to families.

6. Teachers and other practitioners can often make a difference in the lives of economically disadvantaged children when they encourage children and offer particular kinds of support. Which one of the following tactics is *not* one of the textbook's recommendations for working with children from low-income families?
    a. Fostering a sense of belonging
    b. Conveying clear and consistent expectations for children's behavior
    c. Communicating high expectations for children's success
    d. Treating economically poor children exactly as they would children from middle-income families

Essay

7. Imagine that, as a teacher, you have been selected by the school principal to head a "Family Involvement Task Force" at your school. What kinds of recommendations (derived from Chapter 5) might you offer to promote *more effective partnerships* between teachers and students' families?

8. Select two different *family structures*, and indicate the *strengths* and *challenges* that each might offer children.

Family Forms	Strengths	Challenges

Answers to Sample Test Questions

1. a—Alternative *a* illustrates an authoritarian style of parenting. In contrast, *b* illustrates authoritative parenting, *c* is permissive parenting, and *d* is uninvolved parenting (see the section "Families' Influences on Children").

2. d—Sibling relationships give children many opportunities for both cooperation and competition. However, they are not essential to healthy development, as "only" children show good adjustment, often developing close relationships with parents and doing quite well in school (see the section "Children's Influences on Families").

3. c—*Reciprocal influences* refer to the mutual effects that members of a family have on one another (see section "Children's Influences on Families").

4. b—Immigrant children seem to adjust most effectively when they learn their new culture while also continuing to observe some of the customs of their previous culture (see section "Ethnicity, Culture, and Gender").

5. b—Educators should not undermine parents' confidence by implying that they will not be effective unless they follow all recommendations of experts (see the section "Forming Partnerships with Families").

6. d—Alternatives *a*, *b*, and *c* are recommendations for working with children from low-income families (see the section "Educating Children from Low-Income Families"). These children can be resilient to the hardships they face in their environment, and they are most likely to be successful when their unique needs are addressed.

7. As the leader on family involvement, you might recommend the following mechanisms of communication (see the section "Forming Partnerships with Families"):
    *   Frequent parent-teacher conferences
    *   Frequent written communication
    *   Use of e-mail and Web sites
    *   Parent discussion groups
    *   School meetings that accommodate parents' work schedules
    *   Invitations to all family members who are active participants in students' lives
    *   Participation of language translators at parent-teacher conferences

8. Responses will differ depending on family structures. The following is an illustration of a possible response:

Family Forms	Strengths	Challenges
Mothers and Fathers	• Presence of two role models (one male, one female) • Possible models of good communication skills and cooperation • Emotional bonds with two parents	• In some cases, presence of conflict between spouses
Divorced Parents	• Termination of frequent and heated arguments between marital partners • Opportunities to help out around the house	• Series of adjustments needed as the family divides • Confusion about reasons for the divorce • Possible loss of access to the non-custodial parent • Possible drop in standard of living

Chapter 6

COGNITIVE DEVELOPMENT: PIAGET AND VYGOTSKY

Chapter Overview

This chapter describes two early theories of cognitive development that have had a significant influence on research and educational practice: (a) Jean Piaget's cognitive-developmental theory, which focuses on how and why children's logical reasoning abilities change with age, and (b) Lev Vygotsky's sociocultural theory, which considers how children's thinking processes originate in social interactions. We look in depth at both of these theories, as well as at subsequent research and theoretical perspectives that Piaget's and Vygotsky's ideas have spawned. Throughout the chapter, we consider implications for professional practice in schools, child care centers, and other settings.

Possible Knowledge, Beliefs, and Misconceptions Related to Chapter Content

Following are three commonly held beliefs that may interfere with an accurate understanding of Piaget's and Vygotsky's theories. As you read Chapter 6, be on the lookout for evidence that contradicts these ideas:

1. Many students who have previously studied Piaget's theory believe that his four stages of cognitive development are truly accurate descriptions of how children think and behave at various ages. In fact, recent researchers have found that children of a particular age sometimes show more advanced reasoning, and at other times show less advanced reasoning, than Piaget proposed (see the section "Current Perspectives on Piaget's Theory").

2. Most people typically use the term *egocentrism* to mean "selfishness" or "thinking only about one's own needs." Piaget instead used this term to refer to an inability to view a situation from the perspective of others. (See the description of *egocentrism* in the discussion of the preoperational stage in the section "Piaget's Stages of Cognitive Development.")

3. Some people think that children's play activities, while certainly enjoyable and entertaining, are not necessarily the best use of children's time; they think that children's early years are more productively spent in structured lessons (e.g., in piano, ballet, or sports) and academic enrichment. In reality, play is quite beneficial for cognitive development (e.g., see the final bullet in the section "Key Ideas in Vygotsky's Theory"). Play promotes social development as well (see Chapter 12).

Suggested Supplementary Readings

The following readings, presented in the final section of this *Study Guide and Reader*, are relevant to Chapter 6:

CHAPTER OUTLINE	FOCUS QUESTIONS

PIAGET'S THEORY OF COGNITIVE DEVELOPMENT
 	
  Key Ideas in Piaget's Theory
 	
  Piaget's Stages of Cognitive Development
 	
  Current Perspectives on Piaget's Theory
 	
  Key Ideas in Neo-Piagetian Theories
 	
  Applying the Ideas of Piaget and His Followers
	• Briefly describe Piaget's *clinical method*.
	
	• In Piaget's view, what predispositions and cognitive processes promote cognitive development? In what ways do children organize what they learn?
	
	• In what ways do interactions with one's physical and social environments promote development?
	
	• What acquisitions and limitations characterize each of Piaget's four stages?
	
	• In what ways was Piaget on target in his descriptions of cognitive development? In what ways was he apparently *not* on target?
	
	• How do prior knowledge, experiences, and cultural background affect the development of children's reasoning skills?
	
	• Is cognitive development as stagelike as Piaget suggested?
	
	• How are neo-Piagetian perspectives similar to, and different from, Piaget's theory?
	
	• What implications do Piaget's theory and post-Piagetian research and perspectives have for professional practice?
	
	• In what ways does *sociocognitive conflict* promote cognitive development? Use the concept of *disequilibrium* to answer this question.

CHAPTER OUTLINE	FOCUS QUESTIONS
VYGOTSKY'S THEORY OF COGNITIVE DEVELOPMENT	• From Vygotsky's perspective, in what ways do adults and other more skilled individuals promote children's cognitive development?
Key Ideas in Vygotsky's Theory	• What is a *cognitive tool*? Identify a variety of cognitive tools that you use in your daily living.
Current Perspectives on Vygotsky's Theory	• What phenomena occur when thought and language merge? How do these phenomena facilitate the *internalization* of social processes?
Applying the Ideas of Vygotsky and His Followers	• In Vygotsky's view, where do complex mental processes originate?
	• What role does *challenge* play in development? What did Vygotsky mean by *zone of proximal development* (ZPD)?
	• What functions does *play* serve for children?
	• Give an example of a child co-constructing meaning with an adult. Give an example of two or more children co-constructing meaning.
	• In what various ways might adults *scaffold* tasks in a child's ZPD?
	• Describe the nature of *guided participation* and *apprenticeships*.
	• What benefits do children gain from teaching what they know to others?
	• What implications do Vygotsky's ideas have for professional practice?
	• Briefly describe *reciprocal teaching*.
	• What are *authentic activities*? What advantages might they have for children's cognitive growth?
COMPARING PIAGETIAN AND VYGOTSKIAN PERSPECTIVES	• What ideas are common to both Piaget's and Vygotsky's theories?
Common Themes	• In what significant ways do Piaget's and Vygotsky's theories differ?
Theoretical Differences	

Chapter Glossary

Accommodation. Process of dealing with a new event by either modifying an existing scheme or forming a new one.

Actual developmental level. Upper limit of tasks that a child can successfully perform independently.

Apprenticeship. Mentorship in which a novice works intensively with an expert to learn how to accomplish complex tasks in a particular domain.

Appropriation. Gradual adoption of (and perhaps also adaptation of) other people's ways of thinking and behaving for one's own purposes.

Assimilation. In Piaget's theory, process of dealing with a new event in a way that is consistent with an existing scheme.

Authentic activity. Instructional activity similar to one that a child might eventually encounter in the outside world.

Central conceptual structure. Integrated network of concepts and cognitive processes that forms the basis for much of one's thinking, reasoning, and learning in a specific content domain.

Class inclusion. Recognition that an object simultaneously belongs to a particular category and to one of its subcategories.

Clinical method. Procedure in which an adult probes a child's reasoning about a task or problem, tailoring questions in light of what the child has previously said or done in the interview.

Cognition. The various mental activities in which a person engages.

Cognitive apprenticeship. Mentorship in which an expert and a novice work together on a challenging task and the expert suggests ways to think about the task.

Cognitive tool. Concept, symbol, strategy, or other culturally constructed mechanism that helps people think more effectively.

Conservation. Realization that if nothing is added or taken away, amount stays the same regardless of any alterations in shape or arrangement.

Constructivism. Theoretical perspective proposing that learners construct a body of knowledge and beliefs, rather than absorbing information at face value.

Disequilibrium. State of being unable to address new events with existing schemes; is accompanied by a feeling of mental discomfort.

Egocentrism. Inability of a child in Piaget's preoperational stage to view situations from another person's perspective.

Equilibration. Movement from equilibrium to disequilibrium and back to equilibrium; a process that promotes the development of increasingly complex forms of thought and knowledge.

Equilibrium. State of being able to address new events using existing schemes.

Goal-directed behavior. Intentional behavior aimed at bringing about an anticipated outcome.

Guided participation. Active engagement in adult activities, typically with considerable direction and structure from an adult or other more advanced individual; children are given increasing responsibility and independence as they gain experience and proficiency.

Individual constructivism. Theoretical perspective that focuses on how people construct meaning from events on their own.

Inner speech. "Talking" to oneself mentally rather than aloud.

Internalization. In Vygotsky's theory, the gradual evolution of external, social activities into internal, mental activities.

Level of potential development. Upper limit of tasks that a child can successfully perform with the assistance of a more competent individual.

Mediated learning experience. Discussion between an adult and a child in which the adult helps the child make sense of an event they have mutually experienced.

Neo-Piagetian theory. Theoretical perspective that combines elements of Piaget's theory with more contemporary research findings and suggests that development in specific content domains is often stagelike in nature.

Object permanence. Realization that objects continue to exist even when they are out of sight.

Operation. In Piaget's theory, an organized and integrated system of logical thought processes.

Reciprocal teaching. Approach to teaching reading in which students take turns asking teacherlike questions of their classmates.

Scaffolding. Support mechanism, provided by a more competent individual, that helps a child successfully perform a task within his or her zone of proximal development.

Scheme. In Piaget's theory, an organized group of similar actions or thoughts that are used repeatedly in response to the environment.

Self-talk. Talking to oneself as a way of guiding oneself through a task.

Social constructivism. Theoretical perspective that focuses on people's collective efforts to impose meaning on the world.

Sociocognitive conflict. Situation in which one encounters and has to wrestle with ideas and viewpoints different from one's own.

Sociocultural theory. Theoretical perspective that focuses on children's learning of tools and communication systems through practice in meaningful tasks with other people.

Sociodramatic play. Play in which children take on specific roles and act out a scenario of events.

Symbolic thought. Ability to represent and think about external objects and events in one's mind.

Working memory. Component of memory that enables people to actively think about and process a small amount of information.

Zone of proximal development (ZPD). Range of tasks that one cannot yet perform independently but *can* perform with the help and guidance of others.

Table 6–1. Applying Concepts in Child Development: Examining Challenges That Promote Cognitive Development

This table is a complete version of the table that appears at the end of Chapter 6 in the textbook. Compare your entries in the blank cells in the textbook table with our entries here. Keep in mind that there isn't necessarily a single "right" entry for any particular cell.

Age	A Youngster's Experience	Developmental Concepts *Identifying the Nature of the Challenge*	Implications *Facilitating Cognitive Growth*
Infancy (Birth–2)	Eighteen-month-old Julia is becoming frustrated that the tower she's trying to build with wooden blocks keeps toppling over. Her caregiver sits on the floor beside her and helps her stack the blocks in such a way that the tower is more stable.	Building a block tower is in Julia's *zone of proximal development*: She can do it successfully only with assistance.	Observe infants and toddlers as they try new tasks. If they repeatedly struggle and seem frustrated in their efforts, provide assistance, but let them do as much of the task as possible on their own.
Early Childhood (2–6)	Four-year-old Jacob is trying to put together a simple picture puzzle. His progress is slow, but he persists. As he works, he continually makes comments such as, "Nope, doesn't fit," "Where's that green one?" and "Maybe if I turn it this way. . ."	Jacob is engaging in *self-talk* as a way of guiding himself through a difficult task.	Encourage rather than discourage self-talk, because it enables children to perform some difficult tasks without the assistance of others.
Middle Childhood (6–10)	"Metal always sinks, because metal is heavier than water," 9-year-old Rachel emphatically states. Her teacher shows her a postcard of a large cargo ship and says, "This ship is made almost entirely of metal. Why is it floating?" Rachel pauses, squinches her face, and thinks. "Wow, I don't know. Why *does* it float? That doesn't make sense!"	Rachel is experiencing *disequilibrium*, because she can't assimilate the new information into an existing scheme (i.e., her belief that metal sinks).	Present information that conflicts with what children currently believe as a way of helping them acquire more sophisticated understandings of the world.

table continues

Table 6–1 continued

Age	A Youngster's Experience	Developmental Concepts *Identifying the Nature of the Challenge*	Implications *Facilitating Cognitive Growth*
Early Adolescence (10–14)	As part of an assignment for his eighth-grade journalism class, 14-year-old Jamal shadows a local newspaper reporter for a day. The reporter gives Jamal a steno pad similar to the one she herself uses and encourages him to take notes as she interviews the mayor and police chief. Periodically she looks at Jamal's notes and offers suggestions on how he might improve them. At the end of the day, Jamal helps the reporter write a story for the paper using the notes they've both taken.	As a newcomer to the world of journalism, Jamal does not have the training he would need to write a newspaper story on his own. However, he can certainly contribute in meaningful ways to a story. The reporter is engaging Jamal in *guided participation* in an adult activity.	Engage children and adolescents in typical adult activities, for instance by introducing authentic activities in the classroom or by giving them opportunities to take on tasks in community agencies and businesses.
Late Adolescence (14–18)	A high school social studies teacher in a wealthy school district presents some alarming statistics about the number of people living in poverty in the local community. When he asks his students to suggest some possible solutions to the situation, a heated debate ensues: "Some people are just lazy." "No they aren't! We just need to find them all jobs so they can earn a decent living." "Some people can't work because they have disabilities. How about if every rich family 'adopted' a poor family and helped it out?"	The students' diverse opinions about the problem reflect *sociocognitive conflict* that should promote disequilibrium and motivate the students to think about the matter more deeply. Yet some of the responses (e.g., finding jobs for everyone, asking rich families to "adopt" poorer ones) may be unrealistic, consistent with the *idealism* so typical of adolescence.	Engage adolescents in debates about controversial issues. Create an atmosphere in which they feel free to express diverse opinions (e.g., encourage them to "agree to disagree"). Ask them to reflect on whether their suggestions are realistic in today's world.

Application Exercise #1: Identifying Typical and Atypical Behaviors

In the following scenarios, which individuals are exhibiting behaviors typical for their age-group, and which ones are not? Justify your decisions on the basis of Piaget's theory or subsequent research related to his theory.

1. On Monday morning, 4-year-old Susan tells an adult what she did over the weekend. "We drove to the McAllisters' farm and rode Betsy," she says. When the adult explains that he doesn't know the McAllisters and wonders what kind of animal Betsy is, Susan is puzzled by his ignorance about these things.

2. The students in a ninth-grade biology class have just learned that mammals, birds, reptiles, amphibians, and fish are all vertebrates. The teacher asks, "So what do you think: Are there more fish in the world, or more vertebrates?" Jimmy responds, "There are more fish, because the oceans cover more than half the earth."

3. As he sits in his infant seat, 7-month-old David reaches for some of the brightly colored toys nearby and tries to suck on them and chew them.

4. When a fourth-grade teacher describes decimals, her students are totally confused. She tries several different ways of teaching the concept *decimal,* but without much success.

5. A 7-year-old comes to softball practice upset about a neighbor who was killed in a drive-by shooting the night before. "The world would be a much better place if people didn't have guns," she says despondently.

6. In a high school physics lab, students are instructed to design and conduct an experiment to determine whether or not *weight* affects the speed at which something falls. As the students compare the speed with which objects of different weights fall, they are careful to use objects that are similar in size and shape, and they make sure that they drop all of them from the same height at exactly the same time.

7. Five-year-old Ethan watches his after-school child care provider pour poster paint from a tall, thin jar into a short, wide aluminum cup so that Ethan can dip his brush into the paint more easily. The child care provider asks if there is the same amount of paint in the cup as there had been in the jar. Ethan says yes, although he cannot explain why he thinks so.

8. Several 4-year-olds are working on an art project at the same table; they have only two pairs of scissors and one bottle of glue to share among them. Martin wants to keep the glue and one pair of scissors to himself; he doesn't understand why he must let the other children use them as well.

9. A third-grade class is studying different denominations of money and has learned what pennies, nickels, dimes, and quarters are worth. As the children watch, the teacher places ten nickels in a stack and spreads another ten nickels all around on the floor. "Which set of nickels would you rather have?" Nine-year-old Louise says she would rather have the ten nickels stacked up because there are more of them.

10. Fifteen-year-old Nancy asserts that if the United Nations took a strong stand on dealing with world hunger, no child would ever go hungry again.

11. Three-year-old Maria is surprised to discover that her preschool teacher has children of his own. "You can't be a daddy!" she says. "You're a teacher."

12. A third-grade class is watching a video about Alaska, and the video's narrator mentions that on a particular day the outside temperature is "minus 40 degrees." The teacher stops the video at this point and says, "Minus 40 degrees. That's *really* cold, because it's 40 degrees *below* zero." The children look puzzled, and Alexis asks, "Zero means nothing at all. How can anything be less than that?"

13. In a unit on commerce, a high school social studies teacher explains the law of supply and demand: "When the supply of a product is low and the demand for it is high, the product is very expensive. When the supply is high, the price comes down, especially if the demand for the product is low." Although the students can memorize and repeat back what their teacher has told them, they seem unable to apply the principle to real-life problems.

14. Six-year-old Marianne sees a mother rabbit run into its hole and thinks that because the mother no longer exists, her babies must now be orphans with no one to take care of them.

15. Plainview is a farming community, and most of the students at Plainview Middle School live and work on family farms. When the eighth-grade science teacher asks students to conduct experiments to determine whether weight, length, or strength of push determines how fast a pendulum swings, most of the students seem unable to separate and control variables. Then the teacher assigns a different problem: "Design an experiment to find out whether amount of water, use of fertilizer, or type of soil (or perhaps some combination of these) affects the growth of a new variety of corn." Despite their failure on the pendulum problem, most of the students design appropriate experiments in which they examine the effects of each variable while keeping the other two constant.

Answers to Application Exercise #1

1. Typical. Susan's behavior reflects an inability to view situations from another person's perspective—that is, it reflects *egocentrism*—which is common during Piaget's preoperational stage.

2   Not typical. Class inclusion—recognizing that something can simultaneously belong to a category and one of its subcategories—emerges at the beginning of Piaget's concrete operations stage, sometime around age 6 or 7. The teacher's question is similar to the wooden-beads-versus-brown-beads question presented in the textbook.

3. Typical. From a very early age, children try to assimilate new objects into their existing schemes. David is trying to assimilate the toys to his "sucking" and "chewing" schemes.

4. Typical. Decimals are proportions. From Piaget's perspective, proportional thinking doesn't appear until the beginning of the formal operations stage, when children are, on average, about 11 or 12.

5. Not typical. From Piaget's perspective, reasoning about contrary-to-fact ideas does not appear until the formal operations stage, beginning around age 11 or 12.

6. Typical. The students are demonstrating separation and control of variables, a characteristic of Piaget's formal operations stage.

7. Typical. Children in the later years of Piaget's preoperational stage can sometimes think logically, but they are often unable to explain their reasoning.

8. Typical. Egocentrism, the inability to view the world from another person's perspective, is common during Piaget's preoperational stage.

9. Not typical. Conservation of number appears in early concrete operations, sometime around age 6 or 7.

10. Typical. Idealism is common among adolescents in Piaget's formal operations stage, but their idealistic suggestions may not be realistically accomplishable.

11. Typical. Children in Piaget's preoperational stage often have difficulty with class inclusion—that is, with recognizing that things can belong to two or more categories at the same time.

12. Typical. Piaget proposed that most 8- and 9-year-olds are in the concrete operations stage. Children in this stage have difficulty understanding negative numbers, which have no obvious basis in physical reality.

13. Typical. The teacher is describing the supply of law and demand in an abstract manner. Although Piaget proposed that abstract thought emerges at around age 11 or 12, more recent researchers have found that formal operational capabilities emerge only gradually over the adolescent years.

14. Not typical. Object permanence—recognizing that things continue to exist even when they disappear from sight—develops quite early. From Piaget's perspective, it appears late in the first year of life. More recently, researchers have found that it emerges even earlier.

15. Typical. Piaget proposed that the ability to separate and control variables appears at the beginning of the formal operations stage. But more recently, researchers have found that adolescents can more easily apply formal operational abilities to topics about which they have a great deal of knowledge.

Application Exercise #2: Recognizing a Child's Zone of Proximal Development

Which of the following individuals are working within their *zone of proximal development*?
Defend your choices.

1. Selena is learning how to play the trumpet. She still has trouble with some of the high notes but does better when her teacher reminds her what she needs to do.

2. A soccer coach is teaching 6-year-old boys the basics of soccer. She describes the different positions that team members might play and explains the specific roles that players in each position have. She breaks the group into two teams and assigns each boy a specific position on the field. Yet once the ball is in motion, everyone on the field immediately flocks to it, resulting in a game of "magnet ball." The coach repeatedly stops the game and asks the boys to return to their assigned positions, but each time the game resumes, they all run to the ball once again.

3. A high school service club goes door to door selling chocolate bars to raise money for college scholarships for students from low-income families. The advisor for the group finds that he doesn't have to provide any assistance, as the group has conducted candy sales on several previous occasions and so knows exactly how to proceed.

4. When Mr. Marino asks his fifth graders to write a short story, they seem to be at a loss for ideas. But when he suggests that they write a "Just So" story explaining why the elephant has such a big trunk or why the giraffe has such a long neck, they are each able to write a story with a main character, plot, conflict, and resolution.

5. Sarah Jones, an infant caregiver, shows 10-month-old Jaleeza a Jack-in-the-box. Jaleeza is greatly amused when "Jack" pops out. Sarah shows Jaleeza how to turn the crank, places Jaleeza's hand on the knob of the crank, and encourages her to turn it. Jaleeza holds the knob and pulls it toward her, but she lacks the strength and coordination to turn it a full circle.

6. Julian can locate virtually any place on the globe if he knows its latitude and longitude.

7. An art teacher demonstrates how to paint with watercolors and then walks around the room to watch his students work. He offers guidance when he sees someone having trouble creating new colors or keeping different colors from running together on the paper.

8. Regina is quite adept at algebra problems. While her peers are busy solving for x on paper, she quickly arrives at the correct answer in her head.

9. A librarian asks a group of 9-year-olds to read an article in a recent issue of *Time* magazine. He describes the main point of the article before the children begin reading it, and he gives them several questions that they should try to answer as they read. Even so, the children are unable to understand what they are reading.

10. Kris is playing with her 23-month-old cousin Amy. Kris holds up a stuffed dog:

    Kris: What is it?
    Amy: Doggie.
    Kris: What?
    Amy: Doggie.
    Kris: A doggie, yeah. (Picks up elephant.) What is this?
    Amy: Doggie.
    Kris: What?
    Amy: Baby.
    Kris: (Prompts Amy.) No. Uh—. Uh—.
    Amy: Pig.
    Kris: Uh—. Elephant.
    Amy: Elephant.
    Kris: Yeah elephant. (dialogue from Miller, 1982, p. 74; format adapted)

    (Note: We'll revisit this dialogue in our discussion of language development in Chapter 9.)

11. In her unit on genetics, a high school science teacher has students working with fruit flies. Because the students are initially confused about what they are supposed to do, she writes specific instructions on the chalkboard and then circulates around the room, assisting students who are having trouble identifying males and females correctly.

Answers to Application Exercise #2

1.   Yes. Selena plays the high notes successfully only with her teacher's assistance.

2.   No. Even with assistance, the boys are unable to play their respective positions.

3.   No. Group members can easily perform the task without any help.

4.   Yes. The students can write a short story successfully only when Mr. Marino structures the task for them and gives them some ideas about characters and plots.

5.   No. Jaleeza cannot turn the crank even when shown how to do it and given some guidance and encouragement.

6.   No. Using latitude and longitude is obviously an easy task for Julian, because he needs no help from anyone else.

7.   Yes. The students are sometimes having trouble with watercolor technique and benefit from their teacher's assistance.

8.   No. Regina is solving the problems quickly and easily, without help from anyone else.

9.   No. Even with the librarian's assistance, the children are unable to comprehend the article.

10. Yes. Amy seems to be able to recall new words when her older cousin gives her encouragement, an occasional hint, and feedback.

11. Yes. The students are able to proceed only with their teacher's instructions, and some of them are having difficulty sex-typing the flies without her assistance.

Application Exercise #3: Identifying Developmentally Appropriate Practices

Which of the following practices are appropriate for the age level, and which are not? Defend your choices.

1. A high school science teacher asks students in a chemistry lab to answer the question "Does water boil faster when more heat is applied?" He gives them the equipment they need and shows them how to use it safely, and he monitors their procedures to make sure they're following his safety guidelines. The students are able to conduct their investigations fairly independently but seem to benefit from the teacher's occasional guidance about how they might modify their procedures in order to get clear-cut results.

2. As she sits in her high chair, 6-month-old Deena keeps throwing the toys her father places on her tray, despite her father's pleas that she stop. Exasperated, the father scolds Deena and puts her in her crib—where there are no toys at all—to show Deena that toys are not meant to be thrown.

3. When a third-grade class takes a field trip to Rocky Mountain National Park, a park ranger gives a short lecture explaining how the Rocky Mountains were formed by forces pushing upward from within the earth.

4. A high school gymnastics coach describes the steps a person should take when executing a difficult dismount from the parallel bars. As team members begin practicing the dismount, the coach encourages them to whisper the steps to themselves as they proceed.

5. A preschool teacher makes sure that she fills the day with a sequence of structured activities designed to help her 3- and 4-year-olds acquire basic reading and mathematics skills. "I plan every minute of the day," she tells parents.

6. An eighth-grade science teacher describes how geologists divide rocks into three main categories: sedimentary, igneous, and metamorphic.

7. After reading a children's book that describes Columbus's voyage to the New World in 1492, a first-grade teacher asks students to consider what might have happened if Columbus had never made the trip.

8. An eleventh-grade mathematics teacher asks students to solve for x in problems such as this:
$$^3/_7 = {}^{12}/_x$$

9. When working with a small group of students who have poor reading comprehension skills, a fourth-grade teacher meets with them several times a week and has them ask one another questions about the book the group is reading. For instance, one student might ask the others, "Who can summarize the last page?" or "What do you think will happen next?"

Answers to Application Exercise #3

1. Appropriate. From Piaget's perspective, high school students are capable of formal operational thought and so should be able to separate and control variables. They should be able to demonstrate the effect of more or less heat while keeping other variables (size and shape of container, amount of water, etc.) constant. Keep in mind, however, that more recent researchers have found that adolescents don't always separate and control variables as readily as Piaget proposed. The teacher's occasional guidance here can scaffold the students' experimentation efforts.

2. Not appropriate. Piaget observed that infants and toddlers tend to repeat newly acquired behaviors over and over, and in doing so they learn that their actions have certain effects (see the textbook's description of Piaget's sensorimotor period). Rather than discourage Deena from throwing toys, her father should provide toys that she can throw safely (small stuffed animals, foam balls, etc.).

3. Not appropriate. The ranger is describing processes that the children have never directly observed; thus, the ideas he is presenting require abstract thought. Third graders tend to have difficulty with strictly abstract ideas.

4. Appropriate. According to Vygotsky, self-talk is not limited to young children. It is common for people of any age when they are performing a difficult task for the first time.

5. Not appropriate. The teacher is not giving the children any time to play. From Piaget's perspective, children need time to freely explore their physical environment and interact socially with their peers. From Vygotsky's perspective, play gives children a chance to experiment with adult roles and let their thoughts and imaginations guide their actions.

6. Appropriate. According to Vygotsky, adults should convey how culture interprets the world, and the concepts *sedimentary*, *igneous*, and *metamorphic* are cognitive tools that can help youngsters better understand the properties of various rocks. Furthermore, eighth graders, who are typically at least 13 years old, are capable of both class inclusion (a characteristic of Piaget's concrete operations stage) and some degree of abstract thought (a characteristic of Piaget's formal operations stage).

7. Not appropriate. From Piaget's perspective, students in the early elementary grades are not yet capable of reasoning about ideas that are contrary to fact. The teacher is asking the children to imagine a situation opposite to what they know to be true.

8. Appropriate. Research indicates that proportional thinking emerges in early adolescence. Within the framework of Piaget's theory, eleventh graders should be in the formal operations stage and so should be capable of proportional thought.

9. Appropriate. The teacher is engaging the children in reciprocal teaching, an effective means of promoting reading comprehension.

Sample Test Questions

Use the following multiple-choice and essay questions to evaluate and strengthen your understanding of selected concepts in the chapter.

Multiple-Choice

1. Irene knows how to count to 10. She counts the coins she has in her pocket (2 quarters, 5 dimes, and 3 nickels) and says, "I have 10 cents." From Piaget's perspective, Irene is:
   a. Accommodating the counting task to take into account the values of different coins
   b. Assimilating the counting task to the way she has counted things in the past
   c. Experiencing disequilibrium about how to count money
   d. Showing insufficient physiological maturation to perform the task correctly

2. Which one of the following best illustrates Piaget's concept of *symbolic thought* as it appears in the latter part of the sensorimotor stage?
   a. Crying about a teddy bear unintentionally left behind at a restaurant
   b. Climbing a chair to obtain an enticing toy visible on a high shelf
   c. Sucking on a carrot in the same way that one would suck on a bottle
   d. Becoming angry at being put to bed at night

3. Researchers who have examined various aspects of Piaget's theory have concluded that Piaget was *most* accurate about
   a. The abilities of preschoolers
   b. The abilities of elementary school children
   c. The abilities of adolescents
   d. The order in which various logical thinking abilities appear

4. From Robbie Case's neo-Piagetian perspective, cognitive development involves
   a. Becoming increasingly capable of counter-intuitive reasoning
   b. Emergence of new neurological structures in subcortical areas of the brain
   c. Acquiring an integrated network of concepts and cognitive processes related to specific knowledge domains
   d. Acquiring increasing knowledge about the nature of thinking, the result being that children can more effectively regulate their thinking

5. Three of the following are good examples of *cognitive tools*. Which one is *not* what Vygotsky would consider to be a cognitive tool?
   a. The scientific method
   b. A battery-operated chainsaw
   c. A strategy for writing a good short story
   d. The formula for determining the circumference of a circle

6. Imagine that you are a young adolescent in the seventh grade. You and your friends have certain opinions about issues being addressed in an upcoming election, and you all agree to communicate your opinions by writing a group letter to the editor of the local newspaper. An adult encourages you all to brainstorm different strategies for expressing your thoughts in a logical and persuasive manner and then guides you in developing an outline of the major points that you all want to make in the letter. In doing these things with your group, the adult is demonstrating the value of both brainstorming and outlining as strategies for developing a persuasive essay. The adult's approach can best be described as
   a. Teaching a task outside children's zones of proximal development
   b. Helping children separate and control variables
   c. The process of equilibration
   d. A cognitive apprenticeship

Essay

7. Compare and contrast Piaget's and Vygotsky's theories with respect to each of the following:
   • The role of language in cognitive development
   • The kinds of social interactions that are most critical for cognitive development
   • The influence of culture

8. Choose a particular age level of children or adolescents with whom you might someday be working. Then, using Piaget's theory and the findings of researchers who have investigated various aspects of his theory, identify at least *four* cognitive abilities (or *in*abilities) that youngsters at this age level are likely to have. Finally, explain how at least *two* of these abilities (or inabilities) would influence the ways in which you would teach or interact with these youngsters.

Answers to Sample Test Questions

1. b—Irene is showing assimilation: She is addressing a new situation in a way that is consistent with something she already knows how to do.

2. a—Piaget conceptualized symbolic thought as the ability to mentally represent and think about objects and events. Symbolic thought enables a child to think about something that is not necessarily in his or her immediate view.

3. d—Researchers have found support for the general developmental sequence that Piaget suggested, but they have discovered that Piaget probably underestimated the capabilities of youngsters in early and middle childhood and overestimated the capabilities of adolescents.

4. c—Alternative *c* describes Case's notion of *central conceptual structures*.

5. b—Cognitive tools are culturally constructed mechanisms for helping people think more effectively. Alternatives *a*, *c*, and *d* all enhance people's abilities to perform mental tasks. In contrast, a chainsaw is useful for carrying out strictly physical tasks.

6. d—In a cognitive apprenticeship, an expert and one or more novices work together to accomplish a challenging task. In the process, the expert models effective ways to think about the task.

7. Following are ideas that a comprehensive response to the question might include:
    *   *Role of language*: From Piaget's perspective, language provides labels for schemes and thus facilitates symbolic thought. It also enables the social interaction so important for learning about other people's ideas and perspectives and for creating the disequilibrium essential for cognitive growth. From Vygotsky's perspective, language (via self-talk and inner speech) provides the means through which social interactions are internalized into thought processes. Language also embodies many of the cultural interpretations of the world that one generation passes along to the next.
    *   *Social interaction*: Both Piaget and Vygotsky believed that social interactions with people of all ages are important for cognitive development. However, Piaget stressed interactions with peers (who provide opportunities for conflict and thus create disequilibrium), whereas Vygotsky placed greater importance on interaction with adults and other more advanced individuals (who can support children as they work within their zone of proximal development and can help them interpret experiences in culturally appropriate ways).
    *   *Influence of culture*: Piaget proposed that the progression of cognitive development (acquisition of conservation, abstract thought, etc.) is universal across cultures. In contrast, Vygotsky emphasized that different cultural groups—by passing along certain conceptual frameworks, belief systems, religions, and so on—teach children to interpret the world in very different, culture-specific ways.

8. There are many possible answers to this question. Check your response against the chapter's sections on "Piaget's Stages of Cognitive Development," "Current Perspectives on Piaget's Theory," and "Applying the Ideas of Piaget and His Followers."

Chapter 7

COGNITIVE DEVELOPMENT: COGNITIVE PROCESSES

Chapter Overview

This chapter describes recent theoretical perspectives and research findings related to cognitive development. The early sections of the chapter focus largely on *information processing theory*, an approach that considers the development of perception and memory, the specific ways in which children think about (i.e., process) new information, and children's knowledge and beliefs about how they think and learn. After looking at such topics, we draw on both information processing theory and sociocultural theory to discover how adults and children often coordinate their attention, recollections of past events, and cognitive strategies. In a later section, we consider *theory theory*, an approach that describes the integrated belief systems (theories) that children construct about various content domains. Finally, we look at three groups of children—those with learning disabilities, attention-deficit hyperactivity disorder, and autism—who have special educational needs related to information processing.

Possible Knowledge, Beliefs, and Misconceptions Related to Chapter Content

Following are a number of commonly held beliefs that may interfere with an accurate understanding of cognitive processes. As you read Chapter 7, be on the lookout for evidence that contradicts these ideas:

1. Many people erroneously believe that things in "short-term memory" (an alternative term for *working memory*) last for several hours, days, or weeks. In reality, information processing theorists believe that information that does not go beyond working (short-term) memory is remembered for *less than a minute*. (See the section "Key Ideas in Information Processing Theory.")

2. Many people are unaware of the important role that attention plays in the learning process and mistakenly believe that someone can remember things even when not paying attention to it. (Once again see "Key Ideas in Information Processing Theory.")

3. Many people think that repeating something over and over (rehearsal) is the most effective way to learn and remember it. Although repeated practice of information and skills is important for automatization (see the section "Working Memory and the Central Executive"), rehearsal for a limited time (e.g., repeating a fact several times in a row) is much less effective than such strategies as organization and elaboration, in part because the latter strategies help children integrate new ideas with information already in their knowledge base.

4. Many people, including many college students, have relatively naive beliefs about the nature of knowledge and learning. For instance, they may believe that knowledge about a topic is an unchanging, absolute "truth" or that it consists of a collection of isolated facts. Such beliefs are contrasted with more sophisticated views in Table 7-1 on page 254 of the textbook.

111

5. Many teachers and other professionals who work with children think that changing children's misconceptions about a topic is simply a matter of giving children more accurate information about the topic. In fact, children's existing misconceptions influence how they interpret new information and so often remain intact even after more accurate information has been presented. (See the discussion of conceptual change in the section "Facilitating Children's Theory Construction.")

Suggested Supplementary Readings

The following readings, presented in the final section of this *Study Guide and Reader*, are relevant to Chapter 7:

CHAPTER OUTLINE	FOCUS QUESTIONS
DEVELOPMENT OF BASIC COGNITIVE PROCESSES Key Ideas in Information Processing Theory Sensation and Perception Attention Working Memory and the Central Executive Long-Term Memory Thinking and Reasoning Facilitating Basic Cognitive Processes	• Compare and contrast the *sensory register*, *working memory*, and *long-term memory*. Explain how information flows from one component to the next. • What roles does the *central executive* play in children's thinking and behavior? • What sensory and perceptual abilities are present soon after birth? What abilities emerge later? • In what ways does children's ability to pay attention change with age? • How does working memory change over time? Why is it helpful for children to *automatize* basic skills? • What developmental changes take place in long-term memory? What roles do *schemas* and *scripts* play in cognition? • What general developmental trends are seen in thinking and reasoning? What do gestures sometimes indicate about children's cognitive development? • How can teachers and other adults help children process information effectively?

CHAPTER OUTLINE	FOCUS QUESTIONS
DEVELOPMENT OF METACOGNITION AND COGNITIVE STRATEGIES Learning Strategies Problem-Solving Strategies Strategy Development As "Overlapping Waves" Metacognitive Awareness Self-Regulated Learning Epistemological Beliefs Interdependence of Cognitive and Metacognitive Processes Promoting Metacognitive and Strategic Development	• Define *metacognition* in your own words. • Describe *rehearsal*, *organization*, and *elaboration*. At about what age does each of these learning strategies typically emerge? How does a child's environment influence strategy development? • Give an example of how children's problem-solving strategies become increasingly sophisticated with age. • Why is the development of strategies sometimes described as "overlapping waves"? • In what ways does children's *metacognitive awareness* change over time? • What skills and abilities does self-regulated learning involve? • In what ways are children's *epistemological beliefs* different from those of skillful adult learners? How do such beliefs influence learning and cognitive processes? • Describe at least three different ways in which children's cognitive and metacognitive processes are interdependent. • How can adults foster metacognitive and strategic development?
ADDING A SOCIOCULTURAL ELEMENT TO INFORMATION PROCESSING THEORY Intersubjectivity Social Construction of Memory Collaborative Use of Cognitive Strategies Enhancing Information Processing Through Social Interaction	• Describe *intersubjectivity*. Explain how it is reflected in *joint attention* and in *social referencing*. • Explain how memories can be socially constructed. What advantages and disadvantages do socially constructed memories have? • Use Vygotsky's theory to explain how co-regulated learning can facilitate self-regulated learning. (Before answering this question, you may want to review the discussion of Vygotsky's theory in Chapter 6.)

CHAPTER OUTLINE	FOCUS QUESTIONS

CHILDREN'S CONSTRUCTION OF THEORIES
 	
   Children's Theories of the Physical World
 	
   Facilitating Children's Theory Construction
	• What evidence supports the belief that children construct their own theories about certain topics?
	
	• Describe some basic understandings of physical phenomena that infants seem to have.
	
	• Give two examples of how children's theories are sometimes inaccurate. What factors in the environment might promote such misconceptions?
	
	• What implications does theory theory have for teaching and working with children?

COMPARING AND CRITIQUING CONTEMPORARY APPROACHES TO COGNITIVE DEVELOPMENT	• Why is it important for teachers and other practitioners to draw on a variety of theories of cognitive development, rather than limiting themselves to only one theoretical approach? • What questions about cognitive development currently remain unanswered?

EXCEPTIONALITIES IN INFORMATION PROCESSING
 	
   Learning Disabilities
 	
   Attention-Deficit Hyperactivity Disorder
 	
   Autism
 	
   Working With Children Who Have Information Processing Difficulties
	• What characteristics are associated with a *learning disability*? with *attention-deficit hyperactivity disorder*? with *autism*?
	
	• What strategies can adults use to help children and adolescents who have information processing difficulties?

Chapter Glossary

Attention-deficit hyperactivity disorder (ADHD). Disability characterized by inattention, by hyperactivity and impulsive behavior, or by all three characteristics.

Autism. Disability characterized by infrequent social interaction, little awareness of one's own and others' thoughts, communication impairments, repetitive behaviors, narrowly focused interests, and a strong need for a predictable environment.

Automatization. Process of becoming able to respond quickly and efficiently while mentally processing or physically performing certain tasks.

Central executive. Component of the human information processing system that oversees the flow of information throughout the system.

Cognitive strategy. Specific mental process that people use to acquire or manipulate information.

Comprehension monitoring. Process of checking oneself to make sure one understands what one is studying.

Conceptual change. Revision of one's knowledge and understanding of a topic in response to new information about the topic.

Co-regulated learning. Process through which an adult and child share responsibility for directing various aspects of the child's learning.

Elaboration. Process of using prior knowledge to embellish on new information and thereby learn it more effectively.

Epistemological beliefs. Beliefs regarding the nature of knowledge and knowledge acquisition.

Infantile amnesia. General inability to recall events that have occurred in the early years of life.

Information processing theory. Theoretical perspective that focuses on the specific ways in which people mentally think about ("process") the information they receive.

Intersubjectivity. Awareness of shared perceptions and understandings that provide the foundation for social interaction.

Joint attention. Phenomenon in which two people (e.g., a child and caregiver) simultaneously focus on the same object or event, monitor's each other's attention, and coordinate their responses.

Knowledge base. One's knowledge about specific topics and the world in general.

Learning disability. Significant deficit in one or more cognitive processes, to the point where special educational services are required.

Learning strategy. Specific mental process used in acquiring new information.

Long-term memory. Component of memory that holds knowledge and skills for a relatively long period of time.

Metacognition. Knowledge and beliefs about one's own cognitive processes, as well as efforts to regulate those cognitive processes to maximize learning and memory.

Metacognitive awareness. Extent to which one is able to reflect on the nature of one's own thinking processes.

Nativism. Theoretical perspective proposing that some knowledge is biologically built-in and present at birth or soon thereafter.

Organization. Process of identifying interrelationships among pieces of information as a way of learning them more effectively.

Rehearsal. Attempt to learn and remember information by repeating it over and over.

Schema. Tightly integrated set of ideas about a specific object or situation.

Script. Schema that involves a predictable sequence of events related to a common activity.

Self-regulated learning. Directing and controlling one's own cognitive processes in order to learn successfully.

Sensory register. Component of memory that holds incoming information in an unanalyzed form for a very brief time (2–3 seconds or less).

Social referencing. Looking at someone else (e.g., a caregiver) for clues about how to respond to a particular object or event.

Symbol. Mental entity that represents an external object or event, often without reflecting its perceptual and behavioral qualities.

Theory theory. Theoretical perspective proposing that children construct increasingly integrated and complex understandings of physical and mental phenomena.

Working memory. Component of memory that enables people to actively think about and process a small amount of information.

Table 7–1. Applying Concepts in Child Development: Identifying Children's Cognitive Processes

This table is a complete version of the table that appears at the end of Chapter 7 in the textbook. Compare your entries in the blank cells in the textbook table with our entries here. Keep in mind that there isn't necessarily a single "right" entry for any particular cell.

Age	A Youngster's Experience	**Developmental Concepts** *Identifying Cognitive Processes*	**Implications** *Promoting Effective Processes*
Infancy (Birth–2)	One Monday morning, 13-month-old Miguel meets his child care provider's new kitten for the first time. Miguel isn't sure what to make of this creature. When he sees that his caregiver is happily petting the kitten, he smiles and reaches out to touch the kitten's head.	Miguel is engaging in *social referencing*, checking to see how a trusted adult reacts to the new kitten and then responding in a similar way. Social referencing is an aspect of *intersubjectivity*, in which participants in a social situation have some awareness of what other participants are looking at, thinking, or feeling.	As you introduce infants to new people, animals, and objects, model appropriate ways of interacting with and responding to them.
Early Childhood (2–6)	A kindergarten teacher is reading Mercer Mayer's *What Do You Do with a Kangaroo?* to his class. As he often does during story time, he picks up a globe and points to the spot where the story takes place—in this case, Australia. "Most kangaroos live here in Australia," he says. "How come they don't fall off the world?" 5-year-old Andrea asks.	Like virtually all children her age, Andrea has already constructed a *theory* about her physical world. Because the teacher frequently uses a globe to show students different geographical locations, Andrea's theory includes the idea that the earth is a sphere. In her theory, however, gravity does not pull objects toward the center of the earth, but instead pulls them "downward" toward the south pole or into the open space "beneath" it.	Listen carefully to children's comments for clues regarding their beliefs about their physical and social worlds. With age-appropriate explanations, nudge them toward more accurate understandings.

table continues

Table 7–1 continued

Age	A Youngster's Experience	Developmental Concepts *Identifying Cognitive Processes*	Implications *Promoting Effective Processes*
Middle Childhood (6–10)	Although 10-year-old Kendall seems quite capable of doing typical fifth-grade work, he rarely stays on task for more than a few minutes during the school day. He is especially distractible during small-group activities and on other occasions when class activities are fairly noisy. He tends to remember very little of the material that is presented during such times.	*Attention* is critical for getting information into working memory and then (with further processing) into long-term memory. Distractibility is common for children in the preschool and early elementary years, but it is unusual for a boy as old as Kendall. Quite possibly Kendall has an undiagnosed *learning disability* or *attention-deficit hyperactivity disorder*.	When children have difficulty paying attention, minimize distractions and give them frequent opportunities to release pent-up energy. Use high-interest, hands-on activities to keep them mentally engaged in learning classroom subject matter.
Early Adolescence (10–14)	When Faith was in elementary school, she was a conscientious student who earned mostly As and Bs. Now, as a 13-year-old seventh grader, she often forgets to do her homework—sometimes she doesn't even know what her homework assignments are—and her grades have slipped to Cs and Ds. "I need to get my grades up," she tells the school counselor, "because I want to go to college. Next year I promise to work harder."	Faith apparently has not acquired many *self-regulated learning* skills: setting goals, planning study time, and so on. Such skills become increasingly important as students move through the grade levels and are expected to work more independently.	When students show a decline in academic achievement in middle school or junior high, assume that lack of self-regulation skills, rather than lack of motivation, is the culprit. But don't expect students to acquire self-regulated learning skills on their own. Instead, actively *teach* goal setting, self-motivation strategies, comprehension monitoring, and so on.
Late Adolescence (14–18)	After failing the first exam in his Advanced Placement biology class, 17-year-old John tells his science teacher, "I've never done so poorly on a test before, and I studied really hard for it. I repeated everything over and over until I knew it cold!" The teacher looks at John's notebook for the class and responds, "I think I see what the problem is. Your class notes are nothing more than facts and definitions. But my test asked you to apply what you've learned to real-life situations and problems."	Like many high school students, John has depended largely on *rehearsal* to study for his test. Any *comprehension monitoring* probably involved testing himself on facts and definitions rather than checking to see whether he could apply the material to new situations. Quite possibly John's *epistemological beliefs* about school subject matter include the idea that "knowing" something simply means being able to recite specific facts.	Especially at the high school level, encourage students to organize and make sense of information, rather than simply to repeat it verbatim. Help them discover that true mastery of a topic involves understanding how concepts and ideas relate to one another and to real-world situations and problems.

Application Exercise #1: Identifying Typical and Atypical Behaviors

In the following scenarios, which youngsters are exhibiting behaviors typical for their age-group, and which ones are not? Justify your choices on the basis of what you have learned about cognitive processes and cognitive development.

1. A second-grade class in Colorado takes a field trip to the Denver Museum of Natural History, where the students see a large skeleton of a brontosaurus. Ophelia says to her teacher, "I know how we can remember that word. *Brontosaurus* sounds like the Denver Broncos [the local football team], and the Broncos are really big just like this dinosaur is!"

2. Sixteen-year-old Amie is very distractible at school and at her part-time job. Any little noise seems to draw her attention away from what she is supposed to be doing.

3. Ten-year-old Martin studies his spelling words by repeating the letters of each word over and over again.

4. Eighteen-year-old Rita attends weekly counseling sessions to help her get an eating disorder under control. In an attempt to identify the origins of Rita's eating problems, the counselor asks her to recall her early childhood. Rita cannot seem to remember anything that happened to her before she was 2, and her memory of the preschool years is vague at best.

5. A police officer visits a preschool class one morning to talk to the children about safety procedures at home and in the neighborhood. She discusses the importance of staying away from electrical outlets, not putting electrical appliances in the bathtub, looking both ways before crossing the street, and so on. Later in the day, the children's teacher asks them to describe some of the things they learned from the police officer. The children don't seem to remember much of what she said, but several of them comment on her shiny badge, and a couple of girls say that they really liked the pretty barrette she wore in her hair.

6. A seventh-grade teacher gives her students a five-page reading assignment in their social studies textbook; the following day, she gives them a quiz over what they have read. She is pleased at her students' excellent performance on the quiz and asks them what they did when they read and studied the assignment. The strategies they describe are similar to things she did when she studied as a college student.

7. Seven-year-old Lori asks, "Why don't sailors fall off the earth when they get to the end of the ocean?"

8. A preschool teacher has a map of the world displayed prominently on one wall of her classroom. She asks 4-year-old Isaiah to find Europe, Asia, and Africa on the map, and he accurately points to each of the three continents. She then asks Isaiah, "If you are in Europe, which direction would you go to get to Asia?" He looks at the map, thinks for a moment, and answers, "East."

9. Twelve-month-old Darren crawls toward the edge of a large hole where a building contractor is preparing to pour the foundation for a new house. He looks down at the hole and then, oblivious to the danger, begins to crawl forward again as if the hole weren't there. Fortunately, an older child pulls him away in the nick of time.

10. A first-grade teacher places 15 different objects on his desk and asks his students to look at them carefully. He says, "I'm going to cover these up in just a few seconds. How many things do you think you will be able to remember five minutes from now?" His students confidently agree that they will be able to remember almost all of the objects. As it turns out, they can remember an average of only 6 or 7 objects apiece.

11. Fifteen-year-old Jonathan studies for three hours for his geography test and thinks that he knows the material well. His low test score the following day indicates that he doesn't understand it at all.

12. When 12-year-old Rita reads a novel, she reads it very slowly, pointing at each word and stopping to sound out such words as *enough*, *together*, and *potato*.

13. In a discussion about different occupations, a child care provider asks 3-year-old Renée where her mother works. Renée thinks for a moment and then responds, "I forgot." That afternoon, the child care provider mentions the incident to Renée's mother, who responds, "I'm a social worker at the county welfare department. I've never told Renée what I do for a living, because I figured she was too young to understand what social work involves. She couldn't possibly 'forget' something she never knew."

14. Seventeen-year-old Harry is studying for the final exam in his physics class. He tries to make sense of some of the material by thinking about how he might apply it to new situations. He organizes other material by identifying categories (e.g., various types of machines) or cause–effect relationships (e.g., *acceleration* leads to increased *velocity*). But some material (e.g., formulas) he simply tries to memorize by repeating it over and over.

15. Four-month-old Cynthia doesn't seem to distinguish among the various people in her life, and so she responds to anyone who approaches and talks to her—her mother, her father, her pediatrician, a 3-year-old neighbor, or a complete stranger—in essentially the same way.

16. In a discussion of dinosaurs, a fifth-grade teacher shows his class a picture that illustrates what some paleontologists think a newly discovered dinosaur species probably looked like. Ten-year-old Kareem raises his hand and says, "That's only what *some* scientists think. I read in my dinosaur book at home that other scientists think it looked a lot different than that. I guess scientists will have to look harder and find more bones. Maybe they'll figure out how it really looked, and maybe they won't."

Answers to Application Exercise #1

1. Not typical. Ophelia is demonstrating considerable *elaboration*: She is intentionally trying to embellish on information as a way of helping her learn it. Elaboration, at least when used intentionally as a learning strategy, is rare before early adolescence.

2. Not typical. Although children are easily distracted during the early elementary years, they become increasingly able to focus their attention as they grow older.

3. Typical. Rehearsal is a common learning strategy during the later elementary school years.

4. Typical. People tend to remember little if anything of the first two years of life—a phenomenon known as *infantile amnesia*. Furthermore, they have difficulty remembering much of what happened during the preschool years, in part because such memories may be in a form (perhaps nonverbal) that is difficult to retrieve.

5. Typical. Most young children have only limited ability to focus attention on tasks that adults give them, and they shift their attention frequently from one thing to another.

6. Not typical. Adolescents become increasingly knowledgeable about effective study strategies throughout the high school years. Seventh graders use relatively ineffective strategies in comparison to those that high school and college students are likely to use.

7. Typical. Misconceptions about the physical world are common throughout the elementary grades and are often derived from how things *appear* to be. For instance, in our everyday experiences, the world appears to be flat rather than round.

8. Not typical. Young children have very limited ability to understand and interpret symbols such as maps.

9. Not typical. Studies with a *visual cliff* indicate that infants show fear and avoidance of heights as early as 6 months of age. (Caregivers should not rely on this predisposition to fear heights, however. They should always make sure that infants and young children are at a safe distance from potentially dangerous drop-offs.)

10. Typical. Children in the early elementary grades tend to be overly optimistic about how much they will be able to remember.

11. Typical. Many students overestimate what they have learned, even at the high school level. Often students' overconfidence is the result of poor *comprehension monitoring*; that is, they don't regularly assess what they can remember and understand of what they've studied.

12. Not typical. Most 12-year-olds have been reading for about six years and have *automatized* identification of most common words, and so they can read the words quickly and effortlessly.

13. Typical. Three-year-olds are likely to talk about "forgetting" something they never knew to begin with.

14. Typical. Harry is displaying *elaboration*, *organization*, and *rehearsal*. Of the three, rehearsal typically emerges first (i.e., in middle childhood) but is least effective. Children and adolescents often continue to use their early strategies (though perhaps less frequently) even when they acquire more advanced ones, reflecting the concept of *overlapping waves*.

15. Not typical. Within the first week of life, infants begin to show a preference for their mother's voice. Also in the first week or so, their visual acuity (although far from perfect) is sufficient to enable them to recognize the contours of their mother's face and to imitate other people's facial expressions. Keep in mind that although 4-month-olds should be able to distinguish among different people, they will not necessarily be afraid of people they don't recognize; such *stranger anxiety* won't appear until later (see Chapter 11).

16. Not typical. Kareem's views of the nature of knowledge (his *epistemological beliefs*) are quite advanced for a 10-year-old. He acknowledges that differing viewpoints may have equal validity and that knowledge about a topic continues to evolve over time; such understandings are rare before high school.

Application Exercise #2: Identifying Developmentally Appropriate Practices

Which of the following practices are appropriate for the age level of the youngsters, and which are not? Defend your choices.

1.   To discourage 18-month-old Forrest from playing with the kitty litter box, his father holds his nose and says "Yucky!" every time the two of them are near the box.

2.   The director of an after-school child care center divides all the 6- and 7-year-olds into several small groups and gives each one a creative activity to pursue (writing a play, making an invention, composing a song, etc.). She allots a two-hour period for this activity and then pulls the children back together to find out what each group has accomplished.

3.   An eighth-grade language arts teacher encourages students to study their new vocabulary words by repeating the definitions over and over to themselves.

4.   Ms. Jackson's second graders are having a dress rehearsal for a Halloween play tomorrow. Marcella plays the lead character but still doesn't know most of her lines. "Don't worry, Ms. Jackson, I'll have my dad read them to me once tonight, so I'll be sure to remember them tomorrow." Ms. Jackson feels reassured but nevertheless calls Marcella's father to make sure that he *will* read Marcella her lines at least once.

5.   When giving his high school students their evening's reading assignment, Mr. Rodriguez provides a list of questions to answer as they read.

6.   Four-month-old Randall is hospitalized for several weeks after a serious car accident. To minimize his exposure to germs in his vulnerable state, his adult caregivers stay away from his crib, but they fill it with carefully sanitized plastic toys.

7.   A seventh-grade geography teacher is preparing her students for an upcoming quiz on Western Europe and the British Isles. "If you want to do well on the quiz," she tells them, "you should know the capital cities, important waterways, and major imports and exports of each of the countries we've studied."

8.   On a nice day in early May, an infant home-care provider takes the 2-year-olds in her care into her backyard to play. A corner of the yard is fenced off so that she will be able to plant a garden in June. As a game, she tosses several durable plastic toys into the garden area and shows the children how to bring them within reach using a small toy rake. She then encourages the children to do likewise.

9.   Mr. Flick has just taken a job as a history teacher at Maplewood High School. He opens the textbook the school district has purchased for his world history class and turns to the chapter on World War II. "Wow," he thinks, "the book covers at least 20 different battles of the war. If I spend about three or four minutes of class time talking about each one, then I can get through them all in a reasonable time."

Answers to Application Exercise #2

1. Appropriate. At his age, Forrest should be quite capable of *social referencing*, in which he looks to others for clues about how to respond to various objects.

2. Not appropriate. Young children have trouble maintaining attention on any one task for very long, and they have few self-regulation skills for completing lengthy independent tasks.

3. Not appropriate. Rehearsal is a common strategy in the elementary grades. But older students are capable of elaboration, which is a more effective strategy.

4. Not appropriate. Young children tend to overestimate how much they will be able to remember. Once through is probably insufficient even for an adult, let alone for a 7-year-old, but Marcella is unlikely to be aware of this fact. Marcella needs much more practice.

5. Appropriate. Students of all ages, even those in high school, often think they have learned things that they really haven't learned. By giving students questions they must answer from their reading assignment, Mr. Rodriguez is providing them with a way of testing themselves to find out what they actually do and do not understand. In other words, he is facilitating their comprehension monitoring.

6. Not appropriate. By 3 months, infants show a definite preference for human faces over other objects, and by 4 months, they prefer looking at human movements over other movements. Randall's caregivers should take precautions to prevent infection (e.g., wearing a mask, using sanitized gloves), but depriving him of interaction with other human beings is not the answer. (For more on the importance of early human relationships, see the discussion of *attachment* in Chapter 11.)

7. Not appropriate. The teacher is asking her students to memorize a list of isolated facts. By early adolescence, students are increasingly integrating the information they have learned about the world, and focusing on isolated facts can hardly facilitate such integration. Furthermore, the teacher may be fostering the immature epistemological belief that learning is nothing more than committing information to memory in a piecemeal fashion.

8. Appropriate. Two-year-olds show some ability to use tools to solve problems. For instance, if shown how, they can use a rake or other long object to get something that is out of reach.

9. Not appropriate. Adolescents' working memory capacities may be slightly larger than those of younger children, and their larger knowledge bases and more sophisticated learning strategies allow them to learn new material more effectively than younger children. Nevertheless, high school students (adults too, for that matter) can think about only so much information at once. Describing 20 different battles in one or two class periods will undoubtedly be too much information for students to learn and remember.

Sample Test Questions

Use the following multiple-choice and essay questions to evaluate and strengthen your understanding of selected concepts in the chapter.

Multiple-Choice

1. Which one of the following best describes the role that the *central executive* plays in children's cognitive development?
    a. As children grow older, they increasingly control their thinking processes.
    b. Children's gestures often precede the emergence of new reasoning abilities.
    c. As children grow older, they have more knowledge to which they can relate new experiences.
    d. As children grow older, they increasingly understand the nature of maps, diagrams, and other symbolic representations.

2. Which one of the following is the best example of a *script*?
    a. Knowing how to ride a bicycle
    b. Knowing that robins, seagulls, and ostriches are all birds
    c. Knowing the typical sequence of events at a birthday party
    d. Knowing that certain four-letter words are unacceptable at school

3. *Metacognitive development* can best be described as
    a. Becoming increasingly capable of abstract thought
    b. Developing the neurological structures that underlie complex cognitive processes
    c. Acquiring an integrated network of concepts and cognitive processes related to specific knowledge domains
    d. Acquiring increasing knowledge about the nature of thought and increasing proficiency in using effective learning strategies

4. Which one of the following statements is most accurate regarding how *culture* affects cognitive development?
    a. Different cultures foster different learning strategies.
    b. Some cultures explicitly teach children to use their working memories to solve problems; other cultures do not.
    c. Automatization is more common in industrialized countries than in developing nations.
    d. Despite their widely varying experiences, children of all cultures develop similar metacognitive strategies.

5. Three of the following illustrate *epistemological beliefs*. Which one is *not* an epistemological belief?
   a. Believing that "knowing" geography is nothing more than remembering the capitals of countries, provinces, and states
   b. Believing that Jane Austen's *Pride and Prejudice* was the best novel ever written
   c. Believing that anything that appears in a library book must definitely be true
   d. Believing that one's ability to learn is largely uncontrollable

6. Shane has autism. Given this information, you would expect that Shane probably has
   a. A poor sense of rhythm
   b. Poor visual-spatial skills
   c. Trouble communicating with other children
   d. Intense curiosity about new and exciting places and events

Essay

7. As a college student, you probably study a lot more effectively than you did when you were in high school. Identify three different reasons why high school students don't necessarily study classroom subject matter very effectively. Base your response on developmental trends and research results presented in the textbook.

8. In two or three sentences, describe the *theory theory* approach to cognitive development. Then, drawing from either information presented in the textbook or your own experiences with children, give an example of a young child's theory about the biological world, physical world, or nature of thought.

Answers to Sample Test Questions

1. a—The central executive is the general "overseer" of the information processing system and increasingly "takes charge" as children grow older.

2. c—A script is knowledge about the predictable sequence of events related to a common activity.

3. d—Metacognition encompasses knowledge and beliefs about one's own cognitive processes, as well as the use and regulation of those cognitive processes to maximize learning. Metacognitive development, then, involves improvements in such knowledge and capabilities with age.

4. a—Research shows evidence of cross-cultural differences in children's use of rehearsal and in their ability to remember word lists, orally transmitted stories, and spatial arrangements.

5. b—Alternatives *a*, *c*, and *d* all reflect beliefs about the nature of knowledge and learning.

6. c—Children with autism typically show impairments in communication.

7. Your response should include at least three of the following ideas:
    *   For some topics, students may have an insufficient knowledge base to make sense of new ideas and concepts; in such situations, they may have little choice but to resort to rehearsal.
    *   Some basic skills essential for more complex tasks may not yet be automatized, leading to occasional "overload" in working memory.
    *   Students may erroneously believe that rote memorization (e.g., rehearsal) is the most effective way to learn.
    *   Students may have poor self-regulation skills (e.g., they may not know how to set goals for a study session or how to keep themselves motivated during tedious study tasks).
    *   Students may not engage in comprehension monitoring.
    *   Students may have relatively unsophisticated epistemological beliefs (e.g., they may believe that learning something means memorizing isolated facts or that learning happens quickly or else not at all).
    *   Classroom assessment tasks may encourage rote memorization (e.g., by asking students to recall information word for word).

8. From the perspective of theory theory, children construct integrated belief systems about living things, physical objects, and psychological phenomena. Such theories may include erroneous beliefs that distort children's interpretations of new information and experiences. The textbook presents examples of children's theories regarding living things (see the dialogue about apples versus pears), the physical world (see the dialogue about cups versus bowling balls, as well as the section "Children's Theories of the Physical World"), and the mind (see the section "Metacognitive Awareness"). If your example came from your own experiences, it should reflect a child's beliefs (perhaps correct, perhaps not) related to one of these domains.

Chapter 8

INTELLIGENCE

Chapter Overview

Chapter 8 examines various theoretical perspectives on the nature of intelligence and describes some of the ways in which psychologists and other practitioners typically try to assess children's intellectual development. It explores possible hereditary and environmental factors affecting children's IQ scores and suggests several reasons why the relative effects of nature and nurture are difficult to disentangle. Later, the chapter considers several sources of diversity in children's IQ scores (gender, socioeconomic status, ethnic background, giftedness, mental retardation) and offers suggestions for accommodating such diversity in schools and other settings.

Possible Knowledge, Beliefs, and Misconceptions Related to Chapter Content

Following are several beliefs that college students sometimes have before they study the nature and development of intelligence—beliefs that can interfere with an accurate understanding of the information students encounter in a textbook. As you read Chapter 8, be on the lookout for evidence that contradicts these commonly held ideas:

1. In recent years, Howard Gardner's theory of intelligence has gained considerable popularity among teacher educators, who may convey the message that human intelligence definitely consists of multiple and relatively independent intelligences. In fact, the data supporting the existence of eight or nine distinctly different intelligences are limited, leading many experts to disagree with Gardner's views.

2. Many people think of IQ scores as fixed numbers that reflect permanent characteristics. In fact, IQ scores are at best only rough estimates of a person's current level of intellectual functioning, and they can (and often do) change over time.

3. Some people believe that IQ tests have no usefulness in instructional settings. In fact, when such tests are used as part of a larger diagnostic testing battery and are accompanied by information obtained in other ways (e.g., through observations of children and interviews of parents), they can be helpful in determining why some children are having difficulty in school and elsewhere.

4. Some people think that intelligence is almost entirely inherited. Other people believe that intelligence is exclusively the result of environmental factors. Both nature and nurture affect intelligence (see the section "Effects of Heredity and Environment on Intelligence").

5. When some people read that identical twins' IQs are more highly correlated than fraternal twins' IQs, they misinterpret the higher correlation coefficients to mean that identical twins have higher IQs than fraternal twins. In reality, the higher numbers indicate a stronger *relationship* between two sets of IQ scores; they do not indicate higher IQ scores per se.

6. When average differences among groups are described, many people think of these differences as being much larger than they really are. For example, when they hear about gender differences in verbal ability or spatial skills, they might think that most boys are better than most girls, or vice versa. In reality, group differences, when found, are small enough that one can *never* make predictions about individual children and adolescents based on group membership alone (e.g., see Figure 8-7 on page 298 of the textbook).

7. When people discover that intelligence has an inherited component, they may mistakenly conclude that heredity explains differences among *groups* as well as differences among individuals. In fact, although a few theorists have argued that average group differences in intelligence are due to heredity, most experts believe that group differences are usually the result of environmental variables (see the section "Ethnic and Racial Differences").

8. Some people believe that intelligence tests are culturally biased any time that one ethnic or cultural group performs at a higher level on the test than another group does. In fact, a test has *cultural bias* only when it is a *less valid* (i.e., less accurate) measure of intelligence for one group than for another (see the discussion of cultural bias in the section "Ethnic and Racial Differences").

Suggested Supplementary Readings

The following readings, presented in the final section of this *Study Guide and Reader*, are relevant to Chapter 8:

Reading 8-1: Fetal Alcohol Syndrome

Reading 8-2: Adaptive Skills Considered in Identifying Children With Mental Retardation

CHAPTER OUTLINE	FOCUS QUESTIONS
DEFINING INTELLIGENCE	• What qualities does intelligence encompass? • Give an example of how different cultures sometimes have different views of what intelligence is.

CHAPTER OUTLINE	FOCUS QUESTIONS
THEORETICAL PERSPECTIVES OF INTELLIGENCE Spearman's *g* Cattell's Fluid and Crystallized Intelligence Gardner's Multiple Intelligences Sternberg's Triarchic Theory Distributed Intelligence	• What evidence supports the idea of a *general factor* (*g*) in intelligence? What evidence leads some theorists to reject the notion of *g*? • How are *fluid intelligence* and *crystallized intelligence* different? • Describe Gardner's theory of multiple intelligences, and explain why educators find it so appealing. • Summarize the three factors that, in Sternberg's view, affect intelligence: environmental context, prior experience, and cognitive processes. • What do theorists mean by *distributed intelligence*? In what ways is this concept different from Spearman's *g*?
MEASURING INTELLIGENCE Tests of General Intelligence Specific Ability Tests Dynamic Assessment Assessing the Abilities of Infants and Young Children	• For what purposes are intelligence tests most commonly used? • Describe several different kinds of questions or tasks that you might find on an intelligence test. • In what important way is the UNIT different from the WISC-IV and the Stanford-Binet? • How are IQ scores derived? What does a score of 100 mean? a score of 85? a score of 130? • How are specific ability tests different from intelligence tests? • How does *dynamic assessment* differ from a traditional intelligence test? What are the strengths and weaknesses of this approach? • What kinds of tasks are typically used to assess the cognitive development of infants and young children? What concerns does the textbook raise about *school readiness tests*? • To what extent do various measures of intelligence and more specific cognitive abilities have high *validity*? To what extent do various measures have high *reliability*?

CHAPTER OUTLINE	FOCUS QUESTIONS

EFFECTS OF HEREDITY AND ENVIRONMENT ON INTELLIGENCE
 	
   Evidence for Hereditary Influences
 	
   Evidence for Environmental Influences
 	
   How Nature and Nurture Interact in Their Influence on Intelligence
	• How do twin studies and adoption studies provide evidence that intelligence has a genetic component? How do they show that environment is a factor as well?
	
	• What additional evidence exists to support the idea that IQ scores are affected by environmental variables?
	
	• What is the *Flynn effect*? What factors might explain it?
	
	• In what ways do heredity and environment interact in their effects on intelligence?
	
	• Explain why *niche-picking* makes it difficult to separate the relative effects of heredity and environment, especially in older children and adolescents.

DEVELOPMENTAL TRENDS IN IQ SCORES	• Why do IQ scores not increase with age even though children obviously become more intelligent as they get older? • What developmental trends are seen in IQ scores? • Why should adults *not* use early IQ scores to make long-term predictions about school performance?

GROUP DIFFERENCES IN INTELLIGENCE
 	
   Gender Differences
 	
   Socioeconomic Differences
 	
   Ethnic and Racial Differences
	• What two principles are essential to keep in mind when looking at group differences in IQ?
	
	• In what ways are males and females similar in their cognitive abilities? In what ways, and to what extent, are they different, and why?
	
	• On average, children from low-SES families have lower IQ scores than children from middle-SES families. To what factors do theorists attribute this difference?
	
	• At what age do ethnic and racial differences in IQ scores appear? To what factors do theorists attribute these differences?

CHAPTER OUTLINE	FOCUS QUESTIONS
CRITIQUE OF CURRENT PERSPECTIVES ON INTELLIGENCE	• What concerns do the textbook authors have about current approaches to conceptualizing and measuring intelligence?
IMPLICATIONS OF THEORIES AND RESEARCH ON INTELLIGENCE	• What strategies can adults use to maintain their optimism for every child's success in the classroom and elsewhere? • In what various ways might intelligence reveal itself in children's behavior?

EXCEPTIONALITIES IN INTELLIGENCE
 	
  Giftedness
 	
  Mental Retardation
	• What qualities does *giftedness* encompass? What characteristics are frequently seen in children who are gifted?
	
	• Why should educators not rely exclusively on intelligence tests when identifying potential candidates for gifted programs?
	
	• What two characteristics must be present for a diagnosis of mental retardation? What other characteristics are frequently associated with mental retardation?
	
	• What biological and environmental factors may contribute to mental retardation?
	
	• What strategies can teachers and other practitioners use in working with children who are gifted? What strategies can they use when working with children who have been identified as having mental retardation?

Chapter Glossary

Adaptive behavior. Behavior related to daily living skills and appropriate conduct in social situations.

Crystallized intelligence. Knowledge and skills accumulated from prior experience, schooling, and one's culture.

Cultural bias. Extent to which an assessment instrument offends or unfairly penalizes some individuals because of their ethnicity, gender, or socioeconomic status.

Distributed intelligence. Thinking facilitated by physical objects and technology, social support, and concepts and symbols of one's culture.

Dynamic assessment. Systematic examination of how a child's knowledge or reasoning may change as a result of learning a specific task or performing it with adult guidance.

Fluid intelligence. Ability to acquire knowledge quickly and thereby adapt effectively to new situations.

Flynn effect. Gradual increase in intelligence test performance observed in many countries over the past several decades.

g. General factor in intelligence that influences performance in a wide variety of tasks and content domains.

Giftedness. Unusually high ability in one or more areas, to the point where children require special educational services to help them meet their full potential.

Intelligence test. General measure of current cognitive functioning, used primarily to predict academic achievement over the short run.

Intelligence. Ability to apply past knowledge and experiences flexibly to accomplish challenging new tasks.

IQ score. Score on an intelligence test, determined by comparing one's performance with the performance of same-age peers.

Mental retardation. Disability marked by significantly below-average general intelligence and deficits in adaptive behavior.

Niche-picking. Tendency to actively seek out environments that match one's inherited abilities.

Specific ability test. Test designed to assess a specific cognitive skill or the potential to learn and perform in a specific content domain.

Stereotype threat. Reduction in performance (often unintentional) as a result of a belief that one's group typically performs poorly.

Table 8–1. Applying Concepts in Child Development: Using Various Theories of Intelligence to Understand Youngsters' Behaviors

This table is a complete version of the table that appears at the end of Chapter 8 in the textbook. Compare your entries in the blank cells in the textbook table with our entries here. Keep in mind that there isn't necessarily a single "right" entry for any particular cell.

Age	A Youngster's Experience	Developmental Concepts *Applying Theories of Intelligence to Patterns in Youngsters' Behaviors*	Implications *Helping Youngsters Reach Their Full Potential*
Infancy (Birth–2)	When Meghan was born, features of her face, fingers, and toes made it clear that she has Down syndrome. Now almost 2, Meghan has just a few words in her speaking vocabulary, and she learns new things more slowly than her age-mates. She has only recently learned to walk and also shows delays in learning to feed and dress herself.	Meghan shows early signs of mental retardation, which most children with Down syndrome have to varying degrees. Her slower-than-average development across the board is consistent with Spearman's idea of a *general (g) factor* in intelligence.	When children show delays in many different areas, identify a variety of interventions that can support their development in each domain. (For example, Meghan may need explicit instruction not only in cognitive and linguistic skills but also in adaptive behaviors.)
Early Childhood (2–6)	Five-year-old Robin has discovered many addition and subtraction facts on her own and is now insisting that her mother help her understand what multiplication is. Robin also enjoys taking apart small household gadgets (e.g., ballpoint pens, flashlights) to see how they work. Yet she is a physically awkward child who has had trouble learning such skills as tying shoes, and she seems at a loss about how to play with the other children in her kindergarten class.	Robin shows strengths and weaknesses consistent with Gardner's theory of *multiple intelligences*. In particular, she seems to be stronger in logical-mathematical intelligence than in bodily-kinesthetic intelligence and interpersonal intelligence.	Provide experiences that help children develop both their strong and weak areas. Use their strengths as a way of getting them actively engaged in activities in which they can also work on their weaknesses. (For example, a teacher might ask Robin to work on math or science tasks with one or two other children who have high logical-mathematical intelligence. In such small-group activities, Robin can develop her interpersonal skills.)

table continues

Table 8–1 continued

Age	A Youngster's Experience	Developmental Concepts *Applying Theories of Intelligence to Patterns in Youngsters' Behaviors*	Implications *Helping Youngsters Reach Their Full Potential*
Middle Childhood (6–10)	When it comes to learning and remembering things about African American history, 9-year-old Tyrone is like a sponge, absorbing almost everything he reads. He explains his good memory this way: "When I'm reading something, I keep asking myself questions about it and then try to answer them. If I can't answer a question, I go back and read the stuff again."	Tyrone's ability to engage in comprehension monitoring and reflect on his thought processes is unusual for a 9-year-old (see Chapter 7). The role of specific cognitive and metacognitive processes in intelligence is most evident in Sternberg's *triarchic theory*.	Teach more effective cognitive and metacognitive strategies as one means of helping children think and perform more intelligently. (For example, a teacher might help other students learn as effectively as Tyrone by teaching them how to ask one another thought-provoking questions; see Chapter 7.)
Early Adolescence (10–14)	For a science fair project, 13-year-old Jacquita interviews more than 100 students about their eating habits—how often they eat fresh fruits and vegetables, how often they go to fast-food restaurants, and so on. At first, Jacquita has difficulty organizing and making sense of her data. But after her teacher shows her how to use a computer spreadsheet, she easily summarizes her findings and creates several bar graphs for her science fair poster.	We can probably best explain this situation using the concept of *distributed intelligence*. Jacquita shows more intelligent behavior when she has physical objects (computer technology) and symbolic systems (e.g., bar graphs) at her disposal.	Give youngsters the physical and symbolic tools they need to think and act intelligently. (For example, teachers should share with students the many symbolic systems adults in Western societies use to collect, analyze, and interpret data—questionnaires, spreadsheets, statistical procedures, etc.—and teach students how to use calculators, computers, and other physical tools to make the use of symbolic systems easier and more efficient.)
Late Adolescence (14–18)	Mark is quite motivated to do well in his high school classes. Class material doesn't always come easily to him, but he studies hard and so gains a firm grasp of the subject matter. He is especially knowledgeable about current events, as he spends much of his leisure time reading the local newspaper and such news magazines as *Time* and *The Economist*.	Cattell's theory is relevant here. It appears that Mark has average or above-average, but not exceptional, *fluid intelligence*. However, he has accumulated considerable knowledge (especially about current events), reflecting high *crystallized intelligence*.	Help children and adolescents acquire an in-depth and well integrated knowledge base about topics that will be especially useful in adult life. (For example, teachers should teach classroom subject matter in ways that promote true understanding and integration of ideas, rather than mindless memorization of discrete facts.)

Application Exercise #1: Using Measures of Intelligence and Cognitive Development

In each of the following situations, a teacher or other professional is interpreting the results of a measure of cognitive ability. For each situation, decide whether the inference drawn and/or decision made is appropriate or inappropriate. Defend your choices.

1. A fifth-grade teacher has referred several of his students for possible admission to a special program for gifted students. One of his students, 11-year-old Darcy, earns a score of 123 on the Stanford-Binet, missing the program's cut-off score of 130 by 7 points. The teacher argues vehemently for Darcy's admission to the program. "Her test score doesn't reflect her ability," he tells the teacher of the gifted program. "Darcy is incredibly inquisitive about a wide range of topics, and she voraciously reads anything about science that she can get her hands on. She also has a grasp of abstract mathematical concepts that far exceeds that of most of her classmates."

2. A preschool teacher notices that 3-year-old Samuel can do few of the things his classmates can do; for instance, he doesn't talk much, nor can he hold a large crayon and make scribbles on paper. At the teacher's recommendation, the parents have a psychologist evaluate Samuel, and the psychologist reports unusually low performance on the Bayley Scales. At this point, the teacher urges the parents to enroll Samuel in a community program designed for young children with significant developmental delays. "The program is only three mornings a week," the teacher tells the parents. "Sam can still come to my class every Monday, Wednesday, and Friday afternoon, as well as all day Tuesday and Thursday."

3. After learning that 7-year-old Richard has scored 65 on a recent administration of the Stanford-Binet, his second-grade teacher thinks, "Well, that explains his consistently poor performance in my class. Obviously Richard has mental retardation."

4. When the mother of 14-month-old Emily mentions that Emily was given an Apgar score of 9 at birth, Emily's new child care provider makes sure to lavish a great deal of stimulation on Emily—singing her songs, reading her storybooks, giving her complex toys to play with, and so on, whenever Emily is awake—in an effort to help Emily "make up the deficit."

5. Each spring, the kindergarten teachers in the Springfield school district routinely administer school readiness tests to children who plan to enroll in kindergarten the following fall. "We'll put all of the children in kindergarten next year regardless of their performance," district officials tell the parents. "We use the test results only to help us plan the curriculum."

6. When 14-year-old Lisa earns a score of 82 on the WISC-IV, her guidance counselor thinks, "I'm not surprised. Her two older brothers were also low achievers, and as I recall, one of them scored 76 on the Stanford-Binet a few years ago. I think that low intelligence just runs in the family. It's a hereditary thing."

Answers to Application Exercise #1

1. Appropriate. A single measure of intelligence is always subject to some error (reflecting the test's imperfect validity and reliability). Darcy's behaviors are all consistent with high intelligence.

2. Appropriate. Although tests for infants and young children are not as reliable as tests for older children and adolescents, they can be quite useful in helping practitioners identify significant cognitive delays, especially if used in combination with other information. In this case, the test result corroborates what the teacher has observed in Samuel's behavior at school. Samuel will continue to attend his regular preschool class, so he will have many opportunities to engage in typical 3-year-old activities and interact with his peers, so even if for some reason he is *not* actually delayed in his development, he loses little by participating in the community intervention program.

3. Inappropriate. There are many possible reasons for a low score on an intelligence test, especially for a child as young as 7. Furthermore, for an accurate diagnosis of mental retardation, Richard must show deficits in adaptive behavior, which intelligence tests don't assess.

4. Inappropriate. The Apgar Scale ranges from 0 to 10, so a score of 9 is actually quite good and does *not* reveal a "deficit." Certainly a variety of stimulating activities is beneficial for any child, but the child care provider should be careful not to overwhelm Emily, nor should the provider try to push Emily into activities that are clearly beyond her current capabilities. Furthermore, Emily should have time for unstructured play and exploration *without* the provider's intrusions.

5. Appropriate. School readiness tests correlate only modestly with children's academic performance a year or so later. Most 5-year-olds are ready for some sort of structured educational program.

6. Inappropriate. Even if all siblings in the family perform poorly on measures of cognitive ability, environmental factors (poor nutrition, environmental toxins, little cognitive stimulation at home, etc.) might instead be to blame. When children with similar genetic makeup live in the same home, it is virtually impossible to separate the effects of heredity from those of environment.

Application Exercise #2: Identifying Influences of Nature and Nurture on Intelligence

Some of the following situations provide evidence for genetic influences on intelligence. Others show that environment is also involved in intellectual development. For each situation, decide whether heredity or environment is more likely the cause of the effect(s) described. Defend your decisions.

1. A large city establishes several clinics that provide prenatal health care and nutritious meals for low-income pregnant women. Five years later, a researcher finds that the children of women who received the clinics' services throughout their pregnancies have slightly higher IQ scores than children of the same age whose low-income mothers did not have access to such services.

2. Studies repeatedly find that children with Down syndrome perform relatively poorly on intelligence tests.

3. A researcher conducts a study of more than 1,000 adopted children and discovers that those whose adoptive parents have higher IQs tend, on average, to have higher IQs as well.

4. A publisher of a widely used intelligence test finds that, on average, 10-year-olds who took the test in the year 2000 got more items correct than 10-year-olds who took the test in 1975.

5. When identical twins Nicole and Rachel were born, their parents had just divorced and each parent took one of the girls. Nicole grew up with her mother in Florida; Rachel and her father moved to Minneapolis when Rachel was only a month old. Because the girls' mother and father were not on speaking terms, the girls did not see each other again until they were in their teens. They discovered that, despite their separate lives, they showed remarkably similar talents in mathematics, science, and music.

Answers to Application Exercise #2

1. Environment. If the two groups of women were similar in other ways (e.g., if they had the same ethnic backgrounds, were of approximately the same age, etc.), then the medical and nutritional support services—an environmental intervention—presumably account for the higher IQs.

2. Heredity. Down syndrome is the result of having an extra 21st chromosome (see Chapter 3).

3. Environment. There is no genetic link between the children and their parents, so by default the relationship must be the result of environmental factors. One possible explanation for the relationship is that the parents who have higher IQs are likely to have higher income levels, enabling them to provide more enriching opportunities to foster their children's intellectual growth. Parents with higher IQs also tend to have achieved higher levels of education and thus may be better equipped to interact with their children in ways that promote development of the abilities that intelligence tests measure.

4. Environment. The gradual increase in performance on IQ tests over the years is known as the Flynn effect. Human beings pass along a given set of genetic possibilities (a "gene pool") from one generation to the next; thus, one generation is probably not genetically superior to the preceding generation. The Flynn effect is usually attributed to improvements in the overall environment—for instance, better schooling, greater access to information through television and other media, and so on.

5. Heredity. The girls have been raised in different environments since birth (e.g., they have had different caregivers and gone to different schools), so their similar intellectual talents are probably due to their identical genetic makeup. Note, however, that the evidence for heredity is weak here. For one thing, the girls did share the same prenatal environment for nine months, which may have contributed in some way to their similar abilities in math, science, and music. In addition, we would need to see such similarities in *many* pairs of twins raised apart before drawing a firm conclusion that heredity plays a significant role in intellectual development.

Sample Test Questions

Use the following multiple-choice and essay questions to evaluate and strengthen your understanding of selected concepts in the chapter.

Multiple-Choice

1. Myrna has just obtained a score of 110 on an intelligence test. Which one of the following is the most accurate interpretation of her score?
    a. Myrna answered about 60% of the test items correctly.
    b. Myrna scored at about the 40th percentile on the test.
    c. Myrna performed better on the test than more than half of her age-mates.
    d. Myrna's score would qualify her for a gifted program in most school districts.

2. Which one of the following best illustrates the idea of *niche-picking* in the development of cognitive abilities?
    a. Rudy shows an early aptitude for music and persuades his parents to let him begin piano lessons when he is 4. By the time he is 7, he is taking violin lessons as well, and he uses middle school band as an opportunity to learn to play the clarinet.
    b. Kiki's parents want the best for their daughter and so enroll her in an academically stimulating preschool that emphasizes the development of early literacy and numerical skills.
    c. On average, children from middle-income families have higher IQ scores than children from low-income families.
    d. A third-grade teacher makes sure that he provides individualized activities that challenge each of his students.

3. You have just learned that 5-year-old Jonathan has earned a score of 85 on an intelligence test. Which one of the following is the best interpretation of this test score?
    a. Jonathan's performance suggests that he almost certainly will need special class placement in the years to come.
    b. Jonathan probably has a learning disability that interferes with his ability to process information effectively.
    c. Jonathan's future schooling should focus on preparing him for assembly-line work or other careers that require limited cognitive skills.
    d. Jonathan's test performance, although on the low side, is not necessarily an accurate predictor of what his future cognitive functioning is likely to be.

4. A fifth-grade teacher who wants to apply Gardner's theory of multiple intelligences in classroom practice would be *most* likely to
    a. Lobby the school board to get the funds to buy a laptop computer for every student
    b. Build on students' unique abilities when teaching classroom subject matter
    c. Place considerable emphasis on developing students' vocabulary and reading skills
    d. Continually point out how mathematics is relevant to scientific inquiry

5. A school psychologist at Southboro Middle School identifies seventh graders who are sufficiently advanced in cognitive development that they need special educational services to meet their academic needs. Of the 30 students that the psychologist selects for a new gifted program at the middle school, 24 are girls and 6 are boys. Are such numbers consistent with what we know about gender differences in intelligence?
   a. Yes. On average, girls get higher IQ scores than boys throughout childhood and adolescence.
   b. No. Although girls, on average, obtain higher IQ scores in the elementary years, gender differences disappear at about age 10.
   c. No. On average, boys earn higher IQ scores than girls. We would be more likely to see the opposite: 24 boys and 6 girls.
   d. No. Generally speaking, boys and girls have similar IQ scores.

6. To be identified as having mental retardation, a child must show significant delays not only in cognitive functioning but also in
   a. Skills related to daily living
   b. Maturation of skeletal structures
   c. Height and physical stature
   d. Neurological measures of brain functioning

Essay

7. Research consistently finds that, *on average,* children from African American and Hispanic families have lower IQ scores than children from European American families. Describe at least three factors that may contribute to such group differences.

8. Describe at least three different ways in which teachers or other adults might address the unique needs of children and adolescents who are gifted.

Answers to Sample Test Questions

1. c—An IQ score is determined by comparing a child's test performance to the performance of others of the same age. An IQ of 100 indicates that a child has performed at the 50th percentile (i.e., he or she has performed better than 50% of his or her peers). You can use Figure 8-4 in the textbook to find the exact percentile associated with a score of 110. If you add up all the percentages to the left of the line for 110, you obtain a sum of 74.8%. Thus, Myrna's score of 110 is equivalent to a percentile rank of approximately 75.

2. a—Niche-picking is a phenomenon in which children actively seek out environmental conditions that match their inherited abilities. Only in *a* is a child selecting activities consistent with an early talent that may possibly have a genetic origin.

3. d—IQ scores obtained in the early years are influenced by a variety of unstable and irrelevant factors (e.g., attention span, motivation to perform well on the test) and are often poor predictors of later intellectual performance.

4. b—Gardner's theory of multiple intelligences suggests that different students have strengths in different areas and that individual students are apt to learn more effectively when instruction takes advantage of their strengths.

5. d—Aside from a greater frequency of mental retardation in boys than in girls, in general boys and girls have similar IQ scores.

6. a—The second essential condition for a diagnosis of mental retardation is deficits in *adaptive behavior*, including limitations in practical intelligence (managing the ordinary activities of daily living) and in social intelligence (conducting oneself appropriately in social situations).

7. One likely culprit is the fact that, on average, African American and Hispanic families have lower incomes than European American families. Socioeconomic status may impact nutrition, health care, exposure to toxic substances (e.g., lead-based paint is common in old apartment buildings), and educational opportunities, all of which may influence cognitive growth. Other possible factors suppressing the IQ scores of minority group children are long-term discriminatory practices within society, cultural bias in tests (although most current tests have been constructed to minimize such bias), lack of motivation to perform well on intelligence tests, and stereotype threat.

8. The textbook identifies six strategies; your response should include at least three of them *or* other strategies that you can justify on the basis of what you have learned about children and adolescents who are gifted:
   • Provide individualized tasks and assignments.
   • Form study groups of individuals with similar interests and abilities.
   • Teach complex cognitive skills within the context of specific subject areas.
   • Provide opportunities for independent study.
   • Encourage youngsters to set and strive for high goals.
   • Seek outside resources (e.g., mentors in other institutions and agencies).

Chapter 9

LANGUAGE DEVELOPMENT

Chapter Overview

This chapter summarizes several theoretical perspectives of language development and describes the many ways in which children's and adolescents' ability to understand and converse with others changes over time. It also considers issues related to bilingualism and examines diversity and exceptionalities in language development. Suggestions for educators are interspersed throughout the chapter.

Possible Knowledge, Beliefs, and Misconceptions Related to Chapter Content

Following are several beliefs that college students often have before studying language development, and such beliefs may interfere with an accurate understanding of material in Chapter 9. As you read the chapter, be on the lookout for evidence that contradicts these common misconceptions:

1. Some people mistakenly assume that children's syntactic development is complete by middle childhood and that elementary school students can understand the same complex syntactical structures that adults understand. In fact, many children in the early elementary grades have difficulty comprehending certain syntactic structures, such as sentences with passive verbs or multiple clauses. (See the section "Syntactic Development.")

2. Some people think that exposure to a second language in the very early years (e.g., as is the case for an infant or toddler living in a bilingual household) may confuse children and adversely affect their language development. Although a bilingual environment may initially slow down language development, children become proficient in both languages long before they reach school age and show no long-term deficits. Furthermore, bilingualism facilitates certain aspects of cognitive and social-emotional development. (See the opening case study and the section "Bilingualism.")

3. Some people think that immigrant children are best served by immersing them immediately in an English-only school environment. Whether children do better in such an "immersion" situation or instead in bilingual education depends in large part on the extent to which their out-of-school experiences support continuing development in their native tongue. (See the section "Approaches to Teaching a Second Language.")

4. Many people assume that some dialects of the English language are less complex or in some other way "inferior" to the English that is used in the media, textbooks, and most classrooms. In fact, the various regional and ethnic dialects observed in the English language appear to be equally complex and equally capable of supporting advanced cognitive processes. (See the section "Ethnic Differences.")

143

Suggested Supplementary Reading

The following reading, presented in the final section of this *Study Guide and Reader*, is relevant to Chapter 9:

Reading 9-1:   Teaching Children with Limited English Proficiency

CHAPTER OUTLINE	FOCUS QUESTIONS
Introductory paragraphs	• In your own words, define *phonology*, *semantics*, *syntax*, and *pragmatics*.
THEORETICAL PERSPECTIVES OF LANGUAGE DEVELOPMENT Early Theories: Modeling and Reinforcement Nativism Information Processing Theory Sociocultural Theory Functionalism Critiquing Theories of Language Development	• Describe the *modeling* and *reinforcement* perspectives of language development. What evidence indicates that these perspectives cannot adequately explain language development? • What do nativists mean by *language acquisition device*? What might it include? What evidence supports nativists' belief that language has a biological basis? • From an *information processing* perspective, what cognitive processes play important roles in language development? • In what ways do sociocultural theorists and functionalists broaden our understanding of language development? • On what key issue do nativists disagree with information processing theorists and functionalists? How does *Williams syndrome* bolster the nativist view? • Distinguish between *receptive language* and *expressive language*. Why can theorists not determine which one comes first? • What is *infant-directed speech*? What purposes might it serve?

CHAPTER OUTLINE	FOCUS QUESTIONS

TRENDS IN LANGUAGE DEVELOPMENT
 	
   Semantic Development
 	
   Syntactic Development
 	
   Development of Listening Skills
 	
   Development of Speaking Skills
 	
   Development of Pragmatics
 	
   Development of Metalinguistic Awareness
	• In what ways does children's knowledge of word meanings change over time?
	
	• What semantic difficulties do youngsters exhibit during the preschool years? during the elementary school years? during the secondary school years?
	
	• How do children learn word meanings?
	
	• When does syntax first appear in children's speech? What forms might early syntax take?
	
	• What is *overregularization*? Why does it occur?
	
	• What kinds of syntactical errors are you likely to see in preschoolers? in elementary school students? in middle school and high school students?
	
	• What processes appear to underlie children's acquisition of syntactic categories and rules?
	
	• Describe several ways in which parents and teachers can promote youngsters' semantic and syntactic development.
	
	• How do listening skills change over the course of childhood and adolescence? What cognitive factors facilitate understanding of spoken messages?
	
	• How do speaking skills change with age? What kinds of experiences foster these skills?
	
	• Describe several strategies for promoting young people's listening and speaking skills.
	
	• What are *sociolinguistic behaviors*? What sociolinguistic behaviors are different across cultures? In what ways do people in a particular culture foster certain sociolinguistic behaviors?
	
	• Under what circumstances does *culture shock* occur at school and in other settings? What practices can help keep culture shock to a minimum?
	
	• Describe the nature of *metalinguistic awareness*. Also describe how parents, teachers, and other adults can nurture its development.

CHAPTER OUTLINE	FOCUS QUESTIONS
DEVELOPMENT OF A SECOND LANGUAGE The Timing of Second-Language Learning Bilingualism Approaches to Teaching a Second Language	• Summarize the advantages of learning a second language in early childhood. Summarize the advantages of learning a second language in adolescence or adulthood. • What effects does bilingualism have on children's cognitive and social-emotional development? • Contrast the circumstances in which immersion and bilingual education are preferable for teaching a second language.
DIVERSITY IN LANGUAGE DEVELOPMENT Gender Differences Socioeconomic Differences Ethnic Differences	• In what ways do gender, socioeconomic status, and ethnicity affect language development? • What is a *dialect*? How can adults accommodate dialect differences in the classroom and other settings?
EXCEPTIONALITIES IN LANGUAGE DEVELOPMENT Speech and Communication Disorders Sensory Impairments and Language Development	• Describe the various forms that speech and communication disorders may take. Describe several ways in which practitioners can accommodate such disorders. • How do visual impairments and hearing impairments affect language development? How might teachers and other practitioners accommodate such impairments?

Chapter Glossary

African American English. Dialect of some African American communities that includes pronunciations, grammatical constructions, and idioms different from those of Standard English.

Babbling. Repeating certain consonant-vowel syllables over and over (e.g., "mamamama"); common in the latter half of the first year.

Bilingual education. Approach to second-language instruction in which students are instructed in academic subject areas in their native language while simultaneously being taught to speak and write in the second language.

Bilingualism. Knowing and speaking two languages fluently.

Cooing. Making and repeating vowel sounds (e.g., "oooooo"); common in early infancy.

Correlational feature. Characteristic present in many instances of a concept but not essential for concept membership.

Culture shock. Sense of confusion that occurs when one encounters an environment with expectations for behavior very different from those in one's home environment.

Defining feature. Characteristic that must be present in all instances of a concept.

Dialect. Form of a language characteristic of a particular geographic region or ethnic group.

Expansion. Repetition of a child's short utterances in a more complete and grammatically correct form.

Expressive language. Ability to communicate effectively through speaking and writing.

Fast mapping. Inferring a word's general meaning after a single exposure.

Figurative speech. Speech that communicates meaning beyond a literal interpretation of its words.

Functionalism. Theoretical perspective of language development that emphasizes the purposes language serves for human beings.

Grammatical word. Nonlexical word that affects the meanings of other words or the interrelationships among words in a sentence.

Holophrase. A single word used to express a complete thought; commonly observed in children's earliest speech.

Immersion. Approach to second-language instruction in which students hear and speak that language almost exclusively in the classroom.

Infant-directed speech. Short, simple, high-pitched speech often used when talking to young children.

IRE cycle. Adult-child interaction pattern marked by adult initiation, child response, and adult evaluation; in Western cultures, such a pattern is often seen in instructional settings.

Language acquisition device. Biologically built-in mechanism hypothesized to facilitate language learning.

Lexical word. Word that in some way represents an aspect of one's physical, social, or psychological world.

Metalinguistic awareness. Extent to which one thinks about the nature of language.

Narrative. Verbal account of a temporal sequence of events that are logically interconnected; a story.

Native language. The first language a child learns.

Nativism. Theoretical perspective proposing that some knowledge is biologically built-in and present at birth or soon thereafter.

Overgeneralization. Too broad a meaning for a word, such that it is used in situations to which it doesn't apply.

Overregularization. Use of a syntactic rule in situations where an exception to the rule applies.

Personal space. Personally and culturally preferred distance between two people during social interaction.

Phonemes. Smallest units of a spoken language that signify differences in meaning.

Phonology. The sound system of a language; how words sound and are produced.

Playing the dozens. Friendly, playful exchange of insults, common in some African American communities; also called *joaning* or *sounding*.

Pragmatics. Conventions and strategies used in effective and socially acceptable verbal interactions.

Receptive language. Ability to understand the language one hears or reads.

Semantic bootstrapping. Using knowledge of word meanings to derive knowledge about syntactic categories and structures.

Semantics. The meanings of words and word combinations.

Sociolinguistic behaviors. Social and culturally specific conventions that govern appropriate verbal interaction.

Speech and communication disorders. Disability characterized by abnormalities in producing or understanding spoken language, to the point where special educational services are required.

Standard English. Form of English generally considered acceptable in school (as reflected in textbooks, grammar instruction, etc.) and in the media.

Syntax. Rules used to put words together into sentences.

Telegraphic speech. Short, grammatically incomplete sentences that include lexical (rather than grammatical) words almost exclusively; common in toddlers.

Undergeneralization. Overly restricted meaning for a word, excluding some situations to which the word applies.

Wait time. The length of time a teacher pauses, after either asking a question or hearing a student's comment, before saying something.

Table 9–1. Applying Concepts in Child Development: Assessing Developmental Progress in Language

This table is a complete version of the table that appears at the end of Chapter 9 in the textbook. Compare your entries in the blank cells in the textbook table with our entries here. Keep in mind that there isn't necessarily a single "right" entry for any particular cell.

Age	A Youngster's Experience	Developmental Concepts *Recognizing Typical and Unusual Behaviors for the Age-Group*	Implications *Facilitating Acquisition of Language Skills*
Infancy (Birth–2)	When a caregiver at a child care center exclaims, "Your daddy's here!" 10-month-old Midori looks eagerly in the direction of the door. But despite Midori's apparent understanding of the word *Daddy*, she does not yet say his name, not even a reasonable approximation such as "Dada." Sometimes she says "dadadadada," but rarely when her father is present.	This behavior is typical for the age-group. Although children can understand some words as early as 8 months, on average they don't say their first word until sometime around their first birthday. Midori's repetition of the syllable *da*, apparently without reference to anything in her environment, is an instance of *babbling*.	Regularly engage infants in "conversations" in which they can practice vocalizing, taking turns, maintaining eye contact, and using other basic language skills. Simplify your language somewhat (e.g., use *infant-directed speech*), but use a variety of words in appropriate contexts.
Early Childhood (2–6)	Twenty kindergartners sit quietly and politely as the school principal describes the procedure they should follow during a fire drill. However, many of them are unable to describe the procedure after the principal leaves the room.	This behavior is typical for the age-group. Young children often think that being a "good listener" simply means sitting still and being quiet. They do not necessarily realize that listening also involves understanding and remembering what the speaker says.	Keep in mind that for a variety of reasons (short attention spans, limited learning strategies, etc.), young children often don't remember things that adults tell them. Accompany verbal information and instructions with pictures, hands-on activities, practice opportunities, and other nonverbal approaches.
Middle Childhood (6–10)	Seven-year-old Arthur's sentences are rarely more than two or three words long.	Such speech is unusual for the age-group. Children typically begin putting two words together sometime around age 2, and their sentences become increasingly longer after that. By school age, their sentences are adultlike in many respects.	When a child's speech shows significant developmental delays, consult with specialists (e.g., a speech-language pathologist or school psychologist) about conducting an in-depth evaluation and providing appropriate interventions.

table continues

Table 9–1 continued

Age	A Youngster's Experience	Developmental Concepts *Recognizing Typical and Unusual Behaviors for the Age-Group*	Implications *Facilitating Acquisition of Language Skills*
Early Adolescence (10–14)	In an oral report in his seventh-grade history class, 14-year-old Roy says such things as "John Wesley Powell looked for *gooder* boats to use" and "He *goed* down the Grand Canyon in a canoe."	These errors are unusual for the age-group. Adding *-er* to irregular adjectives and *-ed* to irregular verbs are examples of *overregularization.* Overregularization of such common words as *good* and *go* is often seen in the early elementary years but is rare in adolescence.	When children's syntax and word usage are unusual, consider whether a local dialect or family communication patterns might be the cause. If so, encourage Standard English in formal situations, but allow the dialect in everyday conversation with family and friends. If dialect differences cannot account for what you observe, consult with a specialist about appropriate interventions.
Late Adolescence (14–18)	When talking to members of a high school soccer team just before the first game of the season, a coach says, "Remember, ladies, a chain is only as strong as its weakest link." The girls nod in agreement and vow that they will all try to play their best.	This behavior is typical for the age-group. Most high school students can look beyond literal meanings and understand the figurative nature of common expressions and proverbs.	Use a variety of common expressions when talking with adolescents, but check to be sure that your listeners can see beyond the surface meanings to understand your underlying messages.

Application Exercise #1: Identifying Typical and Atypical Behaviors

In the following scenarios, which youngsters are exhibiting behaviors typical for their age-group, and which ones are not? Justify your choices on the basis of what you have learned about language development.

1. At her child care center, 6-month-old Josie is continually surrounded by adults and children who are talking. Whenever she hears her own name, she perks up and looks around to find the speaker.

2. In his history class, a high school senior writes, "Cortez took a great deal of gold from the Aztecs, although he was exceptionally greedy." He does not understand that he is using the word *although* incorrectly here.

3. Mr. Taylor is a school psychologist at a predominantly African American elementary school in South Carolina. When he is asked to evaluate 7-year-old Albert for a possible learning disability, he asks such questions as "Where do you live?" and "Do you have any brothers or sisters?" Albert doesn't say anything in reply.

4. Two-year-old Philip frequently babbles consonant sounds he has never heard the people around him make.

5. Close friends Tanesha and Louise, both ninth graders, can easily spend a half hour or more talking about a single topic.

6. Six-year-old Bert asserts that a lobster can't possibly be an animal because it doesn't have fur.

7. Twelve-year-old Mick often use the word *more* when he really means *less*.

8. Three-month-old Wayland occasionally vocalizes vowel sounds ("eeeeee," "ooooooooo," etc.) but never vocalizes consonants.

9. Eight-year-old Yolanda talks the same way to her 2-year-old brother as she does to her third-grade classmates. She doesn't seem to realize that her brother may not understand the vocabulary and complex sentences she uses in everyday speech.

10. When an after-school child care provider says to her group of 6-year-olds, "Hmmm, I wonder who left this bottle of glue open here by the sink," the children know that she *really* means she wants the guilty party to put the top back on the bottle and return it to its proper place on the shelf.

11. When 7-year-old Sheyla hears an adult say, "The soldier was shot by the old woman," she thinks that the soldier did the shooting.

12. The Sudbury High School and Pine Grove High School ice hockey teams are playing for the regional championship. When Sudbury's star player is sent to the penalty box for two minutes, the Pine Grove coach shouts, "All right, men, we have the advantage now. Let's make hay while the sun shines!" A couple of team members are confused as to why the coach is talking about hay rather than about the game.

13. Four-year-old Robert has trouble pronouncing his own name, often referring to himself as "Wobert."

14. When she sees an adult eating a snack, 9-year-old Jennifer asks, "What you are eating?"

Answers to Application Exercise #1

1. Typical. Children's attention is drawn to their own name as early as 5 months.

2. Not typical. Children as old as 12 have trouble using connectives such as *although* correctly, but a high school senior would typically not have such difficulty.

3. Typical. Children in some African American communities in the southeastern United States have been taught not to answer a stranger's questions about their personal lives.

4. Not typical. In their early babbling, infants make a wide variety of sounds, but they soon drop the sounds they don't hear in the speech around them. Sometime around their first birthday, they begin speaking words; by age 2, they are putting words together. A 2-year-old who is still babbling sounds that are not part of his native language is way behind schedule.

5. Typical. As children grow older, they become increasingly able to carry on lengthy conversations about a single issue or event.

6. Typical. Young children often have too restricted a meaning of the word *animal*, reflecting undergeneralization of this concept.

7. Not typical. Although young children often confuse such comparatives, we would expect a 12-year-old to have mastered the distinction.

8. Typical. Wayland is *cooing*, which is common at 3 months. Consonants appear in *babbling*, which appears somewhere around 6 months.

9. Not typical. Even 3- and 4-year-olds use simpler language with toddlers than they use with adults and age-mates.

10. Typical. Young children are aware that what a speaker says may be different from what he or she means. They use context clues to interpret a speaker's meaning.

11. Typical. Children in the early elementary grades often have difficulty interpreting passive sentences correctly.

12. Not typical. Most high school students can look beyond the literal meanings of spoken messages and understand the figurative nature of common expressions and proverbs.

13. Typical. Preschoolers often have trouble pronouncing the letter *r*.

14. Not typical. In English-speaking countries, children typically master the correct syntax for questions by age 5.

Application Exercise #2: Identifying Developmentally Appropriate Practices

Which of the following practices are appropriate for the age level, and which are not? Defend your choices.

1. When 2-year-old Miranda exclaims, "Get teddy!" her father asks, "Do you want me to get your teddy bear?"

2. Mr. Petzinger includes a unit on jokes and puns (e.g., "What did the dog say when he licked a piece of sandpaper?" "Rough! Rough!") in his middle school language arts class.

3. So as not to overstimulate the 6-month-old infants in her room at a child care center, Ms. Brown rarely speaks to them.

4. Ms. Zimmer insists that the 5- and 6-year-olds in her kindergarten class look her in the eye when she is talking to them. That way, she can be sure they are paying attention.

5. Lamont and Jimmy, both 9, go to Ms. Washington's house after school each day. After doing their homework, the two boys often watch television until their parents come to pick them up. Ms. Washington sometimes joins the boys in front of the TV. When commercials make outrageous claims for certain products, she is quick to point out that they may be stretching the truth—for instance, by saying, "That's ridiculous! Why would having that toy make you 'the envy of all your friends'?"

6. High school English teacher Mr. Moody never corrects his students when they say "I swum" rather than "I swam" or "I buyed" rather than "I bought."

7. When the director of an infant care center learns that 1-year-old Leslee is deaf, she suggests that Leslee's parents learn American Sign Language and begin using it to communicate with their daughter as soon as she turns 4.

8. Ms. James, a second-grade teacher, explains two craft projects that her class will be working on in preparation for a Valentine's Day party. Even though she thinks she has explained the procedures clearly, she encourages her students to ask questions if they are unsure about what to do next.

9. Mr. Bennett teaches at a middle school in a largely African American neighborhood in Philadelphia. He sometimes overhears students telling outrageous stories about how they "ate a whole cow for breakfast" or "saw a mouse as big as a horse." He actively discourages such exaggeration, encouraging them instead to stick close to reality in describing their experiences.

10. Child care provider Mr. Malowitz speaks in shorter sentences, and in a slightly higher pitched voice, when speaking to the infants and toddlers in his care.

11. When teaching the concept *reptile*, Ms. Wang shows her fourth graders pictures of lizards, alligators, dinosaurs, and snakes. She then shows them pictures of frogs and salamanders and says, "These are *not* reptiles; they're amphibians instead. Let's talk about some of the differences between reptiles and amphibians."

12. When Mr. Markley hears 16-year-old Suzy stuttering as she tries to say a particular word, he gently finishes her sentence for her.

13. A middle school offers a class in introductory Russian that sixth and seventh graders can take as an elective.

14. With parents' permission, staff members at a child care center in an English-speaking community consistently speak Spanish to the toddlers and preschoolers in their care. "They hear plenty of English at home," the staff members reason. "This way they can learn Spanish as well."

Answers to Application Exercise #2

1. Appropriate. The father is engaging in *expansion*: He is repeating Miranda's request in a syntactically more mature form.

2. Appropriate. As children grow older, they become increasingly creative in their use of language. By the time they reach middle school, they recognize that words often have multiple meanings. A unit that focuses their attention on multiple meanings should enhance their metalinguistic awareness.

3. Not appropriate. Although young infants are not yet capable of speaking, by the time they are 4 months old, they eagerly engage in verbal interactions, first by cooing and later by babbling. When they hear others speak, they learn and begin to mimic the stress patterns that are common in their language. Furthermore, by engaging in "conversations" with others, they can practice turn-taking and other basic pragmatic skills.

4. Not appropriate. Although some of the children may feel quite comfortable looking an adult in the eye, those from certain cultures may have explicitly been taught to look down in the presence of adults as a way of showing respect.

5. Appropriate. By the time they reach school age, most children know that people may say things that aren't necessarily true, but they sometimes have difficulty distinguishing between fact and fiction. Ms. Washington is encouraging *critical listening*.

6. Not appropriate. High school students do not always hear correct word usage in those around them. They are more likely to master the subtle irregularities of the English language when they are explicitly taught these irregularities. Mr. Moody should, of course, provide corrective feedback in a way that does not embarrass students about their errors or in other ways discourage students from speaking openly in class.

7. Not appropriate. For normal language development, children with hearing impairments ideally need exposure to language as early as possible, and certainly before age 4.

8. Appropriate. Many children in the early elementary grades don't realize that they should ask questions when they don't understand. Ms. James is trying to teach them that asking questions in such circumstances is appropriate.

9. Not appropriate. Such exaggerated descriptions are common in some African American communities. They are perfectly acceptable as long as listeners understand that they reflect creative storytelling rather than actual depictions of events.

10. Appropriate. Adults often use *infant-directed* speech when talking to young children. Some theorists speculate that such speech may facilitate language development. Others suggest that it enhances communication or fosters more affectionate adult–child relationships.

11. Appropriate. Children gain a more accurate understanding of word meanings when they see nonexamples as well as examples.

12. Not appropriate. Children and adolescents with speech and communication disorders are more likely to improve when others allow them to complete their own thoughts.

13. Appropriate. There is no hard-and-fast rule about when to begin studying a second language.

14. Appropriate. Early exposure to two languages promotes bilingualism. It has little negative impact on children's language development over the short run and *no* negative impact over the long run. Furthermore, fluency in two languages enhances children's metalinguistic awareness.

Sample Test Questions

Use the following multiple-choice and essay questions to evaluate and strengthen your understanding of selected concepts in the chapter.

Multiple-Choice

1. Which one of the following is the best example of a *phoneme*?
   a. The "eet" sound in *feet*
   b. The "tum" sound in *bottom*
   c. The "kuh" sound in *cat*
   d. The "ing" sound at the end of *talking*

2. Three of the following affect children's ability to understand the things they hear. Which one does *not* affect listening comprehension?
   a. Working memory capacity
   b. The ability to think abstractly
   c. The ability to articulate specific sounds correctly
   d. Acquisition of schemas, scripts, and other organized forms of knowledge about the world

3. Which one of the following best describes *metalinguistic awareness*?
   a. Thinking about the nature of language
   b. Knowing the past-tense forms of irregular verbs
   c. Knowing when it is and is not acceptable to interrupt someone else
   d. Understanding the subtle differences between words with similar meanings (e.g., *come* versus *go, can* versus *may*)

4. Three of the following statements are accurate descriptions of children who have been raised to be bilingual from the earliest months of life. Which statement is *inaccurate*?
   a. They perform slightly higher on tests of intelligence and creativity.
   b. They may show delays in language development when they are toddlers.
   c. They tend to have greater metalinguistic awareness than monolinguistic children.
   d. Throughout the school years, they frequently confuse the vocabulary and syntax of the two languages.

5. Other things being equal, which one of the following children is most likely to show delays in language development?
   a. Aidan, who is blind
   b. Brian, who has a learning disability
   c. Carlee, who is deaf and whose parents communicate with her in American sign language
   d. Dara, who is deaf and whose parents speak to her exclusively in carefully articulated spoken language

6. Which one of the following children would be most likely to benefit from an *immersion* approach to learning a second language?
   a. Six-year-old Anna and her family move from the United States to Germany, where they plan to settle permanently.
   b. In May, 16-year-old Kendree learns that her family will be spending the following year on a U.S. Air Force base in South Vietnam. Kendree has three months to learn as much Vietnamese as she can.
   c. Eight-year-old Ramon immigrates from Mexico to Los Angeles and enrolls in third grade soon after his arrival.
   d. When 9-year-old Mei-Yau's parents die in a tragic car accident, she moves from Taiwan to Seattle to live with her aunt and uncle.

Essay

7. Some theorists believe that human beings have a specific mechanism, known as a *language acquisition device,* that enables them to learn language relatively easily in the first few years of life. Describe three different kinds of evidence that support their belief in such a mechanism.

8. You have just accepted a position teaching or working with a group of culturally diverse children. Describe three cultural differences in *sociolinguistic behaviors* that you might encounter in your work with the children.

Answers to Sample Test Questions

1. c—Phonemes are the smallest units of spoken language that indicate differences in meaning (e.g., if you change the "kuh" sound in *cat* to a "buh" sound, the word changes to *bat*).

2. c—Alternatives *a*, *b*, and *d* are cognitive factors that influence listening comprehension. Alternative *c* affects expressive language rather than receptive language.

3. a—Metalinguistic awareness is the ability to think about the nature of language and the functions it serves.

4. d—In the preschool years, elements of one language may occasionally intrude into children's use of the other language, but by elementary school, children generally keep the languages separate.

5. d—Children with hearing impairments often show significant delays in both semantic and syntactic development, especially if the impairment has been present since early in life and if the children have little or no exposure to manual forms of language.

6. b—Immersion is most effective when students already have a solid foundation in their first language and will continue to have frequent opportunities to use that language.

7. Your response should include at least three of the following ideas:
   - Even very young infants can detect subtle differences among very similar speech sounds.
   - Infants seem to have a few built-in concepts (e.g., certain colors) that predispose them to categorize the world in certain ways.
   - Languages worldwide have more similarities than would be expected by chance—a finding that leads some theorists to believe that human beings inherit a Universal Grammar that facilitates their acquisition of syntax.
   - Children from diverse cultural and linguistic backgrounds reach milestones in language development at similar ages.
   - Babbling is a universal phenomenon across cultures, even for children who are born deaf.
   - Certain areas of the brain appear to specialize in language functions.
   - There appear to be sensitive periods for some aspects of language development.
   - Children who have Williams syndrome acquire age-typical speech despite significant delays in their overall cognitive development (as reflected in IQ scores of 50–70).

8. Your response should include at least three sociolinguistic behaviors that are different from one culture to another. Following are some examples:
   - Not saying hello or good-bye
   - Hiding feelings when speaking (e.g., displaying a "poker face")
   - Being silent rather than making small talk
   - Being reluctant to initiate conversation with an adult
   - Looking down as a way of showing respect
   - Maintaining very little personal space during conversations
   - Waiting several seconds or more before responding to a question, even an easy one
   - Interrupting others frequently

Chapter 10

DEVELOPMENT IN THE CONTENT DOMAINS

Chapter Overview

Whereas the preceding chapter focused on oral language (listening and speaking), the first part of Chapter 10 focuses on development of written language (reading and writing), as well as on development in math, science, social studies, art, and music. The foundations for most academic domains are laid in infancy and early childhood. For instance, children learn a great deal about reading and writing when adults read them storybooks and when they see other people engaged in various reading and writing activities. And even young infants have some awareness of quantity (upon which a sense of number will build), appear to have an intuitive understanding of certain basic principles of physics (e.g., two objects cannot occupy the same space at the same time), and enjoy music.

Youngsters develop in many ways in the various content domains. In reading they gain greater phonological awareness, increasingly automatize word recognition, and acquire strategies that facilitate comprehension of written materials. In writing they become increasingly proficient in handwriting, spelling, grammar, and composition. In mathematics they learn (and sometimes invent for themselves) procedures for adding, subtracting, and multiplying numbers and, eventually, for solving complex problems involving these and other operations. In science they construct increasingly sophisticated theories about their physical and biological worlds and continue to refine their scientific reasoning skills. As they study history and geography, they gain an appreciation for the nature of historical time and become better able to deal with maps as symbolic representations of physical space. Their artistic and musical talents grow by leaps and bounds during childhood and (especially with instruction) may continue to develop in significant ways in adolescence. As youngsters grow older, metacognitive knowledge, beliefs, and skills affect their proficiency in many of these domains.

Possible Knowledge, Beliefs, and Misconceptions Related to Chapter Content

Following are beliefs that many college students have before studying development in the content domains. Such beliefs are likely to interfere with an accurate understanding of ideas presented in Chapter 10. As you read the chapter, be on the lookout for evidence that contradicts these widely held ideas:

1. Some people who plan to work primarily with older children or adolescents may assume that these youngsters know how to read effectively. In fact, reading skills continue to develop throughout childhood and adolescence. Instructors of middle school and high school students will help their students learn more effectively if they also teach and scaffold effective reading comprehension strategies.

2. A common misconception, often perpetuated by the media, is that dyslexia involves reading "backward"—for instance, reading *tab* as *bat*. The majority of youngsters with dyslexia actually have a very different problem: They have trouble hearing the individual sounds within words and so have difficulty making the connections between how words are pronounced and how they appear on paper.

3. When many college students think about *editing* their own written work, they think primarily about checking for errors in spelling, grammar, and punctuation. In fact, a good editor also looks for organizational problems, ambiguities in meaning, and logical flaws. Such an approach to editing is rare even in the high school years but can certainly be nurtured by skillful teachers.

4. Some future secondary school teachers think that writing instruction is something that only language arts teachers must concern themselves with. In fact, writing takes different forms in different academic disciplines, and so its development is best nurtured in *all* academic classrooms.

5. Many people think of mathematics as a collection of procedures that should be memorized. In fact, a key element in mathematical development is an understanding of *why* various procedures take the forms that they do. Good mathematicians understand the logic behind mathematical operations; they also recognize that there are often two or more equally correct ways of solving a particular problem.

6. College students who have studied Piaget's theory in previous classes may mistakenly believe that scientific reasoning skills (e.g., separation and control of variables) are fully developed by puberty or shortly thereafter. In fact, scientific reasoning continues to develop throughout the high school years and (if applicable) in undergraduate and graduate studies as well.

7. Some college students have epistemological beliefs about science, history, and geography that interfere with a true understanding of these disciplines—for instance, that mastering them involves little more than memorizing discrete facts.

8. Many people think of artistic and musical talents as being largely inherited. Although biological factors probably influence youngsters' talents to some degree, environmental factors—especially instruction—play a significant role in the development of artistic and musical abilities.

Suggested Supplementary Readings

The following readings, presented in the final section of this *Study Guide and Reader*, are relevant to Chapter 10:

CHAPTER OUTLINE	FOCUS QUESTIONS

READING
 	
    Emergent Literacy
 	
    Phonological Awareness
 	
    Word Recognition
 	
    Reading Comprehension
 	
    Metacognition in Reading
 	
    Diversity in Reading Development
 	
    Promoting Reading Development
	• What is *emergent literacy*? In what various ways is it manifested in children's prereading and prewriting behaviors?
	
	• In what ways can caregivers and teachers nurture literacy development in early childhood?
	
	• What effects do children's early literacy experiences have on later reading and writing development?
	
	• What is *phonological awareness*? Describe how it improves in the preschool and early elementary school years. Also describe how parents and teachers can nurture it.
	
	• What specific skills does word recognition typically involve? How does children's word recognition ability change over time?
	
	• In what ways does reading comprehension improve during childhood and adolescence?
	
	• What roles does *metacognition* play in reading comprehension?
	
	• How are literacy skills likely to be different for children who are gifted? for children with mental retardation? for those with visual impairments? for those with hearing impairments?
	
	• What specific deficits are often observed in children with dyslexia?
	
	• In what ways, and to what extent, do reading skills differ for boys and girls? different socioeconomic groups? different ethnic groups? speakers of different languages?
	
	• Identify several general strategies that teachers might use to promote children's reading development in the elementary grades. Identify several additional strategies appropriate for middle school and high school students.

CHAPTER OUTLINE	FOCUS QUESTIONS

WRITING
 	
    Handwriting
 	
    Spelling
 	
    Syntax and Grammar
 	
    Composition Skills
 	
    Metacognition in Writing
 	
    Diversity in Writing Development
 	
    Promoting Writing Development
	• What knowledge about written language might young children's *pseudowriting* reflect?
	
	• How does handwriting change during childhood and adolescence?
	
	• Describe developmental changes in spelling between kindergarten and the middle elementary grades.
	
	• What developmental changes are seen in the *syntax* of children's writing?
	
	• What general trends characterize the development of composition skills?
	
	• Explain the difference between *knowledge telling* and *knowledge transforming*. Why is knowledge transforming considered to be superior?
	
	• In what ways does *metacognition* contribute to the writing process? How metacognitively sophisticated are high school students likely to be?
	
	• Describe at least three different sources of diversity in children's writing development.
	
	• What strategies can teachers and other adults use to promote writing development?

CHAPTER OUTLINE	FOCUS QUESTIONS

MATHEMATICS
 	
  Number Sense and Counting
 	
  Mathematical Concepts and Principles
 	
  Basic Arithmetic Operations
 	
  More Advanced Problem-Solving Procedures
 	
  Metacognition in Mathematics
 	
  Diversity in Mathematics Development
 	
  Promoting Development in Mathematics
	• What evidence indicates that even infants have some awareness of *number*?
	
	• What counting skills are 3-, 4-, and 5-year-olds likely to have?
	
	• How well do youngsters of various ages understand fractions?
	
	• Describe how children's understanding of addition and subtraction improves over infancy, early childhood, and the elementary school years. Also explain why the *part-whole principle* might be an important component of children's understanding of these processes.
	
	• Apply the concept of *overlapping waves* (see Chapter 7) to describe children's increasing competence in multiplication.
	
	• Explain Case's *central conceptual structure* for number, and describe how it changes with age.
	
	• Why is it important that children make sense of, rather than simply memorize, mathematical procedures?
	
	• In what ways are many high school students metacognitively naive about mathematics?
	
	• What gender and cultural differences have been observed in mathematical development?
	
	• Describe several general strategies for nurturing mathematical development in children and adolescents.

CHAPTER OUTLINE	FOCUS QUESTIONS

SCIENCE
 	
  Children's Theories about the Physical and Biological Worlds
 	
  Scientific Reasoning Skills
 	
  Metacognition in Science
 	
  Diversity in Science Development
 	
  Promoting Development in Science
	• What evidence do some theorists use in support of a *nativist* view of science development?
	
	• In what ways do children's theories about living and nonliving things change over the course of infancy and childhood?
	
	• How do youngsters' scientific reasoning skills change with age? In what ways is the development of scientific reasoning skills still incomplete in the high school years?
	
	• How are adolescents' epistemological beliefs about science likely to affect their study strategies?
	
	• Identify sources of diversity in science development related to youngsters' sensory impairments, gender, and cultural backgrounds.
	
	• Describe several general strategies for promoting children's and adolescents' development in science.

CHAPTER OUTLINE	FOCUS QUESTIONS

DEVELOPMENT IN OTHER CONTENT DOMAINS
 	
  History
 	
  Geography
 	
  Art
 	
  Music
	• In what context do children first gain some understanding of history? At what age do they begin to understand the nature of historical time? At what age might they grasp the true nature of history as an academic discipline?
	
	• What difficulties do young children have in interpreting maps?
	
	• What strategies can teachers use to promote development in history and geography?
	
	• What characteristics are common in children's early drawings? In what ways does their artwork change over the course of childhood and adolescence?
	
	• In what various ways does a child's environment affect artistic development?
	
	• To what extent and in what ways do infants appreciate music?
	
	• In what ways might a young child represent music either on paper or with physical objects?
	
	• Describe evidence in support of the view that music development is affected by both nature and nurture.

USING CONTENT AREA STANDARDS TO GUIDE INSTRUCTION	• In your own words, describe the nature of content area *standards*. • What are the benefits of using content area standards in classroom instruction? What are potential drawbacks?

Chapter Glossary

Absolute pitch. Ability to recall the precise pitch of a particular note in music.

Dyslexia. Inability to master basic reading skills in a developmentally typical time frame despite normal reading instruction.

Emergent literacy. Knowledge and skills that lay a foundation for reading and writing; typically develops in the preschool years from early experiences with written language.

Invented spelling. A child's early, self-constructed word spelling, which may reflect only some of the word's phonemes.

Knowledge telling. Writing down ideas in whatever order they come to mind, with little regard for communicating the ideas effectively.

Knowledge transforming. Writing ideas in such a way as to intentionally help the reader understand them.

Music literacy. Ability to read and understand musical notation.

Part-whole principle. Idea that any single number can be broken into two or more smaller numbers, and that any two or more numbers can be combined to form a larger number; central to children's understanding of addition and subtraction.

Phonological awareness. Ability to hear the distinct sounds within words.

Scientific reasoning. Cognitive processes central to conducting scientific research and interpreting findings appropriately.

Sight vocabulary. Words that a child can immediately recognize while reading.

Standards. In education, general statements regarding the knowledge and skills that students should gain and the characteristics that their accomplishments should reflect.

Story schema. Knowledge of the typical elements and sequence of a narrative.

Substance schema. General view of all physical phenomena as being either touchable substances or properties of those substances.

Visual-spatial ability. Ability to imagine and mentally manipulate two- and three-dimensional figures.

Table 10–1. Applying Concepts in Child Development: Identifying Building Blocks for Later
         Acquisitions in the Content Areas

*This table is a complete version of the table that appears at the end of Chapter 10 in the textbook.
Compare your entries in the blank cells in the textbook table with our entries here. Keep in mind that
there isn't necessarily a single "right" entry for any particular cell.*

Age	A Youngster's Experience	Developmental Concepts *Identifying Knowledge and Skills on Which Later Acquisitions Can Build*	Implications *Helping Youngsters Acquire a Solid Foundation in the Content Domain*
Infancy (Birth–2)	As she sits in her highchair, 14-month-old Selena keeps throwing the toys that are on her tray. She seems upset when she no longer has the toys, yet as soon as her caregiver returns them to the tray, she throws them again.	By continually seeing objects move in particular directions (away from her and down to the floor), Selena is learning that certain actions lead to predictable results. Her observations in this and similar circumstances will provide a knowledge base to which she can later relate such concepts as *force*, *momentum*, and *gravity*.	Let infants and toddlers manipulate objects in ways you hadn't anticipated, provided that their actions are not dangerous to themselves or others.
Early Childhood (2–6)	As 5-year-old Rico builds a Lego house, he tells his teacher that he needs more red Legos. Seeing an opportunity for Rico to practice addition, the teacher says, "I see you have three red ones already. If I give you two more, how many red ones will you have altogether?" Rico counts three and then two more on his fingers and then happily responds, "Five!"	Many 4- and 5-year olds invent strategies for handling simple addition and subtraction problems. By using his fingers to keep track of and count Legos, Rico can more easily solve the problem. More sophisticated arithmetic strategies (e.g., retrieving number facts from memory) will build on these early ones. As Rico masters more efficient strategies, he will gradually abandon his finger-counting strategy of his own accord.	Encourage children to use any invented mathematical strategies that yield accurate results. Teach children more efficient strategies, and encourage automaticity for basic math facts, but allow children to use their previously acquired, more concrete strategies until they feel comfortable with the new ones.

table continues

Table 10–1 continued

Age	A Youngster's Experience	Developmental Concepts *Identifying Knowledge and Skills on Which Later Acquisitions Can Build*	Implications *Helping Youngsters Acquire a Solid Foundation in the Content Domain*
Middle Childhood (6–10)	Seven-year-old Leila's second-grade class is studying the *ight* "family" in spelling this week, so Leila is learning how to spell such words as *fight, tight,* and *bright*. In one assignment, Leila writes a short story she calls "The Bright Nightlight," in which she uses as many *ight* words as she can.	Through repeated practice, Leila is gradually automatizing the *ight* spelling pattern. By automatizing basic spelling and grammatical rules, Leila will be able to focus more effectively on (i.e., she can devote more working memory capacity to) composition skills and effective communication in her writing.	Provide a variety of activities in which children can automatize basic reading, writing, and math skills. Such activities are typically more effective when they are authentic and motivating in their own right.
Early Adolescence (10–14)	A middle school history teacher asks students to "write a biography of a person in history as a real person who has both strengths and weaknesses." In a biography of Franklin Delano Roosevelt, 13-year-old Jesse describes Roosevelt's struggle with polio and determination to hide the severity of his disability when running for president.	By understanding that historical figures were in most respects just ordinary human beings (who were perhaps in extraordinary circumstances), Jesse will be able to apply his general knowledge of human thoughts, motives, and emotions to make sense of history—that is, to understand why historical events unfolded in particular ways.	Encourage youngsters to draw on what they know about human nature to understand why various historical figures acted as they did.
Late Adolescence (14–18)	As her high school literature class discusses Carl Sandburg's poem "The Road and the End," 15-year-old Zia discovers that reasonable people may interpret the same information in distinctly different ways.	Zia may be able to apply her newly acquired understanding to other domains in addition to poetry. For instance, she can now more easily understand that scientists might formulate two or more different theories to explain a particular phenomenon. She may also realize that eye witnesses at an historical event might give divergent and possibly contradictory reports on what happened.	Use group discussions as a way of enhancing youngsters' ability to look at situations and phenomena from multiple perspectives.

<u>Application Exercise #1: Identifying Typical and Atypical Behaviors in Reading and Writing</u>

In the following scenarios, which youngsters are exhibiting behaviors typical for their age-group, and which ones are not? Justify your decisions based on what you have learned about literacy development.

1. After reading an account of John F. Kennedy's assassination, 15-year-old Sanford says, "This author thinks that Lee Harvey Oswald acted alone in the shooting, but the evidence she presents to support her case isn't very convincing."

2. Ten-year-old Olivia has trouble hearing the sounds "kuh," "ah," and "rrr" in the word *car*.

3. Four-year-old Liam holds a storybook open, slowly turns the pages, and narrates a story that corresponds loosely to the pictures he sees.

4. When asked to write an essay about the pros and cons of nuclear energy in her high school English class, 16-year-old Marika writes six sentences that are only loosely connected to one another and don't reflect a logical train of thought.

5. As $1\frac{1}{2}$-year-old Magda sits in her high chair at a restaurant, her father gives her the crayons and coloring book that the restaurant hostess has provided. Magda scribbles aimlessly on some of the pages but does not make any attempt to color between the lines.

6. Eight-year-old Alexandria can write many simple words (e.g., *cat, dog, mommy, book*) but cannot yet write her own name.

7. When Ms. Marston's high school seniors read Shakespeare's *Romeo and Juliet*, they interpret it only as a simple love story and seem puzzled when Ms. Marston suggests that it's also a story about prejudice.

8. Four-year-old Rashad writes some scribbles across a sheet of paper and tells his preschool teacher, "This says 'I love you, Grandpa.'"

9. Twelve-year-old Mei-Win recognizes the word *look* because, she says, "the word looks like a pair of glasses, with two round circles in the middle for the lenses and two sticks at either end to go around the ears."

10. Virgil loves to write and hopes to become a novelist someday. When he is 10, his handwriting is neat and easy to read. By the time he is 16, however, his handwriting is so sloppy that he is often the only one who can read it.

11. When trying to write the word *wagon*, $5\frac{1}{2}$-year-old Daniella writes it as "YGN."

12. As 14-year-old Andrea reads the assigned pages in her science textbook, her mind often wanders to other topics (such as yesterday's fight with her best friend) as her eyes move down each page. It doesn't occur to Andrea that she should reread the paragraphs she really wasn't paying attention to the first time.

Answers to Application Exercise #1

1. Typical. Adolescents often read with a critical eye.

2. Not typical. Most children can detect individual phonemes in words by age 6 or 7.

3. Typical. Preschoolers often pretend to read storybooks. Liam's behaviors show some knowledge of the nature of books and reading, reflecting his *emergent literacy*. He is also showing the beginnings of a *story schema*.

4. Not typical. Children become increasingly able to write a cohesive composition as they grow older. Most adolescents are capable of writing organized, integrated text.

5. Typical. At 18 months, toddlers can scribble randomly on paper. More controlled movements (e.g., drawing shapes and pseudowriting) come later as psychomotor coordination increases.

6. Not typical. Children usually learn how to write their own name in early childhood or by the beginning of middle childhood.

7. Not typical. Most adolescents can look beyond the superficial aspects of a story to see underlying themes and symbolism.

8. Typical. Preschoolers don't always understand that writing must take a particular form to have meaning.

9. Not typical. Identifying words in this fashion is fairly common at age 5. Long before age 12, however, children should be making connections between the specific letters and sounds within a word.

10. Typical. The quality of handwriting often decreases in adolescence, in part because teenagers write more quickly than younger children do.

11. Typical. Kindergartners and first graders often create invented spellings that represent some but not all of the phonemes in a word. Daniella probably used the letter *y* because its name ("why") and *wagon* both begin with a "wuh" sound.

12. Typical. Although many adolescents use effective metacognitive strategies (e.g., comprehension monitoring, rereading), many others do not.

Application Exercise #2: Identifying Typical and Atypical Behaviors in Math, Science, Social Studies, Art, and Music

In the following scenarios, which youngsters are exhibiting behaviors typical for their age-group, and which ones are not? Justify your decisions based on what you have learned about development in the content domains.

1. Seven-year-old Monty believes that pebbles are "babies" that eventually grow up to be large rocks. "Rocks grow just like people do," he says.

2. When 13-year-old Hadassah is asked which note Barry Manilow's song "Mandy" begins with, she can hum the exact note.

3. As Heather and Farah work together on a problem in their high school algebra class, they can be heard arguing: "This is the way we need to solve the problem." "No, we need to do it *this* way." "But we get the same answer either way." "Maybe so, but the teacher will say *your* way is wrong."

4. A researcher creates an apparatus that makes it appear to an infant that a moving red ball sets a blue ball in motion even though the two balls never touch each other. Nine-month-old Mason seems quite surprised when he sees the effect the red ball seems to have on the blue ball.

5. Eight-year-old Janine can count to 10 but often gets confused about the order of numbers after that, perhaps counting "... ten, twelve, thirteen, eleven...."

6. When $4^1/_2$-year-old William is given paper and some crayons, he scribbles aimlessly and produces no recognizable shapes. "That's all he ever does at home," his mother says.

7. Fifteen-year-old Alison reads in her history book that automobiles became common in the United States only after Henry Ford instituted the use of assembly lines in 1913. "Wow," she thinks, "that means that my mom and dad didn't have any cars when they were little."

8. Six-year-old Wallace has never seen written music. When asked to "draw" a simple melody he hears, he draws a wavy line across the page. "The line goes up when the music goes up," he says, "and it goes down when the music goes down."

9. A high school mathematics teacher asks, "Which number is bigger, the difference between 9 and 7 or the difference between 6 and 2?" Sixteen-year-old Adam incorrectly responds, "The difference between 9 and 7 is bigger."

10. On a cold winter day, 12-year-old Penny is shivering. "The heat just got sucked right out of me," she says.

11. Thirteen-year-old Breck is given this problem: "What is 24 divided by $\frac{1}{6}$?" Breck quickly responds, "Oh, that's easy! The answer is 4." He is quite surprised when his teacher tells him that the answer is actually 144.

12. When asked to draw a picture of her house, 10-year-old Mattie draws a two-story house with several windows and a door. Below the house is a thin strip of green, which she says is her yard. At the very top of the paper is a thin strip of blue, which she says is the sky.

13. In preparation for a field trip to Cahokia Mounds, the site of an ancient Native American community, Ms. Jackson tells her second graders, "The trip will take us about an hour. We will leave Missouri and go to Illinois, which is another state." She shows her class where Cahokia Mounds is on a map. Later, as the class travels across the state line, 7-year-old Travis looks out the bus window in search of the big black line that marks the state boundary.

14. Mack and Reynold are working together on an experiment in their high school chemistry lab. Following their teacher's instructions, they use a small thermometer to measure the temperature of the air inside a jar. Then they soak a piece of steel wool in vinegar for a minute, squeeze most of the vinegar out of the steel wool, place both the wool and the thermometer inside the jar, and screw a lid on the jar. Five minutes later, they take the thermometer out and discover that the temperature in the jar has risen several degrees. "How can that be?" Mack asks. "We must have measured wrong the first time," Reynold responds.

Answers to Application Exercise #2

1. Not typical. By age 3 or 4, most children know that living and nonliving things are distinctly different entities, and that nonliving entities don't grow in the same way that living ones do.

2. Not typical. Hadassah is showing *absolute pitch* (also known as *perfect pitch*). Such an ability is more common in infants and preschoolers than in older children and adolescents. Quite possibly Hadassah began music lessons at an early age.

3. Typical. A common epistemological belief among high school students is that there's only one right way to solve any particular math problem.

4. Typical. Even much younger infants have some basic knowledge of classic physics, including the principle that one object can influence another only when the two objects come into contact.

5. Not typical. In Western culture, even many 5-year-olds can count well beyond 10.

6. Not typical. When children have regular experience with drawing materials, they typically begin to produce recognizable shapes (e.g., circles, rectangles, triangles) by age 3.

7. Not typical. Even if Alison's parents are on the elderly side, they were certainly born well after 1913. Alison seems to have little understanding of historical time—something that most children begin to grasp sometime around age 10.

8. Typical. As early as age 4, children can, when asked, devise ways of representing music on paper.

9. Not typical. Robbie Case's description of a *central conceptual structure* for numbers tells us that children should be able to answer such a question correctly at about age 10.

10. Typical. Penny is apparently thinking of heat as something that has physical substance. Many children and adolescents think of phenomena such as heat, light, and force as being physical entities (i.e., they misapply their *substance schema*).

11. Typical. When young adolescents work with fractions and other proportions, they often misapply rules for whole numbers. Breck probably thinks that anytime a number is divided by another number, the result must be a *smaller* number—a rule that holds true for whole numbers. With his misconception in mind, he has probably divided 24 by 6 and gotten what he thought was a reasonable result.

12. Not typical. Depicting the ground and the sky in this manner is common in 5- and 6-year-olds. By age 10, we would expect Mattie to be representing depth in her drawings, which would include putting the yard and sky "behind," as well as below and above, the house.

13. Typical. Travis apparently thinks that the state boundaries shown on the map reflect actual markings on the earth. Many children in the early elementary years take what they see on a map quite literally.

14. Typical. The boys are showing *confirmation bias*—a try-to-prove-what-I-already-believe attitude—rather than being open-minded about what they might observe. Confirmation bias is quite common in both children and adolescents. (In this situation, the vinegar removed the wool's protective coating and allowed the iron in the steel to rust. Rusting is a chemical reaction in which iron combines with oxygen. In the process, heat is released.)

Application Exercise #3: Identifying Developmentally Appropriate Practices

Which of the following practices are consistent, and which are inconsistent, with what you've learned about development in the content domains and about cognitive development more generally? Defend your choices.

1. Ms. Bergeron, a high school math teacher, presents basic principles of geometry in a largely abstract manner.

2. As Mr. Valerio reads storybooks to his preschoolers, he often stops to elicit the children's thoughts and opinions about characters and events in the stories.

3. Ms. Olenick gives her eighth-grade history students twenty minutes to write an essay describing the events leading up to the American Revolutionary War. She tells them that she expects correct spelling and punctuation throughout the essay.

4. Ms. Greene makes sure that all writing implements are well out of reach of the toddlers in her care, as she doesn't want them to mark up the storybooks that she keeps in the playroom.

5. Each week, Mr. Marquis, a sixth-grade science teacher, gives students a list of new terms and definitions they should try to memorize for a Friday quiz. "Knowing these things will help you become better scientists," he says.

6. Mr. Weinstock is asking his ninth graders to write their first research paper. He gives them a specific format to follow: (1) an introduction that provides an overview of the paper; (2) a presentation of research findings, including at least three sections on three different aspects of the topic (with each section having its own subheading); and (3) a conclusion that summarizes and identifies implications of the research described in the paper.

7. Many of the 4-year-olds in Ms. Warner's preschool class have had little prior experience with books and other written materials. She begins reading instruction by using flash cards that can teach them how to recognize simple, phonetically regular words such as *cat*, *bed*, and *duck*.

8. The math and social studies teachers at a middle school have eighth graders work in teams to create floor maps of their school. The students use graph paper to depict the school's layout on a one-centimeter-for-every-meter scale, with different team members working in pairs to construct maps of each classroom wing, the cafeteria, the gymnasium, the main office, and so on. Eventually the members of each team convene to assemble their individual maps into overall school maps.

9. Ms. Oliver gives her students free rein whenever they come to her middle school art classes. "I want them to be able to express themselves without any restraints," she says. "I can best help them develop their natural talents by letting them pick their own materials and subject matter each day."

10. Mr. Beruchi encourages his second graders to use only the words they know how to spell when they write their short stories.

11. Mr. DeSeife allows his seventh-grade language arts students to choose their next book from among several classic works of literature (e.g., *The Yearling, To Kill a Mockingbird, The Red Pony*). Over the next two weeks, students who are reading the same book get together in small groups to discuss the book.

12. A child care center for infants and toddlers has several school pets (a rabbit, a small lizard, and several gerbils) that the older children can handle with their teachers' guidance.

13. Ms. Judson occasionally sees a few of her fourth graders counting on their fingers as they work on math problems but does nothing to discourage this behavior.

14. Mr. Holliday asks his high school biology students to write a two-page paper describing the processes involved in human digestion. "The best approach is just to write down the things you've learned about digestion as various thoughts come to mind," he tells them.

15. A preschool provides twice-a-week violin lessons for all of its 4-year-olds.

16. Mr. Strauch asks his kindergartners to think of words that rhyme with *goat*.

17. Teachers at an after-school care program create a home page on the school district's Web site. On the page, children in the program can "publish" the stories they have written about events at school and in the local community.

18. Ms. Tan has her ninth-grade history students read Stephen Crane's *The Red Badge of Courage*, a novel that depicts a young man's thoughts and fears as he joins the army and fights in the U.S. Civil War.

19. Mr. Smart is working to help the 3-year-olds in his preschool class learn about numbers and counting. Once they have learned to count to 10, he begins asking questions such as "Which is more, 3 or 7?" and "Which is less, 5 or 7?"

20. After her seventh-grade math students have solved word problems that require the use of fractions, Mr. Ganota asks them to explain why they used the particular problem-solving strategies they did.

Answers to Application Exercise #3

1. Not consistent. Although most high school students are capable of some degree of abstract thinking, even at this level they benefit from concrete manipulatives that can help them tie abstract ideas to concrete reality.

2. Consistent. Such discussions can help children make better sense of a story.

3. Not consistent. The students probably have time for only one draft of the essay. Students may have insufficient working memory capacity to worry about writing mechanics at the same time that they worry about getting their thoughts on the page in a coherent fashion.

4. Not consistent. Children should have access to writing tools as soon as they are old enough to use them. If she is concerned about keeping the storybooks free from pencil and crayon marks, she might establish separate areas of the playroom for reading and writing. She might also provide materials that the children can write and scribble in—perhaps coloring books and writing tablets.

5. Not consistent. Mr. Marquis is promoting the belief that science is largely a matter of memorizing discrete facts. Certainly he should help his students master important scientific concepts, but he can also do that by having them use the concepts regularly in more authentic scientific tasks (see Chapter 7).

6. Consistent. Giving students a structure to follow provides the scaffolding that many of them will need to guide their writing efforts. Such a structure becomes less necessary over time, as students gain experience with various forms of writing.

7. Not consistent. Authentic literacy activities (e.g., reading children's stories) tend to be more beneficial for young children than activities involving drill and practice of isolated skills.

8. Consistent. The students can learn a great deal about maps (e.g., the importance of scale) by creating their own maps of a place they know well. Furthermore, they can practice basic mathematical skills (e.g., in measurement and use of simple proportions) in an authentic activity.

9. Not consistent. Although some youngsters seem to have a "natural" talent for art, most are more likely to develop their artistic skills when they have explicit instruction in various skills (e.g., as is provided in China and Japan).

10. Not consistent. Many experts urge teachers and other adults to have children focus initially on getting their thoughts on paper in whatever form they can. Children can address writing mechanics, including correct spelling, in later drafts.

11. Consistent. Students who are interested in what they read use more sophisticated metacognitive strategies while reading and so remember more content. The group discussions should help the students construct meaning from what they read.

12. Consistent. Young children learn more about the biological world when they can interact safely with a variety of animals.

13. Consistent. Children occasionally rely on early strategies, such as counting on fingers to add and subtract, even after they've acquired more sophisticated ones. As the new strategies become increasingly efficient, children gradually leave the old ones behind. If the teacher has concerns that her students *aren't* learning more advanced strategies, then she should provide whatever instruction and practice is necessary to help them master these strategies. However, she does not need to discourage the use of strategies that, although slow and cumbersome, are dependable and accurate backups.

14. Not consistent. Mr. Holliday is asking students to engage in knowledge telling, a process that is unlikely to help them organize their thoughts into a cohesive whole.

15. Consistent. There is no hard-and-fast rule about when children should begin music lessons. Beginning early may help the children retain or acquire absolute pitch.

16. Consistent. Rhyming activities can enhance children's phonological awareness, which contributes to reading success.

17. Consistent. The teachers are engaging children in authentic writing tasks.

18. Consistent. History becomes more meaningful when youngsters can think of historical events as involving ordinary people with typical human characteristics.

19. Not consistent. Making *more* and *less* comparisons among numbers is considerably more difficult than counting. Neo-Piagetian researcher Robbie Case found that the ability to make such comparisons appears sometime around age 6.

20. Consistent. Ideally, children should understand (rather than simply memorize) the mathematical procedures they use. Asking students to reflect on and explain their procedures should encourage a focus on such understanding. As young adolescents, seventh graders should be capable of reflecting on their own thought processes (see the discussion of *metacognition* in Chapter 7).

<u>**Sample Test Questions**</u>

Use the following multiple-choice and essay questions to evaluate and strengthen your understanding of selected concepts in the chapter.

Multiple-Choice

1. Which one of the following most clearly illustrates *phonological awareness*?
    a. Knowing that *less* is the opposite of *more*
    b. Knowing that the sounds "duh" and "og" make *dog*
    c. Knowing that *did* is the past tense of *do*
    d. Knowing that apostrophes sometimes are used for contractions and at other times are used for possessive nouns

2. Children who grow up in Italy learn how to read and spell sooner than children who grow up in the United States primarily because
    a. Italian schools are more likely to teach reading using flashcards.
    b. Italy begins systematic literacy instruction when children are 3 years old.
    c. Italian culture values literacy to a greater extent than American culture does.
    d. Italian word spellings are more consistent and predictable than English word spellings.

3. Children with dyslexia are *most* likely to have difficulty in
    a. Perceiving the order in which letters appear within a word
    b. Distinguishing between similarly shaped letters, such as *M* and *N*, or *p* and *q*
    c. Relating new ideas to what they have previously learned
    d. Hearing the individual phonemes that make up words

4. As children get older, they are increasingly likely to engage in *knowledge transforming* rather than *knowledge telling* when they write. Which of the following statements is the best description of how knowledge transforming is different from knowledge telling?
    a. The writer focuses on helping the reader understand the ideas being presented.
    b. The writer explains how his or her ideas about a topic have changed over time.
    c. The writer presents ideas in a nonchronological order (e.g., as a series of flashbacks).
    d. The writer translates ideas that he or she has read in one or more books into his or her own words.

5. Which one of the following best illustrates the *part-whole principle* in mathematics?
   a. In counting, each number is exactly one more than the number it follows.
   b. When you count a group of objects, you need to count one and only one number each time you point to an object; also, you must point to each and every object one time only.
   c. A set of 10 objects can be divided into two sets of 5 objects each or, perhaps instead, into three groups, one with 4 objects and two more with 3 objects each.
   d. If you want to divide one fraction by another fraction (say, dividing $^3/_5$ by $^6/_7$), you flip the numerator and denominator in the second fraction (in the same example, changing $^6/_7$ to $^7/_6$) and multiply.

6. Which one of the following research findings is most consistent with a *nativist* view of science development?
   a. Even very young infants seem to know that an object maintains its size and shape as it moves.
   b. Most 4-year-olds understand that many living things can move themselves but that most nonliving things cannot.
   c. Many 10-year-olds wonder why people and animals near the South Pole don't fall off the earth into outer space.
   d. Children and adolescents often try to confirm what they already believe rather than to seek out disconfirming evidence.

7. "In certain respects, children *lose* musical ability as they grow older." Which one of the following is an accurate example of this statement?
   a. Infants are more likely than adults to notice when a simple melody is played twice with subtle differences.
   b. Children can best understand written music when they are exposed to it before age 3.
   c. Four-year-olds can more easily carry a tune than eight-year-olds.
   d. Young children are more aware of complex musical patterns than teenagers are.

Essay

8. Describe *emergent literacy*, including three or four different kinds of knowledge that it may encompass. Describe a behavior that reflects emergent literacy related to *reading*. Also, describe a behavior that reflects emergent literacy related to *writing*.

9. As children get older, they write longer compositions and spell more words correctly. Describe five *additional* ways in which children's writing changes with age.

10. Children and adolescents often have relatively unsophisticated epistemological beliefs about academic subject matter. Describe two such beliefs in two different content domains (e.g., in math, science, history, or geography) and explain how these beliefs are apt to affect youngsters' learning and classroom performance.

Answers to Sample Test Questions

1. b—Phonological awareness is the ability to hear the distinct sounds (phonemes) within words.

2. d—In Italian, how a word is spelled indicates precisely how it is pronounced, and vice versa. English spelling patterns are less consistent; for instance, the letter combination *ough* is pronounced differently in different words.

3. d—The majority of children with dyslexia appear to have deficits in phonological awareness.

4. a—In knowledge transforming, the writer tries to communicate ideas in a way that a reader is likely to understand.

5. c—The basic idea of the part-whole principle is that any number can be broken into two or more smaller numbers.

6. a—Nativists suggest that some scientific knowledge is biologically built-in. The older that children are, the more likely it is that their knowledge has come from experience rather than biology (i.e., from nurture rather than nature).

7. a—Infants seem to pick up on slight changes in a melody more easily than adults do. Adults are often fairly oblivious to changed notes that remain consistent with the key used to play the melody.

8. Emergent literacy is a fundamental understanding of the nature of reading and writing in children who cannot yet actually read or write. It includes knowing such things as these:
   • Print has meaning and conveys information.
   • Different kinds of printed matter serve different purposes.
   • Spoken language is represented in a consistent fashion in written language.
   • Written language includes predictable elements and conventions.
   • In English, words proceed from left to right, and from the top of the page to the bottom.
   Examples of prereading behaviors that reflect emergent literacy are pretending to read a storybook and correctly identifying words in familiar contexts (e.g., on cereal boxes or fast-food restaurant signs). Examples of prewriting behaviors that reflect emergent literacy are making squiggles or letterlike forms on paper, perhaps accompanied by the claim that these marks have a particular meaning. (You may have identified other legitimate examples of emergent literacy.)

9. Your response should include at least five of the following ideas:
   - Smaller and more controlled handwriting (with a possible decrease in legibility in adolescence due to fast-paced writing)
   - Increasing automatization of spelling
   - More complex syntactic structures
   - Increasing knowledge and automatization of punctuation and capitalization rules
   - Greater development of a particular topic
   - Increasing tendency to take one's audience into account
   - Increasing cohesiveness
   - Increasing tendency to knowledge-transform rather than knowledge-tell
   - Increasing tendency to plan what one is going to write
   - Increasing ability to revise one's own work

   Alternatively, your response might include ideas related to changes in language development more generally—for instance, children's increasing ability to use figurative language (a developmental change described in Chapter 9).

10. Following are examples of unsophisticated (and ultimately counterproductive) epistemological beliefs in various content domains:

    Mathematics:
    - Mathematics is a collection of meaningless procedures to be memorized.
    - Problems always have one and only one right answer.
    - There is only one right way to solve any particular problem.
    - A person will either solve a problem within a few minutes or else not solve it at all.

    Science:
    - Science is a collection of discrete facts to be memorized.
    - Theories are "facts" that don't change over time.

    History and geography:
    - History is a collection of knowledge about what definitely happened, rather than a body of interpretations about how things *might* have happened and about what events *might* have caused other events.
    - Mastering geography means memorizing places (e.g., the capital of Spain is Madrid) and topographical features (e.g., the Rocky Mountains) and their locations on a map.

    The specific effects on learning and classroom performance that you mention will, of course, depend on the particular epistemological beliefs that you identify. Many of the beliefs just listed should lead students to memorize, rather than try to understand, the subject matter and to accept class material at face value rather than to critically evaluate it. Some of the epistemological beliefs about mathematics may lead students to apply mathematical procedures without understanding what they are doing, to get nonsensical problem solutions, and to give up easily when faced with a challenge.

Chapter 11

EMOTIONAL DEVELOPMENT

Chapter Overview

Chapter 11 examines the emotional lives of children. We begin the chapter with a description of Erik Erikson's theory of the challenges individuals face as they progress through life—for example, determining as infants that parents are reliably warm and responsive, concluding as children that they themselves are able to complete everyday tasks, and making commitments as adolescents to particular values and long-term goals. In the second section, we suggest that secure attachments to caregivers help children feel loved, ready to explore the world, and inclined to interact productively with peers and others outside the family. In the third section, we examine developmental changes in children's emotional expression and the difficulty some youngsters experience in dealing with their emotions. In our final section, we examine the stylistic ways that individual children express themselves in social environments, such as being socially outgoing and confident or shy and fearful. Throughout the chapter, we recommend tactics for supporting children's emotional development—specifically, in fostering secure attachments to caregivers, teaching children to express their emotions constructively, offering encouragement and accommodations to children who face emotional problems, and adjusting to children's individual personalities.

Possible Knowledge, Beliefs, and Misconceptions Related to Chapter Content

Your relationships with your own parents and your style of expressing yourself may affect your understanding of concepts in this chapter. Consider how the following specific ideas may affect your interpretation of chapter concepts:

1. Consider a personal loss or traumatic event that you experienced sometime over the last few years. Perhaps you lost a grandparent, were a victim of a crime, had a debilitating illness, or witnessed a serious accident. How did you cope? Adults have many ways to deal with difficult circumstances, yet their front-line technique is often one that has worked well since infancy—seeking reassurance from a loved one. You can draw from such an experience to appreciate why small children flock to familiar caregivers when scared, hurt, angry, or unsure of themselves (see the section "Attachment").

2. Most of us have learned that parents and extended family members are targets of infants' affection. You may be surprised to learn that infants also form close bonds with adults outside the family (such as employed caregivers in child care settings). Caregivers' sensitivity is especially important to children when parents are not consistently responsive (see the section "Attachment").

3. How do you feel when other people show their anger, fear, sadness, and happiness? Some adults are uncomfortable with strong displays of emotions, yet emotions are an important part of everyone's lives. You will learn in this chapter how to help children to express emotions constructively (see the section "Emotion").

4. Some readers will expect that emotional problems in youngsters are rare. In reality, teachers and other practitioners routinely work with children who find it difficult to deal with their emotions. Some youngsters are overly anxious or seriously depressed. Other youngsters respond impulsively to anger by lashing out at peers or adults. Because emotional problems are more common than you might realize, we suggest that you learn to recognize how these difficulties are manifested and acquire strategies that assist troubled youngsters (see the section "Emotion").

5. Some readers may not be aware that children are born with certain temperamental dispositions, such as an inclination to be inhibited and shy or expressive and exuberant. You can increase your effectiveness with children if you begin to watch for such stylistic variations in children's social behaviors and their responses to changes in routines and new intellectual challenges. The section "Temperament and Personality" offers ideas on how to detect and address these qualities in children.

Suggested Supplementary Readings

The following readings, presented in the final section of this *Study Guide and Reader*, are relevant to Chapter 11:

CHAPTER OUTLINE	FOCUS QUESTIONS
ERIKSON'S THEORY OF PSYCHOSOCIAL DEVELOPMENT	• How does Erikson describe the progression of challenges people undertake as they grow?
Lessons Learned from Life's Challenges	• What strengths have been noted in Erikson's theory?
Contemporary Perspectives on Erikson's Theory	• In what areas has Erikson's theory been criticized?

CHAPTER OUTLINE	FOCUS QUESTIONS
ATTACHMENT Developmental Course of Children's Attachments Individual Differences in Children's Attachments Origins of Attachment Security Attachment Security and Later Development Multiple Attachments Implications of Attachment Research	• What does it mean for children to form *attachments* to their parents and caregivers? • How does an infant respond to a parent or other primary caregiver before an attachment is firmly in place? • How do attachments change during infancy, childhood, and adolescence? • Describe the following attachment classifications: secure attachment, insecure-avoidant attachment, insecure-resistant attachment, disorganized and disoriented attachment, and other serious problems with attachment. • What styles of care lead infants to form secure attachments to caregivers? • What other factors contribute to an infant's attachments? • Can infants attach to more than one person at a time? • How does attachment security affect a child's long-term well-being? • How can practitioners support children and families when children's attachments to families are weak?

CHAPTER OUTLINE	FOCUS QUESTIONS

EMOTION
 	
    Developmental Changes in Emotions
 	
    Group Differences in Emotions
 	
    Promoting Children's Emotional Development
 	
    Emotional Problems in Children and Adolescents
	• What functions do emotions serve for children?
	
	• How do emotions change with development?
	
	• What kinds of changes occur in *emotional regulation*?
	
	• How are different groups socialized to express emotions? Specifically, how do gender, family, culture, and socioeconomic status influence emotional expression?
	
	• What can adults do to help children express their feelings constructively?
	
	• Describe the struggles experienced by youngsters with depression, anxiety disorders, and conduct disorders.
	
	• How can educators support youngsters who have serious emotional problems?

TEMPERAMENT AND PERSONALITY
 	
    Elements of Temperament and Personality
 	
    Helping Children to Be Themselves
	• Define *temperament* and *personality*, and suggest how these two concepts may be related.
	
	• What are some possible dimensions of temperament?
	
	• How do nature and nurture affect children's temperament?
	
	• Describe the five dimensions of personality and indicate how educators might adjust to especially low or high levels on these dimensions.

Chapter Glossary

Anxiety. Emotional state characterized by worry and apprehension.

Anxiety disorder. Chronic emotional condition characterized by excessive, debilitating worry.

Attachment. An enduring emotional tie uniting one person to another.

Conduct disorder. Chronic emotional condition characterized by lack of concern for the rights of others.

Depression. Emotional condition characterized by significant sadness, discouragement, hopelessness, and in children, irritability.

Disorganized and disoriented attachment. Attachment classification in which children lack a single coherent way of responding to attachment figures.

Emotion. Affective response to an event that is personally relevant to one's needs and goals.

Emotional contagion. Tendency for infants to cry spontaneously when they hear other infants crying.

Emotional regulation. Strategies to manage affective states.

Empathy. Capacity to experience the same feelings as another person, especially when the feeling is pain or distress.

Ethological attachment theory. Theoretical perspective that emphasizes benefits to children, particularly protection from harm and a secure base from which to explore the environment, derived from close bonds with caregivers.

Insecure-avoidant attachment. Attachment classification in which children appear somewhat indifferent to attachment figures.

Insecure-resistant attachment. Attachment classification in which children are preoccupied with their attachment figures but gain little comfort from them when distressed.

Need for relatedness. Fundamental need to feel socially connected to, and loved and respected by, other people.

Personality. Characteristic way a person behaves, thinks, and feels.

Psychosocial stages. In Erikson's theory, eight periods of life that involve age-related challenges.

Secure attachment. Attachment classification in which children use attachment figures as a source of comfort in times of distress and as a secure base from which to explore.

Self-conscious emotion. Affective state that reflects awareness of a community's social standards (e.g., pride, guilt, shame).

Stranger anxiety. Fear of unfamiliar adults in the latter half of the first year and into the second year of life.

Table 11–1. Applying Concepts in Child Development: Nurturing Youngsters' Emotional Development

This table is a complete version of the table that appears at the end of Chapter 11 in the textbook. Compare your entries in the blank cells in the textbook table with our entries here. Keep in mind that there isn't necessarily a single "right" entry for any particular cell.

Age	A Youngster's Experience	Developmental Concepts *Identifying Emotional Qualities*	Implications *Nurturing Emotional Development*
Infancy (Birth–2)	Edel is a healthy 1-year-old girl with Down syndrome. Her mother is going back to work and enrolls Edel in a child care center. During the first few weeks, when Edel is first dropped off in the morning, she clings to her mother and cries loudly as her mother leaves. When her mother returns in the afternoon, Edel is usually sitting quietly and mouthing and handling toys. Upon noticing her mother, Edel crawls to her, demands to be picked up, and snuggles into her arms.	Edel is showing several *attachment* behaviors. She shows *stranger anxiety* with the new caregivers at the child care center, she protests her mother's departure, and she welcomes her mother happily when she returns.	Be especially reassuring to infants when they first enter your care. Hold them gently, pamper them when they cry, and look after them with utmost sensitivity. Expect them to protest separations from parents, realizing that they eventually will form attachments to you.
Early Childhood (2–6)	Mr. Bono notices that one of his preschool students, Phyllis, seems somewhat anxious at school. Phyllis appears timid and shy, and she stands on the fringes of group activities. She does not interact easily with other children and has no regular friends in the class. With a change in routine, such as missing story time because of a fire drill or having to stay inside during a bitter snow day, Phyllis is obviously upset.	As with all children, Phyllis has her own unique *temperament* and a budding *personality*. Depending on the particular constellation of temperamental or personality characteristics being considered, Phyllis might be described as emotionally intense, showing negative affectivity, or having an inclination toward neuroticism.	When children seem timid, shy, and nervous, offer them reassurance that everything is fine. Provide them with a well-structured learning environment, and when possible, explain ahead of time about changes in regular activities. When children have trouble making friends, help them ease into social groups.

table continues

190

Table 11–1 continued

Age	A Youngster's Experience	Developmental Concepts *Identifying Emotional Qualities*	Implications *Nurturing Emotional Development*
Middle Childhood (6–10)	A third-grade teacher returns children's graded mathematics assignments. Most children did well on the assignment, but two children, Brenda and Billy, had trouble keeping their attention on the task and so received low grades for their work. When Brenda receives her low grade, she cries and broods over the poor score for the remainder of the day. Billy, on the other hand, smiles when he gets the assignment back, says, "Oh well," but he later gets in trouble during recess for disruptive behavior.	Brenda and Billy seem to exhibit typical *gender differences in emotions.* Brenda responds negatively to her poor performance and frets about it all day. Billy seems to deny that there is a problem, but his disruptive behavior later in the day may be a sign that he is, in fact, trying to put on a self-confident front to mask his disappointment.	Help children acquire new, more effective ways of dealing with disappointment and distress. Also help them discover that they can make progress with additional instruction, effort, and practice.
Early Adolescence (10–14)	Thirteen-year-old Adam has confronted many hardships in his life, including his parents' divorce, economic poverty, and the death of a baby sister. Despite facing adversity, Adam is a reasonably happy and healthy young man. When he is sad or anxious, he makes a point to go for a ride on his bicycle and talk openly about his feelings with his parents and close friends. Sometimes when he feels particularly stressed, he goes to the movies with a friend or drops in to the neighborhood youth center to play pool.	Adam seems reasonably well adjusted, perhaps due in part to the fact that he has learned a range of helpful techniques for *emotional regulation.*	Teach and encourage effective ways of regulating emotions. When adolescents are particularly troubled, remind them of the strategies that have helped them in the past, including expressing feelings to others, exercising, and distracting themselves with enjoyable activities.
Late Adolescence (14–18)	Seventeen-year-old Nate broke up with his steady girlfriend. He appears despondent and tells his father and friends that he can't bear it anymore. He says he feels terrible, drinks alcohol excessively, and searches the Internet for Web sites about suicide.	Nate is showing some warning signs that he might be at risk for *suicide.* None of these indicators is definitive, but collectively they do suggest he is in serious trouble and needs immediate attention.	When youngsters show warning signs of suicide, contact a school psychologist, other mental health professional, or supervisor *immediately.* These professionals will be able to provide appropriate interventions.

Application Exercise #1: Identifying Typical Developmental Characteristics of Emotional Development

In each of the following vignettes, determine whether the description of children's emotional development is *typical* for the age group or represents an *unusual* response.

1. Nine-month-old Vincent struggles when his father drops him off at the child care center. As his father prepares to leave the room, Vincent crawls after him. Vincent sobs as Dad walks out the door.

2. Two-year-old Angelica is deeply attached to her parents and her caregiver at the child care center. When she is upset, she often seeks comfort from her parents or her caregiver, depending on which of these adults is nearby.

3. Since entering middle school, 12-year-old Maggie has spent every free moment with friends. When she is upset about something, Maggie now goes exclusively to her friends for reassurance, and she is gradually phasing out the relationships she has had with her parents.

4. Seven-year-old Trinisha adores her loving and responsive mother. Mother encourages Trinisha to make new friends, but Trinisha's secure relationship with her mother interferes with the girl's desire to make friends at school.

5. Marshall is a 18-month-old toddler who is beginning to show genuine emotion. Up until recently, he cried when he was hungry, tired, or hurt but did not show any happiness, fear, interest, or other emotions. Now Marshall is smiling, showing anger when parents curtail his actions, and noticing other people's facial expressions.

6. Nine-year-old Sebastian appreciates that he and other people know how to control their emotional displays. He understands that people do not always show their true feelings.

7. The boys in Ms. Pierson's third-grade class dwell on the mistakes they make, whereas the girls maintain a pretense of confidence, brushing off failures and problems.

8. In his first year of junior high school, Will is somewhat moody. His maturing body, increased difficulty with schoolwork, and uncertainty about how peers view him are sources of stress.

Answers to Application Exercise #1

1. Typical. Concern about separating with parents is a common response beginning in the second half of the first year and continuing for several months and sometimes a few years (see the section "Developmental Course of Children's Attachments").

2. Typical. It is common for young children to be attached to several caregivers, including family members and child care providers (see the section "Multiple Attachments").

3. Unusual. Adolescents spend increasing time with peers and rely on close friends when troubled, but they also typically preserve their ties to parents and other family members and appreciate behind-the-scenes family support (see the section "Developmental Course of Children's Attachments").

4. Unusual. A secure relationship with parents is associated with children's easy adjustment at school and productive relationships with peers and teachers (see the section "Attachment Security and Later Development").

5. Unusual. Infants show contentment, interest, and distress within the first 6 months of life and then add other emotions. Infants begin to observe and imitate other people's facial expressions in the first year of life. The emotions Marshall shows are more typical of a younger infant's abilities than those of a toddler (see the section "Developmental Changes in Emotions").

6. Typical. During middle childhood, children learn that they and other people can regulate their emotions and often put on a "face" that masks what they feel inside (see the section "Developmental Changes in Emotions").

7. Unusual. This gender difference is the reverse of what is typically seen. Girls would typically be more inclined to dwell on their failures and boys to brush them off as being insignificant (see the section "Group Differences in Emotions").

8 Typical. The onset of puberty and a new, unfamiliar school environment can trigger new anxieties (see the section "Developmental Changes in Emotions").

Application Exercise #2: Identifying Developmentally Appropriate Practices

In the following scenarios, distinguish those practices that are *appropriate*—those that nurture children's emotional development—from those that are *inappropriate*.

1. A caregiver notices that one of her 2-year-olds, Simon, seems far more independent than other children in her group. When his parents drop him off in the morning, Simon doesn't protest much, whereas the other children generally fuss for a few moments before settling down. The caregiver believes that Simon *should* protest; she assumes he must be *insecurely attached*. One afternoon when Simon's parents pick him up, she tells them that she is concerned that Simon has failed to bond with them.

2. Two 9-year-old children, Istu and Rossa, are arguing on the playground. The playground supervisor, Ms. Stockholm, observes their scuffle. Istu pushes Rossa, and Rossa kicks Istu in return. Ms. Stockholm is not happy to see the fighting but believes that children must find an honest and open way to express their emotions and so does not intervene.

3. One-year-old Dakota is upset when he arrives at his new child care center in the morning, and he cries and wails for a good 10 minutes after his parents drop him off. He seems to be slowly growing accustomed to his new caregiver, Ms. Sampson. Ms. Sampson understands that he will slowly adjust to her, to the new environment, and to separation from his parents. She holds him at the window and waves good-bye to his parents, cuddles him with his favorite blanket, and reassures him gently throughout the day.

4. Mu-En's child care provider, Ms. Huang, is concerned that baby Mu-En is growing attached to her. He wriggles when he sees her in the morning, smiles and babbles, leaps into her arms, and frequently seeks her attention, contact, and reassurance. Ms. Huang worries that Mu-En will lose his bond with his parents if he becomes too attached to her and so tries to discourage much physical contact.

5. Sixteen-year-old Penda is worried about her upcoming class presentation on African history. Her teacher, Ms. Purdy, is aware of Penda's apprehension because of her performance during a previous oral presentation. Ms. Purdy tells Penda that she is willing to work with her individually or give her time to practice the presentation with a classmate so that she can gain confidence in her ability to present it to the other students.

6. Fourteen-year-old Jara appears deeply troubled. Her history teacher, Mr. Branson, is worried about her. Mr. Branson recalls that Jara was actively involved in class activities earlier in the semester and seemed to be reasonably happy. Now she's quiet, detached, and withdrawn, and she often draws pictures of tombstones, coffins, and skulls in her notebook. When Mr. Branson tells her he's concerned about her, she asks him not to worry because her troubles are almost over. He contacts the school counselor immediately.

Answers to Application Exercise #2

1. Inappropriate. Simon's caregiver is misinterpreting Simon's behavior. Even though Simon shows one of the qualities of being "insecure-avoidant" (he seems indifferent to his parents' departures), it is also possible that Simon has grown adjusted to his parents' daily departures and simply feels comfortable in the child care center (see sections "Individual Differences in Children's Attachments" and "Multiple Attachments").

2. Inappropriate. Ms. Stockholm understands that children are learning to express their emotions. However, she does not realize that she can help them to express their anger in ways that are more constructive than physical aggression (see the section "Promoting Children's Emotional Development").

3. Appropriate. Ms. Sampson realizes that Dakota will gradually adjust to her. She provides appropriate comfort, establishing a pleasant, familiar routine and encouraging him to bring a reassuring item from home (see the section "Attachment").

4. Inappropriate. Ms. Huang does not realize that young children often form attachments with several caregivers. Mu-En's attachment to her will not displace the bond that he has with his parents (see the section "Multiple Attachments").

5. Appropriate. Ms. Purdy realizes that Penda's anxiety may be overwhelming. She offers to give Penda support so that she can build her confidence in presenting to the class (see the sections "Promoting Children's Emotional Development" and "Emotional Problems in Children and Adolescents").

6. Appropriate. Jara is showing a few signs that she is deeply depressed and might be considering suicide. Mr. Branson is taking an appropriate step by contacting the school counselor (see the section "Emotional Problems in Children and Adolescents").

Sample Test Questions

Use the following multiple-choice and essay questions to evaluate and strengthen your understanding of selected concepts in the chapter.

Multiple-Choice

1. Erikson's theory of psychosocial stages makes which of the following contributions to our understanding of social-emotional development?
   a. Erikson's eight stages define the universal assets that people gain simply by growing older.
   b. Erikson's eight stages give a general sense of the challenges that people face at particular age levels.
   c. Erikson's eight stages underscore the importance of autonomy at all age levels.
   d. Failure to replicate Erikson's eight stages indicates that nothing definite can be said about social-emotional development.

2. Which one of the following styles of behavior would be classified as a *secure attachment* according to *ethological attachment theory*?
   a. The child explores the environment in a superficial manner, seems indifferent to a parent's departure, and goes willingly to strangers.
   b. The child clings to parents, is alarmed when parents leave the room, takes a long time to settle down when reunited with them, and protests the presence of strangers.
   c. The child actively explores the surroundings, protests when a parent leaves the room, but settles down when the parent returns.
   d. The child does not have one coherent style, occasionally expressing fear of the parent and at other times willingly receiving comfort from the parent.

3. Which one of the following statements is an accurate summary of *individual differences in attachment*?
   a. Children's own temperaments are the primary factors affecting security of attachment.
   b. Attachment patterns are similar across all cultures.
   c. Security of attachment, established in early childhood, inevitably persists into adulthood.
   d. Children's security of attachment develops largely in response to caregivers' sensitivity and warmth and can be changed with exposure to a new style of care.

4. *Emotional regulation* refers to which one of the following?
   a. Strategies used to manage affective states
   b. A tendency to share the distress of others, as when infants cry when they hear other infants crying
   c. An affective state that reflects understanding of a community's standards for appropriate behavior
   d. A tendency to look at other people's faces for indications of their emotional states

5. Ms. Getel has three students in her middle-school advisee group who appear to have emotional problems:
   - James bullies his way through interactions with peers, doesn't seem to care about others' feelings, and has been caught throwing rocks at school windows.
   - Jordan appears sad and discouraged most of the time.
   - Jill is constantly worrying about one thing or another, and she seems to be overwhelmed with distress.

   How might you describe the emotional problems of these three adolescents?
   a. James seems to suffer from emotional contagion, Jordan may have trouble with social referencing, and Jill seems to feel inferior.
   b. James may be responding to an anxiety disorder, Jordan seems to be depressed, and Jill seems to be externalizing her problems.
   c. James seems to have a secure attachment, and the other two students seem to have insecure attachments.
   d. James may have a conduct disorder, Jordan may be depressed, and Jill may have an anxiety disorder.

6. Which one of the following statements is not one of the recommendations in the book for accommodating children's temperaments and personalities?
   a. Consider children's temperaments when forming groups.
   b. Allow children to apply their natural strengths, but also encourage them to try out new strategies for learning.
   c. Convince children that everyone should adopt the temperamental style of being calm and compliant.
   d. Help children to cope with changes in routines.

Essay

7. Provide three illustrations of environmental influences on children's emotional development. For example, you might talk about the effects of culture, parental relationships, or classroom processes.

8. Describe one problem that sometimes occurs in youngsters' emotional development. Suggest strategies that teachers and other practitioners can use to promote healthier development.

9. Describe Erikson's theory of psychosocial stages. How is the theory supported or refuted by research?

Answers to Sample Test Questions

1. b—Erikson's theory provides a general sense of the major challenges that people face at particular age levels, but the theory does not give detailed information about how culture and context interact with developmental progressions.

2. c—According to ethological attachment theory, a secure attachment in infancy means that children protest separation from caregivers but are reassured when reunited with them. Infants use caregivers as a secure base from which to explore the world (see the section "Individual Differences in Infants' Attachment"). Alternative *a* describes the "insecure-avoidant" classification, *b* describes the "insecure-resistant" classification, and *d* describes the "disorganized and disoriented" classification.

3. d—The quality of children's attachment to their parents depends on caregivers' sensitivity, warmth, and responsiveness in meeting children's needs. Alternative *a* is incorrect because parents are generally able to be sensitive to a wide range of temperaments and characteristics in children. Alternative *b* is incorrect because cultural differences have been observed in the relative frequency of various attachment styles. Alternative *c* is incorrect because the quality of attachment can change over time (see sections "Individual Differences in Children's Attachments," "Origins of Attachment Security," and "Attachment Security and Later Development").

4. a—Emotional regulation is defined in option *a*. Option *b* describes *emotional contagion, c* describes *self-conscious emotion*, and *d* describes *social referencing*.

5. d—This alternative accurately describes the symptoms that all three children are showing. It would be important, however, for Ms. Getel to seek the perspective of a trained counselor before drawing conclusions about adolescents' mental health.

6. c—To some degree, genetic factors affect temperament, and it is probably neither possible nor desirable for all children to have the same temperament.

7. Following are some examples of environmental influences on youngsters' social-emotional development:
   - Children's secure attachments to parents, other family members, and caregivers outside the family are cultivated by warm, responsive, sensitive care (see the section "Origins of Attachment Security").
   - Styles of attachment vary somewhat in different cultural groups (see the section "Origins of Attachment Security").
   - High-quality attachments with caregivers can compensate for weak family relationships (see the sections "Multiple Attachments" and "Implications of Attachment Research").
   - Children's emotional responding is affected by socialization by family members and others (see the section "Group Differences in Emotions").
   - Boys and girls are sometimes socialized to respond differently with regard to emotional regulation (see sections on "Group Differences in Emotions").
   - Teachers and other practitioners can help children express their emotions in socially appropriate ways (see the section "Promoting Children's Emotional Development").

- Some emotional problems occur in response to, or are exacerbated by, family interactions (see the section "Emotional Problems in Children and Adolescents").

8. Several possibilities are described in Chapter 11. For example, you might discuss problems with attachment (e.g., insecure-avoidant and resistant attachments) or emotional problems (e.g., depression, anxiety disorder, or conduct disorder). Recommendations will vary depending on the problem selected. As an example, readers who focus on children's insecure attachments may describe their intentions to treat children with utmost sensitivity and care, model affectionate caregiving for family members, and scaffold parents' interpretations of and responses to children's behavior.

9. Erikson's theory describes major challenges that people face during particular age periods. Erikson's eight stages are as follows:
   - Trust versus mistrust (infancy)
   - Autonomy versus shame and doubt (toddler years)
   - Initiative versus guilt (preschool years)
   - Industry versus inferiority (elementary school years)
   - Identity versus role confusion (adolescence)
   - Intimacy versus isolation (young adulthood)
   - Generativity versus stagnation (middle age)
   - Integrity versus despair (retirement years)

Researchers have identified several problems with Erikson's theory, including its failure to adequately address the influences of culture, its assumption that identity issues are resolved at the end of adolescence, and its neglect of the perspectives of girls and women. However, the theory does provide a useful way to think about the global tasks that individuals are apt to face during particular age periods.

Chapter 12

DEVELOPMENT OF SELF AND SOCIAL UNDERSTANDING

Chapter Overview

Chapter 12 examines the nature of children's and adolescents' beliefs about themselves and other people. In its exploration of *sense of self*, the chapter looks at the development and effects of youngsters' self-concepts, self-esteem, sense of identity, and overall sense of self-worth. The chapter also discusses the development of *social cognition*—how youngsters of various ages perceive and interpret the actions of other people—and interpersonal behaviors. The chapter offers numerous suggestions for enhancing children's self-confidence, understanding of others, and social skills.

Possible Knowledge, Beliefs, and Misconceptions Related to Chapter Content

Following are beliefs that many college students have about children's sense of self and social understanding. Such beliefs are likely to interfere with an accurate understanding of ideas presented in Chapter 12. As you read the chapter, be on the lookout for evidence that contradicts these commonly held ideas:

1. Some people believe that self-esteem is a stable trait. In reality, children's feelings about themselves depend very much on their recent experiences in school and elsewhere. For example, youngsters just entering a new school environment—perhaps beginning first grade or the first year of junior high school—are likely to wonder how well they fit in and measure up to their teachers' expectations and peers' performance. Initially, they may feel somewhat insecure and evaluate their own abilities as being weak. Once they've discovered that they can successfully meet new standards, they regain their positive self-perceptions. (See the section "Changing Nature of the Self Over Childhood and Adolescence.")

2. Many people in teacher education programs believe that to promote positive self-concepts and high self-esteem, teachers should never give negative feedback. In fact, students must know what they are doing wrong as well as what they are doing right. The trick is to provide negative feedback while also communicating high expectations for future performance and providing scaffolding for students' future efforts, so that youngsters have reason to believe they can improve. (See the section "Enhancing Children's Sense of Self.")

3. Many adults like to think of children as being naturally kind and accepting of others. If you hold this view, you may be surprised to learn that some negative social biases, such as prejudice, emerge fairly early. In the section "Social-Cognitive Bias and Prejudice," you will learn that, with age, children have increasing opportunities to discover the unique qualities of different members of a particular group. As children learn that members of any particular ethnic or racial group are in many ways quite different from one another, their biases and prejudices may diminish. In some instances, however, the adults in children's lives tend to verbalize and thereby *increase* negative stereotypes of certain groups.

200

4. One misconception that some adults hold is that infants are asocial—stuck in their own little worlds, oblivious to others. In the section "Interpersonal Behaviors at Different Ages," you will see some of the early social gestures that infants make to other children. You will also learn that young children, who often play side by side without interacting very much, are nevertheless learning a lot about one another's activities, and they put this information to use as their interactions with peers increase.

5. Another common misconception is that adolescents are often the unwilling victims of peer pressure. That is, some people assume that if a well-mannered teenager gets into trouble, undue pressure from unruly peers must be the cause. As you will learn, adolescents do influence one another's behaviors, but adolescents themselves also choose the peers with whom to affiliate, and they don't always take their age-mates' messages at face value.

6. Many adults are surprised to see small children helping one another, as they don't expect young children to sense another person's pain or offer meaningful comfort. In the section "Development of Prosocial Behavior and Aggression," you will learn that young children often display concern for others in distress and that caregivers can cultivate this disposition.

7. Some readers will recall boys and girls who were *bullies* who continually harassed others in their neighborhoods and schools. These children ridiculed classmates, stole lunch money, and were in some instances physically aggressive in order to get something they wanted or to communicate a general sense of power. As someone preparing to work with young people, you may appreciate that it is your responsibility to stop aggressive children from hurting others. What you may not realize, but will learn in Chapter 12, is that aggressive children usually lack social skills. They act aggressively, in part, because that is how they have learned to relate to others.

8. A related misconception is that aggressive children will, of their own accord, outgrow their nasty habits. Unfortunately, extremely aggressive children tend *not* to outgrow this trait without systematic instruction in alternative social strategies. Unusually aggressive children may develop reputations that are difficult to shed, they may become reinforced by the power (and perhaps even the pain) they cause others, and they may not know alternative ways to interact with other people. Thus, youngsters who are exceptionally aggressive desperately need intervention. You will learn some ways in which you can help aggressive children in the section "Fostering Effective Interpersonal Skills."

Suggested Supplementary Readings

The following readings, presented in the final section of this *Study Guide and Reader*, are relevant to Chapter 12:

Reading 12-1: Children's Conceptions of Society

Reading 12-2: Conceptions of Self in the Early Years

Reading 12-3: Selman's Theory of Social Perspective Taking

Reading 12-4: The Social Benefits of Gossip

CHAPTER OUTLINE	FOCUS QUESTIONS

SENSE OF SELF
 	
   Effects of Children's Sense of Self
 	
   Factors Influencing Sense of Self
 	
   General Trends in Children's Sense of Self
 	
   Changing Nature of the Self Over Childhood and
     Adolescence
 	
   Diversity in Sense of Self
 	
   Enhancing Children's Sense of Self
	• Distinguish among the terms *self-concept*, *self-esteem*, *self-worth*, and *self-efficacy*.
	
	• What effects is a child's sense of self apt to have on the child's behavior? Why might a child occasionally *self-handicap*?
	
	• What factors influence children's self-perceptions?
	
	• Describe several ways in which a child's sense of self changes with development.
	
	• Describe at least two characteristics of sense of self at each of the five developmental levels: infancy, early childhood, middle childhood, early adolescence, and late adolescence.
	
	• How might the concepts *imaginary audience*, *personal fable*, and *identity* be reflected in adolescents' behavior?
	
	• What gender differences are you likely to see in children's and adolescents' sense of self? Explain how *self-socialization* might partly contribute to these differences.
	
	• What benefits might a strong *ethnic identity* have?
	
	• What strategies are likely to enhance youngsters' sense of self? Why is telling children that they are "good" or "smart" or "special" *unlikely* to be effective?

CHAPTER OUTLINE	FOCUS QUESTIONS
SOCIAL COGNITION Theory of Mind Social Information Processing Social-Cognitive Bias and Prejudice Diversity in Social Cognition Fostering the Development of Social Cognition	• What is *social cognition*? What forms might it take? • What is a *theory of mind*? What abilities and beliefs does it encompass at different ages? • What environmental factors promote the development of a child's theory of mind? • Describe the steps that might be involved in *social information processing*. Using a concrete example, illustrate how a child might go through these steps in a social situation. • What is a *social-cognitive bias*? In what circumstances might it be helpful? When is it likely to interfere with effective social functioning? • What strategies can teachers and other adults use to help youngsters think effectively about social situations and interactions?
INTERPERSONAL BEHAVIORS Interpersonal Behaviors at Different Ages Development of Prosocial Behavior and Aggression Diversity in Interpersonal Behaviors Fostering Effective Interpersonal Skills	• Describe the interpersonal behaviors and social skills that are typical for each of the five developmental periods: infancy, early childhood, middle childhood, early adolescence, and late adolescence. • In Chapter 6 you discovered the advantages of sociodramatic play for cognitive development. What benefits does sociodramatic play have for social-emotional development? • To what extent does *peer pressure* actually influence adolescents' behavior? • How do nature and nurture contribute to children's helping and hurting behaviors? • What developmental trends are seen in children's prosocial behavior? • What various forms can aggression take? What factors seem to contribute to aggressive behavior? • What gender and cultural differences are you likely to see in youngsters' prosocial behavior and aggression? • What strategies are effective in helping children acquire productive interpersonal skills?

Chapter Glossary

Aggression. Action intentionally taken to hurt another either physically or psychologically.

Androgyny. Tendency to have some characteristics that are stereotypically female (e.g., nurturance) and others that are stereotypically male (e.g., assertiveness).

Autobiographical self. Mental "history" of events important in one's life.

Contingent self-worth. Overall sense of self that is highly dependent on others' opinions.

Ethnic identity. Awareness of being a member of a particular ethnic or cultural group and willingness to adopt certain behaviors characteristic of that group.

Gender schema. Self-constructed body of beliefs about the traits and behaviors of males or females.

Hostile attributional bias. Tendency to interpret others' behaviors as reflecting hostile or aggressive intentions.

Identity. Self-constructed definition of who one is, what things one finds important, what one believes, and what goals one wants to accomplish in life.

Imaginary audience. Belief that one is the center of attention in any social situation.

Intentionality. Engagement in an action congruent with one's purpose or goal.

Peer mediation. Approach to conflict resolution in which one child or adolescent (the mediator) asks peers in conflict to express their differing viewpoints and then work together to identify an appropriate compromise.

Peer pressure. Tactics used to encourage some behaviors and discourage others in age-mates.

Personal fable. Belief held by many adolescents that they are unique beings invulnerable to normal risks and dangers.

Physical aggression. Action that can potentially cause bodily injury.

Prejudice. Display of negative attitudes, feelings, and behaviors toward particular individuals because of their membership in a specific group.

Proactive aggression. Deliberate aggression against another as a means of obtaining a desired goal.

Prosocial behavior. Action intended to benefit another person rather than oneself.

Reactive aggression. Aggressive response to frustration or provocation.

Recursive thinking. Thinking about what other people may be thinking about oneself, possibly through multiple iterations.

Relational aggression. Action that can adversely affect interpersonal relationships.

Self-handicapping. Action that undermines one's own success as a way of protecting self-worth during difficult tasks.

Self-socialization. Tendency to integrate personal observations and others' input into self-constructed standards for behavior and to choose actions consistent with those standards.

Sense of self. Knowledge, beliefs, judgments, and feelings about oneself as a person.

Social cognition. Process of thinking about how other people are likely to think, act, and react and choosing one's own interpersonal behaviors accordingly.

Social information processing. Series of cognitive steps applied to understanding and responding to social events.

Social perspective taking. Imagining what someone else might be thinking or feeling.

Social skills. Strategies used to interact effectively with others.

Social-cognitive bias. Mental shortcut in thinking about other people or social events.

Stereotype. Rigid, simplistic, and erroneous characterization of a particular group.

Sympathy. Feeling of sorrow and concern about another's problems or distress.

Theory of mind. Awareness that people have an inner, psychological life (thoughts, beliefs, feelings, etc.).

Table 12–1. Applying Concepts in Child Development: Determining How Children Are Thinking About Themselves and Others

This table is a complete version of the table that appears at the end of Chapter 12 in the textbook. Compare your entries in the blank cells in the textbook table with our entries here. Keep in mind that there isn't necessarily a single "right" entry for any particular cell.

Age	A Youngster's Experience	Developmental Concepts *Identifying Youngsters' Existing Understandings of Self or Others*	Implications *Promoting Development in Sense of Self and Social Cognition*
Infancy (Birth–2)	When 18-month-old Marvin sees his reflection in the mirror, he rubs his cheek to wipe off the lipstick his mother left when kissing him good-bye earlier in the day.	Marvin understands that he is a physical entity separate from the objects and people around him. Furthermore, he recognizes his image in the mirror, indicating that he has some awareness of his own appearance.	Help infants and toddlers learn about their physical selves not only by holding them in front of mirrors but also by showing them photographs of themselves and talking with them about various body parts ("Show me your nose!", "Did you fall and hurt your knee?").
Early Childhood (2–6)	Arriving early at preschool one morning, 3-year-old Kesia helps her teacher reorganize the art supplies. At the teacher's instruction, she moves the colored markers from a bookshelf to the bottom drawer of a cabinet. Later she is quite surprised when her friend Darla looks for the markers on the shelf. "They're in the drawer, silly!" she exclaims.	Like Kesia, young preschoolers often mistakenly assume that other people know what they themselves know. Not until age 4 or 5 do children appreciate that others may have *false beliefs* based on prior learning experiences.	Encourage young children to look at situations from other people's perspectives. For example, ask them to speculate about what various characters in storybooks might be thinking and feeling.
Middle Childhood (6–10)	When a classmate accidentally brushes past him on the way to the pencil sharpener, Douglas angrily shouts, "You *meant* to do it! I'll get you for that!"	Douglas is exhibiting a *hostile attributional bias*, a tendency to interpret ambiguous (and possibly accidental) behaviors as having malicious intent. Such a bias is often seen in aggressive children.	Help children interpret social situations in accurate and productive ways. For instance, role-play situations in which a person's behavior is ambiguous, then have children brainstorm possible interpretations, responses, and long-term outcomes.

table continues

206

Table 12–1 continued

Age	A Youngster's Experience	Developmental Concepts *Identifying Youngsters' Existing Understandings of Self or Others*	Implications *Promoting Development in Sense of Self and Social Cognition*
Early Adolescence (10–14)	Soon after beginning junior high school, 13-year-old Robert begins dressing as he sees some of his peers do—for instance by wearing oversized pants that hang low on his hips and balloon around his legs. And when he sees a few older boys secretly smoking cigarettes in a far corner of the schoolyard, he asks if he can "take a drag."	Robert appears to have constructed a *gender schema* for "what teenage boys should be like" that includes wearing certain clothes and smoking cigarettes. He is not necessarily experiencing any peer pressure to dress and behave as he does. Quite possibly his standards for behavior are self-imposed, reflecting *self-socialization*. (Possibly he may also mistakenly believe that his peers are watching his every move, reflecting the *imaginary audience* so common in early adolescence.)	Expose youngsters to a wide variety of models of "acceptable" behavior, with particular emphasis on peers who maintain a "cool" image while engaging in healthful and productive activities.
Late Adolescence (14–18)	As a 15-year-old, Rita is quite proud of her Puerto Rican heritage. She belittles certain extracurricular activities at her school, especially athletics and the National Honor Society, saying that they are "entirely too White" for her.	On the road to forming an *ethnic identity*, some adolescents may, like Rita, initially adopt a rigid, inflexible one that rejects the perceived values of other ethnic groups. Eventually, however, she is apt to become more open-minded about behaviors that are acceptable for her. In general, youngsters with a strong ethnic identity have high self-esteem.	Help youngsters discover the many good things about various cultural groups, and encourage them to take pride in their own cultural heritage. Also communicate that a wide variety of activities are equally appropriate for people of diverse backgrounds. Make sure that extracurricular groups are not dominated by a particular group and are truly open to all who wish to participate.

Application Exercise #1: Identifying Typical and Atypical Behaviors

In the following scenarios, which youngsters are exhibiting behaviors typical for their age group, and which ones are not? Justify your decisions based on what you have learned about sense of self, social cognition, and interpersonal behaviors.

1. Sixteen-year-old Beatrice is trying to figure out who she is. One week she's studying hard to get into a good college so that she can become a teacher, and the next week she thinks she'd be happier getting married and becoming a "stay-at home mom" right after high school.

2. When one infant at a child care center begins to cry, several other babies start to cry as well.

3. Fourteen-year-old Tesha is shocked to hear that her swimming coach's father died yesterday. "That can't be!" she exclaims. "Coach smiled at me this afternoon, so she's obviously happy, not sad."

4. When another child tries to take 3-year-old Lexee's stuffed alligator, she yells, "No, mine!"

5. Larinda, an eighth grader, suddenly discovers that her black felt-tip pen has leaked all over her blouse. She's so upset that she has little interest in rejoicing about the high grade she just got on a challenging science assignment.

6. When 15-year-old Larry gets a poor grade in his high school math class, he quickly jumps to the conclusion that he is not a good student—that he probably won't do well in any of his other classes (in science, Spanish, physical education, etc.) either—and that he is in many other respects an inferior person.

7. Eight-year-old Chip is well known for his obnoxious behavior in the school lunchroom. He delights in knocking other students' lunch trays onto the floor, thereby making the lunches inedible. When Ms. McCartney confronts Chip about his behavior, he shows no comprehension of the fact that his classmates might go hungry for the rest of the school day.

8. In a region in eastern Europe that is currently experiencing many hostile interactions among various ethnic groups, 4-year-old Mila expresses hatred for children who belong to groups other than her own.

9. Eleven-year-old Darren says to his friend Lucas, "I guess you're sad that your dog died, huh? But maybe you're glad that she's not in pain anymore."

10. Even though all the ninth graders at Harrison High School must take a required health class, many of them ignore the teacher's remarks about the dangers of unprotected sex. "I won't get pregnant," one girl says to a classmate, "and AIDS is something that only poor people get."

11. At 20 months old, Bret sometimes says, "I know dat!" when his babysitter tells him it's time for bed.

12. Natalie's first year of middle school has been an adjustment for her. Although she has previously been a fairly happy, self-confident student, she now worries that she doesn't belong at her new school.

13. As 5-year-old Xavier watches his mother nurse his new baby sister, he says, "I remember when you first brought me home from the hospital. I was really little then, wasn't I?"

14. Sixteen-year-old John forgets to drive his friend Sam home after school—something he had told Sam he would do that day. The following day he apologizes to Sam, saying, "You must have thought that I decided to blow off my promise to you. That wasn't the case at all; I was so upset about my fight with Janice that I simply forgot."

15. Eight-year-old Gabriella is preoccupied with who she is and what she truly believes and values. She also wonders what she will become and how she will fit into society.

16. Thirteen-year-old Molly is obviously quite upset about something. When her teacher tries to find out what's wrong, Molly replies, "I need to talk to my best friend Tara. No one else can possibly understand."

17. Many of the children in Ms. March's kindergarten class claim that they're one of the best readers in the class. By the time they reach Mr. Galuzzo's third-grade class, however, only a few of them think so.

18. Just before his first graders go outside for recess, Mr. Salazar tells them, "I'm going to put the supplies for this afternoon's art project in the bottom drawer of my file cabinet." After the children leave the room, however, he discovers that the supplies won't fit in the drawer. He asks Mary, a student who's misplaced her jacket and so has asked to stay indoors, to help him put the supplies in the box. That afternoon, Mr. Salazar asks another student, Jimmy, to get the supplies. Mary is quite surprised when Jimmy goes to the file drawer rather than to the cardboard box.

19. In his final year of high school, Paco begins to compare his academic performance with that of his classmates. Previously optimistic about what he could accomplish in school, he now is more cautious in his expectations.

20. When her friend Mamie cries after tripping over a toy, $1\frac{1}{2}$-year-old Ruth offers her a cookie as if to console her.

21. Twelve-year-old Ramon refuses to go to school after he chips two front teeth in an ice hockey accident. "Everyone will laugh at me until I get these fixed," he laments.

Answers to Application Exercise #1

1. Typical. Adolescents frequently struggle with identity issues, including their future life paths.

2. Typical. Such a response to a peer's distress is common in young infants.

3. Not typical. By middle childhood, most youngsters are aware that people's outward expressions don't always reflect their true feelings.

4. Typical. Three-year-olds often lay claims to what is "mine." Such possessiveness is possibly an important precursor to sharing.

5. Typical. For many young adolescents, physical appearance is of far greater concern than academic performance.

6. Not typical. Youngsters usually make distinctions among various aspects of themselves. This is especially true at the high school level, when they are likely to realize that they may be more capable in some areas than in others.

7. Not typical. Unlike most 8-year-olds, Chip shows little ability to take other people's perspectives.

8. Typical. Preschoolers can often identify members of other ethnic groups, and they tend to attribute undesirable qualities to those people. In a more peaceful, democratic society, Mila might shed some of her prejudice as she grows older; in her present life circumstances, however, she very well may not.

9. Typical. By early adolescence, children understand that people can have mixed emotions about an event.

10. Typical. Characteristic of the *personal fable* so common during adolescence is a belief that one is invulnerable to life's normal risks.

11. Not typical. Words such as *know* and *think* tend to appear at around $2^{1}/_{2}$ to 3 years of age.

12. Typical. Youngsters who change school systems often show a temporary drop in self-esteem.

13. Not typical. Children remember very little of their lives before age $3^{1}/_{2}$, and their memories of their first two years are almost nonexistent.

14. Typical. John is engaging in *recursive thinking* ("I think that you think that I think..."), which emerges in early adolescence.

15. Not typical. Gabriella's quest to define her identity is more typical of adolescence than it is of middle childhood.

16. Typical. Adolescents often have close, intimate friends with whom they share their innermost thoughts. They may also exhibit a *personal fable*—a belief that they are completely unique and no one else (certainly not a teacher) has ever had the feelings or problems that they themselves have.

17. Typical. Young children often overestimate their abilities, perhaps in part because they continue to see improvements in what they can do. But as they move through middle childhood, they begin to compare their performance with that of their peers and realize that they are not necessarily at the top of the heap.

18. Not typical. By age 5 or 6, children realize that others can have a *false belief*—to believe something different from what they themselves know to be true.

19. Not typical. Youngsters usually begin to compare themselves to peers in middle childhood. Paco is showing this trend quite late in the game.

20. Typical. At 18 months, children have some awareness of other people's mental states, and they realize that their own behaviors can influence other people's emotions.

21. Typical. Ramon is exhibiting a phenomenon known as the *imaginary audience*—the belief that everyone's attention is focused entirely on him. The imaginary audience is most prevalent in early adolescence.

Application Exercise #2: Identifying Developmentally Appropriate Practices

In the following scenarios, distinguish between those practices that are developmentally appropriate—those that are consistent with general principles and trends in sense of self and social cognition—and those that are *not* appropriate.

1.   Twelve-year-old Cassie dislikes mathematics. She is behind most of the other students in Ms. Adams's seventh-grade math class, sees herself as "dumb" in math, and doesn't expect improvement. Ms. Adams is aware of Cassie's negative attitudes toward math. She points out concepts and skills that Cassie has mastered and gives Cassie concrete suggestions about how she might improve her performance in the future.

2.   Ms. Rudolph knows that objects from home (teddy bears, blankets, etc.) are often a source of comfort to young children. But she also wants to encourage a "spirit of community" in her preschool classroom, and so she insists that the 3-year-olds in her care share their possessions with others while they're at school.

3.   Mr. Rogers has high standards for his high school composition courses. He firmly believes that writing skills are vital to many jobs. He gives students plenty of written feedback, circling misspelled words, marking lapses in grammar, and noting in the margins where he spots problems in topic sentences, definitions of terms, and flow of logic. Mr. Rogers tells his students, "I don't expect that any of you will ever become good writers, but I do expect you will want to get better at writing. Read my comments on your papers."

4.   Nine-year-old Dylan has a mild disability that affects his learning. Dylan's teacher has learned that it helps him if she breaks up assignments into smaller chunks, explains exactly what's expected for each chunk, and gives him specific feedback about what he's doing well and how he needs to improve. Lately it's become obvious that Dylan needs support in his peer interactions as well. On one occasion, Dylan threw a can of soda at another boy, Everett, who was teasing him, and Everett received a gash in the head. School policy required that Dylan be suspended for his intentional act of physical aggression. Before he was sent home, the principal reminded him of the rules in the school conduct manual, being sure to describe these rules in concrete terms. The principal also asked Dylan to reflect on the harm that he had caused Everett. When Dylan returned to school after his suspension, his teacher coached him on basic social skills, such as expressing disagreement and anger tactfully and appropriately. She praised Dylan privately whenever she noticed he was trying out these social strategies. She also placed him in cooperative groups with peers and encouraged him to join an after-school club.

5.   Immediately after lunch, Mr. Wright reads a chapter from E. B. White's *Charlotte's Web* to help his second graders settle down before beginning afternoon lessons. He occasionally stops to ask questions such as "Why do you think Charlotte said that?" or "What must Wilbur be feeling when the sheep tell him why the farmer wants him to gain weight?"

6.   Knowing that many of the infants in her care have little awareness of other people's thoughts and emotions, Ms. Johnson makes a point of not using "thinking" and "feeling" words (e.g., *know, remember, happy, sad*) when she talks with them about everyday events.

7.   When a classmate accidentally brushes by her in the hallway, 10-year-old Lucy explodes in anger and shouts, "Just you wait! I'll get you back after school!" Knowing that such incidents are typical for Lucy, Ms. Bergeron finds time to speak with her about how she misinterpreted the classmate's intentions. She also arranges for Lucy to meet with the school counselor to address her aggressive tendencies.

8.   Ms. Walker, a first-grade teacher, believes that nurturing children's self-esteem is far more important than teaching academic skills. "Students cannot learn academic skills until they feel good about themselves as people," she says, "especially for this age-group."

9.   At age 9, Queenie is a "girl's girl." She wears pretty dresses, plays with dolls, and avoids recess activities that are rough or physically taxing. She carries her traditional femininity into academic subject matter as well, claiming that she's "no good at math." Her teacher appreciates Queenie's feminine traits but makes a point to encourage her to put some effort into her math homework.

10.   At Happy Valley High School, heated arguments and physical fights are growing in frequency and seriousness. After conferring about the problem, the school staff initiates a peer mediation program. Over the next few weeks, an increasing number of students are trained to mediate their classmates' conflicts by helping the feuding parties (a) define their problem, (b) explain their own perspectives and needs, (c) describe the viewpoints and desires of the individual(s) on the other side of the argument, and then (d) formulate one or more solutions that everyone agrees might resolve the problem.

11.   Two-year-old Ally loves to play in the sand box. She sometimes shovels and pats the sand so enthusiastically that she gets sand in other children's eyes. Her teacher, Mr. Brach, believes that she is not doing this on purpose and therefore there is nothing he can do.

12.   Ms. Cranwell, a third-grade teacher, tries to motivate Wayne to write his cursive letters more neatly. She tells him, "Look at how your writing compares to Jeremy's. See how his letters are neat and yours are messy?"

Answers to Application Exercise #2

1. Appropriate. Ms. Adams is focusing Cassie's attention on her own improvement rather than on how she is performing in comparison to peers. She is also providing scaffolding to increase Cassie's chances of success on future assignments.

2. Not appropriate. Although learning to share is certainly a worthwhile long-term goal, possessiveness about certain personal items being *mine* is quite common in early childhood and is probably a natural part of children's development of sense of self.

3. Not appropriate. Mr. Rogers is not focusing students' attention on skills in which they are improving. His feedback is entirely critical, suggesting that the assignments may be beyond the capabilities of his students. He does not communicate an expectation that they are capable of doing well.

4. Appropriate. Dylan's principal and teacher have taken many appropriate actions. Dylan's principal made sure that Dylan understands that physically aggressive acts are *not* permitted at school. The principal also talked with Dylan about the negative consequences of his aggression for Everett, getting him to focus on the pain that Everett endured (as you will discover in Chapter 13, this strategy is known as *induction*). Later, Dylan's teacher coached him on basic social skills in interacting with peers and dealing with negative emotions.

5. Appropriate. By asking students to think about the characters' thoughts and feelings, Mr. Wright is fostering development of *social perspective taking* and *theory of mind*.

6. Not appropriate. Children are more likely to acquire an awareness of other people's mental and emotional states if adults talk regularly about them.

7. Appropriate. Lucy is exhibiting a *hostile attributional bias*, a tendency to interpret ambiguous interpersonal behaviors as reflecting aggressive intentions. Active intervention is often necessary to promote more socially beneficial interpretations.

8. Not appropriate. Ms. Walker may be overrating the importance of self-esteem as a target for educators. Academic skills are vital as well. Helping youngsters to master academic skills is one of the most effective ways of enhancing their sense of self.

9. Appropriate. Queenie's teacher is showing acceptance of her feminine interests, but she is also encouraging her to branch out and achieve in nontraditional areas.

10. Appropriate. Peer mediation programs are often effective in helping children and adolescents to develop strategies for resolving their own and others' interpersonal conflicts.

11. Not appropriate. It is essential for caregivers to supervise interactions among small children. Mr. Brach does need to take action, possibly to move Ally to another area of the sand area, and to continue to remind her to use "gentle" hands and to keep her shovel close to the sand so that other children remain safe. If Ally continues to spray the sand in other children's

eyes, Mr. Brach might remove the shovels from the sandbox. Mr. Brach can help Ally to see the effects of her actions; by modeling his sympathy for children who are hurt, Mr. Brach also can help Ally to develop concern for other people's distress.

12. Not appropriate. As children move through the elementary grades, they increasingly compare their performance to that of their peers *on their own*, and those who find themselves coming up short may have diminished self-esteem. Rather than exacerbate this situation, Ms. Cranwell might comment on how Wayne's writing has improved in recent weeks (if it has) or give him some constructive suggestions about what he might do to improve.

Sample Test Questions

Use the following multiple-choice and essay questions to evaluate and strengthen your understanding of selected concepts in the chapter.

Multiple-Choice

1. Which one of the following best illustrates an *imaginary audience* at work?
    a. Annette thinks that none of her friends can possibly understand how badly she feels about not having a date for the homecoming dance.
    b. Betsy doesn't like working in cooperative groups because she often has trouble understanding new concepts and doesn't want other students to think she's stupid.
    c. Christa doesn't think she could ever become a teacher because she doesn't like speaking in front of groups.
    d. Darlene is convinced that everyone in school has noticed that one of her ears sticks out more than the other.

2. Three of the following teachers are likely to enhance their students' sense of self. Which one is *least* likely to do so?
    a. Mr. Alvaro teaches students a technique that enables them to solve their geometry proofs more successfully.
    b. Ms. Berkowitz holds a class spelling bee to see which student is the best speller in the class.
    c. Ms. Caruso teaches her students how to do the butterfly stroke in swimming.
    d. Mr. Davidson uses a role-playing activity to help his students develop better interpersonal skills.

3. When Sal unintentionally knocks over Mark's bicycle, Mark screams, "You meant to do that!" and punches Sal in the stomach. If you look at this situation from the perspective of *social information processing*, which one of the following is your best conclusion?
    a. Mark has not learned appropriate ways of releasing his aggressive impulses.
    b. Mark has interpreted the situation inaccurately and so has retrieved an inappropriate response.
    c. Mark's parents have taught him that aggression is always the best way to solve a problem.
    d. Mark obviously places greater value on his bicycle than on his relationship with Sal.

4. In its discussion of children's social cognition, the textbook suggests that the appearance of prejudice in young children is:
    a. Almost always due to hearing other people's derogatory remarks about particular groups of people
    b. Rarely observed except in children with certain mental illnesses or deficiencies
    c. Often an unfortunate result of children's natural tendency to categorize their experiences
    d. Usually the result of bad experiences with members of a particular group of people

5. *Prosocial behavior* can best be described as:
   a. A developmental precursor to sharing fantasies in sociodramatic play
   b. A way to break into an existing social group
   c. A method for establishing intersubjectivity
   d. An action intended to help another individual

6. Which one of the following most accurately describes the difference between *proactive aggression* and *reactive aggression*?
   a. Proactive aggression refers to a deliberate hurtful act to obtain a desired goal; reactive aggression is provoked out of frustration.
   b. Proactive aggression refers to hurtful acts designed to achieve a long-term prosocial purpose (e.g., mercy killing); reactive aggression is designed to achieve malicious intent (e.g., hurting others for the purpose of witnessing their pain).
   c. Proactive aggression represents physical acts of hurting; reactive aggression refers to social-exclusionary behaviors, such as gossiping.
   d. Proactive aggression refers to physical acts that are immediate in their effects on victims; reactive aggression refers to acts that have delayed but long-term effects.

Essay

7. As a teacher or other professional who works with children or adolescents, how might you enhance their understandings of adults and peers? Describe at least three specific things you might do.

8. Imagine that you have been asked to give a presentation on how to foster good social skills in children. What key points might you make?

Answers to Sample Test Questions

1. d—The concept *imaginary audience* refers to the belief that one is the center of everybody else's attention.

2. b—Teachers can better foster a positive sense of self by focusing students' attention on their own improvement, rather than on peers' performance.

3. b—Social information processing involves thinking about and interpreting social situations, retrieving potential responses, and making decisions about which response is apt to be most productive.

4. c—Prejudice is an example of a *social-cognitive bias*, a mental "shortcut" that enables people to deal with their environment quickly and efficiently.

5. d—*Prosocial behavior* is an action taken to help another, such as sharing or comforting.

6. a—*Proactive aggression* is a planned, calculated event; *reactive aggression* occurs in response to frustration or provocation.

7. Your response is likely to depend on the age of children or adolescents with whom you are most familiar, but it might include some of the following strategies:
   - Talk with youngsters about your thoughts and feelings, use psychological terms, and discuss other people's viewpoints.
   - Conduct group discussions in which youngsters share differing perspectives about an issue or problem.
   - Talk with youngsters about the various nonverbal cues (e.g., the "body language") that may be indicators of people's emotional states.
   - Ask youngsters about their interpretations of literature, historical events, and scientific data sets. Point out the existence of different perspectives on the same information.
   - As a way of breaking down stereotypes, help youngsters discover that members of any single cultural group are often quite different from one another, and that most members of any particular group have many strengths and other positive qualities.
   - Explain what prejudice is and actively work to reduce it.
   - Provide extra assistance and support to those youngsters with disabilities who have trouble understanding other people, making inferences about others' perspectives, or figuring out how people's actions are guided by their perceptions and intentions.

8. Teachers and other practitioners can use a variety of strategies to teach social skills. In formulating your response, you might draw from material in the section "Fostering Effective Interpersonal Skills" and from the Development and Practice feature "Teaching Social Skills." The section "Fostering the Development of Social Cognition" and the feature "Encouraging Social Perspective Taking" may also be helpful, in that advancements in social cognition should also lead to advancements in social skills. Following are examples of strategies you might mention:

    • Teach children specific social skills, such as how to start a conversation, say positive things to another person, ask for help, and express disagreement. Adults can do this by modeling, describing desirable ways to make social overtures, and giving children feedback on their initial attempts at new social behaviors.

    • Ask children to brainstorm various approaches to solving social dilemmas.

    • Give children concrete feedback about the effective and ineffective ways in which they interact with their peers.

    • Encourage children to solve some social problems themselves, while also being available to provide assistance if conflicts escalate.

    • Label appropriate social behaviors (e.g., "Thank you for *cooperating* with Susan").

    • Provide structure for cooperative learning groups. For instance, teachers can assign roles that children can adopt, enabling every group member to contribute to the group's overall success.

    • Notice and recognize children's positive social actions. When adults notice that children are caring for peers, sharing belongings, and using kind words, they can acknowledge these good behaviors.

    • Expose children to numerous models of prosocial behavior (e.g., through educational television programs such as *Barney and Friends*).

    • Involve children in community service projects.

    • Establish rules that prohibit physical aggression. Children must learn that their schools and organized social groups do not tolerate hitting, fighting, or weapon use.

    • Implement a peer mediation program.

Chapter 13

DEVELOPMENT OF MOTIVATION AND SELF-REGULATION

Chapter Overview

Once children have acquired an ability to do something, their motivation is a key factor in whether they actually *use* that ability. Although youngsters are sometimes motivated by the reinforcers and punishments that follow various behaviors, oftentimes their motivation comes from *within*—for instance, from their interests, goals, priorities, and natural curiosity about the world. Their beliefs about whether they can be successful in various endeavors also come into play: Few children are likely to persevere at a task when they believe they have insufficient ability to do it well.

The "within" aspects of motivation—aspects collectively known as *intrinsic motivation*—are important elements of *self-regulation*, the process of directing and controlling one's own actions in productive ways. Yet to regulate their own learning and behavior, youngsters need skills as well as motivation. For instance, they must set reasonable goals for themselves, have strategies for keeping themselves on task for lengthy periods, and evaluate their own performance in accordance with appropriate criteria. Such skills develop only gradually over time, and not all youngsters acquire them.

Ideally, self-regulation also involves behaving in ways that are consistent with general principles of right and wrong. Beliefs about what actions are morally right and wrong continue to evolve over the course of childhood and adolescence, and often throughout much of adulthood as well.

Possible Knowledge, Beliefs, and Misconceptions Related to Chapter Content

People often have many misconceptions about motivation, self-regulation, and moral development, and such misconceptions may interfere with an accurate understanding of the material presented in Chapter 13. As you read the chapter, be on the lookout for the following:

1. Many adults think of low-achieving youngsters as being "unmotivated." Actually, children and adolescents are almost always motivated in one way or another. However, some may be less interested in the activities that adults have in mind for them (e.g., mastering academic subject matter) than they are in other things (e.g., extracurricular activities or social relationships). Furthermore, many youngsters *do* want to do well in school but do not believe they have the ability to be successful, and so they may misbehave in class, skip school, or in other ways avoid tasks at which they expect to do poorly.

2. Educators often use the term *reinforce* to mean giving students additional information or providing additional experiences related to a topic (e.g., "We can reinforce children's

knowledge of math facts by giving them lots of practice"). They then confuse this meaning of the term with the behaviorist meaning of the term, which is quite different (see the section "Effects of Extrinsic Rewards and Punishments").

3. Many people think of motivation as a relatively stable characteristic that "resides" exclusively inside of children. In fact, motivation is often situation-specific and can be enhanced in a variety of ways (see the section "Motivating Children and Adolescents").

4. Some aspiring professionals who plan to work with children and adolescents think that failure invariably leads to low self-esteem. Actually, failure can sometimes be motivating *if* youngsters attribute it to factors they can change, such as the amount of effort they put forth or the particular strategies they use to tackle a task (see the section "Development of Attributions").

5. Many prospective teachers and coaches think that competition among children is motivating. In reality, very few youngsters perform at their best when they must compete with their peers (e.g., when they are asked to see who can be the "best" or "fastest," or when they are graded on a curve). Most young people learn more effectively when they focus on mastering skills rather than on being better than others (see the discussion of *mastery goals* and *performance goals* in the section "Development of Goals").

6. As youngsters move to the secondary school grades (and especially as they begin high school), many formerly high-achieving students begin to flounder—perhaps skipping classes, "forgetting" homework, and the like. Although many teachers interpret their declining performance as reflecting lack of motivation, oftentimes it is instead the result of insufficient *self-regulation* skills (see the section "Development of Self-Regulation").

7. Some readers will be surprised at how early in life children acquire a basic sense of right and wrong. In the section "Developmental Trends in Morality," you will learn that children acquire some basic ideas about goodness and naughtiness even before age 2. Thus, like in so many developmental areas, children show rudimentary abilities in the very early years, but with age and experience, they continue to expand on these abilities, refine them as limitations surface, and extend them to new contexts.

8. Religious beliefs certainly influence youngsters' judgments about right and wrong. Some readers may be surprised to learn that many researchers have examined children's moral reasoning *without* also considering children's religious beliefs. As a general rule, developmental psychologists who study moral development tend to focus on how children's moral reasoning may develop somewhat independently of religious upbringing.

9. Some readers may think that peers typically have a negative influence on moral development, especially in adolescence. Yet by and large, peer interactions have a *positive* rather than negative effect. Discussions and arguments with peers can lead young people to acquire increasingly sophisticated ideas about what is fair and right. When adults insist on high behavioral standards, children and adolescents must often comply without argument, knowing that they will be disciplined if they're disobedient. With peers, however, youngsters are on equal ground and so can openly exchange opinions and feelings; in the process, they may encounter perspectives different from theirs and, as a result, change their *own* perspectives on various issues (see the section "Factors Affecting Moral Development").

10. Some readers may have seen or heard media accounts about the "declining moral values" of our society, and particularly in young people. There is no evidence to indicate that moral values have declined in the past few decades, or even in the past few centuries. Furthermore, some of the methods that prominent political and religious figures have proposed (e.g., executing firm control over children's behavior or giving specific instruction in moral values) are relatively *ineffective* in promoting moral development (Turiel, 2002). You should note, too, that advanced moral reasoning is *not* something that parents and teachers can easily impose on young people; instead, adults are more likely to promote moral development if they build on youngsters' current levels of moral reasoning and help them to gradually construct more complex understandings (see the section "Promoting Moral Development").

Suggested Supplementary Readings

The following readings, presented in the final section of this *Study Guide and Reader*, are relevant to Chapter 13:

Reading 13-1: The Need for Physical Affection: Wire "Mothers" Aren't Enough

Reading 13-2: The Nature of Negative Reinforcement

Reading 13-3: Using Punishment When You Must

Reading 13-4: Cognitive-Developmental Perspectives on Moral Development: Piaget's and Kohlberg's Theories

Reading 13-5: Do No Harm: When Children Ignore an Authority Figure

Reading 13-6: Children's Understanding of Moral Versus Conventional Transgressions

Reading 13-7: Justice Versus Care Orientations in Moral Reasoning

Reading 13-8: Just Communities

CHAPTER OUTLINE	FOCUS QUESTIONS

MOTIVATION
 	
    Effects of Extrinsic Rewards and Punishments
 	
    Development of Intrinsic Motivation
 	
    Development of Goals
 	
    Development of Attributions
 	
    Diversity in Motivation
 	
    Motivating Children and Adolescents
	• In what various ways might motivation manifest itself in children's and adolescents' behavior?
	
	• Explain how *extrinsic motivation* and *intrinsic motivation* are different. Give an example of each.
	
	• In one or two sentences, summarize the nature of operant conditioning. Distinguish between *primary reinforcers* and *secondary reinforcers*.
	
	• Why is the ability to delay gratification important?
	
	• What are *vicarious reinforcement* and *punishment*?
	
	• What factors seem to underlie intrinsic motivation? How does intrinsic motivation change with age?
	
	• Why might intrinsic motivation for learning school subject matter decrease over the school years?
	
	• Why are *mastery goals* more beneficial for children's learning and development than *performance goals*?
	
	• What forms might youngsters' *social goals* take?
	
	• In what various ways do children and adolescents try to juggle their multiple goals?
	
	• What are *attributions*? What kinds of attributions lead children to be optimistic about future success?
	
	• Describe the difference between an *entity view* and an *incremental view* of ability.
	
	• How do attributions change with age?
	
	• Characterize children who have a *mastery orientation* versus those who have *learned helplessness*.
	
	• What environmental factors lead children to acquire various kinds of attributions?
	
	• Describe several ways in which motivation may differ for children of different genders and cultural groups?
	
	• What strategies can adults use to foster motivation in children and adolescents?
	
	• Who are *students at risk*? What strategies can educators and other adults use to help them succeed?

CHAPTER OUTLINE	FOCUS QUESTIONS
SELF-REGULATION Developmental Trends in Self-Regulation Conditions That Foster Self-Regulation Diversity in Self-Regulation Promoting Self-Regulation	• What capabilities does *self-regulation* involve? • What trends characterize the development of self-regulation? • What environmental conditions tend to promote self-regulation? • What strategies can adults use to help young people become more self-regulating?
MORAL REASONING AND BEHAVIOR Developmental Trends in Morality Factors Affecting Moral Development Diversity in Moral Development Promoting Moral Development	• What developmental trends are seen in children's moral reasoning and behavior? • How are *moral transgressions* and *conventional transgressions* different? Might they require different kinds of interventions in the classroom? • What emotions accompany children's awareness that they have not lived up to moral standards? • What is a *moral dilemma*? Can you think of moral dilemmas that you've encountered in your own life? • Summarize Kohlberg's three levels of moral development, and give an example of reasoning at each level. • Describe several factors that promote moral development. • In what ways, and to what extent, might youngsters' moral reasoning differ as a function of their gender and cultural background? • What strategies can parents, teachers, and other adults use to promote children's moral development?

Chapter Glossary

Attribution. Belief about the cause of one's success or failure.

Care orientation. Focus on nurturance and concern for others in moral decision making.

Conventional morality. Acceptance of society's conventions regarding right and wrong; behaving to please others or to live up to society's expectations for appropriate behavior.

Conventional transgression. Action that violates society's general guidelines (often unspoken) for socially acceptable behavior.

Delay of gratification. Foregoing small immediate rewards for larger ones at a future time.

Distributive justice. Beliefs about what constitutes people's fair share of a valued commodity.

Entity view of ability. Belief that ability is a "thing" that is relatively permanent and unchangeable.

Extrinsic motivation. Motivation provoked by the external consequences that certain behaviors bring.

Guilt. Feeling of discomfort when one inflicts damage or causes someone else pain or distress.

Incremental view of ability. Belief that ability can and does improve with effort and practice.

Induction. Act of explaining why a certain behavior is unacceptable, usually with a focus on the pain or distress that someone has caused another.

Internalized motivation. Adoption of behaviors that others value, whether or not one's environment reinforces those behaviors.

Intrinsic motivation. Motivation resulting from personal characteristics or inherent in the task being performed.

Justice orientation. Focus on individual rights in moral decision making.

Learned helplessness. General belief that one is incapable of accomplishing tasks and has little or no control of the environment.

Mastery goal. Desire to acquire additional knowledge or master new skills.

Mastery orientation. General belief that one is capable of accomplishing challenging tasks, accompanied by an intent to master such tasks.

Moral development. Advancements in reasoning and behaving in accordance with self-constructed standards of right and wrong.

Moral dilemma. Situation in which there is no clear-cut answer regarding the morally right thing to do.

Moral transgression. Action that causes damage or harm or in some other way infringes on the needs and rights of others.

Motivation. State that energizes, directs, and sustains behavior.

Performance goal. Desire to look good and receive favorable judgments from others.

Personal interest. Long-term, relatively stable interest in a particular topic or activity.

Postconventional morality. Behaving in accordance with self-developed abstract principles regarding right and wrong.

Preconventional morality. A lack of internalized standards about right and wrong; making decisions based on what is best for oneself, without regard for others' needs and feelings.

Primary reinforcer. Stimulus or event that satisfies a built-in biological need.

Reinforcer. Consequence of a response that leads to an increased frequency of that response.

Secondary reinforcer. Stimulus or event that becomes reinforcing over time through its association with one or more other reinforcers.

Self-efficacy. Belief that one is capable of executing certain behaviors or reaching certain goals.

Self-evaluation. Judging one's own performance in accordance with predetermined criteria.

Self-instructions. Specific directions that one gives oneself while performing a complex behavior; a predetermined form of *self-talk*.

Self-monitoring. Process of observing and recording one's own behavior.

Self-motivation. Intentionally using certain strategies to keep oneself on task during a dull but important activity.

Self-regulation. Directing and controlling one's own actions.

Self-reinforcement. Self-imposed pleasurable consequence for a desired behavior.

Sense of self-determination. Belief that one has some choice and control regarding the future course of one's life.

Shame. Feeling of embarrassment or humiliation after failing to meet certain standards for moral behavior.

Situational interest. Interest evoked temporarily by something in the environment.

Social goal. Goal related to establishing or maintaining good relationships with other people.

Student at risk. Student who has a high probability of failing to acquire the minimal academic skills necessary for success in the adult world.

Value. Belief that a particular activity has direct or indirect benefits.

Vicarious punishment. Phenomenon in which a child decreases a certain response after seeing someone else punished for that response.

Vicarious reinforcement. Phenomenon in which a child increases a certain response after seeing someone else reinforced for that response.

Table 13–1. Applying Concepts in Child Development: Observing Motivations in Youngsters' Behaviors

This table is a complete version of the table that appears at the end of Chapter 13 in the textbook. Compare your entries in the blank cells in the textbook table with our entries here. Keep in mind that there isn't necessarily a single "right" entry for any particular cell.

Age	A Youngster's Experience	Developmental Concepts *Identifying Motivational Phenomena*	Implications *Motivating Productive Behaviors*
Infancy (Birth–2)	Now that she can easily crawl from place to place, 9-month-old Regina is into everything. Her child care provider once found her trying to stick a couple of house keys into an electrical outlet. And all the cleaning supplies under the sink are a particular source of interest.	Even in infancy, children have a natural *curiosity* about their world and are eager to learn as much as they can about it. Children are especially intrigued by new and unusual objects, which evoke *situational interest*.	Make infants' and toddlers' environments safe for exploration. For example, put plastic plugs in electrical outlets and child-proof safety latches on cabinet doors.
Early Childhood (2–6)	When her mother returns to work after a lengthy maternity leave, 3½-year-old Laura begins attending an all-day preschool. Laura's teachers find her behavior to be a challenge from the very first day. "She shows no patience or self-restraint," one teacher says. "When she wants something, she wants it *now*, and she'll throw a tantrum if she doesn't get it. If I immediately go to her, I can usually calm her down. But I never know when she might explode again."	Like many young children, Laura shows an inability to *delay gratification*. Her teacher is possibly *reinforcing* her tantrums with immediate attention. Perhaps Laura's mother or other caregivers have previously reinforced such tantrums, giving Laura little reason to learn to control her impulses or acquire other self-regulation skills.	Reinforce young children for appropriate behaviors (e.g., give a child one-on-one attention when she is engaged in a productive activity). Impose mild punishments for inappropriate behaviors (e.g., place an unruly child in a short "time-out" situation in which she gets no attention from others). Also teach strategies for delaying gratification (e.g., suggest that a child repeatedly tell herself, "I can play with the toy longer if I wait for my turn").
Middle Childhood (6–10)	After years of struggling with basic reading skills, 10-year-old Kellen becomes increasingly irritable and soon stops doing his homework. One day his mother finds him curled up under his desk, crying and saying, "I can't do this anymore." Mother takes him to a psychiatrist, who concludes that Kellen has dyslexia. (This is the same Kellen whose story appears at the beginning of Chapter 12.)	After repeated failures despite his best efforts, Kellen has developed *learned helplessness* about his ability to read. Learned helplessness is common in children with dyslexia and other learning disabilities.	Give children the guidance and support they need to be successful. Seek the advice of specialists when children show unusual delays in acquiring certain skills. Do *not* dismiss chronic problems as being just a "phase" that children will "grow out of."

table continues

Table 13–1 continued

Age	A Youngster's Experience	Developmental Concepts *Identifying Motivational Phenomena*	Implications *Motivating Productive Behaviors*
Early Adolescence (10–14)	During his third-period class, a middle school teacher often sees 12-year-old JoBeth passing notes to one or more of her classmates. Inevitably, the other students giggle after reading what she has written. Before class one day, the teacher takes JoBeth aside and tells her, "This note passing has to stop. It's getting to be a distraction to the entire class." JoBeth looks down sheepishly. "I'm sorry, Mr. Roberts," she says. "I'm just trying to make the other kids like me. Jeremy Smith tells jokes all the time, and he's one of the most popular kids in the school."	JoBeth's desire for popularity reflects a *social goal*. In observing Jeremy's success telling jokes, JoBeth is experiencing *vicarious reinforcement*, which leads to an increase in her own joke-telling behavior.	Provide opportunities for young adolescents to interact with their peers and in other ways achieve their social goals. Teach them social skills that will help them interact effectively with others.
Late Adolescence (14–18)	Even as a preschooler, Emmanuel showed a keen interest in basketball, and throughout his childhood and early adolescence, he spent many hours playing basketball with his friends at a nearby Boys' Club. Since beginning high school, he's twice tried out for the varsity high school team, but without success. "I'm just too short," he reasons. "Anyway, it's probably better that I focus on my schoolwork, which will help me get into a good college."	Emmanuel has a *personal interest* in basketball. However, his failure in making the varsity team decreases his *self-efficacy* for the sport. He places less *value* on it and instead turns his attention to academic achievement, which he perceives to be more useful in helping him achieve his long-term goal of attending a prestigious college.	Incorporate teenagers' personal interests into academic subject matter. Provide outlets through which *all* youngsters can pursue interest areas that are apt to promote their physical and psychological well-being (e.g., create nonselective intramural programs for all who want to participate in team sports).

Application Exercise #1: Analyzing Motivational and Self-Regulatory Processes

Explain each of the following scenarios using concepts and principles of motivation, self-regulation, or moral development.

1. Mr. Quah assures his high school chemistry students that they can master the symbols for each of the elements (e.g., *O* is oxygen, *Au* is gold, *Hg* is mercury, etc.) if they study them a little bit each night. But Myra insists that she can't. "I'm just no good at remembering science stuff," she says.

2. Just before he begins his piano practice, 10-year-old George asks his mother for a bag of M&M candies. "I'm going to put one in my mouth each time I finish one of the songs that my piano teacher assigned," he tells her.

3. Three-year-old Ramon is riding a tricycle in the play yard at his preschool and accidentally sideswipes Dara, scraping her leg. As a tearful Dara is being patched up by a teacher, Ramon, looking sheepish, approaches her and offers her his teddy bear for comfort.

4. Fourteen-year-old Jasmine usually sits in class slouched in her seat with a defiant "you-can't-make-me-do-anything" attitude. After repeated efforts to motivate her have failed, her science teacher Mr. Jones finally tells her, "OK, Jasmine, you don't have to do a thing in this class if you don't want to. Let's move your desk to the very back of the room, where you can just sit quietly for the entire class. If you change your mind and decide you want to start learning something, you can join us." Jasmine initially seems delighted with this new arrangement and spends the first few days of her newfound freedom pretending to nap. Meanwhile, Mr. Jones and the other students have learned to ignore her and go about their business. After a week or so, Jasmine approaches Mr. Jones and says, "I think I'm ready to join the class now."

5. Although 17-year-old Jacqueline doesn't always put a lot of effort into her homework assignments, she works very hard to perfect a personal essay for her college application.

6. When Father bakes a cake for 2-year-old Sabella's birthday, Sabella asks for a piece. Father explains that they need to save the cake for later in the day, when other family members will be home to help them celebrate. "Cake now!" Sabella screams.

7. When a fifth grader tells 6-year-old Emmy that it's OK to punch a classmate in the stomach, Emmy replies, "No, it's not. It's not nice to hurt other kids."

8. The students in Ms. Chotkowski's middle school art class willingly clean up their materials and work spaces at the end of class each day, even though they don't necessarily enjoy doing so.

9. Four-year-old Laqueesha tells you quite emphatically that she wants to be a veterinarian. Yet a month later she tells you with equal assurance that she plans to be an airplane pilot.

10. Sixteen-year-old Tony will work long hours trying to fix a car engine that doesn't work properly, yet he gives up quickly when he can't solve a math problem.

11. Nine-year-old Richard often impulsively blurts out answers in class, thus preventing other students from having a chance to respond. One day his teacher takes him aside to mention the problem and then gives him a sheet of graph paper to tape to the corner of his desk. "Just make a check mark in one of the squares every time you find yourself calling out an answer," she tells him. Richard willingly complies, and within a week his behavior has improved markedly.

12. The day that Marta turns 6, she brings a box of cupcakes to her kindergarten class so that everyone can celebrate with her. When she distributes the cupcakes at snack time, she finds that she has three left over and so gives a second one to herself and to her friends Annie and Elizabeth. "That's not fair!" several of the other children call out. "Yes, it is," Annie responds, "because I'm Marta's best friend."

13. When a stray dog runs into Mr. Landy's fifth-grade classroom, all the children immediately stop what they are doing to watch the dog.

14. When 2-year-old Matthew lifts his arms up and yells "Up!" a caregiver at his child care center picks him up and gives him attention. Lisette, also 2, watches the process. Shortly thereafter, she reaches toward the same caregiver and says, "Up!"

15. When 13-year-old Rachel does poorly at a dance recital, she says to her dance instructor, "I practiced really *hard* for the recital, honestly I did. But I wasn't feeling very well that night. I think I might have been coming down with the flu." In reality, Rachel was feeling fine that evening but hadn't adequately practiced for the recital.

Answers to Application Exercise #1

1. Mr. Quah and Myra have different *attributions* for success at the task. Mr. Quah attributes students' success to reasonable effort that is spread out over a period of time, but Myra attributes it to a relatively permanent ability that she doesn't have.

2. George is engaging in *self-reinforcement* for practicing his assigned piano music.

3. Ramon is showing *guilt* about the fact that he was the cause of Dara's discomfort.

4. By giving Jasmine the choice to participate or not participate in class, Mr. Jones is enhancing her *sense of self-determination*. Perhaps Jasmine rejoins the class because she finds it interesting (it must certainly be more interesting than doing nothing at the back of the room). Furthermore, participating in class allows Jasmine to interact with her peers, thus addressing her *need for relatedness*.

5. An important factor in intrinsic motivation is *value*: Youngsters believe that there are direct or indirect benefits of performing a task. In this situation, Jacqueline believes that writing a good essay is going to help her meet her long-term *goal* of going to the college of her choice.

6. Like most 2-year-olds, Sabella has trouble *delaying gratification*.

7. Emmy is using *internal standards* to evaluate the appropriateness of punching another child. By age 4, most children realize that causing harm to someone else is wrong regardless of what another person might tell them. Meanwhile, by advocating punching, the fifth grader is showing a definite delay in moral development. One possibility is that this child has a conduct disorder (see Chapter 11).

8. The students are displaying *internalized motivation*: They have adopted behaviors that their teacher values.

9. Young children give little thought to their career goals and change them frequently.

10. Children and adolescents are more likely to persist at a task for which they have high *self-efficacy*. Tony appears to have high self-efficacy for solving automotive problems but low self-efficacy for solving math problems.

11. Richard is engaging in *self-monitoring*, which often leads to improvements in behavior.

12. The children are concerned about *distributive justice*. Like Annie, young children often think that any form of distribution that meets one's own needs and desires is "fair." Some of the other children may be equally concerned about *their* needs, or they may be beginning to view distributive justice as involving equal treatment for everyone. In this situation, the teacher should have suggested an alternative for the three extra cupcakes, perhaps giving them to other staff members (e.g., the principal, the school nurse) or sending them back

home for Marta's family to enjoy. (*Note:* Teachers should be aware of any dietary restrictions students may have—for instance, some may be diabetic—before serving cupcakes or other sweets in class.)

13. New, unusual, and surprising events often evoke *situational interest*.

14. Lisette imitates Matthew's behavior after she sees Matthew being reinforced for it. *Vicarious reinforcement* has been at work here.

15. Many adolescents are aware that different *attributions* elicit different responses from others. Rachel knows that she is more likely to get a sympathetic response from her instructor if she attributes her failure to something beyond her control (e.g., an illness).

Application Exercise #2: Applying Distinctions in Moral Reasoning

In the following scenarios, youngsters are faced with various moral issues. Use one or more of the following italicized concepts from Chapter 13 to explain people's perspectives:
   • Form of transgression: *moral* or *conventional*
   • Level of moral reasoning (Kohlberg): *preconventional*, *conventional*, or *postconventional*
   • Orientation (Gilligan): *justice* or *care*

1.   Two 12-year-olds argue about the meaning of a school rule. The rule states, "Use kind and respectful words." Glenda interprets this rule to mean that people should say nice things to one another. Being kind and respectful, according to Glenda, is being polite and affirming— saying things that make a person feel good. For her, the rule should be interpreted from the perspective of nurturing other people and maintaining positive relationships. Ricky has an entirely different view. He interprets this rule to mean that one should be honest. For him, it is not respectful to hide feelings of anger or dissatisfaction. He sees it as his right to talk honestly, even if his words are hurtful, and it is the listener's right to hear the truth rather than a lie. How do Ricky and Glenda use differing *orientations* in their reasoning?

2.   Mr. Myles talks with his middle-school advisee group about the name-calling he often hears when he walks through the halls. He reminds students about the school's rules regarding appropriate behavior. He explains that these rules have been designed to protect everyone's basic human rights. When he's done, Missy whispers to Bernard, "We'd better stop talking when we see Mr. Myles coming down the hall." How does *level of moral reasoning* help us to understand how Mr. Myles and Missy view name-calling?

3.   Mukta's family has recently moved to the United States from India, and he enrolls as a third grader at Middleton Elementary School. Mukta seems stunned by the menu at lunch and is equally shocked at the eating habits of his American peers. Mukta's classmates do not understand why he is agitated, and some of them find *his* eating habits a little odd. How might variations in perceptions of *form of transgression* help to understand this scenario?

4.   Members of a high school service club work hard to earn money to benefit children with cystic fibrosis. Ms. Waxler, the English teacher who serves as advisor for the group, notices that some club members talk about their responsibility to help people whose health is compromised. Yet other members seem more interested in getting Ms. Waxler's approval or gaining recognition in the local newspaper. How can we use *level of moral reasoning* to explain the various motives that the club members have to help others?

5.   Brenda, a socially outgoing 7-year-old, sees her neighbor in the school auditorium. The neighbor, Ms. Mannie Franklin, is the school librarian and computer specialist. Brenda knows the woman as "Mannie," as Mannie and Brenda's mother are good friends, and Brenda has been encouraged to refer to her by her first name whenever they've talked in the neighborhood. She does so in the auditorium, saying, "Hi, Mannie!" Brenda's friends are taken by surprise. "Her name is Ms. Franklin," one girl reminds her. What *form of transgression* seems to be operating here?

6. Jennifer, who has a cognitive disability that affects her social judgments and behaviors, is excluded from many of the social interactions in her class. Her peers dismiss her as "weird" and don't invite her to join their recess activities, lunch groups, or after-school get-togethers. They believe they have every right to choose whom they do and do not spend their time with, whereas their teacher, Ms. Sample, worries that they are hurting Jennifer's feelings. How is *orientation* relevant here?

7. Mr. Arias has organized his fourth-grade class into cooperative learning groups for science lessons. His students seem willing to help one another only if they believe they are being helped in return. What *level of moral reasoning* do these students exhibit?

Answers to Application Exercise #2

1. Glenda seems to be operating out of a care orientation. Ricky, in contrast, seems to be operating out of a justice orientation.

2. Mr. Myles is talking about abstract principles of human rights, which is a reflection of Kohlberg's Level 3, postconventional morality. Missy does not want to get caught and so seems to be operating at Level 1, preconventional morality.

3. It is possible that the menu and eating habits in the American school are at odds with Mukta's moral code (e.g., in the Hindu religion, cattle are sacred and must not be slaughtered, let alone eaten) and so in his mind are moral transgressions. In contrast, to the extent that the other students find Mukta's eating habits strange, they are apt to interpret his preferences as reflecting different conventions.

4. Some club members seem motivated to obtain approval from their leader or recognition from the community. They are at Level 2, conventional morality, and more specifically at Stage 3, "Good boy/good girl." Other members appear to be operating at Level 3, postconventional morality, and more specifically at Stage 5, "Social contract." They believe they have a moral obligation to help others in need.

5. The children believe that Brenda is violating the convention of using a title (e.g., "Mr." or "Ms.") when referring to an adult at school.

6. Ms. Sample sees the children's exclusion of Jennifer as a care issue. In contrast, the children are taking a justice perspective and see the matter as one in which personal human rights (including the right to choose companions) take precedence.

7. Students in Mr. Arias's class seem to be operating at Level 1, preconventional morality. Specifically, they are at Stage 2, "Exchange of favors." They help one another, but this arrangement breaks down when it appears not to be reciprocal.

Application Exercise #3: Identifying Developmentally Appropriate Practices

Which of the following practices are appropriate for the age level, and which are not? Defend your choices using concepts and principles related to motivation, self-regulation, or moral development.

1. When he finds two 7-year-old boys fighting, a teacher on playground duty tells them, "I don't know what's going on here, but as far as I could tell, Jeremy started it. Jeremy, you sit down by that big tree over there, and stay there for 20 minutes. Brian, you sit on that bench for 10 minutes. I don't want to hear a peep out of either one of you until your times are up. After that, you can resume what you were doing before, but I want you to stay away from each other for the rest of the day."

2. In his tenth-grade art class, Mr. Ramirez asks his students to submit six projects each semester. During fall semester, he sets the due dates for the projects, spacing the dates evenly throughout the semester. During spring semester, he lets his students set their own due dates for their projects, with the stipulation that they set the dates at least a week apart from one another.

3. When working with his junior high school cross-country team, Mr. Cummins assures team members that they all have the ability to be good long-distance runners but that daily practice is essential for helping them build up their endurance.

4. When 3-year-old Juliet hits a playmate hard enough to make him cry, her child care provider yells, "Bad! Don't do that! That's against the rules."

5. Mr. Guyver teaches a mixed-age classroom of fourth and fifth graders. He sees many advantages to the multi-age grouping, including the chance to build on children's understandings and concepts over a two-year period, form cooperative student work groups, and give considerable attention to basic literary skills before students move on to middle school. However, the large variations in students' social behaviors puzzle him. He is particularly amazed about the many beliefs that the students express regarding what's right and wrong, and why. Mr. Guyver deals with this diversity by giving repeated explanations about students' rights and obligations. He tells his students that they are a "mini-society" and need to live as such, seeking equality, justice, and human rights for everyone.

6. At age $1\frac{1}{2}$, Anson tries to feed his mother a cookie that has fallen on the floor. Mom makes a face and says, "No, I don't want that. It's all dirty and might give me a tummy ache."

7. High school mathematics teacher Ms. Shump frequently points out how certain algebraic procedures might be used in such diverse occupations as nursing, carpentry, and retail sales.

8. In his efforts to get his second graders excited about learning how to spell, Mr. Timlin tells them how important spelling is in many careers.

9. When 3-year-old Angie asks Mr. Werner if he will help her put on her jacket for outdoor play time, he is surprised, because he knows that Angie is perfectly capable of putting on her own jacket. Nevertheless, he agrees to help her.

10. Ms. Bergeron tells her fourth graders that they do not need to ask permission to leave the room every time they want to get a drink of water or use the restroom. Instead, they sign themselves out on a small dry-erase board by the door and sign themselves back in when they return. She reminds them that they should keep their trips short: only a minute for getting a drink, and a maximum of five minutes for a trip to the restroom.

11. A high school driver education teacher warns his students, "Be sure to stay within the speed limit. After all, there may be a traffic officer lurking in wait when you least expect one."

12. Ms. Andersen is a home care provider for several 2-year-olds who live in her neighborhood. She has been trying to teach the children to bring their cups and plates to the kitchen after they've finished their lunches, but so far she's had little success. She decides to give them dessert (usually a piece of fruit, low-fat cookie, or box of raisins) only when they bring their dishes to the kitchen.

13. Brittney, a junior high school student, asserts that skipping school occasionally is OK because her older brother says that it is. Mr. Castaneda responds by saying, "Let's think about that for a minute. For many years now, the rule in this country has been that children must go to school until they're at least sixteen years old. Lawmakers know that our society will function more smoothly if its citizens know how to read and write."

14. On Monday morning, Ms. Murphy tells her 3- and 4-year-old preschoolers, "If everyone can play nicely this week, with *no fighting*, we will all go to Baskin Robbins for ice cream cones on Friday afternoon."

Answers to Application Exercise #3

1. Not appropriate. Each boy should have a chance to explain his side of the conflict; in doing so, the two boys might acquire a better understanding of each other's perspectives, as well as better perspective-taking ability more generally (see Chapter 12). Furthermore, the teacher should talk with the boys about the physical harm they might have inflicted on each other if the fight had escalated (*induction*). Note, too, that the teacher has imposed greater punishment on Jeremy than on Brian without knowing for sure that Jeremy was truly more at fault than Brian; in doing so, the teacher is modeling inequitable treatment of others.

2. Appropriate. By giving students control over an aspect of classroom life, Mr. Ramirez is promoting a sense of self-determination, which should enhance their intrinsic motivation. The students have already had some experience with completing art projects, so they should have a reasonable understanding of how long it takes to do each one.

3. Appropriate. By adolescence, young people in Western cultures attribute their successes and failures more to ability than to effort. Mr. Cummins is acknowledging that cross-country running *is* partly a function of ability but pointing out that effort, too, will make an appreciable difference.

4. Not appropriate. Certainly Juliet must have some kind of consequence for hitting another child. But simply yelling at her for breaking a rule is unlikely to promote moral development. A better approach would be to point out that she has caused pain to someone else (induction) and impose an appropriate consequence for her misbehavior (perhaps a short time-out away from peers and toys).

5. Not appropriate. Mr. Guyver is focusing his moral arguments at an abstract, postconventional level, whereas the majority of his students are probably reasoning in preconventional and conventional ways. Mr. Guyver needs to communicate with his students on various levels, perhaps by clarifying rules they need to follow, imposing consequences for breaking them, and establishing expectations for fairness. He needs to do so in a concrete fashion, as his students are unlikely to understand his abstract exhortations about justice and human rights. One possible strategy is to set up a concrete system of student government through which students can have firsthand experiences related to the principles he espouses.

6. Appropriate. Mom is using *induction* to explain why a behavior is undesirable (it might make her sick). In addition, she's using the verb *want*, which may enhance Anson's theory of mind by helping him learn that other people's thoughts and feelings are not necessarily the same as their own (see the discussion of theory of mind in Chapter 12).

7. Appropriate. Adolescents increasingly value activities and skills that will help them reach their long-term goals.

8. Not appropriate. Young children have trouble conceptualizing a "future" that is abstract and many years off. They are more likely to respond to the need for good spelling in their current activities (e.g., in writing stories for their classmates or letters to their relatives).

9. Not appropriate. Children are more likely to become self-regulating when adults give them age-appropriate opportunities to be independent. Mr. Werner might ask Angie if there is a particular reason why she needs help today, but he should not help her perform a task she is able to do on her own.

10. Appropriate. Children need age-appropriate opportunities for independence, and 9- and 10-year-olds are certainly capable of following the procedures Ms. Bergeron has described.

11. Not appropriate. The teacher is focusing on the benefits of staying within the speed limit only for students themselves; he is not helping students look at the broader picture of why speed limits are important. At the high school level, most students understand that rules and conventions help society run more smoothly and that excessive speed endangers people's safety. From Kohlberg's perspective, most high school students reason at the conventional level—they define right and wrong in terms of meeting someone's approval (Stage 3) or obeying society's rules (Stage 4). By focusing on the potential punishment for speeding, the teacher is using preconventional reasoning with these students. Ideally, he should be presenting reasons for following the speed limit that reflect reasoning one stage above where students are (i.e., Stage 4 reasoning for some students and Stage 5 reasoning for others).

12. Appropriate. Extrinsic reinforcers can be quite effective when children have no intrinsic motivation to behave in a desired manner.

13. Appropriate. Challenging children's beliefs about controversial topics helps children acquire more advanced reasoning. From Kohlberg's perspective, Brittney is reasoning at Kohlberg's Stage 3, looking to an authority figure (her older brother) for guidance about what's right and wrong. Mr. Castaneda is using Stage 4 reasoning (law and order)—an argument just one stage above that of Brittney's reasoning.

14. Not appropriate. Young children have difficulty delaying gratification. They are more likely to respond to small, immediate rewards than to larger, more delayed ones.

<u>Sample Test Questions</u>

Use the following multiple-choice and essay questions to evaluate and strengthen your understanding of selected concepts in the chapter.

Multiple-Choice

1. Five-year-old Marjorie discovers that by throwing a temper tantrum she can get whatever she wants from her parents. Her 3-year-old brother Jacob sees what happens when Marjorie throws a tantrum, and before long he too is throwing tantrums to get the things he wants. Jacob is showing the effects of
    a. Intermittent reinforcement
    b. Intrinsic motivation
    c. Vicarious reinforcement
    d. An external attribution

2. Which one of the following teenagers has a *mastery goal*?
    a. Alyssa really enjoys going to scary movies.
    b. Brenda loves ballet and so practices hard to make her movements as controlled and graceful as possible.
    c. Craig is taking two advanced placement courses to increase his chances of getting into a good college.
    d. Darrell studies auto mechanics with the hopes that he can get a job at his uncle's auto repair shop after he graduates.

3. From the perspective of *attribution theory*, an adult who tells a teenager "Good luck at your track meet" is
    a. Fostering extrinsic rather than intrinsic motivation
    b. Enhancing the teenager's self-efficacy about doing well at the meet
    c. Decreasing the teenager's self-efficacy about doing well at the meet
    d. Communicating the message that success will be due to external, uncontrollable factors

4. Three of the following strategies are likely to help children become more self-regulating. Which strategy, though possibly beneficial in other ways, is *unlikely* to promote *self-regulation*?
    a. Praising children for closely following an adult's instructions
    b. Giving children criteria they can use to evaluate the quality of their performance on a task
    c. Holding standards for behavior while also taking children's needs and desires into account
    d. Teaching children to give themselves a half-hour of free time after they finish their homework

5. Nancy intentionally bumps into another girl on the playground and hurts the girl's arm. A teacher who sees the aggressive episode is likely to view Nancy's act negatively. What kind of transgression is the teacher likely to perceive the bump to be?
   a. A moral transgression, because Nancy has hurt the other girl
   b. A transgression of shame, since Nancy should feel ashamed of her behavior
   c. A conventional transgression, because Nancy has broken a school rule
   d. A moral dilemma, because the teacher doesn't know whether or not to ignore the situation

6. Which one of the following statements is an example of *induction* as developmental theorists define the term?
   a. "As soon as everyone has settled down, you can all go to lunch."
   b. "Under no circumstances will cheating be tolerated in this classroom."
   c. "When you shout out the answers to my questions, you prevent anyone else from answering them."
   d. "Someone spilled blue paint all over the floor without telling me, and I think I know who that 'someone' is."

7. Which one of the following statements most accurately summarizes what researchers have learned about *cultural diversity* in moral development?
   a. Regardless of culture, youngsters reach Kohlberg's postconventional stage, on average, somewhere around age 18.
   b. Kohlberg's stages characterize moral development in Europe and North America but not in predominantly Hindu and Islamic countries.
   c. Diversity is apparent in children's behavior but not in their moral reasoning.
   d. Some cultural differences in children's moral reasoning exist, but respect for individual rights and concern for others' needs are seen across cultures.

8. Which one of the following is *least* likely to promote children's moral development?
   a. Modeling proper behavior and helping actions
   b. Telling children about the harm that a certain behavior has caused others
   c. Encouraging children to listen to one another's perspectives about a conflict
   d. Explaining to children what it means to think at the highest levels of moral reasoning

Essay

9. Explain how *intrinsic motivation* is different from *extrinsic motivation*, and describe three ways in which children's intrinsic motivation changes with age.

10. Define *students at risk* and describe at least four characteristics that these students are likely to have. Then, suggest four strategies that educators and other adults can use to help such students be successful.

Answers to Sample Test Questions

1. c—Vicarious reinforcement is a phenomenon whereby a child increases the frequency of a behavior that he or she has seen someone else reinforced for.

2. b—A mastery goal is an internally based desire to acquire additional knowledge or master new skills.

3. d—Attribution theory focuses on the explanations that people have for successes and failures. Adults often communicate messages that include such attributions; this adult, though certainly well-meaning, is implying that success or failure is due to luck, something that is external and out of the teenager's control.

4. a—Alternatives *b* and *d* reflect self-evaluation and self-reinforcement, respectively. Alternative *c* encompasses aspects of authoritative parenting. Alternative *a*, while potentially helpful in other ways, will not necessarily promote self-regulation.

5. a—Nancy's act is a *moral transgression* because she intentionally inflicts physical harm on someone else.

6. c—Induction involves giving a reason why a behavior is unacceptable.

7. d—There is some evidence of cultural differences in moral reasoning, but the emphasis on both individual rights and concern for other people seems common across cultures.

8. d—Lectures to children seem to be less effective in promoting moral development than the other actions listed. Adults can also encourage children to wrestle with moral dilemmas and consider the merits of opinions that are slightly more advanced than their own current views.

9. Intrinsic motivation emerges from factors within the individual (e.g., a child has a strong interest in something) or from factors inherent in the task being performed (e.g., an activity is fun or exciting). In contrast, extrinsic motivation results from factors external to the individual and unrelated to the task at hand (e.g., a child gets allowance—an external consequence—for washing the dishes after dinner each night). Children who are intrinsically motivated are more likely to use effective learning strategies and achieve at higher levels. The textbook describes several trends that in one way or another affect intrinsic motivation; your response should include at least three of them:
    *   As children gradually develop beliefs about what they do well and what they do poorly, they increasingly choose activities for which they have high self-efficacy.
    *   Children's interests become increasingly stable.
    *   Children's choices of activities gradually shift from those that are interesting and enjoyable to those that are likely to be useful to them in some way.
    *   Over time, children gradually internalize the motivation to perform certain activities.
    *   Intrinsic motivation for learning school subject matter declines over the school years.

10. Students at risk are students with a high probability of failing to acquire the minimum academic skills necessary for success in the adult world; many of them drop out of school, and many others graduate without basic skills in reading or mathematics. Common characteristics of students at risk are the following (your response should include at least four of them):
    - Special educational needs (e.g., learning disabilities)
    - Cultural backgrounds that don't mesh easily with the dominant culture at school
    - Home environments that don't encourage or support academic achievement
    - History of poor academic achievement
    - Ineffective learning strategies
    - Low self-esteem
    - Poor relationships with teachers
    - Lack of psychological attachment to school

Possible strategies for helping students at risk are the following (your response should include at least four of these, or else other strategies that will directly or indirectly enhance students' motivation to achieve in the classroom):
    - Make the curriculum relevant to their lives and needs.
    - Use students' strengths to promote high self-efficacy in certain domains.
    - Provide extra support for academic success.
    - Communicate optimism for success.
    - Show them how they have been personally responsible for their successes (i.e., promote productive attributions).
    - Encourage and facilitate participation in extracurricular activities (e.g., sports, student government).
    - Involve them in school policy and management decisions.
    - Engage their interest with stimulating activities.
    - Maintain their sense of self-determination when describing rules and giving instructions.
    - Encourage them to shoot for specific goals, with a focus on mastery goals.
    - Downplay the seriousness of failures.
    - Help them address their need for relatedness within the context of productive school activities.
    - Use extrinsic reinforcers if necessary.

Chapter 14

PEERS, SCHOOLS, AND SOCIETY

Chapter Overview

Chapter 14 introduces you to social contexts outside the family—peer groups, schools, and institutions in society—that leave strong impressions on children. In the first section, we describe the benefits of companionship with peers, such as having chances to practice and refine social skills. We suggest that being accepted by peers and having friends are valuable assets for children, and that as youngsters grow, social groups (such as cliques) may affect—not always constructively—youngsters' social roles, pastimes, and tastes in clothing and music. During adolescence, peers become partners for romance and, in some cases, for sexual relationships. In the second section, we relay features of schools that make them enriching environments for children and adolescents—a sense of community, clear values and high expectations, and warm welcomes to new students. In the final section, we look at the experiences children and adolescents have with child care, after-school programs, extracurricular activities, religious and philosophically-based groups, and television and interactive technologies. Throughout the chapter, we make recommendations to teachers and other practitioners for helping children gain productive experiences with peers, schools, and society.

Possible Knowledge, Beliefs, and Misconceptions Related to Chapter Content

As you read Chapter 14, your own experiences with peers, schools, and society will undoubtedly surface. Consider how beliefs such as the following might affect your interpretations:

1. Some adults believe that children and adolescents participate in deviant acts because of pressure from peers. Developmental research reveals a different picture: Young people who join cliques and other groups do not automatically follow the whims of peers but instead evaluate what others ask them to do and ultimately make their own decisions (see the section "Social Groups").

2. Many people see sexual orientation as a voluntary choice. You will find in this chapter that research does *not* confirm this belief. Nature and nurture both appear to affect sexual orientation, and many homosexual and bisexual youth feel that they are different from peers as early as middle childhood (see the section "Romance and Sexuality").

3. Some adults believe that children who struggle in school have something intrinsically wrong with them—perhaps thinking that these children are unprepared for academic challenges, unmotivated to achieve, or unable to follow rules. Without discounting the personal challenges that individual children face, we suggest that children can be bolstered with caring teachers, clear rules, productive classroom environments, and enjoyable school traditions (see the section "Schools").

4. Many readers have had personal experiences with child care, either themselves previously as children or, more recently, as parents employing caregivers to watch over their own children.

These experiences—good, bad, or mixed—will color expectations about the benefits and risks of child care. In the section "Services for Children and Adolescents," we report that child care can be a beneficial environment for children if the quality of care is good, although there is some evidence that child care can slightly increase aggression with peers and resistance to parents' authority.

5. Some people believe that early interventions such as *Head Start* preschool programs are not worth their financial costs because the intellectual advantages they give children fade over time. Chapter 14 explains that high-quality, comprehensive interventions are often quite positive for economically impoverished children, and especially when the programs begin during infancy, are developmentally appropriate, and continue throughout the school years. In cases of well-designed and long-lasting programs, gains in children's cognitive skills appear significant and are evident for a long time (see the section "Services for Children and Adolescents").

6. Your religious upbringing may affect your interpretation of religious development. For example, if you grew up in a deeply religious family, you may see religion as a vital part of children's social-emotional development. If religion was downplayed, or if your family took a nonreligious stance, you may view religious beliefs with curiosity or disapproval. You will find reminders in Chapter 14 about the need to show tolerance for the many religious and nonreligious beliefs held by children and their families (see the section "Services for Children and Adolescents").

7. Some readers will expect that the effects of television on children are exclusively negative ones. Research casts doubt on this belief, showing instead that television can have either positive or negative effects, depending on program content. You will learn that television has its most detrimental effects when it exposes children to racist, sexist, and other stereotypical images, and when it cultivates children's aggressive tendencies (see the section "Television and the Interactive Technologies").

Suggested Supplementary Readings

The following readings, presented in the final section of this *Study Guide and Reader*, are relevant to Chapter 14:

Reading 14-1: Inclusive Social Practices for Children with Special Needs

Reading 14-2: Supporting Children During Times of Trouble and Tragedy

CHAPTER OUTLINE	FOCUS QUESTIONS

PEERS
 	
    Functions of Peer Relationships
 	
    Peer Acceptance
 	
    Friendships
 	
    Social Groups
 	
    Romance and Sexuality
	• What benefits do peers offer to one another?
	
	• Describe the qualities of each of the following classifications of peer acceptance: popular children, rejected children, neglected children, controversial children, and average children.
	
	• How do friendships differ from other kinds of peer relationships?
	
	• How do children's friendships change as children grow?
	
	• What are some things teachers and other practitioners can do to foster children's friendships and other productive peer relationships?
	
	• What characteristics do children's social groups tend to have?
	
	• How do other members of their social groups influence young people?
	
	• What roles do cliques, subcultures, and gangs play in the lives of adolescents?
	
	• How do ideas about romance change with development?
	
	• What variations are present in adolescents' experiences with sexual intimacy?
	
	• What does research indicate about the origin of sexual orientation?
	
	• What can adults do to address adolescents' sexuality?

CHAPTER OUTLINE	FOCUS QUESTIONS
SCHOOLS The School as a Community Socialization in Schools Transitions to New Schools	• What does it mean for children to have a *sense of community* in a classroom or school? • In your own words, describe a warm, supportive classroom atmosphere and its effects on children. • What kinds of instructional methods contribute to children's sense of community at school? • What kinds of school traditions help children develop a positive school spirit? • Describe typical expectations teachers have for how children should behave in their classrooms. Why is it important for teachers to explicitly articulate their expectations for behavior? • How do children respond when teachers have low expectations of them? What can teachers do to ensure they are communicating high expectations of children? • What challenges do children face when they enter elementary school? Secondary school? • How can teachers help students adjust to new schools?

CHAPTER OUTLINE	FOCUS QUESTIONS

SOCIETY
 	
   Services for Children and Adolescents
 	
   Television and the Interactive Technologies
	• How do advocates of high standards in child care define *quality*?
	
	• What seem to be the beneficial effects of high-quality child care? What risks do children encounter if they spend excessively long hours in child care or receive poor-quality care?
	
	• What are *early childhood intervention programs*, and how have these programs helped children from economically disadvantaged families?
	
	• Under what conditions do children gain the greatest benefits from early interventions?
	
	• Describe research evidence on the effects of after-school programs and extracurricular activities.
	
	• What are the qualities of effective after-school and summer programs?
	
	• What can educators do to promote tolerance of diverse religious and nonreligious orientations?
	
	• Describe potentially detrimental effects of television and interactive technologies.
	
	• What are some possible benefits of television and interactive technologies?
	
	• Describe three actions that adults can take to encourage children's productive uses of television and interactive technologies.

Chapter Glossary

Clique. Moderately stable friendship group of perhaps 3 to 10 members.

Community of learners. A classroom in which teacher(s) and students actively and collaboratively work to help one another learn.

Controversial children. Children whom some peers really like and other peers strongly dislike.

Dominance hierarchy. Relative standing of group members in terms of such qualities as leadership and social influence.

Early childhood intervention program. Program designed to foster basic intellectual, social-emotional, and physical development in infants and young children whose heads of family are burdened by economic poverty or other debilitating life circumstances.

Gang. Cohesive social group characterized by initiation rites, distinctive colors and symbols, territorial orientation, feuds with rival groups, and criminal activity.

Interactive technology. Array of electronic, digitally based machines that are operated dynamically by a person whose commands determine emerging program sequences.

Neglected children. Children whom peers rarely select as someone they would either most like or least like to do something with.

Peer culture. General set of rules, expectations, and interpretations that influence how members of a particular peer group behave.

Popular children. Children whom many peers like and perceive to be kind and trustworthy.

Rejected children. Children whom many peers identify as being unfavorable social partners.

Self-fulfilling prophecy. Phenomenon in which an adult's expectations for a child's performance bring about that level of performance.

Sense of community. In a classroom or school, a collection of widely shared beliefs that students, teachers, and other staff have common goals, support one another's efforts, and make important contributions to everyone's success.

Service learning. Activity that promotes learning and skill development through volunteerism or community service.

Sexual harassment. Form of discrimination in which a target individual perceives another's actions or statements to be hostile, humiliating, or offensive, especially pertaining to physical appearance or sexual matters.

Sexual orientation. Particular sex(es) to which an individual is romantically and sexually attracted.

Society. A very large group of people who live in a particular region and share certain customs.

Subculture. Group that resists the ways of the dominant culture and adopts its own norms for behavior.

Table 14–1. Applying Concepts in Child Development: Fostering Children's Acceptance by Peers

This table is a complete version of the table that appears at the end of Chapter14 in the textbook. Compare your entries in the blank cells in the textbook table with our entries here. Keep in mind that there isn't necessarily a single "right" entry for any particular cell.

Age	A Youngster's Experience	Developmental Concepts *Identifying Factors Affecting a Youngster's Acceptance by Peers*	Implications *Promoting Likability in Youngsters*
Infancy (Birth–2)	Noticing other infants in the child care center, 8-month-old Tyler reacts differently from one occasion to the next. Sometimes he smiles at other infants, reaches out to touch their faces, and babbles to them. At other times he seems oblivious to other infants, ignoring their gestures and crawling over their bodies to get to an interesting object.	Tyler is beginning to show an interest in other children. As is typical for his young age, Tyler's curiosity about peers is fleeting but will slowly blossom into a full-fledged desire to interact with peers. With continued opportunities to interact with peers and support from perceptive adults, Tyler is likely to develop *peer acceptance*.	Talk with infants and toddlers about the activities and emotional states you notice in other small children. For example, when a few children are in high chairs, comment on the food you are placing on each tray and everyone's reaction to it ("I guess Ben doesn't want green beans today, but look at how much Hana is enjoying them!"). Gently point out the effect when infants accidentally hurt another child ("Benny, please be careful. Soledad doesn't like it when you poke her eyes. Let's see if she likes having her arm rubbed instead.").
Early Childhood (2–6)	Five-year-old Finian and his family moved into a new community midway through his kindergarten year. Having now spent 2 months in his new kindergarten class, Finian typically stands quietly at the periphery of other children's social interactions. None of the children encourage him to join their play.	Like Finian, children who *transition to a new school* need considerable time to adjust to the school's people and customs. Finian has yet to find a social niche among his peers and has some of the qualities of *neglected children*. That is, he is quiet, keeps to himself, and is not sought after by peers to join their social groups.	Encourage children who are shy or left out of social groups to ease in to group settings. For example, suggest that neglected children join an informal gathering of children in the classroom's dramatic play area. Or when setting up small groups for learning activities (e.g., a structured art lesson), include a socially neglected child with other children who are apt to be friendly and inclusive.

table continues

Table 14–1 continued

Age	A Youngster's Experience	Developmental Concepts *Identifying Factors Affecting a Youngster's Acceptance by Peers*	Implications *Promoting Likability in Youngsters*
Middle Childhood (6–10)	Eight-year-old Kia has no friends in school. Other children find her bossy and rude. For example, on the playground Kia walks up to a group of children who are quietly inspecting a shiny stone, shoves her way into the group, and demands that the children admire her new shoes, which she claims are far nicer than theirs. When the other children appear annoyed and try to move away from her, Kia grabs one girl, insisting that the two of them play on the monkey bars.	Kia is showing qualities of being *rejected* by peers. Rejected children are disliked by other children for a variety of reasons, perhaps for their aggressive, immature, impulsive, or disruptive behaviors. Kia shows these qualities and, as a result, is excluded from other children's play.	Identify and teach missing social skills to rejected children. In Kia's case it would be helpful to coach her in how to enter a social group. Kia could practice standing near other children, politely listening to the focus of their conversation, and then interjecting a comment that is relevant to the topic being discussed. Because rejected children generally have multiple social needs, consider offering ongoing support, including services from a school counselor or psychologist.
Early Adolescence (10–14)	Twelve-year-old Frank is an energetic young man who takes his zeal for life into every setting he inhabits—his middle school classes, the school cafeteria, his after-school track team, and more. Frank has a good sense of humor but occasionally interrupts the class with off-color jokes and snide comments about peers. All the young people in his middle school know of Frank; many like him, but others find him abrasive, callous, and self-centered.	Frank shares the qualities of *socially controversial children*. He is well liked by some peers but avoided by others. Controversial children can be disruptive in some situations yet helpful, cooperative, and socially sensitive in others.	Acknowledge the many strengths that children with mixed social profiles have. Frank's advisor might compliment him on the exuberant way in which he contributes to class and to the school generally. Explain to these children when their behaviors are disruptive and inappropriate. For example, Frank's advisor might talk with him privately about when it is and is not appropriate to tell jokes in class.

table continues

Table 14–1 continued

Age	A Youngster's Experience	Developmental Concepts *Identifying Factors Affecting a Youngster's Acceptance by Peers*	Implications *Promoting Likability in Youngsters*
Late Adolescence (14–18)	As a 15-year-old, Tara seems fairly happy with her social life. She has three close friends, all girls, and she and they increasingly interact with boys at school football games and school dances. Every now and then, Tara becomes annoyed with one of her friends, calls her names, or tries to exclude her from a social event; usually, however, Tara is kind-hearted and sensitive to her friends. Some students who are not Tara's friends think she's a bit snooty, but they do not perceive her to be overly objectionable.	In the parlance of social acceptance, Tara might be considered *average*: She is liked by some peers and moderately disliked by others. Children who are average in their likability tend to exhibit age-typical social skills, be reasonably concerned about other people's welfare, and show occasional lapses of tact and self-control.	Talk with young people about their social lives—how they get along with peers, who their friends are, and what trouble spots they encounter with peers. Acknowledge to average youngsters that they seem to exhibit a healthy social life, and encourage them to continue to develop their prosocial skills, such as being diplomatic with other people, while also continuing to look after their own needs.

Application Exercise #1: Applying Concepts from Contexts of Development

The following scenarios illustrate developmental concepts related to peers, schools, and communities. Explain how each scenario illustrates concepts from Chapter 14.

1. *Peer acceptance*: Jonathan is a new student at Tassef Middle School. His family moved to the community several months into the school year, so Jonathan entered school when other students were already settled into their classes. At his previous school, Jonathan had two close friends, but he has not yet made any friends at the new school, and he remains alone at lunchtime.

2. *Peer acceptance*: Jerome is a 10-year-old boy who seems to have few friends at school. Other children find Jerome to be irritating, aggressive, and self-centered. In the classroom, he pokes other children, copies from their work, and takes snacks from their backpacks. On the playground, he barges into groups, pushes others around, and fails to pick up on social cues.

3. *Peer acceptance*: Alejandro is a friendly 15-year-old student who is well liked by classmates in his high school. Alejandro is doing well in school and is quick to help other students. He has a good sense of humor, moves in and out of groups easily, and is frequently sought out as a partner for lunch. In his neighborhood as well, Alejandro has many friends.

4. *Friendship*: Brenda and Alisha have been close companions since kindergarten. As young children, they lived in the same neighborhood and frequently walked back and forth between their two apartments. When Alisha's parents divorced, Brenda consoled Alisha, and when Alisha lost her grandmother, Brenda was sympathetic. During middle school, Alisha and Brenda continued to remain close friends even as their social worlds expanded to include others. During high school, the two girls swapped secrets, disclosed their insecurities and admiration for particular boys, and shared their hopes and fears about the future.

5. *Social groups*: Fifteen-year-old Julia looks and dresses like the other teenagers she hangs out with after school. Like the other girls, Julia wears skimpy tops and tight jeans and adorns herself with flashy jewelry. She and the other girls and boys in her clique listen to the same music and congregate together on weekend evenings. In other respects, she remains similar to her parents, particularly in her value for education. Julia loves animals and plans to become a veterinarian.

6. *Dating*: At age 11, Clive told his friends he was going out with his classmate Claire. They never really went anywhere together, though they talked to one another during lunch and sent notes back and forth. At age 16, Clive asked Olivia to the prom, and the two teens went on a few dates to the movies and accompanied each other to a few parties before their romance sizzled out. Now, at age 18, Clive has a steady girlfriend named Iris with whom he spends considerable time. Clive and Iris seem to have a mutually respectful relationship.

7. *Religious affiliation:* Ms. Chantou is a principal for a school serving an ethnically and religiously diverse population of children and families. In setting up the school calendar of events (parent meetings, concerts, plays, and so forth), she is careful to consider major religious holidays celebrated by her families. In the school's student handbook, Ms. Chantou

has included references to the need for religious tolerance, implications of the U.S. Constitution's "separation of church and state," and district policies that protect children from denigration for their religious or nonreligious beliefs.

8. *Television and interactive technologies:* When Ashlyn was in elementary school, she watched several hours of TV each night, but her viewing has decreased since she began high school, had increased homework and social obligations, and started working part-time. Now 17, Ashlyn watches little television, but she is an avid computer user who keeps in close contact with friends through electronic mail (e-mail) and instant messaging. Ashlyn also makes frequent use of her cell phone and sends and receives dozens of text messages each day.

<u>Answers to Application Exercise #1</u>

1. In terms of peer acceptance, Jonathan might be classified as a *neglected child*. This quality is often a temporary one, and it is likely that Jonathan will develop new friendships after he spends more time at the new school. In the meantime, he will benefit from friendly gestures from teachers and opportunities to work with other students in small groups (see the section "Peer Acceptance").

2. In terms of peer acceptance, Jerome might be considered a *rejected child*. Other children do not want to be near him because he is impulsive, aggressive, and lacking in social skills. Jerome definitely needs guidance from caring adults (see the section "Peer Acceptance").

3. In terms of peer acceptance, Alejandro might be considered a *popular child*. His friendly nature and good social skills make him well liked by his peers (see the section "Peer Acceptance").

4. Alisha and Brenda exhibit many qualities of good *friends*. They have voluntarily spent time together, comforted one another during difficult times, displayed loyalty, and shared intimate secrets (see the section "Friendships").

5. Julia demonstrates how social groups tend to influence adolescents' preferences for personal appearance, social activities, and music whereas parents often remain influential in matters of education, morality, religion, and careers (see the section "Social Groups").

6. Clive's dating represents the experiences of many youngsters. His initial dating behaviors were simple gestures of spending time together at school but eventually he did go out on dates with girls. Clive's ability as an older adolescent to enter a healthy relationship characterized by mutual regard may have stemmed in part from his secure relationships with family members (see the section "Romance and Sexuality").

7. Ms. Chantou is showing awareness of religious diversity and fostering a climate of tolerance in her school (see the section "Services for Children and Adolescents").

8. Ashlyn's decrease in television watching over the high school years is typical of adolescents. Her use of interactive technologies to stay in touch with friends is another common trend at this age level (see the section "Television and the Interactive Technologies").

Application Exercise #2: Identifying Developmentally Appropriate Practices

For each of the following vignettes, decide whether the practitioner's response is *appropriate* or *inappropriate*. Justify your decisions using concepts from Chapter 14.

1. Ms. LaPointe has two children in her second-grade class who do not pay attention in class, fit in with the other children, or join spontaneous games at recess. One boy is irritable and combative—she has noticed him poking other children with a pencil, scribbling on their work, and trying to pick fights. One girl seems immature and lacking in social skills—the girl speaks loudly when others are absorbed in class projects, pulls other girls' hair to get their attention, and recites nursery rhymes in a sing-song voice that grates on everyone's nerves. Ms. LaPointe knows that some children take longer to develop social skills than do others and hopes that these two children will eventually catch up. Meanwhile, she ignores the two children and focuses her efforts on the other children who are ready to act appropriately at school.

2. In a student conduct handbook, a school includes its sexual harassment policy. The policy explains what sexual harassment is, why it is prohibited, and the various forms it can take.

3. In his high school advisement group, Mr. Torres wants all of his students to feel that they belong and have a place where they can talk about their concerns. He institutes several routines that become enjoyable traditions in his group—he brings fresh cookies on Mondays, lets students take turns choosing musical CDs to play in their group session on Fridays, and celebrates birthdays at the beginning of each month and summer birthdays during the final week of school. Mr. Torres rotates through his list of students and makes sure to speak quietly and individually with each student at least once a month. When he talks with students, he strives to be honest, tactful, caring, and respectful.

4. Every year, several children whose parents are migrant workers enroll in Johnston Elementary School a full month after school has been open. The fifth grade teacher, Mr. Stilton, cannot understand why these children take so long to adjust to school, and he does not think to post his rules or articulate his expectations for student behavior. By watching the other students, the recently arrived children gradually figure out the rules—that they should raise their hands before speaking in the large group, work independently unless instructed to get in groups, and write their names on their papers and turn them in on time.

5. Mrs. Bierdman has a few children in her kindergarten class who have not previously listened to stories with parents, don't know the alphabet, and do not recognize written letters or numbers. Rather than assuming the children are not yet ready to learn, Mrs. Bierdman arranges for the children to listen to stories in small groups and to learn the academic skills that will be necessary for their future academic learning.

6. Teachers and staff at Letterman High School try hard to ease the adjustment of students at school. Students meet with an advisor and a few classmates in a homeroom two or three days a week. Advisors express an interest in students' coursework, grades, and long-term career goals. With help from their principal, teachers meet regularly and plan new ways to engage

students. A small team of teachers works with volunteers in the community to staff a homework hotline for students with questions and concerns about assignments.

7. Several teachers at Trudeau Junior High are concerned about the trouble youngsters are getting into in the afternoons. They decide to develop an after-school program for junior high school students and ask for help from a few local community organizations and church groups. The after-school program incorporates varied activities, including physical activities and arts and crafts, structured service learning opportunities, informal social events, and tutorial support.

8. Ten-year-old Ruth's father is a minister at a local church. Ruth's teacher, Miss Alexander, begins to notice that Ruth is being harassed about her religious beliefs. For example, one boy, said to her, "Ruth, were you born in a church or *what*?" and, "Hey, Ruth, did you pray for *me* today?" Miss Alexander speaks with the children who make such rude remarks and then reminds the entire class about their school's policy of being tolerant of people whose religious and philosophical beliefs are different from their own.

9. In assigning a U.S. history project for his fifth graders, Mr. Stowe advises students of several reputable Web sites that they might examine. He also explains how anyone can create a Web site these days and cautions the children to be wary of sites that are not sponsored by well-known nonprofit organizations, historical societies, government agencies, or other reputable groups.

Answers to Application Exercise #2

1. Inappropriate. The rejected children in Ms. LaPointe's class will not necessarily learn effective social skills without intervention from adults. Rather than waiting for these children to "grow up," Ms. LaPointe can coach them in gaining entry into social groups, curbing their aggressive impulses, and refraining from making annoying social gestures. If the children continue to be rejected by peers, Ms. LaPointe might consult a school counselor or psychologist to obtain additional support for them (see the sections on "Peer Acceptance" and "Friendships").

2. Appropriate. Not all youngsters understand the forms sexual harassment can take or its status as discrimination. Adolescents who might be tempted to harass others need reminders not to do so, and those teens who feel they are being harassed may appreciate clear guidelines so that they have a firm reason for telling others to stop being offensive or, alternatively, reporting the problem to a teacher or principal (see the section "Romance and Sexuality").

3. Appropriate. Mr. Torres is fostering students' sense of community. He establishes a warm setting for his advisees, institutes enjoyable traditions, and cultivates a feeling that school is a fun place where students belong (see the section "The School as a Community").

4. Inappropriate. The children who enter Mr. Stilton's class after the school year has begun do not understand the class's routines, values, or expected student behaviors. Mr. Stilton is assuming the students already know or should be able to figure out the rules or his classroom. He could help the children to adjust more easily if he were to explain desired behaviors and their rationale to students (see the section "Socialization in Schools").

5. Appropriate. Mrs. Bierdman understands that the children who appear delayed in their learning have considerable academic potential but need instruction that addresses their gaps in knowledge (see the section "Transitions to New Schools").

6. Appropriate. Teachers and other staff at Letterman High School are taking several measures that will foster a good adjustment in students. For example, they are personalizing the school environment and creating backup systems for students who need extra help in their academic learning (see the section "Transitions to New Schools").

7. Appropriate. The teachers are designing activities that are likely to entice and engage teenagers. In the section "Providing Community Support for Children and Adolescents," the characteristics of effective programs are outlined.

8. Appropriate. Ms. Alexander does not condone religious intolerance. She is aware that such remarks are discriminatory, educates children privately when they ridicule one another, and reminds the entire class of the need for tolerance (see the section "Services for Children and Adolescents").

9. Appropriate. Mr. Stowe is teaching children to be critical users of the Internet (see the section "Television and the Interactive Technologies").

Sample Test Questions

Multiple-Choice

1. Which one of the following strategies is *not* one of the textbook's recommendations for *fostering friendships and other productive peer relationships*?
    a. A high school biology teacher arranges cooperative learning activities for part of each class meeting.
    b. A kindergarten teacher helps shy children ease into groups of children engaged in pretend play.
    c. A second-grade teacher coaches an aggressive child in using productive social skills.
    d. A middle school advisor arranges his students into pairs and tells the students that they need to be friends with their partner for the remainder of the year.

2. Which one of the following statements most accurately describes the effects of social groups on adolescents?
    a. Members of a social group typically replace parents and other family members as role models for behaviors, values, moral decisions, and goals for the future.
    b. Members of a social group socialize adolescents to follow a group's norms, but the adolescents themselves make their own judgments on what they are asked to do by group members.
    c. Social groups do more harm than good in adolescent development.
    d. Social groups provide a forum for practicing social skills during early and childhood and then lose their developmental significant during adolescence.

3. Which one of the following examples accurately illustrates *service learning*?
    a. A high school history course asks students to learn about military service as one possible way to fulfill the job-shadowing requirement.
    b. A high school requires students to serve as volunteers in a community agency or setting.
    c. A high school requires students to keep a journal on their employment activities, salary, and budget management.
    d. A high school asks students to keep their pencils sharpened and their backpacks organized.

4. Which one of the following is the most accurate summary of research on the effects of *child care* on children?
    a. There are some positive effects, but these effects depend on quality of care, and there is some evidence that child care may slightly increase aggression and noncompliance in some children.
    b. The effects of child care are mostly negative, but this is especially the case for economically poor children, who do better with full-time care at home with their families.
    c. There are only positive effects, but these effects are strongest when children bring their own toys to the center.
    d. Child care undermines children's social independence, in that children fail to receive the support they need to care for their personal needs or assert themselves in groups.

5. According to the textbook, television's major negative influences on children can be summarized as:
    a. Being an enjoyable activity that interferes with doing chores around the house
    b. Provoking children to memorize and repeat annoying jingles from commercials
    c. Distracting children from reading books and completing their homework
    d. Giving children access to, and perhaps perpetuating, stereotyped social images

6. After-school programs and extracurricular activities:
    a. Foster the achievement of children from high-income families but decrease the achievement of children from low-income families
    b. Are generally beneficial for youngsters' social-emotional development but diminish youngsters' academic progress
    c. Seem to decrease high-risk behaviors in children, although the correlational designs of the research make it impossible to be certain about causal effects
    d. Make life easier for parents but show little impact on children

Essay

7. Imagine you are a new teacher preparing for your first teaching job. Identify the grade level you will be teaching and the tactics you might use to help new students adjust to school.

8. Choose *one* of the following contexts of development: child care, after-school programs and extra-curricular activities, or television and interactive technologies. Address this context in two ways:
    a. Describe how this context affects children.
    b. Give one or more practical strategies for making children's experience with this context productive.

Answers to Sample Test Questions

1. d—Friendships are voluntary relationships. Although teachers can facilitate friendly interactions, they cannot mandate friendships per se.

2. b—Social groups are influential to adolescents, but adolescents make their own judgments as to whether they will do what they are asked to do.

3. b—*Service learning* refers to learning and skill development during volunteer activities or community service.

4. a—Children who participate in high-quality child care learn to be socially competent, and child care appears beneficial in promoting intellectual development, especially for children whose home environments are inattentive or impoverished. Some evidence indicates that child care can lead to increased aggression and noncompliance in some children.

5. d—Television often portrays people in stereotyped ways.

6. c—Before- and after-school programs *seem* to benefit children, but the type of research data available does not lend itself to the unequivocal conclusion that these programs, in and of themselves, bring about positive effects.

7. Responses will vary depending on grade level, but they may include options such as these:
    *   Hosting orientations for children and families before the school year begins
    *   Inviting students to visit the classroom prior to their first day of school
    *   Offering individualized instruction and experiences to children who enter school without academic skills
    *   Creating a warm and supportive climate
    *   Offering tutoring for students who find coursework challenging
    *   Giving students opportunities to engage in self-directed activities
    *   Using instructional methods that are engaging and motivating
    *   Creating class traditions that students will find fun and inviting
    *   At the secondary level, making sure that every student has an advisor who advocates for him or her
    *   At the secondary level, creating small groups of students who take some classes together and become familiar with a teacher

8. Your response might look something like one of these rows:

Context	How the Context Affects Children	Practical Applications
Child care	• Infants and small children typically enjoy secure attachments to employed caregivers who are warm and affectionate. • High-quality child care is associated with good cognitive and social-emotional outcomes in children. • Children who spend long hours in child care or experience poor-quality care may become somewhat aggressive and noncompliant with adults.	• Be warm, sensitive, and affectionate with children. • Encourage children's relationships with a few adults in a child care center who get to know the children personally. • Keep child-caregiver ratios reasonably low. • Offer developmentally appropriate activities for children. • Arrange rooms and facilities that are safe and permit children's exploration. • Offer professional development opportunities for caregivers in topics related to child development and early childhood care.
After-school programs and extracurricular activities	• After-school programs seem to foster children's social-emotional development (cultivating positive feelings toward school, discouraging risky behaviors). • Research is not definitive because investigations use correlational designs that do not justify firm conclusions about causality.	• Offer a variety of options to youngsters. • Permit young people to create authentic products. • Get to know youngsters individually. • Include structured activities and firm limits for behavior. • Be respectful of the cultural backgrounds of youngsters.
Television and interactive technologies	• The stereotyped images that children see on television can distort their views about specific groups. • Children can learn to be more aggressive from watching violent television programs. • Interactive technologies provide an attractive medium for staying in touch with friends.	• Encourage parents to monitor their children's television viewing and to initiate discussions about the content of the programs children watch. • Teach children to be critical viewers of television and thoughtful evaluators of Internet Web sites.

Supplementary Readings

Enhancing Children's Physical, Cognitive, and Social-Emotional Development in Head Start Programs

In Chapter 1 of the textbook, we explain that children develop in *physical, cognitive*, and *social-emotional* domains. We suggest that caring adults can help children by nurturing children's progress in each of the domains.

Relationships Among the Developmental Domains

As you progress through the textbook, you will notice that we usually examine these domains separately. We do so because the domains represent different psychological systems with distinct underlying processes, and also because college students are apt to find it easier to consider one domain at a time. Nevertheless, children always develop as integrated wholes, never as fragmented beings. In other words, the three domains are closely interrelated in children's lives. As examples, changes in the brain (in the physical domain) make it increasingly possible for youngsters to anticipate future events (a cognitive ability); having a close relationship with families (in the social-emotional domain) can affect children's relaxation and growth (in the physical domain); and a growing ability to take the perspective of others (a cognitive ability) can affect children's ability to get along with peers (in the social-emotional domain).

Experienced teachers realize just how important it is to address connections among the developmental domains. Thus a fourth-grade teacher might offer concentrated practice with mathematical skills and then send children out for recess to "recharge their batteries." A middle-school teacher might discourage youngsters from gossiping by appealing to their emerging awareness of how others feel when they hear such rude remarks. And a high school teacher can bolster a low-achieving student's self-confidence by encouraging the student to change tactics, ask for help, and expend more effort.

School programs and curricula can also be designed to meet children's needs in the three domains. As an illustration, the Head Start preschool programs offer comprehensive educational services to 3- to 5-year-old children from economically disadvantaged families (U.S. Department of Health and Human Services, Administration on Children, Youth and Families, Head Start Bureau, 2004). Head Start programs address each of the three domains, as you will now see.

Desired Learning Outcomes for Children

Examine the following subset of learning objectives, taken from Head Start's comprehensive framework, and see if you can guess which of the outcomes focus primarily on physical, cognitive, and social-emotional development.

1. Begins to develop and express awareness of self in terms of specific abilities, characteristics, and preferences.
2. Shows increasing levels of proficiency, control, and balance in walking, climbing, running, jumping, hopping, skipping, marching, and galloping.
3. Develops increasing abilities to understand and use language to communicate information, experiences, ideas, feelings, opinions, needs, questions; and for other varied purposes.
4. Demonstrates growing confidence in a range of abilities and expresses pride in accomplishments.
5. Develops growing strength, dexterity, and control needed to use tools such as scissors, paper punch, stapler, and hammer.
6. Shows increasing ability to discriminate and identify sounds in spoken language.
7. Shows progress in expressing feelings, needs, and opinions in difficult situations and conflicts without harming themselves, others, or property.
8. Progresses in physical growth, strength, stamina, and flexibility.
9. Shows growing interest in reading-related activities, such as asking to have a favorite book read; choosing to look at books; drawing pictures based on stories; asking to take books home; going to the library; and engaging in pretend-reading with other children.
10. Increases abilities to sustain interactions with peers by helping, sharing, and discussion.
11. Shows growing independence in hygiene, nutrition, and personal care when eating, dressing, washing hands, brushing teeth, and toileting.
12. Shows progress in associating the names of letters with their shapes and sounds.
13. Demonstrates increasing comfort in talking with and accepting guidance and directions from a range of familiar adults.
14. Builds awareness and ability to follow basic health and safety rules such as fire safety, traffic and pedestrian safety, and responding appropriately to potentially harmful objects, substances, and activities.
15. Expands knowledge of and abilities to observe, describe, and discuss the natural world, materials, living things, and natural processes (U.S. Department of Health and Human Services, Administration on Children, Youth and Families, Head Start Bureau, 2003, excerpts from pp. 11-14).

Classification of Head Start Outcomes for Children

The Head Start programs promote children's *physical development* with outcomes in motor skills and health practices (items 2, 5, 8, 11, and 14). The programs specify outcomes for *cognitive development* in areas of language development, literacy, mathematics, and science (items 3, 6, 9, 12, and 15). Finally, Head Start programs enhance children's *social-emotional development* by attention to self-concept, self-control, cooperation, social relationships, and knowledge of families and communities (items 1, 4, 7, 10, and 13).[1]

---

[1] A few additional outcomes specified by Head Start do not fit easily into a single developmental domain. For example, outcomes in the creative arts and approaches to learning address more than one developmental domain.

Guidance for Teachers and Other Practitioners from the Field of Child Development

The field of child development offers a wealth of insights for adults who work with infants, children, and adolescents. In the textbook, we had *teachers* primarily in mind when we described the majority of applications. In concentrating on teachers, we had hoped to create a coherent perspective on meeting the needs of youngsters in classrooms and schools. Nevertheless, the field of child development can be helpful to almost anyone who works with children. Following are descriptions of the jobs of selected professionals who interact with youngsters, the kinds of concerns they might have, and examples of recommendations in the textbook that address such concerns.

Teachers and Caregivers

Teachers and caregivers work with infants, children, and adolescents in schools, child care settings, and after-school programs. They offer educational instruction and are responsible for the general welfare of infants, children, and adolescents for several hours daily. Teachers and caregivers educate and care for children by helping them meet their basic physical needs, stimulating their intellectual curiosity, and building their sense of self and ability to get along with other people. These professionals include early childhood professionals, K–12 teachers, teacher aides, special education teachers, and early childhood special education teachers. Teachers and caregivers might have concerns such as these:

Concern of a Professional	Applications in the Textbook
My students aren't at all realistic about what it takes to learn something thoroughly. When I ask them to study for spelling tests or read history chapters carefully, they glance briefly at the material. How can I encourage them to become active learners?	• Model and teach effective cognitive strategies. • Give children frequent feedback about their progress, and help them see the relationship between their strategies and their learning and problem-solving success. • Provide opportunities for children to evaluate their own learning, and help them develop mechanisms for doing so effectively. (See pp. 255-259.)
I want to create an environment that is attractive and enriching for the infants in my care. I wonder what they really see and hear. Are fancy decorations really necessary? What kind of stimulation do they need?	• Give infants some choice and control in their sensory experiences. • Be aware of the dangers of too much stimulation. • Read cues. • Recognize that temperamental and cultural differences determine the optimum amount of stimulation for each child. (See p. 238.)

Educational Specialists and Administrators

Educational specialists and administrators work in schools and other educational settings. Some provide hands-on specialized services to children and adolescents, and others offer administrative and supervisory support to teachers and other professionals. Educational specialists and administrators include school psychologists, early-care licensing personnel, school counselors, career and guidance counselors, school librarians, educational technology specialists, school media specialists, early intervention consultants, child development disabilities specialists, principals, and child care center directors. A school counselor might have a concern such as this:

Concern of a Professional	Applications in the Textbook
Some kids are socially excluded at my school. Some of these children have disabilities, and others are just immature, impulsive, or aggressive. Teachers work hard to integrate these children into the classroom, but they aren't sure about the next step—encouraging other kids to include the kids who seem neglected or even rejected. I'm often called upon to offer advice. What can I tell them?	• Help young children ease into social groups. • Set up situations in which youngsters can enjoy friendly interactions with one another. • Minimize or eliminate barriers to social interaction. • Cultivate children's empathy for peers with special needs. • Provide the specific kinds of support rejected children need most. • Help change the reputations of rejected children. • Encourage a general feeling of respect for others. (See pp. 537-539.)

Family Educators

Family educators support and educate family members regarding the care of children and adolescents and the maintenance of healthy relationships within families. They include parent educators, family support specialists, and family advocates. A family educator might have this concern:

Concern of a Professional	Applications in the Textbook
I know that I can have my greatest impact when I form partnerships with families. Several families I work with do not trust me yet and put up emotional walls. How can I work more effectively with them?	• When first meeting with parents and other heads of family, establish rapport. • Be a listener as well as a talker. • Help parents see that the concerns they have about their children often are natural responses to children's developmental challenges. • Step in their shoes. • Remember that most parents view their children's behavior as a reflection of their own competence. • Be alert for cultural differences. • Accommodate language and literacy differences. (See pp. 170-171.)

Mental Health Professionals

Mental health professionals care for the mental health and other psychological needs of children, adolescents, and their families. They consult with families, teachers, and other experts to identify and address individual needs. Mental health professionals include counselors and clinical psychologists, clinical social workers, homeless shelter counselors, child advocates at family crisis centers, and counselors of crime victims. A community counselor might have a concern such as this:

Concern of a Professional	Applications in the Textbook
Many children referred to me have trouble with emotional outbursts—they explode when they're angry. Others seem to internalize their negative feelings—they blame themselves for their problems. It seems as if they've missed some critical lessons about dealing with anger, disappointment, and frustration. How can I help kids express their emotions in healthy ways?	• Offer an atmosphere of warmth, acceptance, and trust. • Encourage young people to express their feelings. • Consider using a research-based curriculum for fostering emotional development. • Offer age-appropriate outlets for emotional expression. • Ask children to guess what emotions people may feel in particular scenarios. • Take cultural differences into account. • Help keep anxiety at a manageable level. • Model appropriate ways for dealing with negative emotions. (See pp. 425-426.)

Youth Service Providers

Youth service providers arrange for legal and institutional interventions for young people. They include family social workers, caregivers in residential treatment facilities, substance abuse specialists, directors of child abuse and prevention centers, drug and alcohol intervention specialists, residential care managers, adoption and foster care agency personnel, law enforcement officers, probation authorities, and other juvenile justice professionals. These professionals help children by addressing serious problems in their families and by guiding them through legal proceedings. They often encounter children who are troubled and need special guidance, and might have a concern such as this:

Concern of a Professional	Applications in the Textbook
Some of the kids I work with are really aggressive. I have also noticed that they don't seem to know how to get along with peers. How can I help?	• Teach specific social skills and social problem-solving strategies. • Label appropriate behaviors as they occur. • Plan cooperative activities. • Expose children to numerous models of prosocial behavior. • Provide opportunities for children and adolescents to make a difference in their community. • Give concrete guidelines for behavior. • Seek intensive intervention for youngsters with a history of aggression. (See pp. 478-480.)

Community Leaders

Community leaders promote the development of youngsters in numerous ways. They include scout leaders, personnel from youth organizations, religious leaders, coaches, recreation directors, directors of museum programs for children, activity directors, community services specialists, and camp counselors. They offer a variety of services, including athletic events, cultural enrichment, religious education, after-school programs, and leisure pursuits. A community leader might face this kind of challenge:

Concern of a Professional	Applications in the Textbook
I work in a community center for low-income children. What can I do to offer meaningful support to these children?	• Invest in children's strengths. • Foster a sense of belonging. • Convey clear expectations for children's behavior. • Communicate high expectations for children's success. • In after-school programs, include a variety of activities, including recreation, academic and cultural enrichment, and opportunities to pursue individual interests. (See pp. 184-185 and p. 558.)

Health Educators and Health-Care Providers

Health educators and health-care providers offer health education programs, diagnostic evaluations, medical treatments, and therapies. These services support the physical and psychological well-being of children and adolescents. Health educators and health-care providers include pediatric nurses, physicians, school nurses, audiologists, speech and language therapists, occupational therapists, physical therapists, family planning specialists, child life specialists, behavioral health advisors, youth exercise specialists, and directors of outpatient services for children. The following concern is a common one encountered by health educators and health-care providers:

Concern of a Professional	Applications in the Textbook
Many adolescents are sexually active, don't use contraception, and engage in other risky behaviors, such as drinking alcohol and using drugs. How can developmental research guide the interventions of health educators?	• Provide healthy options for free time. • Ask adolescents to keep their long-term goals continually in mind. • Implement programs that have demonstrated success with the population of young people with whom you work. • Encourage adolescents to protect themselves. • Encourage adolescents with infections to abstain from sex or to use precautions. (See pp. 134-135.)

Reading #1-3

Inquiring About Child Development as a Team of Teachers

In Chapter 3, we state that a capacity for *developmentally appropriate practice*—adapting instruction and services to the age, characteristics, and developmental progress of individual children—is a lifelong quest for those who are truly committed to the welfare of children. Teachers and other practitioners can strengthen their ability to meet children's needs by continuing to learn about child development. One helpful way to cultivate increasingly deep insights about children is to consult regularly with colleagues.

Teachers and other practitioners often gain a better understanding of the strengths and needs of individual children when they meet to exchange insights and ideas. Through discussion, they may also gain a more optimistic view of their own ability to bring about positive changes in children's social development and academic achievement (e.g., Weinstein, Madison, & Kuklinski, 1995). In an approach that one school uses, 10 to 12 teachers, administrators, specialists, and parents meet once every 2 or 3 weeks to discuss students' developmental needs (Squires, Howley, & Gahr, 1999). The following example illustrates the kinds of insights that can emerge:

> [W]e began to notice recurring patterns of behavior. For example, when Jordan was upset, he would usually withdraw from the group and from me for awhile. Pat pointed out that these behavior patterns are clues...to what the child is working on in his or her development. From...observations I had made, I thought that Jordan was trying to understand how to deal with conflict. Other children were trying to learn about making "friends" with other students, or dealing with issues of responsibility in homework, classwork, and on the playground. All those details that we wrote in our journals started to make more sense as they were woven into recurring patterns.
>
> ...I found it surprising that the children's developmental work generally had little to do with what we were studying in math, science, or social studies....
>
> We discussed this in the group, as others felt the same way.... If Jordan has his own developmental agenda, then, of course, other students in the class did, too. And what I was doing in the classroom, all that content, didn't match well with what they were dealing with. I felt I was trying to show a movie at the beach at noon. It would be difficult for kids to see the movie (the content of the lessons) when the sun (their developmental agendas) was so strong and bright.
>
> ...I found myself searching for and trying different ways to make my classroom and my teaching more attuned to students' needs. (Squires et al., 1999, p. 200)

These dedicated teachers were able to enhance one another's understanding of children's developmental needs. Obviously, not all discussion groups work well—some, especially those that become gripe sessions, may actually do more harm than good. Because groups can vary in their dynamics, it is often worthwhile to enter such groups with a personal goal of learning more about children and their needs. And when others begin to dwell on children's problems and factors beyond the control of teachers and other practitioners, it is a good idea to steer the conversation back to the "developmental agendas" of youngsters.

Reading #2-1

Considering Your Beliefs and Their Implications

What are your beliefs about children and child development? Like other prospective teachers and practitioners, you probably have some well-established beliefs about children, their needs, and optimal ways of interacting with them (Astington & Pelletier, 1996; D. Kagan, 1992; M. F. Pajares, 1992). In Chapter 2, we suggest that your beliefs about children in general affect your interpretations of what individual children say, do, and create.

Common Beliefs About Infants, Children, and Adolescents

Many college students hold favorable beliefs about children. For example, they often see young learners as curious, innocent, and endearing. Those wishing to work with adolescents are frequently drawn to their thoughtful and idealistic nature. Such beliefs can have beneficial effects in actual practice—adults holding these beliefs may communicate positive regard to young people and endeavor themselves to foster good qualities in young people.

Yet adults' beliefs occasionally can be naive and even counterproductive. Consider, for example, that many prospective teachers:

- Are inclined to value the emotional needs of children but neglect the cognitive and academic variables that influence learning and behaving (C. S. Weinstein, 1988).

- Hold unrealistic views about the classroom problems they will face and assume that they already have all the knowledge and skills they need to teach effectively (Brookhart & Freeman, 1992; Pajares, 1992).

- Tend to support conventional teaching practices and see little need for change in education (Edmundson, 1990; Ginsburg & Newman, 1985; Lortie, 1975).

- Find it easy to believe that youngsters who are "different" should adapt to the existing educational system, instead of seeing themselves as social activists who can change the system to reduce discrimination (Nel, 1993).

Examining Your Beliefs About Child Development

Prospective teachers and other practitioners are almost always motivated to learn more about children and to correct any false beliefs they might have. Yet people cannot typically articulate all their beliefs or easily rid themselves of counterproductive beliefs. Many ideas about children are so ingrained that people are not even aware of them; in a sense, these beliefs have gone "underground" (Olson & Bruner, 1996). Furthermore, particular beliefs are interrelated with other values, perceptions, ideals, and emotions and as a result are difficult to disentangle. Thus if any of us were to recognize that we were wrong about a specific belief (e.g., a belief that children cannot learn to read if they have not done so by second grade), we would not necessarily think to revise similar ideas (e.g., a belief that children cannot later excel in mathematics if they were initially delayed in learning to count, add, and subtract). If you remain mindful of such challenges in monitoring your own beliefs, you can become increasingly reflective and ultimately more effective with children. We suggest the following strategies to strengthen your capacity for self-reflection:

• *Identify metaphors that encapsulate your views of children.* Metaphors can be a useful way to distill several related beliefs into a single image. Do you think that children are like any of the following images?

> Empty buckets waiting to be filled
> Dry sponges soaking up whatever moisture comes their way
> Plants in a garden seeking shelter from the elements
> Thoughtful philosophers questioning what they see and hear
> Restless movie-goers wanting to be entertained
> Stray cats following their own mysterious agendas
> Prisoners conspiring against their wardens
> Caged animals needing to be trained

Adults' images affect their behaviors toward children. For example, when teachers view children as empty buckets waiting to be filled, they may expose children to lots of rich information about a topic without first assessing children's existing understandings and motivations. And adults who view children as caged animals may quickly become harsh, restrictive, and punitive with children.

• *Identify metaphors that portray the roles you expect to assume with children.* Do you see yourself as taking any of the following roles with children?

> Friend
> Parent
> Tour guide
> Cheerleader
> Quality control inspector
> Counselor
> Entertainer
> Scientist
> Gardener
> Drill sergeant
> Religious leader
> Doctor

These various metaphors might yield distinct styles in interacting with children. For example, the "counselor" metaphor suggests that a teacher or other practitioner should focus primarily on social and emotional development and pay little attention to cognitive development. The "quality control inspector" metaphor might lead to an emphasis on measuring, rather than improving, children's abilities.

• *Think twice when a child struggles.* When a teacher or other practitioner works with a child who fails to meet a basic standard for behavior or achievement, the adult naturally is motivated to make sense of the unwanted outcome. Usually this means attributing the child's problems to

273

one or more factors. As you think about a child's difficulty, keep tabs on your own beliefs, especially if you are inclined to settle on a single factor (such as a child being unable to do the work because of an inherited condition). In the textbook, we encourage you to take the perspective that nature, nurture, and a child's own experiences are jointly responsible for the child's progress and difficulties. Teachers and practitioners who take a comprehensive stance on a child's development can often make realistic adjustments to their own strategies and thereby increase the child's chances for success.

• *Consider how developmental research may challenge your beliefs.* As you read research results in the various chapters of the textbook, consciously decide whether these findings are consistent or inconsistent with your previous beliefs. By comparing your ideas to the evidence, you increase your chances of meaningful learning.

Everyday Beliefs About Child Development That Are Challenged by Developmental Research

In the following table, we describe beliefs (in the left-hand column) that we have encountered in college students and other adults. These beliefs are not supported by developmental research, as you can see in the middle column. When students have a chance to discuss the evidence, they often willingly revise their beliefs, particularly when they also consider what is at stake for children (right-hand column). We encourage you to be equally open-minded as you read developmental research in the textbook.

Belief	Research Findings That Challenge This Belief	Implication
The wounds of childhood scar people for life.	Many children are remarkably resilient to life's stresses, especially when supported by a caring adult (Cicchetti & Garmezy, 1993; Sameroff, Seifer, Baldwin, & Baldwin, 1993; D. S. Shaw, Vondra, Hommerding, Keenan, & Dunn, 1994). Although adverse circumstances put children at risk, serious negative outcomes are only likely when negative experiences are particularly harsh or persist.	Respond sensitively to children when they face difficult circumstances, but do *not* assume that present hardships doom children to lasting misfortune or failure.
The best way for professionals to help children is to mimic their home environment.	Sometimes it's good for children to experience different kinds of environments at home and school. In one study, middle school students who had few opportunities for independence and decision making at home became better adjusted when schools fostered their initiative and decision-making (J. L. Epstein, 1983).	Keep in mind the compensatory roles that schools and services can play in children's lives. For example, read to young children even when they are not read to at home.
Children and adolescents who fail to make eye contact with adults are devious and disrespectful.	Patterns of language and communication vary from one culture to another. In some cultures, it is disrespectful to look an adult in the eye or to initiate a conversation with an adult (Gilliland, 1988; Irujo, 1988; Lomawaima, 1995). Furthermore, some children with disabilities (e.g., autism) may routinely avoid eye contact.	Learn about the behavior patterns and communication styles of children whose cultural backgrounds are different from your own.

Belief	Research Findings That Challenge This Belief	Implication
Placing children in a literature-rich environment—one with many books and opportunities to listen to stories—virtually ensures they will learn to read by themselves.	Investigations attest to the importance of early reading experiences and easy access to children's literature. However, many children benefit from explicit instruction in letter-sound correspondences, decoding skills, and comprehension strategies; this is especially true for children who come to school with limited experience with books and other forms of written language (Gough & Wren, 1998; Hulme & Joshi, 1998; Stanovich, 2000). Furthermore, without intervention, early difficulties in reading often become more debilitating (Stanovich, 2000).	Immerse children in a literate environment, but also offer them explicit instruction in learning to decode and make sense of text. Be particularly attentive to the needs of children who struggle with reading.
The best environment for young children is an academically rigorous one. Given early training in basic skills, young children get a boost for life.	Some instruction in basic skills can be beneficial for young children, but too much academic pressure is detrimental. Young children thrive in learning environments that build on their natural curiosity; allow them to make choices; incorporate hands-on activities; and encourage play, small-group interaction, and personal expression (L. G. Katz, 1999a, 1999b; Shephard & Smith, 1988).	Temper your zeal in teaching basic skills to young children; give them opportunities to explore, experiment, and play.
Adolescence is a time of storm and stress that must simply be endured by the adults in their lives.	Adolescence is a period of rapid physical, emotional, and social growth. Conflicts increase with parents as youths struggle to carve out individual identities. Yet only in about one in five families does the turmoil of adolescence lead to intense conflict (Montemayor, 1982). Serious, ongoing conflict in adolescence is associated with juvenile delinquency, dropping out of school, and drug abuse (Brook, Brook, Gordon, Whiteman, & Cohen, 1990).	Never underestimate the emotional needs of troubled youth, but remember that juvenile delinquency and drug abuse are not inevitable outcomes of adolescence.
Schools spend too much time teaching students' "left brains." In doing so, they're asking students to use only half of their brain power.	The left and right hemispheres of the human brain have different specializations, as you will learn in Chapter 4. Nevertheless, the two hemispheres are in constant communication, and studies of efforts to strengthen a particular hemisphere indicate that such "training" is relatively ineffective (Ornstein, 1997; Pressley & McCormick, 1995).	Diversify instructional tasks, formats, and materials for all children, but remember that most activities involve both hemispheres of the brain.

Belief	Research Findings That Challenge This Belief	Implication
Adults are smarter than adolescents, adolescents are smarter than children, and children are smarter than infants.	Thousands of research studies document that children become increasingly capable. However, the superior learning and memory capabilities that come with age are sometimes a function of individuals' knowledge rather than age per se. For instance, when children know more about a topic than adults do, their ability to learn and remember new information about the topic surpasses that of adults (Chi, 1978; Rabinowitz & Glaser, 1985). Furthermore, what appear to be limitations in thinking may actually be advantages for development. For example, the naive optimism young children bring to learning tasks may help them to persist despite frequent failure. Likewise, the more limited memory capacity of young children may help them segment language into manageable pieces (Bjorklund & Green, 1992).	Keep in mind that limitations in children's thinking may sometimes serve a purpose in their long-term development.

Reading #3-1

Hush Little Baby, Don't You Cry:
Massage for Infants

Approximately 12 percent of infants in the United States are born preterm (after less than 37 weeks of prenatal development), and 8 percent of infants are born with low birth weight (at less than 5½ pounds) (Field, Hernandez-Reif, & Freedman, 2004). Every baby craves loving, responsive care, but infants who are born early or with low birth weight require exceptional care attuned to their medical conditions and needs for comfort. In recent decades medical specialists have made significant progress in identifying interventions—temperature-controlled sleeping environments, oxygen supplements, ventilators, tube feeding, surgeries, and the like—that sustain life in many fragile newborn infants. Increasingly, psychologists, medical researchers, and specialists in neonatal intensive care also recognize the importance of fulfilling fragile infants' needs for comfort, stress reduction, and—simply—gentle human touch.

Infant massage is a growing trend in hospital care of preterm and low birth-weight babies. The effects of massage therapy have been examined with fragile newborn infants who are medically stable and not suffering serious medical problems (Field et al., 2004). In a series of studies, preterm infants were massaged three times daily over 5 to 10 days. Specialists implemented massage by stroking infants' heads, torsos, and limbs with warm hands, moderate pressure, and rhythmical movements. Infants who were massaged gained weight more rapidly and were discharged from the hospital earlier than non-massaged infants with similar medical conditions. Potentially, parents and other adults might be trained to offer massage, although this therapy does not seem beneficial for all infants and in some cases (such as when stroking is too light or heavy) might even be experienced as unpleasant or stressful by preterm infants (Lester, Bigsby, & Miller-Loncar, 2004).

Another intervention that addresses infants' needs for human contact is called "kangaroo care." Infants in kangaroo care are placed chest to chest with their mothers in cloth carriers for prolonged periods during the day. Newborn infants who receive kangaroo care gain the comfort of skin-to-skin contact, easy access to breastfeeding, and a pleasant, steady temperature (Harrison, 2001; Field et al., 2004). However, this intervention may not be appropriate with extremely small or especially fragile infants.

For many years, it was common practice by nurses in neonatal intensive care units to minimize intrusive physical care (e.g., taking vital signs, changing diapers, bathing) so that infants could sleep and rest. Now pediatric experts are realizing that some kinds of touch are helpful—perhaps even necessary—for optimal development. The preliminary evidence indicates that caressing touch can be therapeutic for infants, yet clearly more research is needed on the short-term and long-term benefits (and any unintended effects) of various kinds of physical human contact.

A Body to Die For:
Body Image and Eating Disorders

In Chapter 4, we explain that *eating disorders* are ongoing problems in eating behaviors that seriously undermine the health of youngsters—usually adolescents but occasionally children in the elementary grades. The three common forms of eating disorders are *anorexia nervosa* (a person eats little or nothing for weeks or months), *bulimia* (a person attempts to enjoy food without gaining weight by eating a large amount of food and then purging it from the body by vomiting or taking laxatives), and *binging* (a person regularly responds to stress by eating excessively and uncontrollably). Without treatment, eating disorders take a serious toll on the body, including triggering hormonal changes, heart disease, imbalance of minerals and electrolytes, nerve damage, digestive problems, teeth and gum problems, diabetes, and gallbladder disease (Mayo Foundation for Medical Education and Research, 2006). For some young people, untreated eating disorders (especially anorexia nervosa) create such serious health complications that they cause death, and people with advanced anorexia nervosa are also at risk for suicide.

Eating disorders appear to originate due to several factors, including distortions in *body image* (perceptions of one's personal physical appearance); sensitivity to appearance after hearing critical comments by parents, peers, and others; exposure to countless media images of slender, well-shaped women and lean, muscular men; emotional problems, such as being depressed, obsessive, and compulsive; and genetic factors (Jensen, 2005). Such separate factors often become intertwined in young people with eating disorders. For example, an adolescent girl with anorexia nervosa may hear critical comments about her weight from her mother and classmates while growing up; the girl becomes depressed, has low self-esteem, and is extremely concerned about flaws in her appearance; and she is bothered by her obvious (in her mind) failure to meet standards of attractiveness she sees in thin supermodels and movie stars.

Although eating disorders most commonly occur in people in their teenage years and early 20s, the precursors to these problems may be evident in childhood. For example, youngsters often develop problems with body image during middle childhood (Ricciardelli, McCabe, Holt, & Finemore, 2003). Beginning at about age 5, children may express dissatisfaction with their body (especially about being "fat") and begin to diet and exercise. During middle childhood, many girls articulate a desire to be thinner, and boys express an interest in becoming more muscular. Unchecked dissatisfaction with body image, particularly when coupled with emotional problems, can evolve into full-fledged eating disorders, excessive exercise, and, in the case of boys especially, steroid use (Stout & Frame, 2004). As we indicate in Chapter 4, eating disorders (and here we add other problems resulting from distorted body images, such as steroid use) often require intensive and long-term treatment.

The Roles of Fathers in Children's Lives

In their research with parents, developmental psychologists have studied mothers more thoroughly than they have studied fathers. For example, there is considerably more research on children's bonds with mothers than bonds with fathers (Cabrera, 2005). Increasingly however, family researchers are recruiting fathers to participate in their investigations and finding that fathers play distinct and meaningful roles in children's lives (Lamb, Chuang, & Cabrera, 2005).

In Chapter 5 in the textbook, we summarize comparisons of the parenting styles used by mothers and fathers. For example, we indicate that mothers are more inclined to be the hands-on caregivers of children, whereas fathers are more physically playful and take a greater role in discipline, especially as children grow. Yet cross-cultural evidence suggests that fathers are not simply casual playmates for children—fathers and men generally spend a lot of time with children and care for children's many needs. In a large-scale observational study of 23 cultures, Mackey (2001) examined more than 55,000 interactions between men, women, and children in public places (stores, playgrounds, and the like). When men and women were together, women interacted more frequently with children than men did, but when men and women were separated, both sexes were actively engaged with children. Men and women were also similar in that they interacted more often with younger children than with older children, touched younger children more often, and kept the little ones close by. And both men and women showed a bias toward being with children of the same gender.

In-depth qualitative studies of fathers around the world confirm that fathers contribute to children's development in ways that sometimes overlap with, and at other times extend, the parenting of mothers. In general, fathers are capable, nurturing, and attentive parents, though the specific roles that individual fathers take on depend on many things, including the temperaments of fathers and children, families' circumstances, and cultural practices. In one intensive observational study conducted over a two-year period with the Batek of Malaysia, fathers took on active, nurturing roles that complemented the positions mothers fulfilled (Endicott, 1992). Infants spent more time with mothers than with fathers but fathers did "...hold, cuddle, and chatter to their sons and daughters with as much obvious enjoyment as is evident in mothers' behaviors" (Endicott, 1992, p. 285). Fathers took up the slack when children were displaced with a baby sibling, and fathers trained older sons to hunt. As occurs in every culture, individual differences were present among Batek mothers and fathers; in both sexes, some parents were inclined to be patient and others short-tempered.

Cultural Variations in Parenting Styles

In Chapter 5, we explain that *parenting styles* are the general patterns of behavior parents use to nurture and guide their children. Initially, developmental psychologist Diana Baumrind identified three distinct parenting styles, which she called *authoritarian, authoritative,* and *permissive*. Since Baumrind's groundbreaking research, other researchers have described a fourth style, *uninvolved*, which lacks the emotional warmth of a permissive style. Yet even these four categories do not adequately capture all of the parenting styles that are observed in families. In the table below, we describe and illustrate seven distinct parenting styles that have been observed in the United States; we also identify characteristics in children that tend to be associated with these styles and suggest implications for teachers and caregivers. Certainly these seven styles are not exhaustive of all methods of parenting, and many parents fluctuate in particular styles they use based on the circumstances—for instance, based on their own moods and those of their children, the kinds of misbehavior children get into, the presence of others, and so forth.

Parenting Styles	Description	Characteristics of Children	Example	Implications
Authoritarian parenting style in *some* American families	Parents convey relatively little emotional warmth, hold high expectations for children's behaviors, establish rules of behavior without regard for children's needs, expect rules to be obeyed without question, and allow little give-and-take in parent-child discussions.	• Unhappy • Anxious • Low in self-confidence • Lacking initiative • Dependent on others • Lacking in social skills and altruistic behaviors • Coercive in dealing with others • Defiant • Healthy outcomes may be present in some children, depending on cultural background and interpretation of parents' motives	A 6-year-old girl hovers around her peers at an after-school recreation center. She alternates between barking orders (which the others ignore) and retreating to be on her own.	Show emotional warmth and explain rules and procedures for classrooms and other settings. Keep in mind that authoritarian parenting styles at home may be adaptive in some cultural settings and in economically impoverished neighborhoods. Keep in mind that some children (depending on temperament and cultural background) may thrive with strict and demanding parenting.

table continues

Parenting Styles	Description	Characteristics of Children	Example	Implications
Authoritative parenting style in *some* American families	Parents provide a loving, supportive home environment, hold high expectations and standards for children's behavior, enforce household rules consistently, explain why some behaviors are acceptable and others are not, and include children in family decision-making.	• Happy • Self-confident • Curious • Independent and self-reliant • Effective social skills • Likable • Respectful of others • Successful and well-behaved at school	During a middle school parent-teacher conference, a father looks directly at his daughter and asks her why she has been disruptive in class and what she thinks she should do to improve her behavior.	Give children input into decision making and explain the reasons for your expectations and actions. Provide age-appropriate opportunities for independent activities and decision making.
Permissive parenting style in *some* American families	Parents provide a loving, supportive home environment, hold few expectations or standards for children's behavior, rarely punish inappropriate behavior, and allow children to make many of their own decisions (e.g., about eating, bedtime).	• Selfish • Unmotivated • Dependent on others • Demanding of attention • Disobedient	A high school student expects his teacher to immediately grade a class research paper that he turned in a month late.	Be warm but firm about expectations for behavior, and consistently apply rewards for obedience and sanctions for disobedience. Explain why certain behaviors are unacceptable, focusing on their impact on self and others. Explain how rules help children protect others' rights, feelings, and property.
Uninvolved parenting style in *some* American families	Parents provide little if any emotional support for children, hold few expectations or standards for behavior, have little interest in children's lives, and seem overwhelmed by their own problems.	• Disobedient • Demanding • Low in self-control • Low in tolerance for frustration • Lacking long-term goals	A 4-year-old girl has a difficult time adjusting to preschool, appears angry during class activities, and impulsively rips the pages from a book she doesn't like.	Show warmth consistently. Be firm in expectations for behavior, and follow through with consequences, conveying caring and respect for children's needs and rights. Explain why some behaviors are not in children's best interests and will not be tolerated. Help children learn to regulate their behavior in socially appropriate ways.

table continues

281

Parenting Style	Description	Characteristics of Children	Example	Implications
Parenting style in *some immigrant Asian* families	Parents train children at a young age to be self-disciplined and hard working. Parents foster a strong sense of familial investment in children; children may perceive that parents' strict controls reveal their interest and affection. Parents may perceive that achieving at high levels in school is the best route to economic security for children.	• Motivated to honor parents and ancestors • Hard-working in school • Reluctant to question parents' authority • Proficient in basic academic skills (e.g., letter recognition, counting) before starting school	A high school student wishes to bring home high grades and test scores to her parents. She is disappointed and hard on herself when she fails to excel.	Do not expect all children from Asian backgrounds to be star academic performers, and realize how much variation there is among Asian American families. Recognize the value of a strong commitment to education when you see it in children, and give them support in areas that may be difficult for them, such as grammar and vocabulary (for recent immigrants).
Parenting style in *some African American* families	Families may be strict *and* warm in disciplining children. Parents are supported by members of the extended family in raising children, and spirituality is often drawn on as a resource. Parents and other family members may teach children about coping strategies for dealing with racism; they may also instill cultural and ethnic pride in children.	• Motivated to comply with parents' requests and commands • Sense of responsibility for family members • Appreciative of extended family members • Knowledgeable of historical events reflecting oppression (e.g., slavery, economic inequities) • Proud of cultural and ethnic accomplishments	A 10-year-old boy is an active member of his church. He worships with his parents, siblings, aunts and uncles, and grandparents. He is fascinated with African history and likes to paint African figures from folklore he has learned.	Build on the strengths that children bring to your setting, such as their substantial knowledge of African history and African American heritage. Invite extended family members to events that showcase children's talents. Extend children's interests in racism and inequity by including writings by African and African American leaders in all fields.

table continues

Parenting Style	Description	Characteristics of Children	Example	Implications
Parenting style in *some immigrant Latino* families	Families may value social skills and focus on helping children learn to cooperate, take turns, and look after one another. Parents may encourage children to be quiet and respectful, rather than outspoken, with authority figures. Parents may be uncomfortable with praise that singles one child out from the group.	• Helpful and cooperative with other children • Sense of responsibility for family members • Concern that property and possessions be shared • Somewhat quiet in class • Presence of siblings and other family members at parent-teacher meetings	An 8-year-old boy walks to school with his two younger sisters. The three children eat or play together whenever their schedules overlap at school. The boy helps other children with routine tasks, such as zipping jackets. He is quiet but cooperative during lessons.	Welcome the helpful actions that you may notice from children. Gently point out particular circumstances, such as examinations, when children must work independently. With younger children, expect that cooperation is valued more strongly than independence.

Sources: Baumrind, 1971, 1982, 1989; Chao, 2000; Deater-Deakard, Dodge, Bates, & Pettit, 1996; Dekovic & Janssens, 1992; Lamborn & Felbab, 2001; Lamborn, Mounts, Steinberg, & Dornbusch, 1991; Maccoby & Martin, 1983; Okagaki & Diamond, 2000; Simons, Whitbeck, Conger, & Conger, 1991; Steinberg, 1993; Steinberg, Elmen, & Mounts, 1989; Stevenson, 1995; Taylor & Roberts, 1995; Trumbull, Rothstein-Fisch, Greenfield, & Quiroz, 2001.

Reading #5-3

Encouraging Family Involvement at School: The Parent Club

Parents and other heads of family typically do several things to prepare children for academic learning at school. Parents may read to their young children and raise them in a literate environment. Many parents teach children to recite the alphabet and count objects, and some parents are able to bring children to musical and dramatic performances, zoos and museums, the local library, and even distant lands. Parents are also apt to help school-aged children by expressing an interest in their schoolwork and helping them complete homework.

In Chapter 5, we suggest an additional way that parents and other family members can support children's education—by getting involved at their children's school. Parents can get involved in a wide range of ways, including coming to parent-teacher-student meetings and school orientations, volunteering in the classroom, helping with fund raisers, driving on field trips, and participating in school accountability groups. Yet parents and other family members tend to participate in school activities only when they receive a specific invitation to do so and are convinced that school personnel genuinely want them to be there. When parents do become involved at school, they may learn more about their children's education, exert a meaningful impact in the school, and develop their own social networks. They also gain informal opportunities to learn of their children's progress and any challenges in learning they might help children with at home.

One strategy for encouraging parent involvement is to establish a "Parent Club," which includes a central location—typically a separate room in the school—where family members can congregate while volunteering or visiting (Epstein, Coates, Salinas, Sanders, & Simon, 1997). One school's experiences with such a club are summarized by Principal Lucretia Coates:

> A Parent Club brings families together in a friendly environment where they feel welcomed and valued. It also may be called a Family Center, Family Resource Room, Parent Room, or another name to designate a place in the school for parents to meet and assist the school, teachers, children, and other families. Volunteers can work in the Parent Club room, or they may be requested to come to classrooms or other school locations. The room may serve as the volunteers' home-base at school.
>
> A Parent Club is not a formal Parent Teacher Association (P.T.A.) or Parent Teacher Organization (P.T.O.). These groups are usually more involved in school policies and decision making. In schools that do not have formal parent associations or have not yet added parents to their Advisory Councils or School Improvement Teams, a Parent Club may serve as a first step in preparing parents to take leadership roles in the school.
>
> A Parent Club must have a leader/advisor/coordinator who serves as a link between home and school. This may be a parent liaison, counselor, teacher, assistant principal, community resource person, or other talented individual. The leader is responsible for recruiting members, setting the tone of the Parent Club meetings, and helping parents feel at ease in the school. The leader must be sensitive to the differences in backgrounds, interests, skills, and talents of parents in order to help all families become contributing members of the Parent Club and helpful volunteers. The leader cannot dominate, but must be able to foster an atmosphere in which everyone feels vital and necessary. The leader conducts regularly scheduled meetings (at least once a week), helps organize activities, and coordinates teachers' requests for volunteers with parents' available times and talents.

Another key player in the organization and success of a Parent Club is the school principal. As an educational leader, the principal is responsible for welcoming parents, helping teachers and school staff understand the importance of parent participation, and encouraging parents to become involved in the Parent Club and other activities. The principal must designate a room for the Parent Club and support the meetings and activities conducted by the Parent Club.

Once parents are active partners, they soon find many ways to assist the school. In this elementary school, Parent Club members were asked to volunteer for a parent-child reading program, assist with a computer drive sponsored by a local grocery store, and assist the school, teachers, children, and administrators in other ways. During Black History month, the Parent Club organized an African Food Tasting Party. They researched African food, served food to students, and provided background information to teachers. They also learned other leadership roles. For example, for the first time, they went to lobby legislators at the state capital for increased education funding.

Although only a few parents attended the first meeting of the Parent Club, almost thirty participated by the end of the school year. When parents feel that they are contributing and needed partners, they become the Club's best recruiters for more volunteers. As a school builds a full program of partnerships, the Parent Club room may serve as a place where many types of involvement activities are conducted in addition to volunteer work. (Epstein et al., 1997, p. 39)

Reprinted with permission. Epstein, J. L., Coates, L., Salinas, K. C., Sanders, M. G., & Simon, B. S. (1997). *School, family, and community partnerships: Your handbook for action*. Thousand Oaks, CA: Corwin Press.

Parents' and Teachers' Beliefs About Child Development

In many respects, parents and teachers view children in a similar light. Yet as we suggest in Chapter 5, parents and teachers do not always see eye-to-eye on the details of children's educational needs. Let's look at some reasons for the similarities and differences in these adults' beliefs about children.

There are probably several reasons why parents and teachers often have similar beliefs about children. For one thing, both groups have considerable experience caring for youngsters. As a result, parents and teachers alike have gained many practical lessons about age-related characteristics of youngsters, such as curiosity in early childhood, an interest in games in middle childhood, and a capacity for introspection during adolescence. Sharing a common culture increases the odds that parents and teachers will have similar views about appropriate goals for children—for instance, trying hard in school, being good citizens, developing artistic or athletic talents, finding spiritual meaning in life, and so on (Goodnow & Collins, 1990). And finally, the daily contact parents and teachers have with youngsters sensitizes both groups to the distinctive temperaments, personalities, and intellectual talents of individual youngsters. For example, a parent and a teacher may both notice that a 14-year-old boy is good-natured, exceptionally talented in mathematics, and modest about his intelligence.

Yet differences in perspective can sometimes be extensive. Parents and teachers clearly have different responsibilities and experiences with children. Parents see children in the family and in the community; teachers see children at school. Parents have permanent and profoundly close relationships with children, whereas teachers care deeply for individual children but are obliged to distribute affection among a classroom of children and to pass on their charges to new teachers the following year. Parents have intimate knowledge of their children; teachers have a realistic sense of how particular children's academic skills compare to those of classmates. Parents come from a variety of educational backgrounds; teachers have college educations based in child development, educational psychology, methods of teaching, and the academic subject matter they teach to children.

To some degree, parents and teachers must develop similar understandings about children if they are to work cooperatively (e.g., Churchill, 1999). Nevertheless, it is rarely productive for teachers to try to convince parents to change their beliefs about children. (For one thing, parents are often right!) An alternative approach is for parents and teachers to share their perspectives and objectives for children. Parents and teachers do have a lot of common ground, including their mutual regard for children. When teachers take the time to build rapport and credibility with parents, they are in a better position to offer suggestions that parents will seriously consider. Chapter 5 offers additional recommendations for fostering good communication and forming effective partnerships with families.

The Six Substages of Piaget's Sensorimotor Stage

Imagine this situation:

> We show a colorful stuffed clown to 6-month-old Elena. Elena reaches for the clown in much the same way that she reaches for her teddy bear and her stacking blocks. She then drops it and squeals in delight as it falls to the floor. We pick up the clown and, as Elena watches, put it inside a box so that it is no longer visible. At this point, Elena seems to forget about her new toy and turns to play with something else.

Elena readily applies several schemes to the clown, including reaching-and-grasping, letting-go, and visually-following-a-moving-object. Yet she acts as if she cannot imagine a clown she cannot actually see: it is out of sight and therefore out of mind. Jean Piaget proposed that infants' early schemes are based primarily on perceptions (e.g., visual tracking) and behaviors (e.g., grabbing, dropping)—hence the label *sensorimotor* for Piaget's first stage of cognitive development. Only gradually do infants become capable of developing *mental* schemes that enable them to think about objects beyond their immediate view.

After extensive observations of infants and toddlers, especially his own three children, Piaget described the sensorimotor stage as a series of six substages. From her actions as well as her age, we can conclude that 6-month-old Elena is presently in the third substage. As we explore the six substages in the upcoming sections, we'll look back in time and follow Elena as she acquires many new capabilities.

Substage 1: Reflexes (Birth to 1 Month)

In the first month of life, infants' behaviors reflect innate and automatic responses to particular stimuli. For instance, if you put something in or near Elena's mouth at this substage, she will suck on it. If you put something against the palm of her hand, her fingers will close around it. Initially, Elena's actions are automatic, reflexive behaviors (like breathing and coughing) that keep her alive. Yet she soon begins to modify some reflexes to better accommodate to her environment. For instance, she quickly learns to distinguish between a nipple and the surrounding areas of a breast or bottle. And other reflexes, such as the tendency to grab onto something placed in her hand, fade away over time.

Substage 2: Primary Circular Reactions (1–4 Months)

In the first few months of life, infants' behaviors are focused almost exclusively on their own bodies (in Piaget's terminology, the behaviors are *primary*) and are repeated over and over again (i.e., they are *circular*). By the time Elena is 3 months old, she has repeated her innate reflexes countless times. She has also begun to refine them and to combine them into more complex actions. For example, she now opens and closes her hand and then puts it in her mouth. Although she is more focused on her own body than on the world around her, she is beginning to anticipate things that will happen based on clues in her environment. For instance, she may cry when hungry, but when her mother appears, she may quiet down as if she knows that she is about to be fed.

Substage 3: Secondary Circular Reactions (4–8 Months)

Sometime around 4 months, infants become more aware of, and more responsive to, the outside world (in Piaget's terminology, their behaviors become *secondary*), and they begin to notice that their behaviors can have interesting effects on the objects around them. For instance, as we saw earlier, at 6 months Elena picks up and then drops the clown; each time her caregiver gives the clown back to her, she may drop it again yet fret that she no longer has it. Elena seems fascinated by the effects of her actions, although at this point she is not necessarily making a conscious connection between the particular things she does and the resulting consequences. If you watch 7-month-old Madison explore a variety of objects in the Emotional Development: Infancy video clip on Observation CD 2, you will notice that her explorations seem similarly spontaneous and unplanned. More purposeful behaviors will appear in Substage 4.

Substage 4: Coordination of Secondary Circular Reactions (8–12 Months)

After repeatedly observing that certain actions lead to certain consequences, infants gradually acquire knowledge of cause-effect relationships. Accordingly, they begin to engage in **goal-directed behavior**: They behave in ways that they know will bring about desired results. For example, as a 9- or 10-month-old, Elena might drop the clown *intentionally*, knowing in advance that it will fall to the floor and waiting eagerly to see this happen.

Infants in the fourth substage also begin to combine behaviors in new ways to accomplish their goals. For example, when Elena sees the string of a pull-toy near her, rather than crawling over to the toy, she may instead reach out and grab the string. She will purposely pull it and will not be surprised that the toy comes to her so she can pick it up. At Substage 4, infants also acquire **object permanence**, the realization that physical objects continue to exist even when they are removed from view. Whereas at 6 months, Elena forgot about the toy clown once it was put in a box, at 10 months she knows where the clown is and may search its hiding place to retrieve it. In the Cognitive Development: Infancy video clip on Observation CD 1, 16-month-old Corwin shows object permanence when he looks for the toy elephant that his mother repeatedly hides.

Substage 5: Tertiary Circular Reactions (12–18 Months)

Beginning sometime around their first birthday, infants show increasing flexibility and creativity in their behaviors, and their experimentation with objects often leads to new outcomes (the term *tertiary* reflects this new versatility in previously acquired responses). For instance, imagine that at age 15 months, Elena is given a tennis ball and a coffee can. She'll explore the two objects thoroughly, rolling them, dropping them, throwing them, putting the ball inside the can, and so on. Her creative explorations now are quite deliberate.

Piaget illustrated tertiary circular reactions with a description of his daughter Jacqueline, then 14 months old:

Jacqueline holds in her hands an object which is new to her; a round, flat box which she turns all over, shakes, rubs against the bassinet, etc. She lets it go and tries to pick it up. But she only succeeds in touching it with her index finger, without grasping it. She nevertheless makes an attempt and presses on the edge. The box then tilts up and falls again. Jacqueline, very much interested in this fortuitous result, immediately applies herself to studying it....

Jacqueline immediatcly rcsts the box on the ground and pushes it as far as possible (it is noteworthy that care is taken to push the box far away in order to reproduce the same conditions as the first attempt, as though this were a necessary condition for obtaining the result). Afterward Jacqueline puts her finger on the box and presses it. But as she places her finger on the center of the box she simply displaces it and makes it slide instead of tilting it up. She amuses herself with this game and keeps it up (resumes it after intervals, etc.) for several minutes. Then, changing the point of contact, she finally again places her finger on the edge of the box, which tilts it up. She repeats this many times, varying the conditions, but keeping track of her discovery: now she only presses on the edge! (Piaget, 1952, p. 272)

Substage 6: Mental Representation (18–24 Months)

Piaget proposed that in the latter half of the second year, young children develop **symbolic thought**, the ability to represent and think about objects and events in terms of internal, mental entities, or *symbols*. They may "experiment" with objects in their minds, first predicting what will happen if they do something to an object, then transforming their plans into action. To some degree, mental prediction and planning replace overt trial-and-error as growing toddlers experiment and attempt to solve problems. By the time Elena is 2 years old, she is forming mental images of objects and events; in essence, she now has an imagination. She's also becoming more efficient at solving problems. Although she still uses her body to explore and experiment, her mind is an important part of the process as well.

The capacity for mental representation is seen in the emergence of **deferred imitation**, the ability to recall and copy another person's behaviors hours or days after their behaviors have been observed. Although infants show some ability to imitate others' actions quite early in life (beginning in the second substage, as Piaget noted), up until now they have imitated only the behaviors they see someone else demonstrating on the spot. Their newly acquired ability to recall and imitate other people's *past* actions enables them to engage in make-believe and pretend play. Thus, we may see Elena "talking" on a toy telephone or "driving" with the toy steering wheel attached to her car seat, even when the people around her are preoccupied with other matters.

As children move into more advanced stages of development, they don't entirely discard sensorimotor ways of interacting with the environment. Even as adults, we continue to use the behavioral and perceptual schemes we acquired as infants (reaching and grasping, following a moving object with our eyes, etc.), and sometimes trial-and-error experimentation is the only way to interact with a new and puzzling object.

Why Do Young Children Talk "Egocentrically"?

In his work with young children, Jean Piaget noticed that children often say things without considering the perspective of the listener—a phenomenon he called **egocentric speech**. For instance, children may leave out critical details as they tell a story, giving a fragmented version that a listener cannot possibly understand. As an illustration, an adult in Piaget's laboratory once told a story and asked a child whom we'll call Giovanna to retell it:

> **The adult's original:** Once upon a time, there was a lady who was called Niobe, and who had 12 sons and 12 daughters. She met a fairy who had only one son and no daughter. Then the lady laughed at the fairy because the fairy only had one boy. Then the fairy was very angry and fastened the lady to a rock. The lady cried for ten years. In the end she turned into a rock, and her tears made a stream which still runs today. (Piaget, 1959, p. 82)

> **Giovanna's version:** Once upon a time there was a lady who had twelve boys and twelve girls, and then a fairy [had] a boy and a girl. And then Niobe wanted to have some more sons. Then she was angry. She fastened her to a stone. He turned into a rock, and then his tears made a stream which is still running today. (Piaget, 1959, p. 102)

Notice that Giovanna never explained who "she," "her," and "he" were—things that couldn't possibly have been obvious to a listener. (She also remembered parts of the story incorrectly—errors that may reflect a limited attention span, elaboration, or other cognitive factors described in Chapter 7.)

Developmental theorists have offered various explanations for young children's egocentric speech. Here we'll consider four possibilities.

Piaget's Explanation

In Piaget's view, egocentric speech reflects the *egocentrism*—the general inability to look at the world from other people's perspectives—that characterizes preoperational thought. In Giovanna's rendition of the story we find one reason why, as Piaget suggested, social interaction is so important for cognitive development. Someone listening to the child's story might express confusion about who was angry and who turned into a rock. Repeated feedback from other people helps children learn that their thoughts and feelings are unique to them—that their perception of the world is not always shared by others and in some cases may not reflect the true state of affairs.

Vygotsky's Explanation

Another early developmental theorist, Lev Vygotsky, suggested that many instances of egocentric speech are better understood as talking to oneself than as talking to someone else. Such *self-talk*, Vygotsky proposed, is most likely to appear when children are engaged in challenging tasks that they must talk themselves through. (See the discussion of Vygotsky's theory in Chapter 6 in the textbook.)

A Language Development Perspective

As early as age 3, children begin to adapt their speech to the characteristics of their listeners—for instance, by using simpler language with toddlers than they use with adults and peers (see Chapter 9 in the textbook). Even so, they sometimes provide insufficient information for their listeners to understand their messages. Researchers who study language development suggest that egocentric speech is sometimes the result of young children's inability to express their thoughts clearly (McDevitt & Ford, 1987). In a nutshell, young children may not always have the words they need to describe objects and events in precise terms.

A Theory of Mind Perspective

As children get older, they acquire increasingly complex understandings of other people's mental states—thoughts, beliefs, emotions, and so on. In other words, children develop an increasingly sophisticated *theory of mind* (see Chapter 12 in the textbook). From a theory-of-mind perspective, egocentric speech may reflect ignorance about how the mind works. In particular, young children may not yet realize that people to whom they are speaking can make sense of new information only to the extent that they have sufficient knowledge to do so (Perner, 1991).

Contrasting Preoperational, Concrete Operational, and Formal Operational Reasoning

Jean Piaget identified many ways in which youngsters think and reason differently at different ages. Our discussion of Piaget's stages in the textbook only skims the surface of Piaget's stages of cognitive development. In the following two tables, we contrast children's thinking at the preoperational, concrete operational, and formal operational stages.

Contrasting Preoperational versus Concrete Operational Thought

PREOPERATIONAL THOUGHT	CONCRETE OPERATIONAL THOUGHT
Egocentrism Inability to see things from someone else's perspective; thinking that one's own perspective is the only one possible. *Example:* A child tells a story without considering what prior knowledge the listener is likely to have.	**Differentiation of one's own perspective from the perspectives of others** Recognition that different people see things differently and that one's own perspective may be incorrect. *Example:* A child asks for validation of his own thoughts (e.g., "Did I get that right?").
Confusion between physical and psychological events Confusion of external, physical objects with internal thoughts; thinking that thoughts have physical reality and that objects think and feel. *Example:* A child is afraid of the "monsters" in a closet and worries that a doll will feel lonely if left alone.	**Distinction between physical and psychological events** Recognition that thoughts don't have physical reality and physical objects don't have thoughts and feelings. *Example:* A child realizes that imagined monsters don't exist and that dolls cannot feel sad or lonely.
Lack of conservation Belief that amount changes when a substance is reshaped or rearranged, even though nothing has been added or taken away. *Example:* A child asserts that two rows of five pennies similarly spaced have equal amounts, but when one row is spread out, it has "more pennies."	**Conservation** Recognition that amount stays the same if nothing has been added or taken away, even when the substance is reshaped or rearranged. *Example:* A child asserts that two rows of five pennies are the same number of pennies regardless of spacing.
Irreversibility Lack of awareness that certain processes can be undone, or reversed. *Example:* A child doesn't realize that a row of five pennies previously made longer by extra spacing can be shortened back to its original length.	**Reversibility** Ability to envision how certain processes can be reversed. *Example:* A child moves the five pennies in the longer row close together again to demonstrate that both rows have the same amount.
Reliance on perception over logic Dependence on how things appear when drawing conclusions. *Example:* A child hears a story about a girl whose uncle gives her a baby rattle as a gift; though sad, the girl smiles so she won't hurt her uncle's feelings. When viewing a picture of the smiling girl, the child concludes that the girl feels happy (Friend & Davis, 1993).	**Reliance on logic over perception** Dependence on conceptual understandings when drawing conclusions. *Example:* A child hearing the story about the inappropriate gift and seeing the picture of the smiling girl concludes that the girl *looks* happy but actually feels sad (Friend & Davis, 1993).

table continues

PREOPERATIONAL THOUGHT	CONCRETE OPERATIONAL THOUGHT
Single classification Ability to classify objects in only one way at any given point in time. *Example:* A child denies that a mother can also be a doctor.	**Multiple classification** Recognition that objects may belong to several categories simultaneously (includes *class inclusion*). *Example:* A child acknowledges that a mother can also be a doctor, a jogger, and a spouse.
Transductive reasoning Reasoning that involves combining unrelated facts (e.g., inferring a cause-effect relationship simply because two events occur close together in time and space). *Example:* A child believes that clouds make the moon grow (Piaget, 1928).	**Deductive reasoning** Drawing an appropriate logical inference from two or more pieces of information. *Example:* A child deduces that if Jane is taller than Mary, and if Mary is taller than Carol, then Jane must be taller than Carol.

Contrasting Concrete Operational versus Formal Operational Thought

CONCRETE OPERATIONAL THOUGHT	FORMAL OPERATIONAL THOUGHT
Dependence on concrete reality Logical reasoning only about concrete objects that are readily observed. *Example:* A child has difficulty with the concept of negative numbers, wondering how something can possibly be less than zero.	**Ability to reason about abstract, hypothetical, and contrary-to-fact ideas** Logical reasoning about things that are not tied directly to concrete, observable reality. *Example:* A child understands negative numbers and is able to use them effectively in mathematical procedures.
Inability to formulate and test multiple hypotheses Identifying and testing only one hypothesis when seeking an explanation for a scientific phenomenon. *Example:* When asked what makes a pendulum swing faster or more slowly, a child states that the weight of the pendulum is the determining factor and disregards any observations she has made that contradict her hypothesis.	**Formulation and testing of multiple hypotheses** Developing and testing several hypotheses about cause-effect relationships related to a particular phenomenon. *Example:* When asked what makes a pendulum swing faster or more slowly, a child proposes that weight, length, and strength of initial push are all possible explanations and then tests the effects of each variable.
Inability to separate and control variables Confounding two or more variables when attempting to confirm or disprove a particular hypothesis about a cause-effect relationship. *Example:* In testing possible factors influencing the oscillation rate of a pendulum, a child adds more weight to the pendulum while at the same time also shortening the length of the pendulum string.	**Separation and control of variables** Testing one variable at a time while holding all others constant, in an attempt to confirm or disprove a particular hypothesis about a cause-effect relationship. *Example:* In testing factors that influence a pendulum's oscillation rate, a child tests the effect of weight while keeping string length and strength of push constant and then tests the effect of length while keeping weight and push constant.
Lack of proportional reasoning Lack of understanding about the nature of proportions. *Example:* A child cannot make sense of the procedure his teacher demonstrates for converting fractions to ratios.	**Proportional reasoning** Understanding proportions and using them effectively in mathematical problem solving. *Example:* A child works easily with proportions, fractions, decimals, and ratios.

Reading #6-4

Using Piaget's Clinical Method

In Chapter 6, the textbook describes Jean Piaget's theory of cognitive development. Piaget pioneered a research technique known as the *clinical method*, in which he presented a variety of problems and tasks and asked children a series of questions to probe their reasoning processes. An experienced practitioner often knows the right questions to ask in order to zero in on a child's beliefs and understandings, but novices sometimes need a little structure and guidance to conduct an effective clinical interview. Following are three examples of interviews you might conduct.

Conservation of Substance

Materials:
- Two equal-size balls of clay
- A small amount of clay on the side

Procedure:

1. Present the two balls of clay. Say <u>Are these balls of clay the same size?</u> If the child says no, then say <u>Then please make them the same size.</u> Allow the child to add or subtract clay until satisfied that the balls are equal.

2. Smash one ball into a pancake shape. Say <u>Does one of these have more clay than the other, or do both balls have the same amount?</u> Record the child's response.

3. Say <u>Can you tell me or show me how you know this is true?</u> Record the child's response.

Interpretation:

Children show conservation of substance if their response indicates an awareness that the two amounts of clay must be equal because nothing has been added or subtracted in the transformation. Examples include:
- Statements such as "Changing shape doesn't change the amount" or "You didn't add any more clay, so they're both still the same."
- Behaviors such as rolling the pancake back into a ball, or flattening the ball into a pancake so that both pieces of clay appear equal again.

Children show a lack of conservation if they say the two pieces of clay are different in amount and justify that conclusion on the basis of the clay's appearance. Examples include:
- Statements such as "The ball is taller" or "The pancake is skinnier."
- Behaviors such as adding more clay to one in order to make the two pieces the "same" again.

Conservation of substance appears early in concrete operations, usually when children are about 6 or 7 years old.

Conservation of Displaced Volume

Materials:
- Two equal-size balls of clay, and a small amount of clay on the side
- Two glasses containing equal amounts of water
- Two rubber bands
- A table knife

Procedure:

1. Present the two glasses of water, with one rubber band around each glass at the level of the water's surface. Say <u>Do both glasses have the same amount of water?</u> If the child says no, say <u>Then please make them the same</u> and allow the child to pour water from one glass to the other until satisfied that the amounts are equal.

2. Present the two balls of clay. Say <u>Are these balls of clay the same size?</u> If the child says no, then say <u>Then please make them the same size.</u> Allow the child to add or subtract clay until satisfied that the balls are equal.

3. Place one ball of clay into a glass of water as the child watches. Say <u>Did you see the water go up? Let's move the rubber band to the place where the top of the water is.</u> Move the rubber band to the level of the water's surface.

4. Take the second ball of clay and second glass of water. Say <u>I'm going to cut this ball of clay into two pieces.</u> Using the knife, cut the ball into two approximately equal pieces.

5. Say <u>How far do you think the water in this glass will go up when I put the two pieces of clay into it? Please move the rubber band up to the spot where you think the water will go.</u> Allow the child to adjust the rubber band until satisfied with its location.

6. Say <u>Tell me why you put the rubber band where you did.</u> Record the child's response.

7. Say <u>Let's see what happens.</u> Drop the two pieces of clay into the glass. Say <u>Were you right?</u> Record the child's response.

8. Say <u>The water in this glass is the same height as the water in the other glass. Can you explain why that is?</u> Record the child's response.

Interpretation:

Children show conservation of displaced volume if their response indicates an awareness that the same amount of water is being displaced in each glass. Examples include:
- Placing the rubber band on the second glass at a level equal with the rubber band on the first glass.
- Statements such as "There's the same amount of clay in each glass." Statements like these are considered to indicate conservation even if the child's original prediction was incorrect.

Children show a lack of conservation if they predict that the water in the second glass will rise to a different height than that in the first glass *and* if they cannot later justify why the two heights are the same. Examples include:
- Placing the rubber band of the second glass higher or lower than that of the first glass.
- Statements such as "There is more clay in the second glass" or "The pieces in the second glass are smaller."

Conservation of displaced volume appears later than most other forms of conservation, usually not until age 11 or 12 at the earliest (Linn & Pulos, 1983; Sund, 1976).

Proportional Reasoning

Materials:
- A piece of poster board or large sheet of thick paper, with a stick figure drawn on each side. One figure, labeled "Mr. Little," is 20 cm tall. The other figure, labeled "Mr. Big," is 35 cm tall.
- Two thin pieces of wood (such as slats or dowels) at least 45 cm (18 inches) long. One (the "greenie" ruler) is marked in green ink at 5-cm intervals. The other (the "reddie" ruler) is marked in red ink at 2-cm intervals.
- A pencil
- A sheet of blank paper

Procedure:

1. Place the greenie and reddie rulers out of sight. Show the child the two stick figures. Say <u>Here is Mr. Little, and here is Mr. Big. I want you to measure how tall they are.</u>

2. Show the child the greenie ruler. Say <u>Here is a special ruler from the planet Xeron. People on planet Xeron don't measure with centimeters or inches, they measure with units they call "greenies."</u> Give the greenie ruler to the child. Say <u>I'd like you to measure how many greenies tall Mr. Little is.</u> Let the child measure Mr. Little, assisting if necessary, until a height of 4 greenies is obtained.

3. Say <u>Now I'd like you to measure how many greenies tall Mr. Big is.</u> Let the child measure Mr. Big, assisting if necessary, until a height of 7 greenies is obtained.

4. Remove the greenie ruler from sight, and bring out the reddie ruler. Say <u>Here is a ruler from the planet Phylus. People on planet Phylus measure with units they call "reddies."</u> Give the child the reddie ruler. Say <u>I'd like you to measure how many reddies tall Mr. Little is.</u> Let the child measure Mr. Little, assisting if necessary, until a height of 10 reddies is obtained.

5. Remove the reddie ruler from sight. Say <u>Now let's review what we know so far. Mr. Little is 4 greenies tall and Mr. Big is 7 greenies tall. Mr. Little is 10 reddies tall. Without measuring, see if you can figure out how tall Mr. Big must be in reddies.</u> Give the child the pencil and blank paper. Say <u>You may use pencil and paper if you wish.</u> Allow the child to work as long as necessary.

6. After the child gives you a prediction for Mr. Big's height in reddies, say <u>How did you arrive at that answer?</u> Record the child's response.

7. Give the child the picture of Mr. Big and the reddie ruler. Say <u>Now measure Mr. Big to see if you are right</u>. Let the child measure Mr. Big, assisting if necessary, until a height of $17\frac{1}{2}$ reddies is obtained. Say <u>Mr. Big is $17\frac{1}{2}$ reddies tall. Can you tell me why that is the correct answer?</u> Record the child's response.

Interpretation:

Children show proportional reasoning if their response indicates the use of multiplication, division, ratios, or fractions. Examples include:
- The correct answer of $17\frac{1}{2}$.
- Statements such as "The ratio of Mr. Big to Mr. Little in reddies is the same as the ratio in greenies" or "4 is to 7 as 10 is to $17\frac{1}{2}$" or "10 is 2.5 times 4, so the answer must be 2.5 times 7." Statements like these indicate proportional reasoning even if the child's original prediction was incorrect.

Children show a lack of proportional reasoning if they use addition or subtraction to obtain an answer *and* if they cannot later explain how the correct answer is obtained. Examples include:
- An incorrect answer (often "13").
- Statements such as "The difference between 4 and 7 is 3, so I added 3 to 10 and got 13" or "4 plus 6 equal 10, so I added 6 to 7."

Proportional reasoning is one aspect of formal operational thinking.

Reading #7-1

Promoting Children's Development Through Modeling

As noted in the discussion of apprenticeships in Chapter 6, one important way in which adults teach children more advanced skills is by demonstrating how to perform those skills. Such **modeling**—exhibiting desired behaviors so that someone else can observe and learn them—is a central focus of *social learning theory*, a perspective introduced in Chapter 1 in the textbook.

You can probably think of many skills that you've acquired by watching other people do them first. For instance, your mother or father may have shown you how to interpret a road map, find certain kinds of books at the library, or make a list for a grocery shopping trip. Your teachers have undoubtedly modeled many skills for you—skills such as how to write a lab report, how to write a persuasive essay, how to conjugate the Spanish verb *estudiar*, or how to solve various kinds of mathematical word problems.

Numerous research studies demonstrate modeling's effectiveness as a means of teaching cognitive and social skills to growing children. Consider these studies as examples:

- Children who have difficulty solving subtraction problems that require regrouping ("borrowing") become more successful problem solvers when they see the procedure modeled by someone else. In one experiment, children actually benefited more from watching a peer solve subtraction problems than from watching a teacher do it (Schunk & Hanson, 1985).

- In another experiment, young children were taught not to speak to strangers. One group of children heard a lecture about the dangers of following strangers and about the things they should do if a stranger tried to entice them; nevertheless, very few of these children tried to resist a friendly stranger who later appeared on the playground. A second group actually observed another child demonstrate techniques for resisting strangers; most of these children resisted the stranger's advances (Poche, Yoder, & Miltenberger, 1988).

- When a teacher models effective reading comprehension techniques—techniques such as summarizing information, asking oneself questions about the information, predicting what a textbook is likely to say next, and so on—children begin to demonstrate these same skills, and their reading comprehension improves, in some cases quite dramatically (see the discussion of *reciprocal teaching* in Chapter 6).

Helping Children Learn From Models

According to social learning theorists (e.g., Bandura, 1977, 1986), four conditions are necessary before children can successfully imitate someone else's behavior:

1. **Attention.** To learn from a model, children must first *pay attention* to the model—they must watch carefully as the model demonstrates proper procedures and techniques. Children's overt behaviors—whether they are remaining quiet and looking directly at the

model—provide some indication of whether they are paying attention to what the model is doing. But appearances can be deceiving. For example, you might be able to think of times when, as a student, you watched a teacher demonstrate a particular skill without thinking at all about what the teacher was doing. Attention, then, is a *mental* as well as physical process.

Adults can gain and maintain children's attention in a variety of ways. For instance, they can ask children to answer questions about actions just demonstrated. They can place especially distractible children close by. And they can give reasons why the modeled skills are important—reasons that make children *want* to pay attention.

2. **Retention.** After paying attention, children must *remember* what the model does—the specific actions required, the sequence in which those actions should be performed, and so on. Social learning theorists propose that children may remember modeled behaviors both as verbal representations (such as step-by-step instructions or labels that described the actions being performed) and as visual images of the behaviors they have seen. These verbal and visual **memory codes** serve as guides when children perform the observed behavior, whether they perform it immediately after the model has illustrated it or at some time in the future. As one illustration of such a memory code, teachers sometimes teach the mnemonic *Please excuse my dear Aunt Sally* to help students remember the order in which they should work with various components of an algebraic expression: expressions within *p*arentheses (*Please*), *e*xponents (*excuse*), *m*ultiplication and *d*ivision (*my dear*), and *a*ddition and *s*ubtraction (*Aunt Sally*). As another example, swimming instructors sometimes use the labels "chicken," "airplane," and "soldier" to describe the different arm positions of the elementary backstroke.

Considerable evidence indicates that learning from a model is easier if children have assistance in forming memory codes for the behaviors they observe (Alford & Rosenthal, 1973; Bandura & Jeffery, 1973; Bandura, Jeffery, & Bachicha, 1974; Coates & Hartup, 1969; Cohen, 1989; Gerst, 1971; Rosenthal, Alford, & Rasp, 1972). For example, in an early study by Rosenthal and his colleagues (1972), 7-year-old children watched an adult model as she formed groups of three objects; each group consisted of a red object, a yellow object, and a blue object. The children learned the procedure most successfully when the model described what she was doing in specific terms, like this:

> So you see, each time I picked one thing of one color, another thing of a different color, and another thing of the last color. So I might pick a blue car, a red block and a yellow wooden bead; or a yellow block, a red car, and a blue wooden bead. (Rosenthal et al., 1972, p. 187)

Children for whom the model either gave a vague explanation ("I'll take one of these, and one of those, and one of those others and put them here") or remained silent throughout the procedure had far less success in learning what needed to be done.

3. **Motor reproduction.** In addition to attention and retention, children must be capable of *physically reproducing* (i.e., successfully copying) the modeled behavior. When an individual cannot reproduce an observed behavior, perhaps because of physical immaturity or disability, this third step obviously cannot occur. For example, a child with articulation difficulties may never be able to pronounce *sassafras* correctly no matter how many times he has heard the word spoken.

Reproduction of an observed behavior as soon as it has been observed facilitates learning for at least two reasons. For one thing, it enables children to encode that behavior, not only in verbal and visual forms, but perhaps in a *motoric* form as well—that is, in terms of the specific actions it encompasses (Cohen, 1989). Furthermore, by modeling a behavior in the presence of the model, children can get feedback about how to improve their performance (Bandura, 1977; Schunk, 1981).[1] For example, when teaching division to children who are having difficulty with mathematics, instruction that includes an opportunity for practice and immediate feedback about the quality of performance is clearly superior to instruction that provides no opportunity for such practice and feedback (Schunk, 1981).

4. **Motivation.** The final necessary ingredient for modeling is motivation to exhibit the modeled behavior: Children must want to demonstrate what they have learned. Children see the adults around them—parents, teachers, and so on—model a wide variety of behaviors every day, but they typically do not imitate all of those behaviors. We authors think of our own children, who have successfully imitated skills such as how to address invitations for a birthday party, how to find a friend's phone number in a telephone book, and how to deposit money in a savings account at the bank. Other skills continue to elude them, however—skills such as how to cook cauliflower, how to keep their bedrooms neat and orderly, and how to keep the kitchen floor sparkling clean—because they have little motivation to master these behaviors.

Identifying Effective Models

Most of the models from whom children learn are **live models**—real people that they actually see doing something. Children acquire many behaviors by watching family members, neighbors, teachers, and peers. In the classroom, for instance, they may learn by watching their teachers solve an algebraic equation on the chalkboard, observing a visiting police officer demonstrate important rules of bicycle safety, or hearing how a peer gives a campaign speech.

Children are also influenced by **symbolic models**—real or fictional characters portrayed in books, in films, on television, and through various other media. For example, they might learn something about military strategy by reading about George Washington's tactics during the battle at Yorktown, or they might learn how to use a certain kind of computer software by watching a video or television show that demonstrates the process.

Social learning theorists have found some consistency in the types of models that children are likely to imitate (Bandura, 1977, 1986; Rosenthal & Bandura, 1978). Effective models typically exhibit one or more of the following characteristics:

- **Competence.** Children typically try to imitate people who do something well, not those who do it poorly.

---

[1]Note, however, that some children may prefer to practice newly learned behaviors in private before showing an adult what they have learned. For instance, this may be the case for many Native American children (García, 1994; Grant & Gomez, 2001; Sanders, 1987; Suina & Smolkin, 1994).

- **Prestige and power.** Children often imitate those who are famous or powerful—perhaps people who are renowned at a national or international level (e.g., a world leader or an Olympic athlete) or perhaps people who are prestigious only within a more local context (e.g., a teacher, scout leader, community center director, or well-respected peer).

- **"Gender-appropriate" behavior.** Children are most likely to model behaviors that they believe are appropriate for their gender. Different children are likely to define "gender-appropriate" somewhat differently, with some holding rigidly to stereotypes as to what is appropriate for males and females.

- **Behavior relevant to one's own situation.** Children are most likely to model behaviors they believe will help them in their own circumstances.

Curiously, in some cases a model who demonstrates a behavior quickly and easily is *not* the most effective model, especially when children have had little or no history of success with the task in question. In these situations, **coping models**—those who struggle with the task at first but eventually complete it successfully—may have a greater impact on children's performance, perhaps because children perceive these models to be more similar to themselves in ability (Schunk, Hanson, & Cox, 1987; Schunk & Zimmerman, 1997).

At school, teachers are, of course, among the most influential models that children are likely to observe and imitate. But teachers can bring other adult models into the classroom as well—perhaps a scientist, newspaper reporter, or novelist—to talk about and demonstrate their areas of expertise. It may be particularly valuable to invite people who engage in nongender-stereotypical careers (e.g., female mathematicians and engineers, male secretaries and nurses) and people who share children's ethnic backgrounds—to broaden children's views regarding what skills are appropriate and relevant for their own circumstances (Huston, 1983; Pang, 1995).

Examples of Information Processing Deficiencies
in Children With Learning Disabilities

As noted in Chapter 7, a child or adolescent with a **learning disability** has significant difficulty with one or more specific cognitive processes. Following are examples of the kinds of difficulties that might be present:

- **Perceptual difficulty:** Difficulty understanding or remembering information received through a particular sensory modality.

- **Memory difficulty:** Lower-than-average capacity to remember information, either over the short or long run; more specifically, a problem with either working memory or long-term memory.

- **Metacognitive difficulty:** Difficulty using effective learning strategies, monitoring one's own comprehension, and in other ways regulating one's own learning.

- **Difficulty processing oral language**: Trouble understanding spoken language or remembering what one has been told.

- **Reading difficulty:** Trouble recognizing printed words or comprehending what one has just read. An extreme form of this condition is known as *dyslexia*. Dyslexia is described in Chapter 10 of the textbook.

- **Written language difficulty:** Problems in handwriting, spelling, or expressing oneself coherently on paper.

- **Mathematical difficulty:** Trouble thinking about or remembering information involving numbers (e.g., a poor sense of time or direction, difficulty learning basic number facts). An extreme form of this condition is known as *dyscalculia*.

- **Difficulty with social perception:** Trouble interpreting other people's social cues and signals (e.g., difficulty perceiving another person's feelings or reactions to a situation), resulting in frequent inappropriate responses in social situations.

Reading #8-1

Fetal Alcohol Syndrome

In its discussion of intelligence in Chapter 8, the textbook points out that children's intelligence can be negatively affected by a variety of toxic substances. One such substance is alcohol. When mothers consume alcoholic beverages during pregnancy, their children's development may be in jeopardy. In extreme cases, children are born with **fetal alcohol syndrome (FAS)**, a condition marked by many of the following characteristics:

- Distinctive facial features (e.g., wide-set eyes and a thin upper lip)
- Visible birth defects (e.g., cleft lip, club foot)
- Defects in the heart and circulatory system
- Abnormalities in joints
- Small teeth
- Hearing difficulties
- Convulsions or epilepsy
- Short attention span
- Poor motor coordination
- Delayed language
- Mental retardation

In *The Broken Cord*, Michael Dorris (1989) described his adopted son Adam, who was eventually diagnosed with FAS. When Adam finished elementary school, he had only the most rudimentary knowledge and skills; he did not yet know the town, state, or country in which he lived, nor could he do simple arithmetic or count money. His difficulties followed him into the secondary grades; very little school subject matter seemed to "sink in," despite intensive instruction both at school and at home.

Throughout Adam's school years, neither his parents nor his teachers understood the nature or extent of his disability. Sadly, some of Adam's teachers assumed that his success or failure at school rested entirely on the parents' effort (or lack of effort) to help their son. On one occasion a social studies teacher sent home a note asking the parents to help Adam study for a test on a particular aspect of the U.S. government. Despite a weekend of intensive—and exhausting—drill and practice at home, Adam answered not a single test item correctly the following Monday. His teacher sent home his test paper with a frowning face and a note saying, ""I *asked* you to help him on this" (p. 129).

The teacher's finger-pointing is an example of an inaccurate *attribution*. In Chapter 13, the textbook describes the nature and effects of children's attributions for their own successes and failures. But the fact is, teachers and other adults also form attributions for children's successes and failures (Reyna, 2000; Weiner, 2000). The teacher attributed Adam's failure to lack of effort—a controllable cause—and so was angry about the parents' apparent noncompliance with what was, to her, a reasonable request. In fact, Adam's difficulties were probably based in biology and so could not be fully overcome, although they could be accommodated with loving and supportive attention, realistic goals, and instruction tailored to his learning abilities.

Reading #8-2

Adaptive Skills Considered in Identifying Children With Mental Retardation

In its discussion of intelligence in Chapter 8, the textbook states that in order to be identified as having mental retardation, children must exhibit two characteristics. First, they must have low intelligence: They typically have IQ scores no higher than 65 or 70, reflecting performance in the bottom 2% of their age group. Second, they must show deficits in **adaptive behavior**: They must have difficulty with basic skills related to daily living. The American Association on Mental Retardation (1992) has described ten adaptive skills that should be considered in assessing adaptive behavior:

- **Communication:** Skills related to understanding and expressing ideas through spoken and written language and through body language.

- **Self-care:** Skills related to hygiene, eating, dressing, and grooming.

- **Home-living:** Skills related to general functioning at home, including housekeeping, laundry, food preparation, budgeting, and home safety.

- **Social:** Skills related to social interaction, including adhering to social conventions for interaction, helping others, recognizing feelings, forming friendships, controlling impulses, and abiding by rules.

- **Community use:** Skills related to using community resources effectively, including shopping, using local transportation and facilities, and obtaining services.

- **Self-direction:** Skills related to making choices, following a schedule, initiating activities appropriate to the context, completing required tasks, seeking needed assistance, and solving problems.

- **Health and safety:** Skills related to personal health maintenance, basic first aid, physical fitness, basic safety, and sexuality.

- **Functional academics:** Skills acquired in the school curriculum that have direct application to independent living, such as reading, writing, and basic arithmetic.

- **Leisure:** Skills related to initiating self-chosen leisure and recreational activities based on personal interests, playing socially with others, and abiding by age and cultural norms for activities undertaken.

- **Work:** Skills related to holding a job, including specific job skills, appropriate social behavior, completion of tasks, awareness of schedules, and money management.

Teaching Children with Limited English Proficiency

Even when families live in an English-speaking country, many of them (several million in the United States) speak a language other than English at home (McKeon, 1994; National Association of Bilingual Education, 1993). Some of these families are recent immigrants to the country, but others (e.g., many Native American, Puerto Rican, and Mexican American families) have been born on U.S. soil (Pérez, 1998b). Some children (like Mario, whose language development is described throughout Chapter 9 of the textbook) have ample exposure to English outside of the home. However, others have little exposure to English prior to their enrollment in school. As a result, they have **limited English proficiency** (**LEP**)—they are fluent in their native language but not in English—and so have difficulty communicating their ideas and understanding others in an English-based classroom. One estimate indicates that more than 5% of the public school population in the United States has limited English proficiency, and the number increases every year (U.S. Department of Education, 1993).

To the extent that children have not encountered English prior to the school years, they are apt to have trouble with schoolwork in an English-based classroom. Research consistently indicates that, on average, students with limited English proficiency achieve at higher levels in bilingual education programs than in English-only classrooms (Garcia, 1995; Snow, 1990; Willig, 1985; Wright, Taylor, & Macarthur, 2000). The optimal bilingual education proceeds through a gradual phase-in of the use of English in students' education, perhaps in a sequence such as the following:

1. LEP students join native English-speakers for classes in subject areas that do not depend too heavily on language skills (e.g., art, music, physical education). They study other subject areas in their native language and also begin classes in English as a Second Language (ESL).

2. Once students have acquired some English proficiency, instruction in English begins for one or two additional subject areas (perhaps for mathematics and science).

3. When it is clear that students can learn successfully in English in these subject areas, they join their English-speaking classmates in regular classes in the subjects.

4. Eventually students are sufficiently proficient in English to join the mainstream in all subject areas, and they may no longer require their ESL classes (Krashen, 1996).

Bilingual education programs are especially effective when they encourage skills in students' native language as well as in English—in essence, when they foster true bilingualism rather than proficiency only in English (Krashen, 1996; Losey, 1995; Pérez, 1998a).

Effects of Reading and Writing on Cognitive Development

Reading and writing are, of course, valuable in their own right. But in addition, reading and writing activities can promote cognitive development more generally. When children and adolescents read regularly, they add to the knowledge base that is so important for helping them interpret and respond to new experiences effectively. Reading also exposes young people to more sophisticated vocabulary than they typically encounter while conversing with others or watching television (Stanovich, 2000).

Writing, too, promotes learning and cognition. For instance, writing about a particular topic enhances children's understanding of the topic (Benton, 1997; Klein, 1999; Konopak, Martin, & Martin, 1990). In addition, various kinds of writing activities may encourage children to engage in and thereby further develop specific cognitive skills, including organization, elaboration, and critical thinking (Baron, 1987; Greene & Ackerman, 1995; Kellogg, 1994). By assigning writing activities in all areas of the school curriculum—in science, mathematics, social studies, and so on, as well as in language arts—and in activities outside of school as well, teachers and others who work with children and adolescents promote development in specific content domains as well as in writing per se.

Our society has a significantly higher literacy rate than it did 50 or 100 years ago (Chall, 1996). Yet even today, many children and adolescents—perhaps because of inherited disabilities or perhaps because of insufficient opportunities and instruction—do not have the reading and writing skills they need to learn effectively in school or to participate fully in adult society. Fortunately, researchers and practitioners are making great strides in discovering how best to promote literacy development in people of all ages.

Reading #10-2

Chall's Stages of Reading Development

As you have discovered in Chapter 10 in the textbook, reading is a complex activity that encompasses numerous skills and abilities. One prominent reading theorist, Jeanne Chall (1996), has proposed that reading development involves six qualitatively distinct stages. At each stage, children and adolescents acquire new knowledge and skills that provide a foundation for any stages that follow. As we describe the stages, we also list ages and approximate grade levels at which they appear. These ages and grade levels typify reading development in many Western, English-speaking schools at the present time; they do not necessarily apply to other cultural contexts or other historical periods (Chall, 1996).

Stage 0: Prereading (To Age 6)

Children develop some awareness of word sounds and learn to recognize most letters of the alphabet. They can pretend to read a book and know enough to hold the book right-side up and turn the pages one at a time. However, these prereading activities depend little, if at all, on actual print. (Chall's Stage 0 encompasses the *emergent literacy* described in the textbook.)

Stage 1: Initial Reading, or Decoding (Ages 6–7, Grades 1–2)

Children focus on learning letter-sound relationships and gain increasing insight into the nature of English spelling. They depend almost entirely on the printed page as they read; in Chall's words, they are "glued to the print."

Stage 2: Confirmation, Fluency, Ungluing from Print (Ages 7–8, Grades 2–3)

Children solidify the letter-sound relationships they learned in Stage 1 and automatize their recognition of many common words. They are beginning to take advantage of the redundancies in language, as well as their general knowledge about the world, and so they are less dependent on each and every letter and word on the page (in Chall's words, they are "ungluing from print"). They become increasingly fluent in their reading and can read silently. Although children now read for meaning, most of what they read confirms what they already know; for instance, they read familiar books and stories but do not yet read textbooks that introduce new ideas.

Stage 3: Reading for Learning the New (Ages 9–14, Grades 4–8 or 9)

Children can now learn new information from the things they read; by the end of Stage 3, reading surpasses listening as a means of acquiring information. Children begin to study the traditional academic content areas (science, history, geography) in earnest and gain much of their knowledge about these subjects from textbooks. They also begin to develop strategies for finding information in chapters, books, and reference materials (looking at headings, consulting indexes, etc.).

Reading materials become increasingly complex, abstract, and unfamiliar during Stage 3, and success at reading and understanding them increasingly relies on children's prior understandings of word meanings and the subject matter. Accordingly, children whose language skills and general world knowledge are relatively limited begin to struggle with reading and learning. This **fourth-grade slump** is often seen in children from low socioeconomic backgrounds, perhaps because they have had less access to reading materials and enriching educational opportunities (museum visits, family travel, etc.) than their more economically privileged peers (Chall, 1996).

Early in Stage 3, children learn best from reading material that presents a single viewpoint in a clear, straightforward manner, and they typically take what they read at face value. As they reach grades 7 and 8, however, they begin to analyze and think critically about what they read.

Stage 4: Multiple Viewpoints (Age 14 on, High School)

In high school, teenagers become more skilled readers of textbooks, reference materials, and sophisticated works of fiction. They can now handle reading materials that present multiple points of view, and they can integrate the new ideas they encounter in text with their previous knowledge about a topic.

Stage 5: Construction and Reconstruction (Age 18 on, College)

Especially if young people go on to college, they may begin to construct their *own* knowledge and opinions (often at a high level of abstraction) by analyzing, synthesizing, and evaluating what others have written. They also read more purposefully; that is, they may read certain parts of a text but skip other parts to accomplish their goals for reading the text as efficiently as possible. Chall has estimated that fewer than 40% of college students develop their reading skills to a Stage 5 level.

In general, then, as young people move through the elementary and secondary grades, they read with greater fluency and flexibility and become able to read increasingly complex, unfamiliar, and abstract material. As they acquire the skills of new stages, however, they do not necessarily lose previously learned skills. For example, even college students proficient at Stage 5 reading may occasionally relax with a mystery novel that they read in a Stage 2 or Stage 3 fashion (Chall, 1996).

Reading #10-3

Storybook Discussions

In Chapter 10, the textbook emphasizes the importance of storybook reading as a way of promoting *emergent literacy* in young children. Even before children are reading books themselves, discussions of storybooks can help them learn that books are to be interpreted and in other ways *thought about* as well as simply read. For example, in the following dialogue, a kindergarten teacher has just read *Goldilocks and the Three Bears* to her students:

Teacher:	What sort of girl is Goldilocks?
Andrew:	She's curious.
Teacher:	What does "curious" mean?
Andrew:	That you get into trouble.
Charlotte:	She's a robber. She eats food and goes into houses.
Mary Ann:	That's right. She could be a robber. Robbers go into people's houses.
Teacher:	Did she plan on robbing the bears?
Jill:	Yes she did. They forgot to lock the door. The father said, "Don't forget to lock the door."
Janie:	She *is* a robber. She could of stoled their money.
Teddy:	Maybe her parents got killed and she was looking for a house.
Franklin:	She just wanted to go in the house. She wanted to sit in a chair because she was tired from walking too much.
Teacher:	Why was she in the woods?
Jonathan:	Probably she got lost and she was looking for a new house.
Jill:	Or looking for blackberries . . .
Mary Ann:	Maybe she was looking for blackberries and she thought this was the way she always went through the woods, but it wasn't.
Teddy:	Maybe she was cutting down wood.
Clarice:	What if she thinks it's her own house?
Charlotte:	She *did* think it's her own house. She probably has the same furniture.
Karen:	That could happen.
Jeremy:	She went in because of being tired. And when she heard footprints she thought it was her mommy and father. And when she woke up it was the bears. (Paley, 1984, pp. 51-52)

Notice how the children piggy-back on one another's analyses. For instance, when Charlotte suggests that Goldilocks might be a robber, Mary Ann provides evidence that this was the case ("Robbers go into people's houses"). And when Teddy speculates about a possible motive for Goldilocks's illegal behavior ("Maybe her parents got killed"), Franklin offers another possible explanation ("[S]he was tired from walking too much"). By tossing around possible interpretations of what they are reading, children often model effective reading and listening comprehension strategies for one another (Anderson et al., 2001).

Reading #10-4

Early Spelling Development

Children learn the correct spellings of a few words (such as their names) almost as soon as they learn how to write letters of the alphabet. But they also acquire several general spelling strategies, which typically appear in the following sequence:

1. **Prephonemic spelling.** Beginning writers, including most kindergarten and first graders, often create and use **invented spellings** that may only vaguely resemble actual words. Invented spellings typically reflect some but not all of the phonemes in a word; for instance, a child might spell *rabbit* as "RT" (Ferreiro, 1990; Gentry, 1982; Treiman, 1998). Sometimes children use a letter's name for clues about when to use it in a word. As an example, a child might spell *work* as "YRK" because both Y (pronounced "why") and *work* begin with a "wuh" sound (Treiman, 1998).

2. **Phonemic spelling.** As children develop greater phonological awareness, they try to represent most or all of a word's phonemes in their spelling (Beers, 1980; Frith, 1985; Gentry, 1982). For example, consider the following piece entitled "My Garden," written by a kindergartner:

   > THIS IS A HWS
   > THE SUN
   > WL SHIN
   > ND MI
   > GRDN
   > WL GRO (Hemphill & Snow, 1996, p. 192)

   Notice how the child's misspellings (e.g., "HWS" for *house,* "WL" for *will,* and "SHIN" for *shine*) capture most or all of the phonemes that the child might hear when listening to the words. (For instance, if you pronounce the word *house* very slowly, dragging out the "hou" part, you might hear a "wuh" sound.)

3. **Orthographic spelling.** Eventually (perhaps in first or second grade), children begin to consider conventional spelling patterns (Beers, 1980; Bryant, Nunes, & Aidinis, 1999; Gentry, 1982). At this point, they use analogies between similar-sounding words—for instance, drawing a parallel between *went* and *sent* or between *nation* and *vacation* (Frith, 1985; Nation & Hulme, 1998). They also apply their increasing knowledge of general spelling rules, such as adding the suffix *-ed* for past tense (Bryant et al., 1999). Thus, they spell the past tense of *pour* as "POURED" (or perhaps "PORED") rather than "POURD." Curiously, many children initially apply the *-ed* rule to irregular verbs (e.g., spelling *felt* as "FELED") and sometimes even to nonverbs (e.g., spelling *soft* as "SOFED"), thus showing the *overregularization* phenomenon described in Chapter 9 (Bryant et al., 1999).

4. **Automatized spelling.** With increasing practice in reading and writing, children learn how various words are actually spelled and can ultimately retrieve many correct spellings quickly and accurately (Rittle-Johnson & Siegler, 1999). Children differ considerably in the extent to which they automatize spelling. Some have mastered most commonly used

311

words by the time they reach the upper elementary grades; others continue to make numerous spelling errors throughout adolescence and into adulthood.

The Development and Practice feature below, "Helping Children Learn Word Spellings," describes several strategies for promoting spelling development.

DEVELOPMENT AND PRACTICE

Helping Children Learn Word Spellings

- When engaging young children in authentic writing activities, write a few important words out for them, and give them the correct spellings of any other words they ask for.

  Example: When children at a childcare center make valentine cards to take home, the teacher shows the children how *valentine* and *I love you* are spelled.

- Teach common spelling patterns.

  Example: A second-grade teacher asks children to study a list of words that end in an "uff" sound. The list, which includes *puff, muff, stuff, rough, tough,* and *enough,* illustrates two common ways of spelling the sound.

- Teach general spelling rules.

  Example: A fourth-grade teacher teaches his students the rule "I before E except after C, or when pronounced 'ay,' as in *neighbor* and *weigh*." But he cautions them that the rule is not completely reliable; for example, the words *either* and *height* are exceptions.

- Encourage older children and adolescents to use dictionaries and computer spell checking programs when they are unsure of how words are spelled.

  Example: As middle school students complete articles for the school newspaper, their faculty advisor shows them how to use the spell check function in the word processing software. She explains that a spell checker is not completely trustworthy; for example, it won't identify situations in which *they're* has been incorrectly used in place of *there* or *their*.

- Stress the importance of correct spelling for a writer's credibility.

  Example: A career counselor points out several obvious spelling errors in a story in the local newspaper. He then asks the high school students with whom he is working to reflect on the impressions that such errors convey about the reporter who wrote the story.

Reading #10-5

Writing Samples at Different Age Levels

It is December, and Dinah Jackson has just earned her Ph.D. in educational psychology. She spends the next few months working as a substitute teacher while she looks for a university teaching position for the following academic year. In some of the classrooms in which she teaches, she finds time during the school day to ask her students to respond in writing to this question:

The land we live on has been here for a very long time, but the United States has only been a country for a little more than 200 years. How did the United States become a country?

Following are a sample of her students' responses (we have kept students' original spelling, punctuation, and indentations):

Linda (first grade):

George mad the country ane he mad us and he levd be for the dinosaurus.

Monica (first grade):

It all staredid in eginggind they had a wore. Thein they mad a bet howevery wone the wore got a ney country. Called the united states of amarica and amaricins wone the wore. So they got a new country

Damion (third grade):

The pilgruns came over in 17 hundreds, when they came over they bilt houses. The Idians thout they were mean. Then they came friends, and tot them stuff. Then winter came, and alot died. Then some had babies. So thats how we got here.

Jonathan (third grade):

The United States began around two hundred years ago, when Colombus saled and found the new world. They settled there for the winter. around 30 men died that winter.
They thought they were the only ones there but they found that Indins lived there. They became friends. The Indians showd them alot, and they had Thanksgiving.

Matt (sixth grade):

In the early days Columbus came to the United States and found Indians. Then we had our first president, Geoge Washington. Then Lincon. After that Thomas Jeresson singed and the Declaration fo Independence. Then Ben Franklin invented electricity. The Henry Ford invented the car.

Wesley (sixth grade):

I think how it became a country is that when colombus found it he went back and brought back more and more people. After awhile there were citys with homes. After awhile there was enough money they had shops to that would do things for money. More people came it expanded and all of the people in North America argeed to make it a country. There were so meny people in

313

North America that they over ruled the English and mabey later on they had a war. The North Americans won and they made their own country called the United States.

Roxanne (eighth grade):

The first people here were what we called the Native Americans they crossed over to America on a land Bridge or as some people say.

In Europue people where thinking the world was flat and if you sailed on and on you would fall of the world but Christopher Columbus did not beleave that he believed it was round. So Christopher Columbus sailed to America soon after Pilgrims came to get away from the Cathalic religion. More people came over and keept pushing the Indians off their land and taking what was not theirs the Indians where willing to share it but americans just took it. Then the people wanted to break away from Brittany. Then Americans fought with each other over many things like slavery. And North won.

Andrea (eighth grade):

A combination of events helped to form our country. First, to gain our own freedom, we found the Revolutionary war. The Revolutionary war was just the beginning, though. I think our country was formed by the determination to keep our country together and fight for it's beliefs. The fighting of the civil war really determined what kind of country we wanted to become. I think the struggle concerning slavery and other struggles pulled us together and made this country become strong and even more independent. The want of individuals made it even more possible to become what this country is today. I think those are just some of the points that aided or country in becoming what it is today.

When children first enter elementary school as kindergartners or first graders, the vast majority of them have mastered many aspects of their native language; for instance, they speak in complete sentences, use and understand the meanings of a large number of words, and effectively communicate their thoughts and needs to those around them. But as the textbook points out in Chapters 9 and 10, language and literacy skills continue to develop throughout the elementary and secondary school years. Following are several trends evident in the students' responses:

• *Vocabulary becomes more extensive and eventually begins to incorporate words that represent abstract ideas.* In Linda's first-grade response, we see a very limited set of words: correcting for spelling this time, we repeat her response:

George made the country and he made us and he lived before the dinosaurs.

We see a wider range of words, including many abstract words, in the older students' responses. For instance, we see the words *expanded, overruled, religion, freedom, determination,* and *concerning* in the sixth- and eighth-grade writing samples.

•*Sentences increase in length and complexity.* Children in the early elementary grades often write in short, choppy sentences; for example, Damion writes (and we translate into correct spelling):

Then some had babies. So that's how we got here.

Their longer "sentences" often consist of two or more independent clauses strung together in a single sentence; for instance, Monica writes (and again we translate):

It all started in England they had a war.

In contrast, adolescents use lengthy sentences that often include dependent clauses; as an example, consider this sentence from Andrea's response:

I think the struggle concerning slavery and other struggles pulled us together and made this country become strong and even more independent.

• *Writing increasingly incorporates correct word spellings and other conventions of written English.* We see many spelling errors in the younger students' responses; for instance, Monica spells *whoever* as "howevery," and Damion spells *taught* as "tot." We see mechanical errors as well; for example, Monica omits a period, and Jonathan neglects to capitalize *around*. In contrast, the older students' responses, although not perfect, more closely resemble conventional written English; for instance, the sixth and eighth graders use correct punctuation and capitalization more consistently, and three of them use indentation to indicate the beginning of a new paragraph.

• *Narratives become longer and more coherent.* As children grow older, they become better able to tell a good story. As a first grader, Monica gives us very little in the way of a sequence of events; she only tells us that George (Washington, we presume) lived before the dinosaurs. Contrast her response with Wesley's, whose response has a definite plot—one that includes Columbus's voyage, the development of cities and shops, increasing migration to the New World, and the eventual dispute with the British.

• *The ideas expressed become more accurate as one's knowledge base increases.* Obviously, children can express themselves more effectively when they know what they're talking about. Although the younger students are at a clear disadvantage here, even the older students don't always have their facts straight. For example, Roxanne has Columbus sailing after the Pilgrims did, and she confuses Britain with Brittany (a region in France).

The last of the trends just listed—the improvement in self-expression as a result of an increasing knowledge base—is just one example of how cognitive development and language development are closely intertwined. Cognitive development is critical for the development of language. Children can talk and write only about things they can first *think* about; for example, they are unlikely to use abstract words correctly until they can think about abstract ideas. But the acquisition of language is equally important for children's cognitive development: It enables them to exchange information and perspectives with the people around them, provides a set of symbols through which they can mentally represent their world, helps them make associations among the various pieces of information they learn, and (from Vygotsky's perspective) helps them internalize many of the processes that adults first share with them in a social context.

Reading #10-6

Scaffolding Revision Processes in Writing

As the textbook points out in Chapter 10, adults can often foster children's and adolescents' writing development by *scaffolding* effective writing processes. One aspect of writing with which youngsters of all ages have difficulty is evaluating and revising what they have written, and scaffolding in these processes can be especially helpful. For example, in a study by De La Paz, Swanson, and Graham (1998), eighth graders with a history of writing difficulties learned the following procedure for evaluating and revising persuasive essays:

First Revision Cycle: Global Evaluation

1. Read the entire paper and choose one of these four evaluations:
   - Ignores obvious point against my ideas
   - Too few ideas
   - Part of the essay doesn't belong with the rest
   - Part of the essay is not in the right order

2. Depending on the evaluation selected, select one of the following strategies:
   - Rewrite something
   - Delete something
   - Add something
   - Move something

3. Execute the strategy selected in step 2. Repeat steps 2 and 3 as many times as necessary.

Second Revision Cycle: Local Evaluations

4. Reread the entire paper and highlight sections that still require revision.

5. For each highlighted section, select one of six evaluations:
   - This one doesn't sound right.
   - This is not what I intended to say.
   - This is an incomplete idea.
   - This is a weak idea.
   - This part is not clear.
   - The problem is _____.

   Fix each problem using one of four strategies: rewrite, delete, add, or move.

Students who learned and followed this procedure revised their work more frequently and effectively and improved the overall quality of their writing (De La Paz et al., 1998).

Problems in Forming Attachments

Chapter 11 indicates that having secure bonds with parents and other caregivers contributes to a child's happy and healthy development. Unfortunately, not every child develops such a bond.

When infants have little or no opportunity to form a secure attachment to a caregiver, they are at greater risk of developing emotional and behavioral difficulties. Research on the tragic circumstances of infants cared for in Romanian orphanages in the early 1990s provides relevant data. At the time, child-to-caregiver ratios in Romanian institutions were about 10:1 for infants and 20:1 for children over age 3 years (McMullan & Fisher, 1992). Adult caregivers were unable to provide individual attention, and as a result, children often failed to form secure attachments to adults. Media attention in North America focused on the infants' deprivation, leading to their adoption by many Canadian and American families.

Two research studies of Romanian adoptees' subsequent adjustment reveal both vulnerability and resilience. In one study (Marcovitch et al., 1997), researchers studied the relationship between attachment quality of 3- to 5-year-old children to adoptive family members and such problem behaviors as aggression, hyperactivity, depression, and social withdrawal. The children had been adopted on average at 6 months. Rates of secure attachment to adoptive mothers were slightly lower than those in the general population. Children who had spent less than 6 months in an orphanage and those who spent 6 months or more there did *not* differ in attachment security. However, parents of children who had spent more than 6 months in Romanian institutions reported slightly more behavior problems than did parents of children who spent less than 6 months there.

A second study showed that length of time in an orphanage (and age at adoption, which correlated with length of stay in the institution) did make a difference (Chisholm, Carter, Ames, & Morison, 1995). Researchers compared three groups of children living in Canadian families: (a) Romanian orphans adopted before they were 4 months old, (b) Romanian orphans adopted after 8 months of age, and (c) a comparison group of Canadian-born children living with their birth families (these children were matched in age to the second group of children). Children adopted after 8 months showed lower attachment security than did the other two groups. Apparently, some of these children had difficulty forming trusting relationships with new parents.

Problems in early relationships are not confined to distant lands or orphanages, of course, and impaired bonds are especially common when parents or other primary caregivers have poor parenting skills (Greenberg, 1999; Zeanah, 2000). Serious attachment problems are often the result of multiple stresses, including family discord, disorganization, and rejection, making it important to identify and support children and their families (Rutter & O'Connor, 1999). In the following case report, twin 2-year-old girls showed serious problems in relationships with their parents:

> **Family Composition**. "The Delaney family consists of the parents, Thomas, age 28, and Janice, age 27. They have twin daughters, Angelina and Abigail, who are 2 years old." (Brown, 2002, p. 73)

Current Situation. "Mr. and Mrs. Delaney, a Caucasian couple, have been together for five years but have only been married for fourteen months...The neighbors called the Department of Children and Family Services (DCFS) and reported that they have heard the parents use very harsh language toward the children. The neighbors report that they hear the children crying and that their cries do not sound normal. The neighbors also report that they have not seen the children in a week or so, and they are afraid the children are being harmed. A child protective services intake investigator investigated the case and substantiated the report of inappropriate parenting skills because, as punishment, the parents would lock the kids up in their room for hours. The parents' rationale was that they did not want to hit the children. The father also stated that he would go two or three days and not talk to the girls, as a way of punishment. He also stated that he would not let the mother hold the girls or give them any kind of attention for a few days until they behaved better. The investigator felt that this family needed parenting skills and there appeared to be other problems that would warrant a worker in the family to ensure child safety....The girls' affect was of sadness, and they appeared to have distant looks on their faces. The investigator also felt that the parents seemed 'too perfect' because they appeared to have calculated answers to all of his questions." (Brown, 2002, pp. 73-74)

Children. The two children both showed problems in adjustment:

Angelina. "Angelina is the older of the twins. She was born ten minutes before Abigail. Angelina appears to be physically developed for her age, but she seems to be listless at times, and her affect is one of sadness. She seems shy around people and often hides under a chair. She does not speak to or look at strangers. According to the day care teacher, Angelina is very bright but shy, and she often becomes fearful when her father picks her up from the center. On several occasions Mr. Delaney has come to the day care." (Brown, 2002, p. 76)

Abigail. "Abigail is the younger twin, smaller in size but more outgoing. According to the day care teacher, she seems different when Mr. Delaney picks her up. It has been brought to the parents' attention that the girls seem different when their father picks them up. According to the center, the parents' response to this was that the girls were playing a game. According to the parents, the game also included Abigail hitting her head against the wall over and over." (Brown, 2002, p. 76)

From Venessa A. Brown *Child Welfare Case Studies*. Published by Allyn and Bacon, Boston, MA. Copyright © by Pearson Education. Reprinted by permission of the publisher.

In this situation, Child Protective Services intervened. The behaviors of the girls, including their failure to explore the environment and displays of fear to their father, seem to reveal serious attachment problems. In such a circumstance—that is, when parents remain committed to raising children who are already beginning to struggle—social workers are faced with the challenge of protecting children and helping parents learn more effective styles of disciplining and interacting with children.

Sometimes, attachment problems are so serious that children are removed from families and placed with adoptive parents, foster parents, or professional caregivers who have special training. When children are removed from abusive and neglectful family environments, they often form positive relationships with their new caregivers. An investigation with toddlers (Howes & Segal, 1993) examined the children's attachment to caregivers in a high-quality emergency shelter home with trained professionals. All children had been abruptly taken from their mothers because of abuse and neglect. A law enforcement or protective service officer had brought them to the shelter, where they stayed until the courts authorized a placement plan. In the shelter, child-to-caregiver ratios were 3:1 during the daytime and $4^1/_2$:1 at night. Even though the children had different caregivers in the morning, afternoon, and night, 10 out of 16 showed secure relationships with one or more caregivers in the shelter, particularly with those who were assessed as being highly sensitive nurturers. The longer that children resided at the shelter, the more likely it was that they formed secure relationships with caregivers there.

Together, the results of these investigations suggest that spending prolonged time in a deprived setting puts children at risk for insecure attachments and social problems. Even so, many children are resilient and later form positive ties to adoptive parents, other adults, and their peers.

Reading #11-2

Learning to Read Emotions

Children gradually learn about emotions. Beginning soon after birth, infants show facial expressions of distress, contentment, and interest, and they gradually add other emotions to their repertoire. Infants' daily experiences with emotions help them develop intuitive understandings of various emotions and what emotional expressions signify in other people. Infants actively observe the facial expressions of familiar caregivers and use these expressions to guide their own behaviors and feelings. For instance, an infant girl may become apprehensive when she sees her mother appear fearful while talking with an unfamiliar man at the front door. As children grow older, they develop an ability to reflect consciously on their own and other people's emotional states. From such reflections, children learn that they and others respond in distinctive ways to particular feelings such as happiness, disappointment, anger, or shame. Children also learn that people sometimes mask their emotional expressions when they think it would be personally embarrassing, risky, or socially improper to show their true feelings. For example, an adolescent boy may show a neutral expression when spotting a low grade on his essay, not wanting to show classmates that he had worked hard, wanted to do well, and now is frustrated and angry.

Many children acquire good insights into emotions and develop constructive habits for responding to their own and others' feelings. But others find it difficult to pick up on subtle social cues and draw reasonable inferences about what other people are feeling. Children who are adept at drawing such inferences tend to be more successful in interpersonal relationships, presumably because they tailor their own behaviors with their knowledge of others' emotions and thereby facilitate productive social interactions. Children who become insightful about emotions may also become increasingly proficient in expressing their innermost feelings authentically; expressing anger, fear, and other unpleasant feelings constructively (e.g., neither exploding turbulently, at one extreme, nor totally denying bad feelings, at the other extreme); and showing their emotions in ways that are reasonably sensitive to other people as well as culturally appropriate.

In Chapter 11 in the textbook, we offer several strategies for promoting children's emotional development. For example, teachers and other practitioners can encourage youngsters to express their feelings. Adults can also offer age-appropriate outlets for emotional expression (e.g., through pretend play in early childhood and personal journals in childhood and adolescence) and provide opportunities to talk about other people's emotions during analyses of literature and history. In the following discussion with third-grade children, an art teacher (T) and several children (C) are thinking about possible ways of capturing people's facial expressions on paper:

T: Have you ever noticed that people's faces change depending on how they are feeling?

C: When my mom is mad, her eyes get real skinny and her mouth closes up tight.

C: I can tell when my grandmother is really happy, because her face goes all soft looking.

T: What parts of our faces are important for showing how we feel? Which parts change? How do those parts change?

C: When my little brother gets surprised, his mouth just drops wide open.

C: When I'm scared, my eyes get much rounder and look as if they are going to drop right out.

T: You've been describing some very strong feelings in which your face changes a lot. What are some other feelings that can make your face change? How can it change?...

C: If I'm confused, my eyes squint, and my mouth feels all wrinkly.

T: So what parts of your face are most important for showing how you are feeling?

C: Eyes. Mouth.

C: But sometimes if I'm puzzlcd, my eyebrows go crooked instead of straight.

C: And when my sister smells something bad, her nose twitches...

T: Here are some mirrors. Let's try to imagine some of the feelings we talked about and see how our faces change. Try out two or three very different feelings. How do your eyes change? What happens to your mouth? Do other parts of your face change too? (Smith et al., 1998, pp. 71-72)

Reading #11-3

You Can't Make Me Do It: Children's Responses to Rules

Chapter 11 describes five dimensions of children's *personality*—extraversion, agreeableness, conscientiousness, neuroticism, and openness—that influence children's behavior and remain relatively stable across time. Children may be high, low, or somewhere in between on each of the dimensions. The wide ranges on the five dimensions create countless personality profiles that make each and every child truly unique. For example, one child may be exceptionally extraverted and socially outgoing, reasonably agreeable, careless with detailed tasks, relaxed and confident, and moderately open to learning new things. Another child may be quiet and shy, irritable, reasonably conscientious, fearful and neurotic, and close-minded when faced with new intellectual challenges. We offer ideas in Chapter 11 as to how teachers and other practitioners might respond to children who are at exceptionally high or low levels on these dimensions.

Occasionally, teachers and other practitioners may find it helpful to think about children's personalities in simpler terms. One straightforward framework of children's personality focuses on orientations to rules (Block, 1971). Psychologist Jack Block has suggested that children's responses to rules are stable and predict their later behavior. He and his colleagues have distinguished three groups of children:

- **Ego-resilient children.** These children have a healthy sense of self and interact effectively with other people. They comply with rules but are not bogged down by them. They can follow instructions while also effectively expressing their own needs and desires.
- **Vulnerable overcontrolled children.** These children are rigidly conforming. They follow rules exactly and are nervous when they think they might be transgressing against rules or not meeting adults' expectations.
- **Unsettled undercontrolled children.** These children are impulsive and antisocial. They disregard rules and give in to immediate desires. They seem not to care about how their actions affect other people.

Block's classification has been verified by numerous researchers and with diverse samples of girls, boys, women, and men from several different countries (Caspi & Silva, 1995; Hart, Hofman, Edelstein, & Keller, 1997; Pulkkinen, 1996; Robins, John, Caspi, Moffitt, & Stouthamer-Loeber, 1996; York & John, 1992). Not everyone fits neatly into one of the groups, but those who do tend to show a consistent response style over time.

There appear to be some enduring consequences of Block's personality types. For example, in research by Block and colleagues, the tendency to be undercontrolled in the preschool years was associated with drug use at age 14 (Block, Block, & Keyes, 1988). As preschool children, youngsters who would later smoke marijuana and use hashish or heroin were unable to delay gratification, moved rapidly between activities, showed rapid shifts between moods, overreacted to what seemed to be minor frustrations, and were easily angered.

Because these personality types persist and can have a significant influence on children's behavior, teachers and practitioners may encounter some consistent individual differences in children's responses to rules. Adults usually find that most children are reasonably receptive to direction and get along well with one another—these would be the ego-resilient children.

Children who are undercontrolled need to learn to *think* before acting and especially to anticipate how their actions will affect others. You can encourage undercontrolled children to set goals for themselves (e.g., to try to sit still in their seats for a specified period of time), keep track of their progress toward these goals, and chart how well they have done. You can also praise them when they are considerate of other people. (You will find strategies for helping children regulate their own behavior according to reasonable standards in Chapter 13.) Overcontrolled children, in contrast, may need a lot of reassurance from adults, particularly in times of stress and change. These children may need gentle reminders that perfection is rarely attainable and that what counts most is their best effort.

Reading #12-1

Children's Conceptions of Society

Individual people are often objects of children's analysis, but so are groups of people—families, peer-group cliques, ethnic and racial groups, community associations, corporate organizations, governments, and so on. Children gradually develop **conceptions of society**, beliefs about the nature, structure, and operation of social institutions (Furth, 1980). As with many conceptual developments, children first apply personalized and concrete notions to the task of understanding various parts of society and then gradually transform their ideas into more comprehensive, integrated, and abstract belief systems, or *theories* (Slonim & Case, 2002; Torney-Purta, 1994; Turiel, 1983). As you've discovered in the textbook, a gradual shift from concrete to abstract representations is seen in a wide variety of developmental progressions.

Researchers have looked in some depth at children's changing conceptions of several aspects of society, including government and politics, industry and commerce, economics, and social stratification and mobility.

Children's Understanding of Government and Politics

Children's understanding of the nature of government and political systems changes quite a bit with age (Slonim, 2001; Slonim & Case, 2002).[1] At age 6 or 7, children typically have little understanding of what government involves or how it facilitates society's functioning; some think of "government" as being a single individual (e.g., a benevolent president or other prominent leader) who essentially takes care of the world. But by the time children are 11 or 12, they understand that a government consists of a group of people, each of whom has a particular function to play in moving society forward and helping it run smoothly. One 11-year-old's definition of *government* illustrates this point:

> [P]eople that are in charge of what they do with the money, with the wages of the police officer, the doctor and the teacher, they enforce laws . . . taxes . . . they're the head of the community, they run things. (Slonim, 2001, pp. 93–94)

As young people reach the later high school years at ages 16 to 18, they realize that a government also reflects and maintains the structure and values of the society it serves. Consider this definition of *government* from an 18-year-old:

> I would say an elected body . . . at least in our society it's elected, it doesn't have to be elected, it's a body that . . . deals essentially with issues that are greater than the individual level, cause you and I can only see so far but . . . we won't be able to agree in terms of a nation, what society thinks they need for each other . . . so they represent your values and beliefs as a collective whole, it won't be individualized but it will be similar, they don't represent you but they represent a group of people. (Slonim, 2001, p. 95)

---

[1]Slonim and Case have suggested that children's understanding of society and government may reflect an underlying *central conceptual structure* (see the discussion of this concept in the section on neo-Piagetian theories in Chapter 6).

Family discussions about controversial political issues enhance young people's understanding of government and politics and can sometimes foster a commitment to civic causes (Chaffee & Yang, 1990). Adults outside the family can be influential as well—for instance, by conducting group discussions about current events and providing opportunities for participation in student government or community service (Chapman, Nolin, & Kline, 1997; Niemi & Junn, 1998). And more generally, parents, teachers, and other adults can promote an appreciation for democracy and equal opportunity by treating all youngsters fairly and equitably, genuinely listening to their ideas and opinions, and insisting that they treat one another in a similar manner (Flanagan & Faison, 2001).

How favorably young people view their country and government is, in part, a function of their group membership. For instance, in the United States, adolescents of European American descent tend to think that their country has, since its beginning, consistently been dedicated to principles of democracy, freedom, and individual rights; many overlook the fact that the majority of citizens (e.g., women and African Americans) were not full-fledged participants until well into the twentieth century. In contrast, teens of African American descent, who are more attuned to injustices their ancestors suffered and perhaps have themselves been targets of inequitable treatment, are more apt to view government institutions and policies as being racist and discriminatory (Epstein, 2000).

Children's Understanding of Industry and Commerce

We get a sense of children's conceptions of the world of industry and commerce from a study by Berti and Bombi (1988). These researchers interviewed 120 Italian children, ages 4 to 13, who lived in Marghera, an industrialized city near Venice. In the following excerpts (translated from Italian), an interviewer asks children about work and industry. We begin with Mara (age $4^1/_2$):

Adult:	What work does your father do?
Mara:	He goes to Venice.
Adult:	And when he gets there what does he do?
Mara:	Works with his friends.
Adult:	What does he do when he works?
Mara:	My mother gives him money.
Adult:	Does he need money to work?
Mara:	Yes. (dialogue from Berti & Bombi, 1988, p. 139)

Mara's limited knowledge of adult work is typical of the youngest children (ages 4 and 5) that Berti and Bombi interviewed. In contrast, children ages 6 to 10 were generally able to describe some of the activities that occur in the workplace. In the following interview, Mauro (age $8^1/_2$) shows some understanding of the employment hierarchy but struggles with issues related to ownership of property:

Adult:	Whose are the toys which they make in the factory?
Mauro:	They take them to the shops and sell them.
Adult:	Who takes them?
Mauro:	The workers.
Adult:	But do the dolls belong to the workers or to the boss?
Mauro:	The boss, I think.
Adult:	You don't seem very convinced?
Mauro:	I'm not really.
Adult:	Why not?

Mauro:	Because it's the workers who make them.
Adult:	Why don't the workers keep them?
Mauro:	Because they have to sell them. (dialogue from Berti & Bombi, 1988, p. 143)

The oldest children, ages 12 and 13, differentiated between bosses, who supervised the workers, and owners, who owned property in the business. In the final interview, we hear from Alessandro (age $12^1/_2$):

Adult:	Does the factory belong to someone?
Alessandro:	Of course, small factories though: Montedison for instance doesn't belong to a single person. I think it belongs to a lot of people. . . .
Adult:	What do the owners do?
Alessandro:	They have to maintain contacts with the middlemen, so that if someone wanted a certain type of shoe they would send their representatives around to show them theirs. . . . I think they would sit in an office with lots of telephones. . . .
Adult:	Whose are the things which they make in the factory?
Alessandro:	They must belong to the owner, who sells them to someone, who then sells them to someone else who has a shop.
Adult:	How come these things belong to the owner?
Alessandro:	Because he pays the workers who do this particular job. (dialogue from Berti & Bombi, 1988, pp. 143–144)

Social experiences certainly influence youngsters' conceptions of industry and commerce. When children have direct contact with the world of work, they become knowledgeable about it at an earlier age. For example, in a series of studies by Jahoda (1979, 1982, 1983), children in Zimbabwe, Africa, had a better understanding of the need for profit in business than their peers in European countries, apparently because many of the Zimbabwean children were actively involved in family farms and retail shops.

Children's Economic Understandings

Many young children have little understanding of the value of money (Furnham, 1994). For instance, when Teresa's son Alex was 6, his Christmas "wish list" included not only two videogame systems, a Lego set, and a model boat but also $50,000. As you can imagine, his college professor parents had neither the means nor the desire to fulfill all of his requests. Young children also have only superficial understandings of economic activities (shopping, banking, etc.), seeing them as rituals that have little or no purpose. As children gain increasing experience with such activities—perhaps shopping with their own money, initiating a savings account, and so on, their understandings gradually become more sophisticated (Furnham, 1994).

Active involvement with local economic activities clearly affects children's knowledge and beliefs about economic systems. For example, in a study by Jahoda (1983), two adults interviewed children from Harare, a township in Zimbabwe that was made up mostly of low-income families. The children's parents either were actively involved in selling goods (some were small traders who purchased items for resale, others were farmers who grew their own produce for sale) or not involved in selling goods. Two researchers performed simple sales transactions in front of the children using props such as boxes of pens, cookies, and balloons; the boxes were labeled with prices. They then asked the children how much the customer paid for the item, how much the shop had to pay the supplier for the item, and what happened to the money in the cash register at the end of the day. In interpreting the children's responses, Jahoda noted whether they understood that the shopkeeper paid the supplier less than the customer paid the shopkeeper (thereby enabling the shopkeeper to make a profit) and considered their explanations for the differing amounts.

Jahoda found that children whose parents were actively involved in selling and who were somewhat involved in selling themselves had a more accurate understanding of profit than children whose families were not regularly involved in sales. Furthermore, Jahoda compared his sample to the performance of English, Scottish, and Dutch children in previous investigations (Furth, 1980; Jahoda, 1979, 1982). The children from Zimbabwe outperformed their European counterparts, presumably because their personal experiences with trading and their frequent exposure to adults' discussions about trading led them to develop an understanding of profit and the mechanisms needed to ensure it. Even those African children who came from nonselling families outperformed the European children, perhaps because the African children grew up in a culture in which trading was a frequent topic of conversation.

Another factor that affects children's conceptions of economic systems is their family's financial circumstances. In a study with 7- to 13-year-olds in England, France, and the United States, Emler and colleagues explored children's judgments about the fairness of income inequalities (Emler, Ohana, & Dickinson, 1990). The researchers asked the children questions about the kinds of salaries that people earned in different professions (i.e., doctor, teacher, bus driver, street cleaner) and the fairness of having some people make more money than others. Across societies in the study, children from lower-income families were more likely than children from middle-income families to say that it would be better to pay people in different types of jobs the same salary. With age came an increasing understanding of why some people have higher salaries than others. Whereas 10- and 11-year-olds mentioned social contributions (how much people help others in their jobs) and the amount of effort a job requires, older participants (12- to 15-year-olds) also mentioned that years of education and possession of certain skills contributed to income level. In addition, those older participants who came from middle-income backgrounds gave more complex justifications for income differences, suggesting that they accepted the legitimacy of such differences.

Children's Understanding of Social Stratification and Mobility

Even 4- and 5-year-olds understand that some people are wealthier than others, but they tend to think in terms of two discrete categories: People are either very rich or quite poor (Delval, 1994). Young children also tend to think that people are poor only because they don't have enough money to "buy" a good job. As children reach the upper elementary grades, they realize that wealth is a continuum rather than an either-or phenomenon and that many families are financially comfortable without necessarily being rich. As they move into the junior high and high school grades, they also begin to understand that social status involves more than just money—that some people have more social status because of higher educational levels and more prestigious occupations (Delval, 1994).

Just as children's conceptions of wealth and status become increasingly complex, so, too, do their understandings of how people gain social status over time. For example, a 6-year-old might tell you that you can make poor people rich by giving them a small amount of money, and that poor people can easily mingle with the upper crust simply by wearing fancy clothes and jewelry. As youngsters grow older, and especially as they reach the secondary grades, they begin to realize that improving one's social status involves more than just having a lot of money—that it also involves gaining more education and securing a better job—and that poor people sometimes encounter insurmountable obstacles to upward social mobility (Delval, 1994).

Enhancing Children's Understanding of Society

Youngsters' understanding of their society depends, in part, on their growing cognitive abilities and on the specific experiences they have had with social and political phenomena (Furnham, 1994; Slonim & Case, 2002). Even so, educators and other adults can do several things to advance their conceptions of society:

• *Bring children to the world of work, commerce, and government.* Children gain considerable knowledge about how their society functions from field trips to the post office, bank, police station, local government offices, and so on, particularly when such trips involve a behind-the-scenes view of the daily activities of such institutions. Field trips have an additional benefit in that they provide a mechanism for involving parents and other family members in children's activities at school and elsewhere. (The importance of family involvement in children's schooling is discussed in Chapter 5 in the textbook.)

• *Bring society's institutions into the classroom.* In preschool and kindergarten settings, teachers and other caregivers can bring assorted props (e.g., supplies from a pizza restaurant, hardware store, hair salon, or veterinary clinic) to extend children's fantasies in pretend play (Ferguson, 1999). In the elementary and secondary grades, teachers might ask students to set up a market economy (e.g., producing, selling, and buying goods), create a student government to make classroom decisions, or establish a classroom courthouse to try mock cases. Furthermore, students of all ages can learn from community members who visit the classroom to describe their day-to-day activities in the workforce.

One activity that's easy to bring into classroom settings is the process of voting. For example, Teresa recalls how, during a presidential election, 5-year-old Alex's kindergarten teacher demonstrated the voting process by having the children mark ballots about their preferred type of cookie, chocolate chip or oatmeal. (Chocolate chip cookies won, hands down.) A systematic introduction to the democratic process can be found in a curriculum called "Kids Voting USA," designed for students in kindergarten through grade 12 (M. McDevitt & Chaffee, 1998). In this curriculum, students have age-appropriate lessons about voting, political parties, and political issues, and they relate what they learn to local election campaigns. For instance, they might conduct their own mock elections, analyze candidates' attacks of opponents, or give speeches in class about particular propositions on the ballot. Participants in the program are more likely to focus regularly on media reports about an election, initiate discussions about the election with friends and family members, and be knowledgeable about candidates and election results. The effects are particularly striking for students from low-income families, who traditionally are less aware of and less involved in local politics than wealthier families: The program narrows the "political awareness" gap among different socioeconomic groups. Curiously, the students' involvement in the program has an impact on their parents as well, in that the children's excitement about political issues and events "trickles up" to other family members. (See Chapter 5 in the textbook for a discussion of children's influences on families.)

• *Examine society's inequities.* Older children and adolescents, especially those from low-income families, may struggle with inequities in income, living conditions, and educational opportunities. Teachers and other adults can help young people from all backgrounds become aware of inequities in their society, identify possible causes of such inequities, and develop solutions for overcoming them. As Flanagan and Faison (2001) have put it, "to promote democracy youth need to know the full story, not just the 'good parts' of history. If they appreciate that history and politics are controversial, they may see the importance of taking a stand and of adding their voice to the debate" (Flanagan & Faison, 2001, p. 3).

Conceptions of Self in the Early Years

Chapter 12 describes some of the ways in which children's self-perceptions change with age; for example, as children move from childhood to adolescence, their sense of self becomes increasingly abstract and differentiated. Yet even toddlers clearly have some awareness of themselves as people separate from others. Researchers have used indicators such as the following to assess self-awareness in toddlers (Levine, 1983):

- Use of personal pronouns (e.g., *I* and *me*) correctly in speech
- Ability to follow directions that include personal pronouns (e.g., "Tickle *my* toes" vs. "Tickle *your* toes")
- Taking another person's perspective into account (e.g., moving a cardboard box so that an adult can see an object)

Another effective research strategy is the rouge-on-the-nose task (Lewis & Brooks-Gunn, 1979). As a young child watches in a mirror, Mother wipes the child's face, leaving a red mark on his or her nose. Children who wipe their own nose immediately afterward apparently realize that the imagine in the mirror is "me."

Researchers have observed possible effects of sense of self in children as young as age 2. For example, in a study involving 2-year-old boys, Levine (1983) used the indicators just described to assess the degree to which each boy had a sense of self. Levine then put the boys in pairs—some pairs had a strong sense of self, whereas others had less self-awareness—and observed how they played together. At the beginning of their play sessions, the boys with strong-self-definitions defined their territory by claiming toys, but then played in a positive manner with each other. Compared to boys with less self-definition, these boys also commented on peers, their behavior, and possessions more often and interacted in a friendlier way. In the following illustration, two of the high self-definition boys initially scuffled over possessions and then resolved the matter:

John: My ball.
Jim: Mine ball.
John: My ball [I] Have this. My ball. No. [This warning came in spite of the fact that Jim had made no move toward his toy.]
Jim: My ball.
John: No.
Jim: No ball.
John: No ball ball. Two ball ball.
Jim: Mine.
John: No.
Jim: My ball. Boon ball. [smiles]
John: Bump!
Jim: Yup!
John: Car's going bump! (Levine, 1983, p. 548)

Initially, both boys persevered in claiming possession, but eventually Jim's funny phrase, "Boon ball," defused the verbal battle and eased the two of them into friendly activity with cars. Levine's research suggests that learning about oneself, including what is *mine*, is a natural part of development and may even be a precursor to sharing.

Reading #12-3

Selman's Theory of Social Perspective Taking

Consider the following situation:

> Holly is an 8-year-old girl who likes to climb trees. She is the best tree climber in the neighborhood. One day while climbing down from a tall tree she falls off the bottom branch but does not hurt herself. Her father sees her fall. He is upset and asks her to promise not to climb the trees any more. Holly promises.
>
> Later that day, Holly and her friends meet Sean. Sean's kitten is caught up in a tree and cannot get down. Something has to be done right away or the kitten may fall. Holly is the only one who climbs trees well enough to reach the kitten and get it down, but she remembers her promise to her father. . . .
> * Does Holly know how Sean feels about the kitten?
> * Does Sean know why Holly cannot decide whether or not to climb the tree? . . .
> * What does Holly think her father will think of her if he finds out?
> * Does Holly think her father will understand why she climbed the tree? (Selman & Byrne, 1974, p. 805)

To answer these questions, you must look at the situation from the perspectives of three different people: Sean, Holly, and Holly's father.

By presenting situations like this one and asking children to view them from various perspectives, Robert Selman (1980; Selman & Schultz, 1990) found that with age, children show an increasing ability to take the perspective of others. He described a series of five levels that characterize the development of perspective taking:

* **Level 0: Egocentric perspective taking.** Children are aware of physical differences among people but have little awareness of psychological differences. They are incapable of looking at a situation from anyone's perspective but their own (hence the reference to Level 0).

* **Level 1: Subjective perspective taking.** Children realize that people have different thoughts and feelings as well as different physical features. However, they view someone else's perspective in a relatively simplistic, one-dimensional fashion (e.g., a person is simply happy, sad, or angry) and tend to equate behavior with feelings (e.g., a happy person will smile, and a sad person will pout or cry).

* **Level 2: Second-person, reciprocal perspective taking.** Children realize that people occasionally have mixed feelings about an event—for instance, that Holly might feel both compassion for the kitten and uneasiness about breaking her promise to her father. At this level, children also understand that people may feel differently than their behaviors indicate and that people may sometimes do things they didn't really want or intend to do.

* **Level 3: Third-person, mutual perspective taking.** Children can take an outsider's perspective of interpersonal relationships: They can look at their own interactions with another person as a third individual might. They appreciate the need to satisfy both oneself

and another simultaneously and therefore understand the advantages of cooperation, compromise, and trust.

- **Level 4: Societal, symbolic perspective taking.** Children realize that people are a product of the many factors in their environments and, furthermore, that people are not always aware of why they act as they do.

Echoing Piaget's description of egocentrism in the preoperational stage, Selman proposed that most preschoolers engage in little or no perspective taking and so are at Level 0. However, young children actually do appear able to consider how other people think and feel about things, even if they do not always exercise this ability; thus, they are not as egocentric as Piaget and Selman proposed. For example, even young preschoolers realize that another person can see an object only if he or she is looking in the object's direction and has a clear, unobstructed view. Older preschoolers also realize that the same object may look different to people viewing it from different angles—for example, that a book that is right-side-up to one person will be upside-down to someone sitting across the table (Flavell, 1992, 2000). Furthermore, in their daily communication, children appear to be truly other-oriented most of the time; that is, they listen to what other people say, respond appropriately, and take into account how their listeners might be thinking and feeling (Garvey & Horgan, 1973; Mueller, 1972; Rubin & Pepler, 1995).

At the same time, adults can gradually nudge young people toward thinking in slightly more advanced ways about the people around them—perhaps "one level up" in terms of Selman's levels of perspective taking. For example, preschool teachers might point out how classmates' feelings may differ from children's own feelings (Level 1). Adults who work with children in the elementary grades can discuss situations in which people may have mixed feelings or want to hide their feelings—situations such as going to a new school, trying a difficult but enjoyable sport for the first time, or celebrating a holiday without a favorite family member present (Level 2). Adults who work with adolescents might, either informally (e.g., in free-flowing conversations) or formally (e.g., in a high school psychology class) explore the many ways in which people are affected by their past experiences and present understandings (Level 4).

Although Selman may not have accurately pinned down when early perspective taking emerges, his five levels nevertheless provide a helpful framework for evaluating individual children's social perspective-taking skills. Accordingly, we describe and illustrate them in the Observation Guidelines table "Using Selman's Levels to Assess Social Perspective Taking" on the next two pages.

Observation Guidelines: Using Selman's Levels to Assess Social Perspective Taking

CHARACTERISTIC	LOOK FOR	EXAMPLE	IMPLICATION
Level 0: Egocentric Perspective Taking (Selman observed this level in most preschoolers and some children in the early elementary grades)	• Awareness that people are different in physical ways (e.g., gender, appearance) • Little if any awareness that people are also different in psychological ways (e.g., in thoughts and feelings); assumption that other people share one's own thoughts and feelings • Indignant responses when other people express differing views	Three-year-old Andrea assumes that her preschool classmates know about her fear of heights. So she expresses surprise and indignation when Rose and Molly ask her to join them in going down the slide.	Encourage children to share their unique perspectives about simple topics. For example, read a story to preschoolers and then ask them to describe how they each felt about various story characters' actions. Point out the variability in the children's opinions ("Isn't it wonderful how much we can learn from hearing all these different ideas?").
Level 1: Subjective Perspective Taking (Selman observed this level in most children in the early and middle elementary grades)	• Realization that other people have thoughts and feelings different from one's own • Overly simplistic perceptions of others' perspectives • Tendency to equate people's outward expressions (e.g., smiles) with their internal feelings	Eight-year-old Li-Wen realizes that her friend Tony is sad about his grandfather's death. However, she does not fully appreciate the depth of his sorrow, nor does she understand his simultaneous relief that the grandfather's physical suffering has ended.	Acknowledge children's perceptiveness in detecting the unique perspectives of others. Extend their understanding by pointing out the complex feelings that people sometimes have.
Level 2: Second-Person, Reciprocal Perspective Taking (Selman observed this level in many children in the upper elementary grades)	• Realization that others may have mixed and possibly contradictory feelings about a situation • Understanding that people may feel differently from what their behaviors indicate and that people sometimes do things they didn't intend to do	Eleven-year-old Pablo understands that his friend Mark may have misgivings about his decisions to experiment with inhalants at a friend's house. Pablo hears Mark bragging but senses some reservations in Mark's tone of voice and body language.	Help children to make sense of the complex motivations that guide people's actions. Communicate the legitimacy of mixed feelings ("I bet you're both excited and sad about your move to a new town").

table continues

Observation Guidelines table continued

CHARACTERISTIC	LOOK FOR	EXAMPLE	IMPLICATION
Level 3: Third-Person, Mutual Perspective Taking (Selman observed this level in many middle school and junior high students)	• Ability not only to see a situation from one's own and another's perspectives but also to look at a two-person relationship from a distance (i.e., as an outsider might) • Appreciation of the need to satisfy both oneself and another simultaneously • Understanding of the advantages of cooperation, compromise, and trust	Two high school freshmen, Jasmine and Alethea, discover that they've both arranged a homecoming party for the same night. They learn that they've sent invitations to numerous mutual friends as well as to each other. Since they were both looking forward to hosting a party, they discuss options for rescheduling one or both of the parties.	Acknowledge children's respect for the rights of others as they pursue their own needs and goals. Help children brainstorm alternative strategies when they have trouble identifying ways for everyone to "win" in certain situations.
Level 4: Societal, Symbolic Perspective Taking (Selman observed this level in some junior high and many high school students)	• Recognition that people are a product of their environment—that past events and present circumstances contribute to personality and behavior • Understanding that people are not always aware of why they act as they do • Emerging comprehension of the true complexity of human behaviors, thoughts, and emotions	In their high school psychology course, Keith and Jerome are preparing a joint oral report on strategies of social persuasion. They find magazine advertisements that are geared toward adolescents and discuss possible images and feelings that advertisers are trying to invoke.	Initiate discussions of psychological motives, perhaps within the context of studying historical events in a history class or works of poetry and fiction in a literature group. For example, encourage adolescents to identify the varying motives that may have converged to affect a character's decisions in a classic work of literature.

Sources: Based on Selman, 1980; Selman & Schultz, 1990.

Reading #12-4

The Social Benefits of Gossip

Although gossip is a form of relational aggression, it can also serve important social functions. For example, gossiping provides a means whereby children and adolescents alike can explore one another's beliefs and priorities; it may also help them establish an emotional bond—a sense of *we-ness*—that unites them against a common "enemy" (Gottman, 1986a, 1986b; Gottman & Mettetal, 1986). As an example, consider how two middle school students use gossip about their teachers to get to know each other better:

A: I have a dumb [life skills] teacher. She goes, "Well, I'd like to try your muffins but I have no sense of taste." I'm going [*makes a disgusted face*].

B: [*Giggle.*]

A: I mean you could tell by her clothes that she had no sense of taste . . . [*Later.*] Yeah, my teacher she shows the dumbest movies. We, Friday we saw a movie about how bread gets moldy. She wants to teach us all about, um, calories and stuff and she's so fat you can tell she needs to learn more than us.

B: [*Giggle.*]

A: There's not a fat person in the class, except for the teacher.

B: [*Giggle.*] About the most sophisticated foreign language teacher we have is our French teacher.

A: I can't stand it.

B: Oh, and she's always going, I say, "Hi, Miss Rickey" and she goes, "Bonjour" [*giggles*].

A: [*Giggle.*]

B: I was walking down steps and I almost fell. I was cracking up. I was going, "OK, whatever you say." (Gottman & Mettetal, 1986, p. 214)

The Need for Physical Affection: Wire "Mothers" Aren't Enough

In its description of operant conditioning in Chapter 13, the textbook talks about reinforcement as an important factor affecting children's motivation. Some reinforcers, known as *primary reinforcers*, satisfy basic biological needs, such as the needs for food, drink, and warmth. Others, known as *secondary reinforcers*, serve no biological purpose but become reinforcing over time through their repeated association with existing reinforcers; examples are money, trophies, and good grades.

Some early behaviorists suggested that physical affection is a secondary reinforcer: Through being associated with primary reinforcers such as milk and warmth, they argued, physical cuddling eventually becomes a reinforcer in its own right. But classic research studies by Harry Harlow (1959; Harlow & Harlow, 1962) indicate that primates (presumably including human beings) have a basic biological need for physical contact and cuddling. Harlow raised rhesus monkeys in complete isolation from other monkeys, including their mothers. In their cages, infant monkeys had two surrogate "mothers": (a) a wire-mesh cylinder with a wooden head and (b) a softer, cuddlier terry-cloth cylinder with a more monkeylike head. A bottle of infant formula was consistently attached to one of the mothers. Regardless of which mother provided the nourishment, the monkeys spent considerable time cuddling against the terry-cloth mother and developed an obvious emotional attachment to "her." Association with a primary reinforcer—the formula—was clearly insufficient to make a wire mom a more appealing companion than a terry-cloth mom.

Reading #13-2

The Nature of Negative Reinforcement[1]

The discussion of reinforcement in Chapter 13 of the textbook is quite brief, and its focus is exclusively on **positive reinforcement**—that is, on desirable stimuli or events that are *presented* after a particular behavior. Whenever children receive food, praise, money, a scratch-and-sniff sticker, or some other pleasant consequence, they are being positively reinforced. But reinforcement can take another form as well. **Negative reinforcement** occurs when certain objects are taken away or certain events stop after a child behaves in a particular way. In other words, negative reinforcement involves the *removal* of a stimulus (usually one that the person finds unpleasant) after a response. Following are some examples:

- Reuben must read *Ivanhoe* for his English literature class before the end of the month. He doesn't like having this assignment hanging over his head, so he finishes it early. When he's done, he no longer has to worry about it.

- Rhonda is in the same literature class. Each time she sits down at home to read *Ivanhoe*, she finds the novel confusing and difficult to understand. She quickly ends her study sessions by finding other things she "needs" to do instead—washing her hair, folding her laundry, playing basketball with the neighbors, and so on.

- Ms. Randolph yells at the rowdy students in her English literature class. They quiet down. By yelling, Ms. Randolph terminates a noisy and unpleasant situation, even if only temporarily.

Notice how, in each example, something *goes away* after a response: Reuben's assignment is no longer hanging over his head, Rhonda's study sessions stop (at least for the time being), and student rowdiness diminishes in Ms. Randolph's classroom.

Teachers and other practitioners will intentionally use negative reinforcement rarely if at all; ideally, they want to create environments in which there are few stimuli that youngsters want to be rid of.[2] But they should realize that negative reinforcement often occurs naturally in classrooms and other day-to-day situations. For example, a child who consistently begins to misbehave or complains of a "tummy ache" just before each day's math lesson may be hoping to escape mathematics for the day by going to the principal's office or school nurse. If the child routinely *does* leave the classroom on each occasion, then misbehaving or complaining about feeling badly (each of which is a behavior) is negatively reinforced (the child escapes the math lesson).

We authors have often heard teachers and other practitioners use the term *negative reinforcement* as a synonym for *punishment*. But in fact, negative reinforcement *increases* the behavior it

---

[1] Much of this reading has been adapted from *Educational Psychology: Developing Learners* (5th ed.), by J. E. Ormrod, 2006, Upper Saddle River, NJ: Merrill/Prentice Hall.

[2] The use of a *time-out*, in which children are placed in a boring situation for a short period of time and then released when behavior improves, comprises a combination of punishment and negative reinforcement. Putting a child *in* a time-out is a form of punishment (most children find lack of stimulation and removal from opportunities to interact with peers a bit unpleasant). Taking a child *out* of time-out contingent on good behavior is a form of negative reinforcement.

follows, whereas punishment is intended to decrease a behavior. Don't let the term *negative* lead you astray here. It refers to the fact that a stimulus is being taken away rather than added; in no way is it meant to reflect a value judgment or indicate that a consequence is undesirable. Quite the opposite, in fact: The *removal* of unpleasant circumstances is a desirable consequence indeed!

In contrast to negative reinforcement, *punishment* takes two forms: either gaining an unpleasant stimulus (perhaps a scolding or spanking) or losing a pleasant one (perhaps being grounded—in which case opportunities for enjoyable activities outside the home are lost—or losing a privilege). The table below can help you distinguish among positive reinforcement, negative reinforcement, and the two forms of punishment. The examples in the rightmost column will show you how each kind of consequence might either enhance or impede a child's growth and development over the long run.

CONSEQUENCE	EFFECT	EXAMPLES
Positive reinforcement	Response *increases* when a new stimulus (presumably one the person finds desirable) is *presented*.	• A child *is praised* for writing an assignment in cursive. She begins to write other assignments in cursive as well. • A boy *gets lunch money* by bullying a girl into surrendering hers. He begins bullying his classmates more frequently.
Negative reinforcement	Response *increases* when a previously existing stimulus (presumably one the person finds undesirable) is *removed*.	• A teenager *no longer has to worry* about a research paper he has completed several days before the due date. He begins to do his assignments ahead of time whenever possible. • A teenager *escapes the principal's wrath* by lying about her role in a recent incident of school vandalism. After this incident, she begins lying to school faculty whenever she finds herself in an uncomfortable situation.
Presentation Punishment	Response *decreases* when a new stimulus (presumably one the person finds undesirable) is *presented*.	• A child *is scolded* for taunting other students. She taunts others less frequently after that. • A child *is ridiculed by peers* for asking a "stupid" question during a lecture. He stops asking questions in class.
Removal Punishment	Response *decreases* when a previously existing stimulus (presumably one the person finds desirable) is *removed*.	• A child *is removed from the softball team for a week* for showing poor sportsmanship. She rarely shows poor sportsmanship in future games. • A child *loses points on a test* for answering a question in a creative but unusual way. He takes fewer risks on future tests.

Using Punishment When You Must[1]

Ideally it is better to entice youngsters to act appropriately, perhaps by creating conditions that lead to intrinsic motivation or perhaps by extrinsically reinforcing youngsters for productive behaviors. But sometimes youngsters exhibit behaviors that must be actively and immediately discouraged, perhaps because they interfere with planned classroom activities or perhaps because they put someone's physical safety or psychological well-being in jeopardy.

Chapter 13 of the textbook defines a *reinforcer* as a consequence of a response that leads to an increased frequency of that response. In contrast, **punishment** is a consequence that *decreases* the frequency of the response it follows. All punishing consequences fall into one of two groups. **Presentation punishment** involves presenting a new stimulus, presumably something a person finds unpleasant and doesn't want. Scoldings and teacher scowls, if they lead to a reduction in the behavior they follow, are instances of presentation punishment. **Removal punishment** involves removing a previously existing stimulus, presumably one a person finds desirable and doesn't want to lose. The loss of a privilege, a fine (involving the loss of money or previously earned points), and "grounding" (when certain pleasurable outside activities are missed) are all possible examples of removal punishment.

Effective Forms of Punishment

As a general rule, parents, teachers, and other practitioners should use only mild forms of punishment with children and adolescents; severe consequences can lead to such unwanted side effects as resentment, hostility, or (when administered by teachers) truancy from school. Researchers and experienced educators have identified several forms of mild punishment that can be effective in reducing undesirable behaviors:

- **Verbal reprimands (scolding).** Although a few youngsters seem to thrive on adult scolding because of the attention it brings, most find **verbal reprimands** to be unpleasant and punishing, especially if they occur infrequently (Pfiffner & O'Leary, 1993; Van Houten, Nau, MacKenzie-Keating, Sameoto, & Colavecchia, 1982). In general, reprimands are more effective when they are immediate, brief, and unemotional; they also work better when they are given in a soft voice and in close proximity to the child, perhaps because they are less likely to be noticed and so less likely to draw others' attention (O'Leary, Kaufman, Kass, & Drabman, 1970; Pfiffner & O'Leary, 1993). Reprimands should be given in private whenever possible: When scolded in front of peers, some youngsters may relish the attention, and others (e.g., many Native American and Hispanic children) may feel totally humiliated (Fuller, 2001).

- **Response cost.** Because it involves the loss either of a previously earned reinforcer or of an opportunity to obtain reinforcement, **response cost** is an instance of removal

---

[1] This reading has been adapted from excerpts from *Educational Psychology: Developing Learners* (5th ed.), by J. E. Ormrod, 2006, Upper Saddle River, NJ: Merrill/Prentice Hall.

punishment. When teachers and therapists work with youngsters who have severe behavior problems, they sometimes incorporate response cost into a point system of some sort: They award points, check marks, plastic chips, or the like for good behavior (reinforcement) and take away these things for inappropriate behavior (response cost). Youngsters who accumulate a sufficient number of points or tokens can use them to "buy" objects, privileges, or enjoyable activities that are otherwise not available. Response cost is especially effective when coupled with reinforcement of appropriate behavior (Iwata & Bailey, 1974; Lentz, 1988; Rapport, Murphy, & Bailey, 1982).

- **Logical consequences.** Something that follows naturally or logically from a youngster's misbehavior, a **logical consequence**, is punishment that fits the crime. For example, if a student destroys a classmate's possession, a reasonable consequence is for the student to replace it or pay for a new one. If two close friends talk so much that they aren't completing assignments, a reasonable consequence is for them to be separated. If a teenager intentionally makes a mess in the cafeteria, an appropriate consequence is to clean it up. The use of logical consequences makes "logical" sense, and numerous research studies and case studies vouch for its effectiveness (Dreikurs, 1998; Lyon, 1984; Schloss & Smith, 1994; Wright, 1982).

- **Time-out.** A misbehaving youngster given a **time-out** is placed in a dull, boring (but not scary) situation—perhaps a separate room designed especially for time-outs or a remote corner of the classroom. A child in time-out has no opportunity to interact with other people and no opportunity to obtain reinforcement. The length of the time-out is typically quite short (perhaps two to ten minutes, depending on the child's age), but the child is not released until inappropriate behavior (e.g., screaming, kicking) has stopped. Time-outs have been used successfully to reduce a variety of noncompliant, disruptive, and aggressive behaviors (e.g., Pfiffner & Barkley, 1998; Rortvedt & Miltenberger, 1994; White & Bailey, 1990). Keep in mind, however, that a time-out is apt to be effective only if ongoing group activities are a source of enjoyment and reinforcement. If, instead, it allows a child to escape difficult tasks or an overwhelming amount of noise and stimulation, it might actually be reinforcing and so *increase* undesirable behavior (Alberto & Troutman, 2003; McClowry, 1998; Pfiffner & Barkley, 1998).

- **In-school suspension.** Like time-out, **in-school suspension** involves placing a child in a quiet, boring room, in this case within the school building. However, it often lasts one or more school days and involves close adult supervision. Students receiving in-school suspension spend the day working on the same assignments that their nonsuspended classmates do and so are able to keep up with their schoolwork. But they have no opportunity for interaction with peers—an aspect of school that is reinforcing to most students. Although in-school suspension programs have not been systematically investigated through controlled research studies, experienced educators report that these programs are often effective in reducing chronic misbehaviors, particularly when part of the suspension session is devoted to teaching appropriate behaviors and tutoring academic skills and when the supervising teacher acts as a supportive resource rather than as a punisher (Gootman, 1998; Huff, 1988; Pfiffner & Barkley, 1998; Sullivan, 1989).

Ideally, adults should individualize their use of punishment. For example, some children enjoy the attention that verbal reprimands bring (as Spencer sometimes does in the final case study in textbook Chapter 13), and others appreciate the peace and quiet of an occasional time-out. If adults find that a certain form of punishment has no noticeable effect on a child's behavior, they should conclude that it isn't really punishing for the child and consider other alternatives.

Ineffective Forms of Punishment

Several forms of punishment are typically *not* recommended:

- **Physical punishment.** Most experts advise against physical punishment for school-age children and adolescents (Doyle, 1990; Zirpoli & Melloy, 2001). Furthermore, its use in the classroom is *illegal* in many places. Even mild physical punishment, such as a spank or slap with a ruler, can lead to such undesirable behaviors as resentment of the adult administering the punishment, inattention to school tasks, lying, aggression, vandalism, avoidance of school tasks, and truancy. When carried to extremes, physical punishment constitutes child abuse and may cause long-term psychological harm and permanent physical damage.

- **Psychological punishment.** Any consequence that seriously threatens a child's self-esteem is **psychological punishment** and is not recommended (Davis & Thomas, 1989; Walker & Shea, 1999). Embarrassing remarks and public humiliation can lead to some of the same side effects as physical punishment (e.g., resentment of the punisher, inattention to school tasks, truancy from school) and have the potential to inflict long-term psychological harm. By deflating children's sense of self, psychological punishment can also lower their expectations for future performance and their motivation to learn and achieve (see the discussion of *self-efficacy* in Chapter 13 in the textbook).

- **Extra classwork.** Asking a student to complete makeup work for time missed in school is a reasonable and justifiable request. But assigning extra classwork or homework beyond that required for other students is inappropriate if it is assigned simply to punish a student's wrongdoing (Cooper, 1989; Corno, 1996). In this case there is a very different side effect: The teacher inadvertently communicates the message that "schoolwork is unpleasant."

- **Out-of-school suspension.** Out-of-school suspension is usually *not* an effective means of changing a student's behavior (Moles, 1990; Nichols, Ludwin, & Iadicola, 1999; Pfiffner & Barkley, 1998). In the first place, being suspended from school may be exactly what the student wants, in which case inappropriate behaviors are being reinforced rather than punished. Second, because many students with chronic behavior problems also tend to do poorly in their schoolwork, suspension involves a loss of valuable instructional time and interferes with any psychological "attachment" to school, thereby decreasing even further the students' chances for academic and social success (Nichols et al., 1999; Skiba & Raison, 1990).

An additional form of punishment—missing recess—gets mixed reviews regarding its effectiveness. In some situations missing recess may be a logical consequence for students who fail to complete their schoolwork during regular class time due to off-task behavior. Yet research indicates that, at least at the elementary level, students can more effectively concentrate on school tasks when they have occasional breaks from academic activities (Maxmell, Jarrett, &

Dickerson, 1998; Pellegrini, Huberty, & Jones, 1995). Perhaps the best piece of advice is to withdraw recess privileges infrequently, if at all, and to monitor the effectiveness of such a consequence on students' classroom behavior over the long run.

Using Punishment Humanely

A frequent criticism of using punishment is that it is "inhumane," or somehow cruel and barbaric. Indeed, certain forms of punishment, such as physical abuse or public humiliation, do constitute inhumane treatment. Adults must be *extremely careful* in their use of punishment in the classroom and elsewhere. When administered judiciously, however, some forms of mild punishment can lead to a rapid reduction in misbehavior without causing physical or psychological harm. And when adults can decrease counterproductive behaviors quickly and effectively—especially when those behaviors are harmful to oneself or others—then punishment may, in fact, be one of the most humane approaches to take (Lerman & Vorndran, 2002). Following are several guidelines for using punishment effectively and humanely:

• *Inform youngsters ahead of time that certain behaviors will be punished, and explain how those behaviors will be punished.* When children are informed of response-punishment contingencies ahead of time, they are less apt to engage in forbidden behaviors; they are also less apt to be surprised or resentful if punishment must be administered (Gottfredson & Gottfredson, 1985; Moles, 1990). Ultimately, youngsters should learn that their behaviors influence the consequences they experience—that they have some control over what happens to them (see the discussion of *attributions* in Chapter 13 in the textbook).

• *Follow through with specified consequences.* One mistake some adults make is to continually threaten punishment without ever following through. One warning is desirable, but repeated warnings are not. The teacher who says, "If you bring that rubber snake to class one more time, Tommy, I'm going to take it away," but never does take the snake away, is giving the message that no response-punishment contingency really exists. Because punishment is effective only when it is actually carried out, after-school detentions can sometimes be problematic: Some students simply cannot stay after school hours (Nichols et al., 1999). Perhaps they have transportation issues, perhaps they are reluctant to walk through certain neighborhoods after dark, or perhaps they must take care of younger siblings until parents get home from work. Unless we can address such concerns, imposing after-school detention is unrealistic.

• *Administer punishment privately.* By administering punishment in private, adults protect youngsters from public embarrassment or humiliation. They also eliminate the possibility that the punishment will draw the attention of peers—a potential reinforcer for the very behavior the adults are trying to eliminate.

• *Explain why the punished behavior is unacceptable.* Adults must explain exactly why a certain behavior cannot be tolerated (perhaps because it interferes with learning, threatens the safety or self-esteem of other people, or damages school property). Punishment is far more effective when accompanied by one or more reasons why the punished behavior is unacceptable (Cheyne & Walters, 1970; Parke, 1974; Perry & Perry, 1983). (See the discussion of *induction* in textbook Chapter 13.)

• *Emphasize that it is the behavior that is undesirable, not the child.* Adults must emphasize that certain behaviors interfere with youngsters' success in the classroom and elsewhere—that youngsters are preventing themselves from becoming the very best they can be.

• *Simultaneously teach and reinforce desirable alternative behaviors.* Punishment of misbehavior is almost always more effective when appropriate behaviors are being reinforced at the same time (Lerman & Vorndran, 2002; Pfiffner & Barkley, 1998). Furthermore, by reinforcing desirable responses as well as punishing undesirable ones, adults give children the positive, optimistic message that, yes, behavior can and will improve. Ultimately, the overall environment adults create for children must be a positive one that highlights the good things children do and de-emphasizes the "bad" (e.g., Smith & Smoll, 1997).

Cognitive-Developmental Perspectives on Moral Development:
Piaget's and Kohlberg's Theories

As you should recall from Chapter 1 in the textbook, *cognitive-developmental theories* focus on the qualitative ways in which children's thinking processes change with age. Often these theories include distinct stages through which children progress over time. Two early, groundbreaking cognitive-developmental theories of moral development were those of Piaget and Kohlberg. Both of them focus on children's *reasoning* about moral issues.

Piaget's Theory of Moral Development

Although Jean Piaget is best known for his theory of cognitive development, in fact his studies extended to the moral domain as well. In Piaget's view, not only do children construct (rather than absorb) knowledge about the world, they also construct moral beliefs and values. Piaget proposed that as children get older, they construct increasingly complex and flexible understandings of "good" and "bad" behavior. For instance, in the early elementary years, children believe that behaviors that are "bad" or "naughty" are those that cause serious damage or harm. By the upper elementary grades, however, children consider people's motives and intentions when evaluating behaviors. As an illustration of this change, consider the following situations:

> A little boy who is called John is in his room. He is called to dinner. He goes into the dining room. But behind the door there was a chair, and on the chair there was a tray with fifteen cups on it. John couldn't have known that there was all this behind the door. He goes in, the door knocks against the tray, bang go the fifteen cups, and they all get broken!

> Once there was a little boy whose name was Henry. One day when his mother was out he tried to get some jam out of the cupboard. He climbed up on to a chair and stretched out his arm. But the jam was too high up and he couldn't reach it and have any. But while he was trying to get it he knocked over a cup. The cup fell down and broke. (Piaget, 1932/1960, p. 118)

A 6-year-old child, whom we'll call "Susan," evaluates the two boys' misdeeds this way (she initially refers to the 15 cups as "plates"):

> Adult: Are those children both naughty, or is one not so naughty as the other?
> Susan: Both just as naughty.
> Adult: Would you punish them the same?
> Susan: No. The one who broke fifteen plates.
> Adult: And would you punish the other one more, or less?
> Susan: The first broke lots of things, the other one fewer.
> Adult: How would you punish them?
> Susan: The one who broke the fifteen cups: two slaps. The other one: one slap.
> (dialogue from Piaget, 1932/1960, p. 121; format adapted)

In contrast, 9-year-old "Greta" takes the boys' motives into account:

> Adult: Which of these two silly things was naughtiest, do you think?

Greta: The one where he tried to take hold of a cup was [the silliest] because the other boy didn't see [that there were some cups behind the door]. He saw what he was doing.

Adult: How many did he break?

Greta: One cup.

Adult: And the other one?

Greta: Fifteen.

Adult: Then which one would you punish most?

Greta: The one who broke one cup.

Adult: Why?

Greta: He did it on purpose. If he hadn't taken the jam, it wouldn't have happened.
(dialogue from Piaget, 1932/1960, p. 125; format adapted)

After interviewing children about a variety of situations—causing damage, telling lies, stealing someone else's possessions, playing games, and so on—Piaget proposed that moral reasoning undergoes qualitative changes that are to some degree dependent on children's developing cognitive abilities. For preschoolers, "good" behavior consists of obeying adults and other authority figures. Around age 5, children begin to judge what is good and appropriate based on established *rules* for behavior. At this point, they see rules as firm and inflexible, as dictates to be obeyed without question (Piaget called this rule-based morality **moral realism**). Sometime around age 8 or 9, children begin to recognize that rules are created primarily to help people get along and can be changed if everyone agrees to the change.

Researchers have found that Piaget was not always accurate about when various aspects of moral reasoning emerge. For example, many preschoolers recognize that certain behaviors (e.g., pushing others or damaging their property) are wrong even if an adult assures them that such behaviors are acceptable (Nucci & Turiel, 1978; Tisak, 1993; Turiel, 1983). However, many developmentalists find value in Piaget's notion that children construct their own standards for moral behavior—often as a result of having discussions with adults and peers—rather than simply adopting the moral guidelines of those around them (Davidson & Youniss, 1995; Kohlberg, 1984; Kurtines, Berman, Ittel, & Williamson, 1995; Turiel, 1998). Furthermore, theorists acknowledge that development of children's moral understandings depends considerably on advancing cognitive capabilities, such as perspective taking and abstract thought (Eisenberg, 1995; Kohlberg, 1969; Kurtines et al., 1995).

Kohlberg's Theory of Moral Development

Like Piaget, Lawrence Kohlberg believed that moral development is very much a constructive process. Kohlberg also found value in Piaget's concept of *disequilibrium*: In Kohlberg's view, children acquire more advanced forms of moral reasoning only when they find that their existing ways of reasoning cannot adequately address the moral issues and dilemmas they confront.

Due to space constraints, the textbook provides only brief descriptions of Kohlberg's three levels of moral development and the two stages within each one. Here in the *Study Guide and Reader*, we describe them in more detail.

Level I: Preconventional morality. Preconventional reasoning is the earliest and least mature form of moral reasoning, in that the individual has not yet adopted or internalized society's conventions regarding what is morally right or wrong. The preconventional person's judgments about the morality of behavior are determined primarily by the consequences of those behaviors. Behaviors that lead to rewards and pleasure are "right"; behaviors that lead to punishment are "wrong." Preconventional individuals will obey people who have control of rewards and punishments; they will not necessarily obey people without control over such consequences. According to early research by Kohlberg and others, preconventional morality is common in preschoolers and most elementary school students, and it is sometimes seen in middle school and high school students as well (Colby & Kohlberg, 1984; Reimer, Paolitto, & Hersh, 1983).

Preconventional morality encompasses two stages:

Stage 1: Punishment-avoidance and obedience. Stage 1 individuals make moral decisions based on what they think is best for themselves, without considering the needs or feelings of other people. For these individuals, the only wrong behaviors are ones that will be punished. Stage 1 individuals follow rules of behavior that are established by people more powerful than themselves, whether these people are adult authority figures (e.g., parents and teachers) or stronger peers. But they may disobey rules if they think that they can avoid punishment in doing so. In a nutshell, individuals in Stage 1 will do anything they can get away with.

Stage 2: Exchange of favors. Individuals in Stage 2 (which Kohlberg often called the *instrumental-relativist* stage) are beginning to recognize that others have needs just as they themselves do. They sometimes address the needs of others by offering to exchange favors ("You scratch my back, and I'll scratch yours"), but they usually try to get the better end of the bargain. To Stage 2 individuals, being "fair" means that everybody gets the same opportunities or the same amount of whatever is being handed out. Adults might hear "That's not fair!" from Stage 2 children who think they're being shortchanged.

Level II: Conventional morality. Conventional morality is characterized by an acceptance of society's conventions concerning right and wrong: The individual obeys rules and follows society's norms even when there is no reward for obedience and no punishment for disobedience. Adherence to rules and conventions is somewhat rigid; a rule's appropriateness or fairness is seldom questioned. According to early researchers, conventional morality occasionally appears in the upper elementary grades but more often emerges in the middle school or junior high school years; many high school students continue to use such reasoning (Colby & Kohlberg, 1984; Reimer et al., 1983).

Like preconventional morality, conventional morality includes two stages:

Stage 3: Good boy/good girl. Stage 3 individuals look primarily to the people they know, and especially to authority figures (e.g., parents, teachers, popular peers), for guidance about what is right and wrong. Stage 3 individuals want to please others and gain their approval; they like being told that they are a "good boy" or a "good girl." They are also concerned about maintaining interpersonal relationships through sharing, trust, and loyalty. For example, they believe in the Golden Rule ("Treat others as you would like to be treated") and in the importance of keeping promises and commitments. Stage 3 individuals can put themselves in another person's shoes and consider the perspectives of others in making decisions. They also acknowledge that someone's intentions must be considered in determining guilt or innocence. As an example, recall 9-year-old Greta's explanation of why the boy who broke one cup was naughtier than the boy who broke 15 cups: "He did it on purpose."

Stage 4: Law and order. Stage 4 individuals look to society as a whole, rather than just to the people they know, for guidelines (conventions) about what is right and wrong. They know that rules are necessary for keeping society running smoothly and believe that it is their "duty" to obey them. They see these rules as set in concrete, however; they do not yet recognize that it may occasionally be more morally justifiable to break laws (perhaps those that legally authorize racial segregation or interfere with basic human rights) than to follow them. Nor do they recognize that, as society's needs change, rules should be changed as well.

Level III: Postconventional morality. Postconventional individuals have developed their own set of abstract principles to define what actions are morally right and wrong—principles that typically include such basic human rights as life, liberty, and justice. Postconventional individuals obey rules consistent with their own abstract principles of morality, and they may *dis*obey rules inconsistent with such principles. According to early researchers, adolescents rarely demonstrate postconventional reasoning before they reach college, and in fact most people never reach this level of moral reasoning at all (Colby & Kohlberg, 1984; Reimer et al., 1983; Snarey, 1995).

Postconventional morality, too, encompasses two stages:

Stage 5: Social contract. Stage 5 individuals view rules that are determined through a democratic process as a *social contract*, an agreement among many people about how everyone should behave. They think of rules as being useful mechanisms that maintain the general social order and protect individual human rights, rather than as absolute dictates that must be obeyed simply because they are "the law." They also recognize the flexibility of rules; rules that no longer serve society's best interests can and should be changed.

Stage 6: Universal ethical principle. Kohlberg (1984) described Stage 6 as an ideal stage that few people ever reach. This stage represents adherence to a few abstract, universal principles that transcend specific norms and rules for behavior. Such principles typically include respect for human dignity and basic human rights, the belief that all people are truly equal, and a commitment to justice and due process. Stage 6 individuals answer to a strong inner conscience, rather than to authority figures or concrete laws, and they willingly disobey laws that violate their own ethical principles. Martin Luther King, Jr.'s "Letter from a Birmingham Jail," excerpted here, illustrates Stage 6 reasoning:

> One may well ask, "How can you advocate breaking some laws and obeying others?"
> The answer lies in the fact that one has not only a legal but a moral responsibility to obey just laws. One has a moral responsibility to disobey unjust laws, though one must do so openly, lovingly and with a willingness to accept the penalty. An individual who breaks a law that conscience tells him is unjust, and accepts the penalty to arouse the conscience of the community, is expressing in reality the highest respect for law. An unjust law is a human law not rooted in eternal law and natural law. A law that uplifts human personality is just; one which degrades human personality is unjust. (King, 1965, cited in Kohlberg, 1981, pp. 318–319)

Reading #13-5

Do No Harm: When Children Ignore an Authority Figure

In his classic theory of moral development, Lawrence Kohlberg suggested that young children are primarily concerned with satisfying their own needs and avoiding punishment by powerful authority figures (see Chapter 13 of the textbook). However, more recent research has suggested that by age 4, most children understand that causing harm to another person is wrong even if an authority figure tells them otherwise. As an example, Laupa (1994) described several hypothetical school situations to 4- and 5-year-olds:

1. Two children are on the playground and want to go down the slide. They disagree about who should go first. A person comes along and tells them which child should go first and which one should go second.

2. Some children can't decide where to sit during snack time. A person comes along and tells them where to sit.

3. Two children are fighting on the playground. A person comes along and tells them that they should stop fighting.

4. Two children are fighting on the playground. A person comes along and tells them that it's OK for them to keep fighting.

For these situations, the person in the story who gave the instructions varied among four possibilities:

- An adult with authority (a teacher)
- An adult without authority (a lady from across the street)
- A peer with authority (a teacher's helper)
- A peer without authority (another child on the playground)

After each situation, Laupa asked, "Is it all right for her to tell them that?" and "Should they do what she tells them to do?" (p. 10). As a general rule, the children were more likely to accept a teacher's instructions than those of a teacher's helper, but they were more likely to accept the instructions of a helper (a peer with authority) than those of a lady from across the street. (Most put little stock in what a child *without* authority had to say.) Thus, both adult status and authority status entered into children's decisions to abide by someone else's instructions. Laupa found an exception to this general pattern in the situations involving fighting, which had the potential to cause physical harm: The children were much more likely to obey a peer authority or adult nonauthority who said to *stop* fighting than to obey a teacher who said that it was OK to continue fighting.

Reading #13-6

Children's Understanding of Moral Versus Conventional Transgressions

Even toddlers know that some behaviors are frowned upon; for instance, a child who inadvertently breaks a lamp might say "Uh-oh!" As children get older, they begin to form two different categories of "wrong" behaviors (Nucci & Nucci, 1982b; Nucci & Turiel, 1978; Turiel, 1983). They intuitively realize that some actions—which theorists call *moral transgressions*— show disregard for other people's rights and needs, perhaps by causing physical or psychological harm or perhaps by violating basic principles of equality, freedom, or justice. In contrast, other actions—which theorists call *conventional transgressions*—violate culturally shared understandings of what is "proper" and "well-mannered"— wearing clothes when going out in public, talking respectfully to an authority figure, saying "thank you" for a gift, and so on. Initially, children distinguish between moral and conventional transgressions only for situations with which they have had personal experience (e.g., a boy bullying children on the playground versus a girl eating dinner with her fingers). By the time they are 6, they make the distinction for less familiar situations as well (Davidson, Turiel, & Black, 1983; Helwig & Jasiobedzka, 2001; Laupa & Turiel, 1995).

In the early elementary grades, children believe social conventions should be followed simply for their own sake. As they grow older, however, they become more aware of the importance of social conventions for maintaining a cohesive society (Turiel, 1983). As an example, imagine that a boy named Peter calls his teacher by her first name. Children and adolescents almost invariably say that such behavior is inappropriate, but they offer differing explanations about *why* it is inappropriate. Let's consider how three boys analyzed the situation:

> **John (age 6):** [He shouldn't have called the teacher by her first name] because what the teacher tells you, you have to obey and it is being nice to call someone what they want to be called. . . . Because he or she is pretty important. (Turiel, 1983, p. 107)
>
> **Bruce (age 11):** Wrong, because the principal told him not to. Because it was a rule. It was one of the rules of the school. . . . Because you should follow the rules. . . . [I]f there wasn't a rule, it wouldn't matter. . . . It wouldn't matter what they called her if there wasn't a rule. (Turiel, 1983, p. 108)
>
> **Richard (age 17):** I think he was wrong, because you have to realize that you should have respect for your elders and that respect is shown by addressing them by their last names. . . . Informally, you just call any of your friends by their first names, but you really don't have that relation with a teacher. Whereas with parents too, you call them Mom and Dad and it's a different relation than the other two. . . . I think he'd have to realize that you have to go along with the ways of other people in your society. . . . (Turiel, 1983, p. 110)

Generally speaking, 6- and 7-year-olds (like John) believe that people should follow rules and conventions in large part because authority figures tell them to do so. In contrast, 10- and 11-year-olds (like Bruce) believe that one should follow rules and conventions simply because they exist, even though they recognize that rules and conventions are somewhat arbitrary. By late adolescence (e.g., at ages 14 to 16), young people realize that conventions help society function more smoothly; for instance, Richard says that "you have to go along with the ways of other people in your society" (Kurtines, Berman, Ittel, & Williamson, 1995; Turiel, 1983).

How Do Children Learn the Difference?

Children appear to learn about the "wrongness" of moral and conventional transgressions in different ways. Consider the following scenarios:

- A number of nursery school children are playing outdoors. There are some swings in the yard, all of which are being used. One of the children decides that he now wants to use a swing. Seeing that they are all occupied, he goes to one of the swings, where he pushes the other child off, at the same time hitting him. The child who has been pushed is hurt and begins to cry. (Laupa & Turiel, 1995, p. 461)

- Children are greeting a teacher who has just come into the nursery school. A number of children go up to her and say "Good morning, Mrs. Jones." One of the children says, "Good morning, Mary." (Laupa & Turiel, 1995, p. 461)

In the first scenario, the child who pushes his peer gets immediate feedback that he has caused harm and distress: The peer cries and is clearly injured. In the second scenario, the child who calls a teacher by her first name may get verbal feedback that such behavior is unacceptable but will not see any concrete evidence of harm. Sometimes children get no feedback that they have violated social conventions, in part because some conventions are situation-specific (e.g., some adults prefer that children call them by their first names). When adults *do* respond to conventional transgressions, they typically respond differently than they do to moral transgressions. For instance, they are more likely to use physical punishment (e.g., a spanking) for moral infringements than for conventional ones (Catron & Masters, 1993). And when adults explain what children have done wrong, they focus on other people's needs and rights for moral transgressions ("You've really hurt Megan's feelings by your unkind remark") but emphasize rules and the need for social order for conventional violations ("We always use our 'indoor' voices when speaking in class") (Chilamkurti & Milner, 1993; Nucci & Nucci, 1982b; Nucci & Turiel, 1978; Smetana, 1989).

Children show a similar distinction in their own reactions to their peers' transgressions (Nucci & Nucci, 1982a, 1982b; Turiel, 1983). They talk about possible injury or injustice in the case of moral transgressions, as the following observation on a playground illustrates:

> Two boys have forcibly taken a sled away from a younger boy and are playing with it. A girl who was watching says to the boys, "Hey, give it back, assholes. That's really even odds, the two of you against one little kid." The girl pulls the sled away from one of the older boys, pushes him to the ground, and hands the sled back to the younger boy. He takes the sled and the incident ends. (Nucci & Nucci, 1982a, p. 1339)

In contrast, children talk about the importance of rules and norms in the case of conventional transgressions. For instance, if a 7-year-old boy sees another child spitting on the grass, he might admonish the child, "You're not supposed to spit" (Nucci & Nucci, 1982a, p. 1339).

Reading #13-7

Justice Versus Care Orientations in Moral Reasoning

In Chapter 13, the textbook describes Carol Gilligan's distinction between two distinctly different orientations in moral reasoning. A **justice orientation** focuses on fairness and equality: People take others' rights into consideration when making moral decisions. In contrast, a **care orientation** focuses on compassion and taking responsibility for others' well-being. In Gilligan's view, a justice orientation predominates in the moral reasoning of males, whereas a care orientation is more common in the moral reasoning of females.

According to Gilligan, the development of a morality of care proceeds through three stages. At the first stage, children are concerned exclusively about their own needs, mostly to ensure their own survival. At the second stage, they show concern for people who are unable to care for themselves, including infants and the elderly. At the third and final stage, they recognize the interdependent nature of personal relationships and extend compassion and care to all human beings (Gilligan, 1977, 1982).

Critics have found several shortcomings in Gilligan's theory. First, most research studies do *not* find major gender differences in moral reasoning (Eisenberg, Martin, & Fabes, 1996; Nunner-Winkler, 1984; Walker, 1991). Furthermore, Gilligan provides only the most general explanation of how gender differences emerge (and has not empirically tested it) and offers no explanation at all about how children might move from one stage to the next (Turiel, 1998; Walker, 1995). Moreover, her early studies involved only small samples of college women discussing a single issue, abortion, which is clouded by women's views on whether an unborn fetus is a living human being (Turiel, 1998). An additional problem is that the women's responses were analyzed in an arguably superficial and subjective fashion, without a systematic means of categorizing the data (Hoff Sommers, 2000; Turiel, 1998; Walker, 1995).

Yet by broadening our view of what moral reasoning may involve, Gilligan has made an important contribution to our understanding of moral development. In addition, the distinction between justice and care orientations may be helpful in understanding some cultural differences in people's behaviors. A cross-cultural study by Miller and Bersoff (1992) provides an example of how the two orientations might be revealed in cultural differences in moral decision making. These researchers presented several moral dilemmas to third graders, seventh graders, and undergraduate students in both the United States and India. An American version of one dilemma was as follows (Indian names and an Indian city were used in the Indian version):

> Ben planned to travel to San Francisco in order to attend the wedding of his best friend. He needed to catch the very next train if he was to be on time for the ceremony, as he had to deliver the wedding rings.
>
> However, Ben's wallet was stolen in the train station. He lost all of his money as well as his ticket to San Francisco.
>
> Ben approached several officials as well as passengers at the train station and asked them to loan him money to buy a new ticket. But, because he was a stranger, no one was willing to lend him the money he needed.
>
> While Ben was sitting on a bench trying to decide what to do next, a well-dressed man sitting next to him walked away for a minute. Ben noticed that the man had left his coat unattended. Sticking out of the man's coat pocket was a train ticket to San

Francisco. . . . He also saw that the man had more than enough money in his coat pocket to buy another train ticket. (Miller & Bersoff, 1992, p. 545)

Participants were asked to choose one of two solutions to the problem and to explain their reasoning. One solution placed priority on individual rights and justice; the other placed priority on caring for others:

Ben should not take the ticket from the man's coat pocket—even though it means not getting to San Francisco in time to deliver the wedding rings to his best friend. (p. 545)

Ben should go to San Francisco to deliver the wedding rings to his best friend—even though it means taking the train ticket from the other man's coat pocket. (p. 545)

Indian participants almost always chose caring solutions over justice solutions. Some American participants also chose caring solutions, but many others put higher value on preserving individual rights.

Just Communities

In its discussion of strategies for promoting moral development in Chapter 13, the textbook briefly describes an approach known as a **just community**, in which young people and adults hold regular "town meetings" to discuss issues of fairness and justice and establish rules for appropriate behavior (e.g., Higgins, 1995; Power, Higgins, & Kohlberg, 1989). Meetings are democratic, youngsters and adults have one vote apiece, and the will of the majority is binding. As an example, consider how a just community at one high school (the Cluster School in Cambridge, Massachusetts) dealt with a stealing incident:

> Nine dollars was taken during a class from someone's purse, and no one would admit to taking the money. A community meeting was convened to discuss the theft. One group of students came to the meeting with a proposal that each member of the school should chip in fifteen cents to make up for the nine dollars stolen from the girl's purse. Phyllis, a girl from this group, offered an elaborate rationale for reimbursing the stolen money. "It's everyone's fault that she don't have no money. It was stolen because people just don't care about the community. Everybody should care that she got her money stolen, (and therefore) we decided to give her money back to her."
>
> Not everyone agreed with the proposal. Bob was worried that if they adopted the proposal, "then anyone can say I lost ten dollars."
>
> Jill asked, "How do you know whether to believe someone who says her money has been stolen?"
>
> Bob and Jill both thought the fault lay not with the community but with the girl for having left her pocketbook unattended. "She gives you a chance to steal it; if you had it in your arms (length), wouldn't you be thinking about stealing it?"
>
> In response, Phyllis reiterated her point. She began with the assumption that Cluster ought to be a community and its members ought to trust one another. If people could not be trusted, it was the group's failure, and they would have to pay for the fault. Some staff members and students both pointed out that the community should put pressure on the guilty party to return the money. The community adopted a compromise. "If the money is not returned anonymously by a certain date, everyone will be assessed fifteen cents." This combined proposal was voted in and in fact proved effective. The person who stole the money eventually admitted it and was given a schedule of repayment. Even though the girl who stole the money only repaid a portion, this incident ended stealing in the Cluster School. A certain level of group trust had been established based on a sense of the group as a true community. There were no thefts in the school in the three years after that meeting. (Higgins, 1995, pp. 67–68)

From "Educating for Justice and Community: Lawrence Kohlberg's Vision of Moral Education" by A. Higgins, in W. M. Kurtines and J. L. Gewirtz (Eds.), *Moral Development: An Introduction*, Boston: Allyn & Bacon, 1995, pp. 67-68. Copyright 1995 by Allyn & Bacon. Reprinted by permission.

Case studies such as the one just presented suggest that just communities not only decrease immoral behaviors but also promote more advanced moral reasoning. For instance, Higgins (1995) reported that after two years of using the just-community model, students at the Cluster School showed an increased understanding of how their own actions impacted others, gained a sense of responsibility for one another's well-being, and were more likely to reason at Kohlberg's Stages 3 and 4.

Inclusive Social Practices for Children with Special Needs

Chapter 14 identifies several important roles that peer relationships play in children's development. Yet not all children are included by peers in conversations, games on the playground, or after-school social events. Children who are not accepted by peers are apt to feel rejected, and these excluded children lack opportunities to practice the social skills that facilitate effective peer interactions.

Some children have disabilities that affect their peer acceptance. For example, classmates at school may harbor negative attitudes (such as pity or disgust) toward children with some disabilities and fail to treat these children with kindness and respect. The story of one elementary student conveys the social isolation that can occur, but it also offers optimism that isolation can be overcome:

> Daniel is a second grader who has multiple disabilities: He has cerebral palsy and a visual impairment, as well as a seizure disorder. Daniel uses a wheelchair and needs to be fed and dressed. To communicate with others, Daniel is learning to use a communication device that speaks for him. When Daniel first attended the preschool special education program at age 3, several staff members who did not work with Daniel wondered why he was in school. Older pupils attending the school stared at Daniel while he was being fed in the lunchroom and even imitated the way food dribbled from his mouth. Now, in a school that values diversity and practices inclusion, Daniel is an appreciated member of Ms. Kilmer's second-grade class. Students in Daniel's school have learned to look beyond Daniel's differences and instead focus on his similarities to them.
> (Snell & Janney, 2000, p. 7)

Initially, Daniel's preschool teachers did not recognize his need to interact with peers and so did little to encourage interaction with classmates. Fortunately, Daniel later joined a classroom where he was made to feel welcome and respected. His teacher, Ms. Kilmer, undoubtedly used a variety of strategies to help the other children see Daniel's positive characteristics.

Clearly, being physically *included* in the classroom and other group settings is not the same as being socially *accepted*. Teachers and other practitioners may find that a series of actions are needed to promote social connections among youngsters with and without disabilities. We offer the following suggestions:

• *Create situations that make social interaction necessary or highly probable.* When nondisabled children select partners with whom to talk, eat, study, or play ball, they often overlook peers who have physical or cognitive disabilities. Teachers and other practitioners can use several strategies to increase social opportunities for children with special needs: assigning "buddies" who can assist them with tasks they cannot complete alone; supporting after-school extracurricular activities that are overtly inclusive (and perhaps explicitly *inviting* children with disabilities to join those activities); and giving all children assigned seats rather than letting them choose where to sit (Snell & Janney, 2000).

• *Teach effective social behaviors.* Children with mental retardation typically have limited experience in the give-and-take of social situations (Greenspan & Granfield, 1992). Adults may be able to teach these children specific social skills—for instance, how to open a conversation, ask for help, and express disagreement. Adults may find it helpful to model these behaviors for children and encourage them to practice the behaviors in specific settings.

• *Teach children to interpret social situations in productive ways.* Children with emotional and behavioral disorders—for example, those who are unusually aggressive—frequently have difficulty understanding other people's perspectives and sometimes mistakenly believe that others are trying to hurt them (Hughes, 1988; Lind, 1994). Children with autism, too, have trouble looking at situations from other people's perspectives (Baron-Cohen, 1993; Hobson, 1993). Children with cognitive disabilities may have difficulty inferring other children's intentions, especially when there is conflict or when harm is inflicted (Leffert, Siperstein, & Millikan, 1999). When adults suspect that children are having trouble with perspective taking and accurate interpretation of social cues, they may want to provide specific (and possibly intensive) training in these areas. (We suggest you examine recommendations in Chapter 12 for fostering children's social understandings and productive interpersonal behaviors and also the strategies in Chapter 11 for supporting youngsters with emotional problems.)

• *Make use of technology.* Sometimes special equipment can help children with physical disabilities communicate more effectively with others. For example, children who have trouble speaking or using sign language might benefit from a communication board with pictures, phrases, and the alphabet on it. Nondisabled peers can learn how to use the equipment as well, and adults can encourage children to respond to the messages communicated by the children with disabilities.

Reading #14-2

Supporting Children During Times of Trouble and Tragedy

We have suggested throughout the textbook, and especially in Chapter 14, that teachers and other practitioners can make a difference in children's lives by being affectionate, offering developmentally appropriate instruction, and establishing enjoyable routines in classrooms and other group settings. Such affirming support is helpful to children in the best of times, and it is most certainly critical when the lives of children and their families are disrupted by a natural disaster such as an earthquake, hurricane, or flood, or by a political tragedy such as terrorism or a society's economic collapse.

Children who live through a disaster or tragedy may have several unsettling experiences, including unexpected hardships and significant personal losses—perhaps a family member dying, their home being destroyed, or the family's sudden relocation to a new city. Teachers and other practitioners can help children deal with such challenging circumstances by expressing their concern, being aware of changes in children's behaviors, reassuring children that they are being protected, encouraging children to express their feelings, and—to the degree possible— carrying on with routines and traditions. Following are five specific recommendations:

• *Be prepared.* Schools and community agencies can develop plans for dealing with disasters— before they occur. Planning may consist of designing prevention checklists, procuring a disaster supplies kit, using security precautions, creating an emergency communications plan, training staff members, posting phone numbers for emergency response agencies, preparing for children's immediate distress and long-term responses to grief and loss, determining how to contact families in an emergency, and implementing drills for fire, tornadoes, and other problems endemic to the area (National Clearinghouse for Educational Facilities, 2003). (In implementing drills, adults should reassure children that they are taking every precaution and that these drills will help keep everyone safe in the unlikely event of a real emergency.)

• *Seek support from mental health agencies.* Overwhelming feelings of fear, anger, and confusion exceed some children's ability to cope. Children may be at risk for developing serious emotional problems, particularly if they are already suffering from depression or anxiety or have personally experienced a momentous change or loss, such as having a parent being sent to active military duty. Counselors, therapists, and other mental health professionals are specially trained to provide support needed by children with various mental health needs.

• *Protect children from graphic images of violence and harm.* Adults can shield children from disturbing television images of disasters and violence. They can also limit the total number of hours during which the television is turned on.

• *Give children age-appropriate reassurance.* The particular reactions that children have during a tragedy will depend on their developmental levels (Families and Work Institute, 2002; National Association of School Psychologists, 2003). Teachers and other practitioners need to focus on youngsters' age-related needs, listen thoughtfully to the concerns children and adolescents raise, and arrange outlets for emotional expression. Following are some specific ways that youngsters of various ages may express their concerns and the tactics adults can use to comfort them (Families and Work Institute, 2002; National Association of School Psychologists, 2003):

Infants. Infants sense changes in routines and apprehension from adults. When adults are under stress, infants may show more irritability than usual. Caregivers can offer the kinds of attention infants always crave—responsive care, affection, and comfort.

Young children. Young children do not always have the capacity to distinguish real threats from their own fantasies. They may respond to stress with bedwetting, thumb sucking, nightmares, sleeplessness, loss of appetite, and heightened fears (e.g., being afraid of the dark, monsters, and kidnappers). Adults can offer young children comfort and familiarity, for example, by maintaining daily routines in child care centers. Adults can encourage children to express their feelings through play and art and reassure children that they are being protected.

School-Age Children. In middle childhood, children can grasp many of the basic, concrete aspects of tragedies. For example, they now understand that military forces fight in war, and that acts of nature can destroy buildings and leave people without clean water, personal possessions, or electricity. Children may struggle with uncomfortable feelings—particularly about why bad things happen—when they believe the world *should* be a benevolent place. Children of this age may be flooded with fear and anger and show distress by becoming irritable, aggressive, clingy, and withdrawn. They may experience sleep disorders, distractibility, nail biting, and loss of appetite. Adults can explain how they are endeavoring to keep children safe in their schools and communities, strive to answer children's questions honestly and kindly, put events in perspective, and remind children of all the things they can do together to care for one another. Finally, adults can read historical accounts that reveal the courage and cooperation that other people have shown during difficult times.

Adolescents. Adolescents struggle with many transitions in everyday life. Uncertainty can turn to anxiety when the surrounding world is in upheaval. Adolescents may understand the reasons and mechanisms behind tragedies and grasp the feelings and motives of soldiers, rescue workers, and victims. Adolescents are apt to analyze the operations of government agencies and be critical of those in power. Adolescents' responses to stress may include sleeping and eating disturbances, physical symptoms such as abdominal pain and headaches, withdrawal from friends and family, irritability, and poor concentration. In addition, adolescents may act out by drinking alcohol or by taking drugs that reduce their feelings of anxiety and depression. Adults can help by keeping routines as familiar and pleasant as possible; talking and listening; encouraging adolescents to help others in need; asking for self-expression through poetry, art, and essays; and relaying the initiatives of positive role models during previous tragedies.

• *Care for yourself*. Should you work with youngsters during a local disaster or tragedy, you will be more effective yourself if you attend to your own physical and emotional needs (American Psychological Association, 2003). You can look after yourself by eating healthful foods, exercising, and resting. Maintaining routines is as important for you as it is for children, and keeping in close touch with family and friends helps everyone (American Psychological Association, 2003). Finally, by helping children in distress, you may feel considerable satisfaction in the contributions you have made to children during trying times.

REFERENCES

Alberto, P. A., & Troutman, A. C. (2003). *Applied behavior analysis for teachers* (6th ed.). Upper Saddle River, NJ: Merrill/Prentice Hall.

Alford, G. S., & Rosenthal, T. L. (1973). Process and products of modeling in observational concept attainment. *Child Development, 44*, 714-720.

American Association on Mental Retardation (1992). *Mental retardation: Definition, classification, and systems of supports* (9th ed.). Washington, DC: Author.

American Psychological Association. (2003). *Resilience in time of war*. Retrieved March 20, 2003, from http://www.helping.apa.org/resilience/war.html.

Anderson, R. C., Nguyen-Jahiel, K., McNurlen, B., Archodidou, A., Kim, S.-Y., Reznitskaya, A., Tillmanns, M., & Gilbert, L. (2001). The snowball phenomenon: Spread of ways of talking and ways of thinking across groups of children. *Cognition and Instruction, 19*, 1–46.

Astington, J. W., & Pelletier, J. (1996). The language of mind: Its role in teaching and learning. In D. R. Olson & N. Torrance (Eds.), *The handbook of education and human development: New models of learning, teaching and schooling* (pp. 593–619). Cambridge, MA: Blackwell.

Bandura, A. (1977). *Social learning theory*. Upper Saddle River, NJ: Prentice Hall.

Bandura, A. (1986). *Social foundations of thought and action: A social cognitive theory*. Upper Saddle River, NJ: Prentice Hall.

Bandura, A., & Jeffery, R. W. (1973). Role of symbolic coding and rehearsal processes in observational learning. *Journal of Personality & Social Psychology, 26*, 122-130.

Bandura, A., Jeffery, R. W., & Bachicha, D. L. (1974). Analysis of memory codes and cumulative rehearsal in observational learning. *Journal of Research in Personality, 7*, 295-305.

Baron, J. B. (1987). Evaluating thinking skills in the classroom. In J. B. Baron & R. J. Sternberg (Eds.), *Teaching thinking skills: Theory and practice.* New York: Freeman.

Baron-Cohen, S. (1993). From attention-goal psychology to belief-desire psychology: The development of a theory of mind and its dysfunction. In S. Baron-Cohen, H. Tager-Flusberg, & D. Cohen (Eds.), *Understanding other minds: Perspectives from autism* (pp. 59–82). Oxford, England: Oxford University Press.

Baumrind, D. (1971). Current patterns of parental authority. *Developmental Psychology Monographs, 4*(1, Pt. 2).

Baumrind, D. (1982). An explanatory study of socialization effects on black children: Some black-white comparisons. *Child Development, 43,* 261–267.

Baumrind, D. (1989). Rearing competent children. In W. Damon (Ed.), *Child development today and tomorrow.* San Francisco: Jossey-Bass.

Beers, J. W. (1980). Developmental strategies of spelling competence in primary school children. In E. H. Henderson & J. W. Beers (Eds.), *Developmental and cognitive aspects of learning to spell: A reflection of word knowledge.* Newark, DE: International Reading Association.

Benton, S. L. (1997). Psychological foundations of elementary writing instruction. In G. D. Phye (Ed.), *Handbook of academic learning: Construction of knowledge.* San Diego, CA: Academic Press.

Berti, A. E., & Bombi, A. S. (1988). *The child's construction of economics.* Cambridge, England: Cambridge University Press.

Bjorklund, D. F., & Green, B. L. (1992). *The adaptive nature of cognitive immaturity. American Psychologist, 47,* 46–54.

Block, J. (1971). *Lives through time.* Berkeley, CA: Bancroft Books.

Block, J., Block, J. H., & Keyes, S. (1988). Longitudinally foretelling drug usage in adolescence: Early childhood personality and environmental precursors. *Child Development, 59,* 336–355.

Brook, J. S., Brook, D. W., Gordon, A. S., Whiteman, M., & Cohen, P. (1990). The psychological etiology of adolescent drug use: A family interactional approach. *Genetic Psychology Monographs, 116,* (No. 2).

Brookhart, S. M., & Freeman, D. J. (1992). Characteristics of entering teacher candidates. *Review of Educational Research, 62,* 36–60.

Brown, V. A. (2002). *Child welfare case studies.* Boston, MA: Allyn and Bacon.

Bryant, P., Nunes, T., & Aidinis, A. (1999). Different morphemes, same spelling problems: Cross-linguistic developmental studies. In M. Harris & G. Hatano (Eds.), *Learning to read and write: A cross-linguistic perspective.* Cambridge, England: Cambridge University Press.

Cabrera, N. J. (2005). Father involvement. In C. B. Fisher & R. M. Lerner (Eds.), *Encyclopedia of applied developmental science* (Vol. 1, pp. 460-461). Thousand Oaks, CA: Sage.

Caspi, A., & Silva, P. A. (1995). Temperamental qualities at age 3 predict personality traits in young adulthood: Longitudinal evidence from a birth cohort. *Child Development, 66,* 486–498.

Catron, T. F., & Masters, J. C. (1993). Mothers' and children's conceptualizations of corporal punishment. *Child Development, 64,* 1815–1828.

Chaffee, S. H., & Yang, S. M. (1990). Communication and political socialization. In O. Ichilov (Ed.), *Political socialization, citizenship, education, and democracy* (pp. 137–157). New York: Teachers College Press.

Chall, J. S. (1996). *Stages of reading development* (2nd ed.) Fort Worth, TX: Harcourt, Brace.

Chao, R. K. (2000). Cultural explanations for the role of parenting in the school success of Asian-American children. In R. D. Taylor & M. C. Wang (Eds.), *Resilience across contexts: Family, work, culture, and community* (pp. 333–363). Mahwah, NJ: Erlbaum.

Chapman, C., Nolin, M., & Kline, K. (1997). *Student interest in national news and its relation to school courses* (NCES 97–970). Washington, DC: U.S. Department of Education, National Center for Education Statistics.

Cheyne, J. A., & Walters, R. H. (1970). Punishment and prohibition: Some origins of self-control. In T. M. Newcomb (Ed.), *New directions in psychology.* New York: Holt, Rinehart & Winston.

Chi, M. T. H. (1978). Knowledge structures and memory development. In R. S. Siegler (Ed.), *Children's thinking: What develops?* Hillsdale, NJ: Erlbaum.

Chilamkurti, C., & Milner, J. S. (1993). Perceptions and evaluations of child transgressions and disciplinary techniques in high- and low-risk mothers and their children. *Child Development, 64,* 1801–1814.

Chisholm, K., Carter, M. C., Ames, E. W., & Morison, S. J. (1995). Attachment security and indiscriminately friendly behavior in children adopted from Romanian orphanages. *Development and Psychopathology, 7,* 283–297.

Churchill, S. L. (1999, April). *Parent and teacher agreement on child and parenting behaviors as a predictor of child outcomes.* Paper presented at the biennial meeting of the Society for Research in Child Development, Albuquerque, NM.

Cicchetti, D., & Garmezy, N. (1993). Prospects and promises in the study of resilience. *Development and Psychopathology, 5,* 497–502.

Coates, B., & Hartup, W. W. (1969). Age and verbalization in observational learning. *Developmental Psychology, 1*, 556-562.

Cohen, R. L. (1989). Memory for action events: The power of enactment. *Educational Psychology Review, 1*, 57-80.

Colby, A., & Kohlberg, L. (1984). Invariant sequence and internal consistency in moral judgment stages. In W. M. Kurtines & J. L. Gewirtz (Eds.), *Morality, moral behavior, and moral development.* New York: Wiley.

Cooper, H. (1989). Synthesis of research on homework. *Educational Leadership, 47*(3), 85–91.

Corno, L. (1996). Homework is a complicated thing. *Educational Researcher, 25*(8), 27-30.

Davidson, P., & Youniss, J. (1995). Moral development and social construction. In W. M. Kurtines & J. L. Gewirtz (Eds.), *Moral development: An introduction.* Boston: Allyn & Bacon.

Davidson, P., Turiel, E., & Black, A. (1983). The effect of stimulus familiarity on the use of criteria and justification in children's social reasoning. *British Journal of Developmental Psychology, 1,* 49–65.

Davis, G. A., & Thomas, M. A. (1989). *Effective schools and effective teachers.* Needham Heights, MA: Allyn & Bacon.

De La Paz, S., Swanson, P. N., & Graham, S. (1998). The contribution of executive control to the revising by students with writing and learning difficulties. *Journal of Educational Psychology, 90*, 448-460.

Deater-Deakard, K., Dodge, K., Bates, J., & Pettit, G. (1996). Physical discipline among African American and European American mothers: Links to children's externalizing behaviors. *Developmental Psychology, 32*(6), 1065–1072.

Dekovic, M., & Janssens, J. M. (1992). Parents' child-rearing style and child's sociometric status. *Developmental Psychology, 28*, 925-932.

Delval, J. (1994). Stages in the child's construction of social knowledge. In M. Carretero & J. F. Voss (Eds.), *Cognitive and instructional processes in history and the social sciences* (pp. 77–102). Mahwah, NJ: Erlbaum.

Dorris, M. (1989). *The broken cord.* New York: Harper & Row.

Doyle, W. (1990). Classroom management techniques. In O. C. Moles (Ed.), *Student discipline strategies: Research and practice.* Albany: State University of New York Press.

Dreikurs, R. (1998). *Maintaining sanity in the classroom: Classroom management techniques* (2nd ed.). Bristol, PA: Hemisphere.

Edmundson, P. J. (1990). A normative look at the curriculum in teacher education. *Phi Delta Kappan, 71,* 717–722.

Eisenberg, N. (1995). Prosocial development: A multifaceted model. In W. M. Kurtines & J. L. Gewirtz (Eds.), *Moral development: An introduction.* Boston: Allyn & Bacon.

Eisenberg, N., Martin, C. L., & Fabes, R. A. (1996). Gender development and gender effects. In D. C. Berliner & R. C. Calfee (Eds.), *Handbook of educational psychology.* New York: Macmillan.

Emler, N., Ohana, J., & Dickinson, J. (1990). Children's representations of social relations. In G. Duveen & B. Lloyd (Eds.), *Social representations and the development of knowledge* (pp. 47-69). Cambridge, England: Cambridge University Press.

Endicott, K. (1992). Fathering in an egalitarian society. In B. S. Hewlett (Ed.), *Father-child relations: Cultural and biosocial contexts* (pp. 281-295). New York: Aldine deGruyter.

Epstein, J. L. (1983). Longitudinal effects of family-school-person interactions on student outcomes. *Research in Sociology of Education and Socialization, 4,* 101–127.

Epstein, J. L., Coates, L., Salinas, K. C., Sanders, M. G., & Simon, B. S. (1997). *School, family, and community partnerships: Your handbook for action.* Thousand Oaks, CA: Corwin Press.

Epstein, T. (2000). Adolescents' perspectives on racial diversity in U.S. history: Case studies from an urban classroom. *American Educational Research Journal, 37,* 185–214.

Families and Work Institute (2002). *Coping and contributing in the aftermath of crisis, tragedy and trauma; An educator's guide.* Stamford, CT: Lifetime Learning Systems, Inc.

Ferguson, C. J. (1999). Building literacy with child-constructed sociodramatic play centers. *Dimensions of Early Childhood, 27,* 23–29.

Ferreiro, E. (1990). Literacy development: Psychogenesis. In Y. M. Goodman (Ed.), *How children construct literacy.* Newark, DE: International Reading Association.

Field, T., Hernandez-Reif, M., & Freedman, J. (2004). Stimulation programs for preterm infants. *Social Policy Report, 17*(1) (Society for Research in Child Development).

Flanagan, C. A., & Faison, N. (2001). Youth civic development: Implications of research for social policy and programs. *Social Policy Report of the Society for Research in Child Development, 15*(1), 1–14.

Flavell, J. H. (1992). Perspectives on perspective taking. In H. Beilin & P. Pufall (Eds.), *Piaget's theory: Prospects and possibilities* (pp. 107–139). Hillsdale, NJ: Erlbaum.

Flavell, J. H. (2000). Development of children's knowledge about the mental world. *International Journal of Behavioral Development, 24*(1), 15–23.

Friend, M., & Davis, T. L. (1993). Appearance-reality distinction: Children's understanding of the physical and affective domains. *Developmental Psychology, 29,* 907–914.

Frith, U. (1985). Beneath the surface of surface dyslexia. In K. E. Patterson, J. C. Marshall, & M. Coltheart (Eds.), *Surface dyslexia: Neuropsychological and cognitive studies of phonological reading.* London: Routledge & Kegan Paul.

Fuller, M. L. (2001). Multicultural concerns and classroom management. In C. A. Grant & M. L. Gomez, *Campus and classroom: Making school multicultural* (pp. 109–134). Upper Saddle River, NJ: Merrill/Prentice Hall.

Furnham, A. (1994). Young people's understanding of politics and economics. In M. Carretero & J. F. Voss (Eds.), *Cognitive and instructional processes in history and the social sciences* (pp. 17–47). Mahwah, NJ: Erlbaum.

Furth, H. G. (1980). *The world of grown-ups: Children's conceptions of society.* New York: Elsevier.

García, E. E. (1994). *Understanding and meeting the challenge of student cultural diversity.* Boston: Houghton Mifflin.

García, E. E. (1995). Educating Mexican American students: Past treatment and recent developments in theory, research, policy, and practice. In J. A. Banks & C. A. M. Banks (Eds.), *Handbook of research on multicultural education.* New York: Macmillan.

Garvey, C., & Horgan, R. (1973). Social speech and social interaction: Egocentrism revisited. *Child Development, 44,* 562–568.

Gentry, R. (1982). An analysis of the developmental spellings in *Gnys at Wrk. The Reading Teacher, 36,* 192–200.

Gerst, M. S. (1971). Symbolic coding processes in observational learning. *Journal of Personality & Social Psychology, 19,* 7-17.

Gilligan, C. (1977). In a different voice: Women's conceptions of self and of morality. *Harvard Educational Review, 47,* 481–517.

Gilligan, C. (1982). *In a different voice: Psychological theory and women's development.* Cambridge, MA: Harvard University Press.

Gilliland, H. (1988). Discovering and emphasizing the positive aspects of the culture. In H. Gilliland & J. Reyhner (Eds.), *Teaching the native American*. Dubuque, IA: Kendall/Hunt.

Ginsburg, M. B., & Newman, M. K. (1985). Social inequalities, schooling, and teacher education. *Journal of Teacher Education, 36*(2), 49–54.

Goodnow, J. J., & Collins, W. A. (1990). *Development according to parents: The nature, sources, and consequences of parents' ideas*. East Sussex, England: Erlbaum.

Gootman, M. E. (1998). Effective in-house suspension. *Educational Leadership, 56*(1), 39-41.

Gottfredson, G. D., & Gottfredson, D. C. (1985). *Victimization in schools*. New York: Plenum Press.

Gottman, J. M. (1986a). The observation of social process. In J. M. Gottman & J. G. Parker (Eds.), *Conversations of friends: Speculations on affective development* (pp. 51–100). Cambridge, England: Cambridge University Press.

Gottman, J. M. (1986b). The world of coordinated play: Same- and cross-sex friendship in young children. In J. M. Gottman & J. G. Parker (Eds.), *Conversations of friends: Speculations on affective development* (pp. 139–191). Cambridge, England: Cambridge University Press.

Gottman, J. M., & Mettetal, G. (1986). Speculations about social and affective development: Friendship and acquaintanceship through adolescence. In J. M. Gottman & J. G. Parker (Eds.), *Conversations of friends: Speculations on affective development* (pp. 192–237). Cambridge, England: Cambridge University Press.

Gough, P. B., & Wren, S. (1998). The decomposition of decoding. In C. Hulme & R. M. Joshi (Eds.), *Reading and spelling: Development and disorders*. Mahwah, NJ: Erlbaum.

Grant, C. A., & Gomez, M. L. (2001). *Campus and classroom: Making schooling multicultural* (2nd ed.). Upper Saddle River, NJ: Merrill/Prentice Hall.

Greenberg, M. T. (1999). Attachment and psychopathology in childhood. In J. Cassidy & P. R. Shaver (Eds.), *Handbook of attachment: Theory, research, and clinical applications* (pp. 469–496). New York: Guilford Press.

Greene, S., & Ackerman, J. M. (1995). Expanding the constructivist metaphor: A rhetorical perspective on literacy research and practice. *Review of Educational Research, 65,* 383–420.

Greenspan, S., & Granfield, J. M. (1992). Reconsidering the construct of mental retardation: Implications of a model of social competence. *American Journal of Mental Retardation, 96,* 442-453.

Harlow, H. F. (1959). Love in infant monkeys. *Scientific American, 200,* 68-74.

Harlow, H. F., & Harlow, M. K. (1962). Social deprivation in monkeys. *Scientific American, 207,* 137-146.

Harrison, L. L. (2001). The use of comforting touch and massage to reduce stress in preterm infants in the neonatal intensive care unit. *Newborn and Infant Nursing Reviews, 1*(4), 235-241.

Hart, D., Hofman, V., Edelstein, W., & Keller, M. (1997). The relation of childhood personality types to adolescents' behavior and development: A longitudinal study of Icelandic children. *Developmental Psychology, 33,* 195–205.

Helwig, C. C., & Jasiobedzka, U. (2001). The relation between law and morality: Children's reasoning about socially beneficial and unjust laws. *Child Development, 72,* 1382–1393.

Hemphill, L., & Snow, C. (1996). Language and literacy development: Discontinuities and differences. In D. R. Olson & N. Torrance (Eds.), *The handbook of education and human development: New models of learning, teaching, and schooling*. Cambridge, MA: Blackwell Publishers.

Higgins, A. (1995). Educating for justice and community: Lawrence Kohlberg's vision of moral education. In W. M. Kurtines & J. L. Gewirtz (Eds.), *Moral development: An introduction.*

Boston: Allyn & Bacon.

Hobson, R. P. (1993). *Autism and the development of mind.* London: Erlbaum.

Hoff Sommers, C. (2000). *The war against boys: How misguided feminism is harming our young men.* New York: Simon & Schuster.

Howes, C., & Segal, J. (1993). Children's relationships with alternative caregivers: The special case of maltreated children removed from their homes. *Journal of Applied Developmental Psychology, 17,* 71–81.

Huff, J. A. (1988). Personalized behavior modification: An in-school suspension program that teaches students how to change. *School Counselor, 35,* 210-214.

Hughes, J. N. (1988). *Cognitive behavior therapy with children in schools.* New York: Pergamon.

Hulme, C., & Joshi, R. M. (Eds.). (1998). *Reading and spelling: Development and disorders.* Mahwah, NJ: Erlbaum.

Huston, A. C. (1983). Sex-typing. In E. M. Hetherington (Ed.), *Handbook of child psychology: Vol. 4. Socialization, personality, and social development* (4th ed.). New York: Wiley.

Irujo, S. (1988). An introduction to intercultural differences and similarities in nonverbal communication. In J. S. Wurzel (Ed.), *Toward multiculturalism: A reader in multicultural education.* Yarmouth, ME: Intercultural Press.

Iwata, B. A., & Bailey, J. S. (1974). Reward versus cost token systems: An analysis of the effects on students and teacher. *Journal of Applied Behavior Analysis, 7,* 567-576.

Jahoda, G. (1979). The construction of economic reality by some Glaswegian children. *European Journal of Social Psychology, 9,* 115–127.

Jahoda, G. (1982). The development of ideas about an economic institution: A cross-national replication. *British Journal of Social Psychology, 21,* 337–338.

Jahoda, G. (1983). European "lag" in the development of an economic concept: A study in Zimbabwe. *British Journal of Developmental Psychology, 1*(2), 113–120.

Jensen, M. M. (2005). *Introduction to emotional and behavioral disorders: Recognizing and managing problems in the classroom.* Merrill/Prentice Hall.

Kagan, D. (1992). Implications of research on teacher belief. *Educational Psychologist, 27,* 65–90.

Katz, L. G. (1999a). *Another look at what young children should be learning.* Champaign, IL. ERIC Clearing-house on Elementary and Early Childhood Education (ERIC Document Reproduction Service No. ED 430 735).

Katz, L. G. (1999b, November). *Current perspectives on education in the early years: Challenges for the new millennium.* Paper presented at the Annual Rudolph Goodridge Memorial Lecture, Barbados, West Indies. (ERIC Document Reproduction Service No. ED 437 212).

Kellogg, R. T. (1994). *The psychology of writing.* New York: Oxford University Press.

Klein, P. D. (1999). Reopening inquiry into cognitive processes in writing-to-learn. *Educational Psychology Review, 11,* 203–270.

Kohlberg, L. (1969). Stage and sequence: The cognitive-developmental approach to socialization. In D. A. Goslin (Ed.), *Handbook of socialization theory and research* (pp. 347–480). Chicago: Rand McNally.

Kohlberg, L. (1981). *The philosophy of moral development: Moral stages and the idea of justice.* San Francisco: Harper & Row.

Kohlberg, L. (1984). *The psychology of moral development: The nature and validity of moral stages.* San Francisco: Harper & Row.

Konopak, B. C., Martin, S. H., & Martin, M. A. (1990). Using a writing strategy to enhance sixth-grade students' comprehension of content material. *Journal of Reading Behavior, 22,* 19–37.

Krashen, S. D. (1996). *Under attack: The case against bilingual education.* Culver City, CA: Language Education Associates.

Kurtines, W. M., Berman, S. L., Ittel, A., & Williamson, S. (1995). Moral development: A co-constructivist perspective. In W. M. Kurtines & J. L. Gewirtz (Eds.), *Moral development: An introduction.* Boston: Allyn & Bacon.

Lamb, M. E., Chuang, S. S., & Cabrera, N. (2005). Promoting child adjustment by fostering positive paternal involvement. In R. M. Lerner, F. Jacobs, & D. Wertlieb (Eds.), *Applied developmental science: An advanced textbook* (pp. 179-200). Thousand Oaks, CA: Sage.

Lamborn, S. D., & Felbab, A. J. (2001, April). *Applying ethnic equivalence and cultural value models to African American teens' perceptions of parents.* Paper presented at the biennial meetings of the Society for Research in Child Development, Minneapolis.

Lamborn, S. D., Mounts, N. S., Steinberg, L., & Dornbusch, S. M. (1991). Patterns of competence and adjustment among adolescents from authoritative, authoritarian, indulgent, and neglectful families. *Child Development, 62,* 1049-1065.

Laupa, M. (1994). "Who's in charge?" Preschool children's concepts of authority. *Early Childhood Research Quarterly, 9,* 1–17.

Laupa, M., & Turiel, E. (1995). Social domain theory. In W. M. Kurtines & J. L. Gewirtz (Eds.), *Moral development: An introduction.* Boston: Allyn & Bacon.

Leffert, J. S., Siperstein, G. N., & Millikan, E. (1999). *Social perception and strategy generation: Two key social cognitive processes in children with mental retardation.* Paper presented at the biennial meeting of the Society for Research in Child Development, Albuquerque, NM.

Lentz, F. E. (1988). Reductive procedures. In J. C. Witt, S. N. Elliott, & F. M. Gresham (Eds.), *Handbook of behavior therapy in education.* New York: Plenum Press.

Lerman, D. C., & Vorndran, C. M. (2002). On the status of knowledge for using punishment: Implications for treating behavior disorders. *Journal of Applied Behavior Analysis, 35,* 431–464.

Lester, B. M., Bigsby, R., & Miller-Loncar, C. (2004). Infant massage: So where's the rub? *Social Policy Report, 17*(1), 8.

Levine, L. (1983). Mine: Self-definition in 2-year-old boys. *Developmental Psychology, 19,* 544–549.

Lewis, M., & Brooks-Gunn, J. (1979). *Social cognition and the acquisition of self.* New York: Plenum.

Lind, G. (1994, April). *Why do juvenile delinquents gain little from moral discussion programs?* Paper presented at the annual meeting of the American Educational Research Association, New Orleans, LA.

Linn, M. C., & Pulos, S. (1983). Male-female differences in predicting displaced volume: Strategy usage, aptitude relationships, and experience influences. *Journal of Educational Psychology, 75,* 86-96.

Lomawaima, K. T. (1995). Educating Native Americans. In J. A. Banks & C. A. M. Banks (Eds.), *Handbook of research on multicultural education.* New York: Macmillan.

Lortie, D. (1975). *Schoolteacher: A sociological study.* Chicago: University of Chicago Press.

Losey, K. M. (1995). Mexican American students and classroom interaction: An overview and critique. *Review of Educational Research, 65,* 283-318.

Lyon, M. A. (1984). Positive reinforcement and logical consequences in the treatment of classroom encopresis. *School Psychology Review, 13,* 238-243.

Maccoby, E. E., & Martin, J. A. (1983). Socialization in the context of the family: Parent-child interaction. In E. M. Hetherington (Ed.), *Handbook of child psychology: Vol. 4. Socialization, personality, and social development.* New York: Wiley.

Mackey, W. C. (2001). Support for the existence of an independent man-to-child affiliative bond: Fatherhood as a biocultural invention. *Psychology of Men and Masculinity, 2(1),* 51-66.

Marcovitch, S., Goldberg, S., Gold, A., Washington, J., Wasson, C., Krekewich, K., & Handley-Derry, M. (1997). Determinants of behavioral problems in Romanian children adopted in Ontario. *International Journal of Behavioral Development, 20,* 17–31.

Maxmell, D., Jarrett, O. S., & Dickerson, C. (1998, April). *Are we forgetting the children's needs? Recess through the children's eyes.* Paper presented at the annual meeting of the American Educational Research Association, San Diego, CA.

Mayo Foundation for Medical Education and Research (2006). *Eating disorders.* Retrieved May 6, 2006, from http://www.mayoclinic.com/health/eating-disorders/DS00294

McClowry, S. G. (1998). The science and art of using temperament as the basis for intervention. *School Psychology Review, 27,* 551–563.

McDevitt, M., & Chaffee, S. H. (1998). Second chance political socialization: "Trickle-up" effects of children on parents. In T. J. Johnson, C. E. Hays, & S. P. Hays (Eds.), *Engaging the public: How government and the media can reinvigorate American democracy.* Lanhan, MD: Rowman & Littlefield.

McDevitt, T. M., & Ford, M. E. (1987). Processes in young children's communicative functioning and development. In M. E. Ford & D. H. Ford (Eds.), *Humans as self-constructing systems: Putting the framework to work.* (pp. 145–175). Hillsdale, NJ: Erlbaum.

McKeon, D. (1994). When meeting "common" standards is uncommonly difficult. *Educational Leadership, 51*(8), 45-49.

McMullan, S., & Fisher, L. (1992). Developmental progress of Romanian orphanage children in Canada [Abstract]. *Canadian Psychology, 33(2),* 504.

Miller, J. G., & Bersoff, D. M. (1992). Culture and moral judgment: How are conflicts between justice and interpersonal responsibilities resolved? *Journal of Personality and Social Psychology, 62,* 541–554.

Miller, P. J. (1982). *Amy, Wendy, and Beth: Learning language in south Baltimore.* Austin: University of Texas Press.

Moles, O. C. (Ed.). (1990). *Student discipline strategies: Research and practice.* Albany: State University of New York Press.

Montemayor, R. (1982). The relationship between parent-adolescent conflict and the amount of time adolescents spend with parents, peers, and alone. *Child Development, 53,* 1512–1519.

Mueller, E. (1972). The maintenance of verbal exchanges between young children. *Child Development, 43,* 930–938.

Nation, K., & Hulme, C. (1998). The role of analogy in early spelling development. In C. Hulme & R. M. Joshi (Eds.), *Reading and spelling: Development and disorders.* Mahwah, NJ: Erlbaum.

National Association of Bilingual Education (1993). Census reports sharp increase in number of non-English speaking Americans. *NABE News, 16*(6), 1, 25.

National Association of School Psychologists (2003). *Helping children deal with tragic events in unsettling times: Tips for parents and teachers.* Bethesda, MD: Author.

National Clearinghouse for Educational Facilities (2003). *Disaster preparedness for schools.* Retrieved March 7, 2003, from *http://www.edfacilities.org/rl/disaster.cfm.*

Nel, J. (1993). Preservice teachers' perceptions of the goals of multicultural education: Implications for the empowerment of minority students, *Educational Horizons, 71*, 120–125.

Nichols, J. D., Ludwin, W. G., & Iadicola, P. (1999). A darker shade of gray: A year-end analysis of discipline and suspension data. *Equity and Excellence in Education, 32*(1), 43–55.

Niemi, R. G., & Junn, J. (1998). *Civic education: What makes students learn.* New Haven: Yale University Press.

Nucci, L. P., & Nucci, M. S. (1982a). Children's responses to moral and social conventional transgressions in free-play settings. *Child Development, 53,* 1337–1342.

Nucci, L. P., & Nucci, M. S. (1982b). Children's social interactions in the context of moral and conventional transgressions. *Child Development, 53,* 403–412.

Nucci, L. P., & Turiel, E. (1978). Social interactions and the development of social concepts in preschool children. *Child Development, 49,* 400–407.

Nunner-Winkler, G. (1984). Two moralities? A critical discussion of an ethic of care and responsibility versus an ethic of rights and justice. In W. M. Kurtines & J. L. Gewirtz (Eds.), *Morality, moral behavior, and moral development.* New York: Wiley.

O'Leary, K. D., Kaufman, K. F., Kass, R. E., & Drabman, R. S. (1970). The effects of loud and soft reprimands on the behavior of disruptive students. *Exceptional Children, 37*, 145-155.

Okagaki, L., & Diamond, K. E. (2000, May). Responding to cultural and linguistic differences in the beliefs and practices of families with young children. *Young Children*, 74-80.

Olson, D. R., & Bruner, J. S. (1996). Folk psychology and folk pedagogy. In D. R. Olson & N. Torrance (Eds.), *The handbook of education and human development: New models of learning, teaching and schooling* (pp. 9–27). Cambridge, MA: Blackwell.

Ormrod, J. E. (2006). *Educational psychology: Developing learners* (5th ed.). Upper Saddle River, NJ: Merrill/Prentice Hall.

Ornstein, R. (1997). *The right mind: Making sense of the hemispheres.* San Diego, CA: Harcourt Brace.

Pajares, M. F. (1992). Teachers' beliefs and educational research: Cleaning up a messy construct. *Review of Educational Research, 62*, 307–332.

Paley, V. G. (1984). *Boys and girls: Superheroes in the doll corner.* Chicago: University of Chicago Press.

Pang, V. O. (1995). Asian Pacific American students: A diverse and complex population. In J. A. Banks & C. A. M. Banks (Eds.), *Handbook of research on multicultural education.* New York: Macmillan.

Parke, R. D. (1974). Rules, roles, and resistance to deviation: Explorations in punishment, discipline, and self-control. In A. Pick (Ed.), *Minnesota Symposia on Child Psychology* (Vol. 8). Minneapolis: University of Minnesota Press.

Pellegrini, A. D., Huberty, P. D., & Jones, I. (1995). The effects of recess timing on children's playground and classroom behaviors. *American Educational Research Journal, 32*, 845-864.

Pérez, B. (1998a). Creating a classroom community for literacy. In B. Pérez (Ed.), *Sociocultural contexts of language and literacy.* Mahwah, NJ: Erlbaum.

Pérez, B. (1998b). Literacy, diversity, and programmatic responses. In B. Pérez (Ed.), *Sociocultural contexts of language and literacy.* Mahwah, NJ: Erlbaum.

Perner, J. (1991). *Understanding the representational mind.* Cambridge, MA: MIT Press.

Perry, D. G., & Perry, L. C. (1983). Social learning, causal attribution, and moral internalization. In J. Bisanz, G. L. Bisanz, & R. Kail (Eds.), *Learning in children: Progress in cognitive development research.* New York: Springer-Verlag.

Pfiffner, L. J., & Barkley, R. A. (1998). Treatment of ADHD in school settings. In R. A. Barkley, *Attention-deficit hyperactivity disorder: A handbook for diagnosis and treatment* (2nd ed., pp. 458-490). New York: Guilford Press.

Pfiffner, L. J., & O'Leary, S. G. (1993). School-based psychological treatments. In J. L. Matson (Ed.), *Handbook of hyperactivity in children* (pp. 234–255). Boston: Allyn & Bacon.

Piaget, J. (1928). *Judgment and reasoning in the child* (M. Warden, Trans.). New York: Harcourt, Brace.

Piaget, J. (1952). *The origins of intelligence in children*. New York: International Universities Press.

Piaget, J. (1959). *The language and thought of the child* (3rd ed.; M. Gabain, Trans.). London: Routledge & Kegan Paul.

Piaget, J. (1960). *The moral judgment of the child* (M. Gabain, Trans.). Glencoe, IL: Free Press. (First published in 1932)

Poche, C., Yoder, P., & Miltenberger, R. (1988). Teaching self-protection to children using television techniques. *Journal of Applied Behavior Analysis, 21*, 253-261.

Power, F. C., Higgins, A., & Kohlberg, L. (1989). *Lawrence Kohlberg's approach to moral education*. New York: Columbia University Press.

Pressley, M., & McCormick, C. B. (1995). *Advanced educational psychology for educators, researchers, and policymakers*. New York: HarperCollins.

Pulkkinen, L. (1996). Female and male personality styles: A typological and developmental analysis. *Journal of Personality and Social Psychology, 70*, 1288–1306.

Rabinowitz, M., & Glaser, R. (1985). Cognitive structure and process in highly competent performance. In F. D. Horowitz & M. O'Brien (Eds.), *The gifted and the talented: Developmental perspectives*. Washington, DC: American Psychological Association.

Rapport, M. D., Murphy, H. A., & Bailey, J. S. (1982). Ritalin vs. response cost in the control of hyperactive children: A within-subject comparison. *Journal of Applied Behavior Analysis, 15*, 205-216.

Reimer, J., Paolitto, D. P., & Hersh, R. H. (1983). *Promoting moral growth: From Piaget to Kohlberg* (2nd ed.). White Plains, NY: Longman.

Reyna, C. (2000). Lazy, dumb, or industrious: When stereotypes convey attribution information in the classroom. *Educational Psychology Review, 12*, 85–110.

Ricciardelli, L. A., McCabe, M. P., Holt, K. E., & Finemore, J. (2003). A biopsychosocial model for understanding body image and body change strategies among children. Applied Developmental Psychology, 24, 475-495.

Rittle-Johnson, B., & Siegler, R. S. (1999). Learning to spell: Variability, choice, and change in children's strategy use. *Child Development, 70*, 332–348.

Robins, R. W., John, O. P., Caspi, A., Moffitt, T. E., & Stouthamer-Loeber, M. (1996). Resilient, overcontrolled, and undercontrolled boys: Three replicable personality types. *Journal of Personality and Social Psychology, 70*, 157–171.

Rortvedt, A. K., & Miltenberger, R. G. (1994). Analysis of a high-probability instructional sequence and time-out in the treatment of child noncompliance. *Journal of Applied Behavior Analysis, 27*, 327-330.

Rosenthal, T. L., & Bandura, A. (1978). Psychological modeling: Theory and practice. In S. L. Garfield & A. E. Beige (Eds.), *Handbook of psychotherapy and behavior change: An empirical analysis* (2nd ed.). New York: Wiley.

Rosenthal, T. L., Alford, G. S., & Rasp, L. M. (1972). Concept attainment, generalization, and retention through observation and verbal coding. *Journal of Experimental Child Psychology, 13*, 183-194.

Rubin, K. H., & Pepler, D. J. (1995). The relationship of child's play to social-cognitive growth and development. In H. C. Foot, A. J. Chapman, & J. R. Smith (Eds.), *Friendship and social relations in children* (pp. 209–233). New Brunswick, NJ: Transaction.

Rutter, M., & O'Connor, T. G. (2000). (1999). Implications of attachment theory of child care policies. In J. Cassidy & P. R. Shaver (Eds.), *Handbook of attachment: Theory, research, and clinical applications* (pp. 823-844). New York: Guilford Press.

Sameroff, A. J., Seifer, R., Baldwin, A., & Baldwin, C. (1993). Stability of intelligence from preschool to adolescence: The influence of social and family risk factors. *Child Development, 64*, 80–97.

Sanders, S. (1987). Cultural conflicts: An important factor in academic failures of American Indian students. *Journal of Multicultural Counseling and Development, 15*(2), 81-90.

Schloss, P. J., & Smith, M. A. (1994). *Applied behavior analysis in the classroom.* Needham Heights, MA: Allyn & Bacon.

Schunk, D. H. (1981). Modeling and attributional effects on children's achievement: A self-efficacy analysis. *Journal of Educational Psychology, 73*, 93–105.

Schunk, D. H., & Hanson, A. R. (1985). Peer models: Influence on children's self-efficacy and achievement. *Journal of Educational Psychology, 77*, 313-322.

Schunk, D. H., & Zimmerman, B. J. (1997). Social origins of self-regulatory competence. *Educational Psychologist, 32*, 195-208.

Schunk, D. H., Hanson, A. R., & Cox, P. D. (1987). Peer-model attributes and children's achievement behaviors. *Journal of Educational Psychology, 79*, 54-61.

Selman, R. L. (1980). *The growth of interpersonal understanding.* San Diego, CA: Academic Press.

Selman, R. L., & Byrne, D. F. (1974). A structural-developmental analysis of levels of role taking in middle childhood. *Child Development, 45,* 803–806.

Selman, R. L., & Schultz, L. J. (1990). *Making a friend in youth: Developmental theory and pair therapy.* Chicago: University of Chicago Press.

Shaw, D. S., Vondra, J. I., Hommerding, K. D., Keenan, K., & Dunn, M. (1994). Chronic family adversity and early child behavior problems: A longitudinal study of low income families. *Journal of Child Psychology and Psychiatry, 35*, 1109–1122.

Shephard, L. A., & Smith, M. L. (1988). Escalating academic demand in kindergarten: Counterproductive policies. *The Elementary School Journal, 89*, 135–144.

Simons, R. L., Whitbeck, L. B., Conger, R. D., & Conger, K. J. (1991). Parenting factors, social skills, and value commitments as precursors to school failure, involvement with deviant peers, and delinquent behavior. *Journal of Youth and Adolescence, 20*, 645-664.

Skiba, R., & Raison, J. (1990). Relationship between the use of time-out and academic achievement. *Exceptional Children, 57*, 36-46.

Slonim, N. (2001). *Children's and adolescents' understandings of society and government.* Unpublished master's thesis, Ontario Institute for Studies in Education, University of Toronto.

Slonim, N., & Case, R. (2002, April). *Children's and adolescents' understandings of society and government.* Paper presented at the annual meeting of the American Educational Research Association, New Orleans, LA.

Smetana, J. G. (1989). Toddlers' social interactions in the context of moral and conventional transgressions in the home. *Developmental Psychology, 25,* 499–508.

Smith, N. R., Cicchetti, L., Clark, M. C., Fucigna, C., Gordon-O'Connor, B., Halley, B. A., & Kennedy, M. (1998). *Observation drawing with children: A framework for teachers.* New York: Teachers College Press.

Smith, R. E., & Smoll, F. L. (1997). Coaching the coaches: Youth sports as a scientific and applied behavioral setting. *Current Directions in Psychological Science, 6*(1), 16–21.

Snarey, J. (1995). In a communitarian voice: The sociological expansion of Kohlbergian theory, research, and practice. In W. M. Kurtines & J. L. Gewirtz (Eds.), *Moral development: An introduction.* Boston: Allyn & Bacon.

Snell, M. E., & Janney, R. (2000). *Social relationships and peer support.* Baltimore, Brookes.

Snow, C. E (1990). Rationales for native language instruction: Evidence from research. In A. M. Padilla, H. H. Fairchild, & C. M. Valadez (Eds.), *Bilingual education: Issues and strategies.* Newbury Park, CA: Sage.

Squires, D. A., Howley, J. P., & Gahr, R. K. (1999). The developmental pathways study group. In J. P. Comer, M. Ben-Avie, N. M. Haynes, & E. T. Joyner (Eds.), *Child by child: The Comer process in education* (pp. 193–207). New York: Teachers College Press.

Stanovich, K. E. (2000). *Progress in understanding reading: Scientific foundations and new frontiers.* New York: Guilford Press.

Steinberg, L. (1993). *Adolescence* (3rd ed.). New York: McGraw-Hill.

Steinberg, L., Elmen, J., & Mounts, N. (1989). Authoritative parenting, psychosocial maturity, and academic success among adolescents. *Child Development, 60,* 1424-1436.

Stevenson, H. C. (1995). Relationships of adolescent perceptions of racial socialization to racial identity. *Journal of Black Psychology, 21,* 49–70.

Stout, E. J., Frame, M. W. (2004). Body image disorder in adolescent males: Strategies for school counselors. Professional School Counseling, 8(20), 176-181.

Suina, J. H., & Smolkin, L. B. (1994). From natal culture to school culture to dominant society culture: Supporting transitions for Pueblo Indian students. In P. M. Greenfield & R. R. Cocking (Eds.), *Cross-cultural roots of minority child development.* Hillsdale, NJ: Erlbaum.

Sullivan, J. S. (1989). Planning, implementing, and maintaining an effective in-school suspension program. *Clearing House, 62,* 409-410.

Sund, R. B. (1976). *Piaget for educators.* Upper Saddle River, NJ: Merrill/Prentice Hall.

Taylor, R. D., & Roberts, D. (1995). Kinship support and maternal and adolescent well-being in economically disadvantaged African-American families. *Child Development, 66,* 1585-1597.

Tisak, M. (1993). Preschool children's judgments of moral and personal events involving physical harm and property damage. *Merrill-Palmer Quarterly, 39,* 375–390.

Torney-Purta, J. (1994). Dimensions of adolescents' reasoning about political and historical issues: Ontological switches, developmental processes, and situated learning. In M. Carretero & J. F. Voss (Eds.), *Cognitive and instructional processes in history and the social sciences* (pp. 103–122). Mahwah, NJ: Erlbaum.

Treiman, R. (1998). Beginning to spell in English. In C. Hulme & R. M. Joshi (Eds.), *Reading and spelling: Development and disorders.* Mahwah, NJ: Erlbaum.

Trumbull, E., Rothstein-Fisch, C., Greenfield, P. M., & Quiroz, B. (2001). *Bridging cultures between home and school: A guide for teachers.* Mahwah, NJ: Erlbaum.

Turiel, E. (1983). *The development of social knowledge: Morality and convention.* Cambridge, England: Cambridge University Press.

Turiel, E. (1998). The development of morality. In W. Damon (Editor-in-Chief) & N. Eisenberg (Vol. Ed.), *Handbook of child psychology: Vol. 3. Social, emotional, and personality development* (pp. 863–932). New York: Wiley.

Turiel, E. (2002). *The culture of morality: Social development, context, and conflict.* Cambridge, England: Cambridge University Press.

U.S. Department of Education (1993). *National excellence: A case for developing America's talent.* Washington, DC: Office of Educational Research and Improvement.

U.S. Department of Health and Human Services, Administration on Children, Youth and Families, Head Start Bureau. (2003). *The Head Start leaders' guide to positive child outcomes.* Author: Washington, DC.

U.S. Department of Health and Human Services, Administration on Children, Youth, and Families, Head Start Bureau (2004). *Head Start Program Fact Sheet.* Retrieved July 27, 2004 at www.acf.hhs.gov/programs/hsb/research/2004.htm.

Van Houten, R., Nau, P., MacKenzie-Keating, S., Sameoto, D., & Colavecchia, B. (1982). An analysis of some variables influencing the effectiveness of reprimands. *Journal of Applied Behavior Analysis, 15,* 65-83.

Walker, J. E., & Shea, T. M. (1999). *Behavior management: A practical approach for educators* (7th ed.). Upper Saddle River, NJ: Merrill/Prentice Hall.

Walker, L. J. (1991). Sex differences in moral reasoning. In W. M. Kurtines & J. L. Gewirtz (Eds.), *Handbook of moral behavior and development: Vol. 2. Research* (pp. 333–364). Hillsdale, NJ: Erlbaum.

Walker, L. J. (1995). Sexism in Kohlberg's moral psychology? In W. M. Kurtines & J. L. Gewirtz (Eds.), *Moral development: An introduction.* Boston: Allyn & Bacon.

Weiner, B. (2000). Intrapersonal and interpersonal theories of motivation from an attributional perspective. *Educational Psychology Review, 12,* 1–14.

Weinstein, C. S. (1988). Preservice teachers' expectations about their first year of teaching. *Teaching and Teacher Education, 40*(2), 53–60.

Weinstein, R. S., Madison, S. M., & Kuklinski, M. R. (1995). Raising expectations in schooling: Obstacles and opportunities for change. *American Educational Research Journal, 32,* 121–159.

White, A. G., & Bailey, J. S. (1990). Reducing disruptive behaviors of elementary physical education students with sit and watch. *Journal of Applied Behavior Analysis, 23,* 353-359.

Willig, A. C. (1985). A meta-analysis of selected studies on the effectiveness of bilingual education. *Review of Educational Research, 55,* 269-317.

Wright, L. S. (1982). The use of logical consequences in counseling children. *School Counselor, 30,* 37-49.

Wright, S. C., Taylor, D. M., & Macarthur, J. (2000). Subtractive bilingualism and the survival of the Inuit language: Heritage- versus second-language education. *Journal of Educational Psychology, 92,* 63-84.

York, K., & John, O. P. (1992). The four faces of Eve: A typological analysis of women's personality at midlife. *Journal of Personality and Social Psychology, 63,* 494–508.

Zeanah, C. H. (2000). Disturbances of attachment in young children adopted from institutions. *Journal of Developmental and Behavioral Pediatrics, 21,* 230–236.

Zirpoli, T. J., & Melloy, K. J. (2001). *Behavior management: Applications for teachers.* Upper Saddle River, NJ: Merrill/Prentice Hall.